# Gender Codes

### IEEE Computer Society Publications

The world-renowned IEEE Computer Society publishes, promotes, and distributes a wide variety of authoritative computer science and engineering texts. These books are available from most retail outlets. Visit the CS Store at *http://computer.org/store* for a list of products.

### IEEE Computer Society / Wiley Partnership

The IEEE Computer Society and Wiley partnership allows the CS Press authored book program to produce a number of exciting new titles in areas of computer science, computing and networking with a special focus on software engineering. IEEE Computer Society members continue to receive a 15% discount on these titles when purchased through Wiley or at wiley.com/ieeecs.

To submit questions about the program or send proposals please e-mail kguillemette@ computer.org or write to Books, IEEE Computer Society, 10662 Los Vaqueros Circle, Los Alamitos, CA 90720-1314. Telephone +1-714-816-2169.

**Additional information regarding the Computer Society authored book program can also be accessed from our web site at *http://computer.org/cspress*.**

# GENDER CODES

## Why Women Are Leaving Computing

Edited by

**Thomas J. Misa**

A John Wiley & Sons, Inc., Publication

Published by John Wiley & Sons, Inc., Hoboken, New Jersey.
Published simultaneously in Canada.

For general information on our other products and services please contact our Customer Care Department within the U.S. at 877-762-2974, outside the U.S. at 317-572-3993 or fax 317-572-4002.

Wiley also publishes its books in a variety of electronic formats. Some content that appears in print, however, may not be available in electronic formats.

*Library of Congress Cataloging-in-Publication Data is available*

ISBN 978-0470-59719-4

Printed in the United States of America

10  9  8  7  6  5  4  3  2  1

In memory of Karen J. Freeze (1945–2009), scholar and colleague, who in her life successfully bridged notable divides between nature and culture, industry and academe, research and family, and East and West.

# Contents

# Foreword

In 1966 there was already a "manpower" shortage of trained (or even untrained) programmers, operators, and software designers. The situation became a crisis when an estimated 50% more programmers would be needed by 1967.

It was an exciting time—the Mercury and Gemini programs sent humans into space and the Apollo program landed them on the Moon and returned them safely to Earth. The effort fulfilled President Kennedy's goal when he said that "no single space project in this period will be more impressive to mankind, or more important for the long-range exploration of space; and none will be so difficult or expensive to accomplish."

With this kind of presidential mandate, there were free-flowing funds in collecting the workers, and there were no barriers to race, religion, political leanings, or gender. Just about anyone who could pass an aptitude test, believed in the mission, and loved challenges in logical thinking was brought on board. The work was centered around the computers and the control systems that launched astronauts into space, and not on ambition or power—it was amazing that so many people could be coordinated and committed so that each person felt he/she had a part in the work. That gave us all a sense of pride.

I was lucky enough to join the ranks in 1965, when the National Aeronautics and Space Administration (NASA) and its subcontractors were hiring a cast of thousands. The desperate need was primarily a call to arms due to the Cold War and the race for space—using a new technology only increased the challenge!

Of course, we must admit that there were hurdles as well as successes. Sadly, the struggles have not always been brought to light, nor have they resulted in learning experiences. Where I worked in 1965, men and women programmers and program designers sat together in offices (pre-cubicle), shared ideas, and acted as sounding boards for each other. We had comfortable and equal working conditions, supplies, and equipment. Following a design, we wrote—by hand—computer program instructions on large coding pads (80 columns per instruction, the same width as a Hollerith punched card). A courier came by twice each day, picking up the coding pads and delivering yesterday's instructions that had been magically translated into a different physical medium—card decks. Put some paper on a cart one day and presto, the next day, a stack of $7\frac{3}{8}$ inch by $3\frac{1}{4}$ inch, stiff paper sheets with holes punched in them were delivered. These cards constituted the program, which was sent to the machine room where operators fed the decks through the card reader. (Remember, this was the mid-1960s.)

What I did not think about then was that the machine room, where the programs ended their journey, was cool (it had to be—the older mainframe computers put out a lot of heat), the operators had some authority, and they were male. By contrast, the "support" room in the basement housed the female keypunchers. It was hot and stuffy and filled with rows and rows of machines where the women sat in front of the card punch machines all day. Keypunching was mind-numbing, the breaks were seldom and short, and the data had no meaning to the keyboardists. (This is not to denigrate the job or the need for it—members of my close family were keypunch "girls.")

Unfortunately, these women were often blamed for errors in the deck, which then became errors in the program—it was easy for a programmer, any programmer, to shift the blame when necessary. This resulted in instituting a verification procedure where each punched card deck had to be rekeyed, using the exact same data, by another woman, making the reward system (based on volume) even less meaningful.

During this time period, I knew several male operators who, without a 4-year degree of any kind, were promoted into the ranks of programmer, seemingly because they were skillful at reading hardware signal lights, fanning card decks, hanging tapes, mounting disks, or even just putting printed output on delivery carts. These were important, necessary activities, carried out by some incredible young men. However, it isn't at all clear how those duties translated into a talent for programming. Keypunchers, who also performed mostly physical tasks, were rarely (never, in my experience) selected for aptitude tests or invited to an interview that could have led to an elevated position. I never knew of a single woman keypuncher who was promoted into any other rank, with the possible exception of women who were elevated to group supervisor, and then they had to stay in the same hot room. I wish I were relating only an individual experience and not the norm, but there is evidence that this situation was prevalent and has been recreated in many ways.

In 1969, the Data Processing Management Association (DPMA) awarded its very first "Computer Sciences Man of the Year" award to U.S. Navy Commander Grace Hopper, eventually to be Rear Admiral Hopper. She was already famous as the "inventor" of COBOL, a programming language that was close to natural speech (English)—for many years the most widely used language in computing. On three different occasions I drove for hours just to hear her captivating and motivating speech. Now she was a role model.

Women continued to enter the field of computing, not only as "keypunch girls" but also as professionals and educators who could employ their mathematical or engineering education or proclivities, in unprecedented numbers during the 1960s and 1970s. Many, maybe most, of them greatly enjoyed their experiences.

There were the pros and cons of being female in the computing field then, just as there are now. The disadvantages still exist, but they have morphed into different ones and are shifting the workforce culture in an unhealthy direction that threatens the future of a profession that still needs diverse participation and input to support our undisputed computer-reliant life.

In this book, the chapters provide a fresh and constructive look at potential reasons for the growing imbalance in gender, exploring the different reasons for the evolution of a profession that has become as male coded as the computing profession now is. While the first wave of programmers and analysts worked in a relatively unsegregated environment, the current computer workforce (across all sectors, including government employees, small business owners, entrepreneurs, chip designers, space-race programmers, and game developers) has become ordered and structured as primarily male.

While Thomas Misa and his colleagues search for answers, they assume no conspiracy theories. There is no diatribe against the male gender, nor does anyone fan the flames of the early feminist movement. It is simply a fact that the last 25 years have seen an increasing imbalance in gender in the computing profession. Most other science and technology sectors actually demonstrate steady growth in the number of female participants. Clearly, something odd happened in computing.

This book is, at times, brutally honest: women are practically absent from the historical literature on computing. They made significant contributions in all segments of the computer industry, yet they had to fight for respect and funding, and too often they lost.

This book gives voice to historians as well as practitioners—those who experienced the heyday, those who are trying to understand it, those who report it, and all those who are trying to change it. The book takes a fair look at this complex issue, is true to history, presents an international perspective, and without judgment explores the strange and unsettling phenomenon that we are now living with: only the male half of the population is working to achieve the potential of computing. And, with the diagnosis that computing's public image is radically out of step with computing's actual practices, the book presents a clear way of moving forward.

If I had had a crystal ball in 1965 and realized what 2009 would look like, it might have been easier, or more obviously important, that we should strive to preserve the culture of the "golden age" of women in computing, while helping it to mature and evolve to meet today's technical challenges. And, by all measures, to be fair.

LINDA SHAFER, CSDP
*IEEE Computer Society Press Chair*

# Preface

We don't normally think of academic publishing as a contact sport, but this volume was born with bruises on my arm. We were planning a workshop at the Charles Babbage Institute (CBI) and enjoying the process of framing a much-needed historical assessment of gender and computing. We knew it was a respectable topic. Scholars from many different backgrounds and traditions had in recent years put gender on the academic map. The exploration of gender and computing history was long overdue. After all, there must be something in the many hundreds of photographs we'd seen over the years showing "white guys with computers."

When introducing the CBI workshop to my colleagues in science and engineering, I explained how gender had become a useful category of analysis in the social sciences, and our aim for bringing gender analysis into the mainstream of computing history. Often, I didn't get more than two or three sentences into the spiel when a female colleague grabbed my arm and said: "no, you don't quite understand—what you are doing, gender and computing, is important, really important." My technical colleagues had gone through graduate school and started their careers in the midst of the women's movement, and many had struggled in their careers and institutions with its ambiguous successes. They wanted to *understand* gender and computing, but they also wanted to *change* the existing state of affairs. This volume took form with both these aims in mind.

We were fortunate to draw on a growing interest in the gendered aspects of computing. Educators, administrators, managers, and scholars share an interest in better understanding how computing has emerged and become part of contemporary culture. Computing educators are justifiably concerned about flagging computer science and engineering enrollments, while administrators and managers at all levels strive to recruit and retain a more gender-balanced workforce. Scholars in computer history can appreciate that gender is a useful category of analysis, and that gender studies of computing are urgently needed.

To identify promising themes and possible contributors, we formed a steering committee consisting of Janet Abbate (Virginia Tech), Veronika Oechtering (University of Bremen), Jeffrey Yost (Charles Babbage Institute), and myself.

Bringing these educators and scholars together for a weekend in May 2008 depended on material support from several sources. At the University of Minnesota, we are grateful for essential financial support from the Institute of Technology Dean's Office, the Computer Science and Engineering Department, the Electrical and Computer Engineering Department, and the Program for the History of Science, Technology and Medicine. International travel was funded by the University's Office of International Programs and the Deutsche Forschungsgemeinschaft (German Research Foundation). Everything we do at the Charles Babbage Institute represents a unique partnership between the founders of CBI, with their prescient vision of supporting a research center for the history of computing, and the longstanding institutional support from the University of Minnesota's Institute of Technology, the University Libraries, and the Program for History of Science, Technology and Medicine.

We are fortunate also for first-rate staff at CBI. R. Arvid Nelson, CBI's archivist, developed a special museum exhibit entitled "Gendered Bits: Identities, Practices, and Artifacts in Computing" in cooperation with in-house professional designer Darren Terpstra. These materials were physically installed in Andersen Library during the summer of 2008 and will be made available permanently via an online exhibit. (Images of the installed exhibit, as well as literature and background materials for the workshop, can be found at **umn.edu/ ~tmisa/gender/**.) Katie Charlet took charge of registration and played an essential role in preparing this volume for publication, including translations from the French (again!), while Jeffrey Yost and Stephanie Crowe assisted with preparations and logistics.

Gender studies of technology and science have an active interdisciplinary journal literature in *Signs, Women's Studies, Gender and Society*, and *Social Studies of Science, Technology & Culture*, as well as key books, including those by Roger Horowitz (editor), *Boys and Their Toys?* (New York: Routledge, 2001); Donna J. Haraway, *Simians, Cyborgs and Women* (New York: Routledge, 1991); Donna J. Haraway, *Modest_Witness@Second_Millennium* (New York: Routledge, 1997); Nina E. Lerman, Ruth Oldenziel, and Arwen Mohun (editors), *Gender and Technology* (Baltimore: Johns Hopkins University Press, 2003); Ruth Oldenziel, *Making Technology Masculine* (Amsterdam: Amsterdam University Press, 2004); and Roger Horowitz and Arwen Mohun (editors), *His and Hers* (Charlottesville: University of Virginia Press, 1998). For computer history, see the special issue introduced by Janet Abbate, "Women and Gender in the History of Computing," *IEEE Annals of the History of Computing*, Vol. 25, No. 4 (2003): 4–8. Our gender and computing bibliography can be found at www.umn.edu/~tmisa/gender/literature.html.

THOMAS J. MISA

*Minneapolis, Minnesota*
*March 2010*

# Contributors

**JANET ABBATE** is an assistant professor in Science, Technology and Society at Virginia Tech. She is the author of *Inventing the Internet* (MIT Press, 1999) and co-editor with Brian Kahin of *Standards Policy for Information Infrastructure* (MIT Press, 1995). She also was guest editor for a special issue on "Women and Gender in the History of Computing," *IEEE Annals of the History of Computing*, Vol. 25, No. 4 (2003). Currently, she is writing a book on women in the computing profession since World War II.

**HILDE G. CORNELIUSSEN** is an associate professor of Digital Culture at the Department of Linguistic, Literary and Aesthetic Studies at the University of Bergen, where she teaches courses in digital culture, gender and ICT, and computer history. Corneliussen holds a Ph.D. in Humanistic Informatics, and she has published on gender and ICT, computer history, computer education, and computer games. She is co-editor of *Digital Culture, Play, and Identity: A World of Warcraft Reader* (MIT Press, 2008).

**GREG DOWNEY** is a professor in the School of Journalism & Mass Communication and the School of Library and Information Studies at the University of Wisconsin–Madison. He is the author of *Telegraph Messenger Boys: Labor, Technology, and Geography, 1850–1950* (Routledge, 2002), and *Closed Captioning: Subtitling, Stenography, and the Digital Convergence of Text with Television* (Johns Hopkins University Press, 2008).

**NATHAN ENSMENGER** is an assistant professor in the History and Sociology of Science Department at the University of Pennsylvania. His current research interests include the social and labor history of computer programming, the history of artificial intelligence, and the use of computers as "decision technologies" in medicine, finance, and government. He is completing a book on the history of software development.

**Thomas Haigh** is an assistant professor in the School of Information Studies at the University of Wisconsin, Milwaukee. He received his Ph.D. in History and Sociology of Science from the University of Pennsylvania and has published on many aspects of the history of computing.

**Caroline Clarke Hayes** is a professor of Mechanical Engineering at the University of Minnesota. She is the first Ph.D. to graduate from Carnegie Mellon's Robotics program in the School of Computer Science. The focus of her research work is how to design effective systems of people and technology; current projects focus on technology for collaboration over distance. She is chair of the University of Minnesota's Women's Faculty Cabinet for 2009–2010 and co-investigator on the university's most recent National Science Foundation ADVANCE proposal.

**Marie Hicks** received her Ph.D. in History from Duke University in 2009. She teaches courses in history, STS, and women's studies at Duke University and North Carolina State University. Her dissertation, *Compiling Inequalities: Computerization in the British Civil Service and Nationalized Industries, 1940–1979*, investigated the understudied, feminized class of machine operators upon whose work the U.K. government built its ambitious national computing projects.

**Serkan Karas** is a Ph.D. student in the Graduate Program in the History and Philosophy of Science, National and Kapodistrian University of Athens and National Technical University of Athens, Greece. A native Cypriot who speaks Turkish, Greek, and English, he is interested in comparative and transnational approaches to the history of technological infrastructures.

**Hara Konsta** is a Ph.D. student in the Graduate Program in the History and Philosophy of Science, National and Kapodistrian University of Athens and National Technical University of Athens, Greece. A high-school teacher of arts and crafts, Konsta is writing her dissertation on the history of co-shaping of computing configurations and work/educational space.

**Theodore Lekkas** is a Ph.D. student in the Graduate Program in the History and Philosophy of Science, National and Kapodistrian University of Athens and National Technical University of Athens, Greece. A computer industry professional, he is working on a dissertation on aspects of the history of software in Greece.

**Thomas J. Misa** is director of the Charles Babbage Institute at the University of Minnesota, where he also teaches in the Ph.D. program in the history of science, technology, and medicine. He is a faculty member in the Department of Electrical and Computer Engineering, and holds the ERA-Land Grant Chair in the History of Technology. He is author or editor of six books, including *Leonardo to the Internet* (Johns Hopkins University Press, 2004).

**Corinna Schlombs** in December 2009 completed her dissertation, a comparative and transnational examination of the transfer of computing technology and culture between the United States and Western European countries from the end of World War II to the late 1960s, in the History and Sociology of Science Department at the University of Pennsylvania. She has published "Toward International Computing History," in *IEEE Annals of the History of Computing*, Vol. 28, No. 1 (2006): 107–108; and "Engineering International Expansion: IBM and Remington Rand in European Computer Markets," in *IEEE Annals of the History of Computing*, Vol. 30 (2008): 42–58.

**ARISTOTLE TYMPAS** is assistant professor of the History of Technology in Modernity at the Department of Philosophy and History of Science, National and Kapodistrian University of Athens, Greece. He specializes in the history of the use of computers in engineering contexts, mechanical, electrical, and biomedical.

**JEFFREY R. YOST** is associate director of the Charles Babbage Institute, University of Minnesota, and Editor-in-Chief of *IEEE Annals of the History of Computing*. He has published books on the history of the computer industry and scientific computing as well as more than a dozen articles and book chapters on the business, social, and cultural and intellectual history of computing, software, and networking.

# Tools for
# Understanding

# Gender Codes
## Defining the Problem

1

THOMAS J. MISA

Women have passionately programmed computers for many decades. Ada Lovelace wrote abstract programs for calculating Bernoulli numbers on Charles Babbage's mechanical computer, and six women mathematicians, known as human "computers," created working programs for the ENIAC computer during the Second World War. In the 1950s the pioneering generation of computer science featured a surprising number of prominent women who led research teams, defined computer languages, and even pioneered the history of computing. The annual Grace Hopper celebration, named for the most prominent of these pioneering women computer scientists, offers "a four-day technical conference designed to bring the research and career interests of women in computing to the forefront"[1]. More recently, Elizabeth "Jake" Feinler defined the top-level domain names—.com, .gov, .org—for the Internet. In 2006, Fran Allen, already the first female IBM Fellow, was the first woman to win the prestigious Turing Award from the Association for Computing Machinery, for her work in optimizing computer code. Two years later, Barbara Liskov was awarded the Turing Award for her foundational work on programming languages. The list of notable women in computing is sizable and expanding. It's strange anyone would think that women don't like computing.

Since the 1970s women have made impressive gains in professional life, but these gains did not extend evenly into the fields of engineering and the physical sciences. Greater gender parity has typified most professions in the past two decades or so, with women making up half or more of all graduate or professional students: this is true for law schools and medical schools as well as most fields in the social and biological sciences. Engineering and physical sciences started with rather few women, at all levels, and have been making slow if steady progress in enrolling more women students and hiring more women faculty and scientists. Retaining women scientists and engineers at mid-career remains a challenge. But when you look at the college enrollments and workforce figures for computing, a strikingly different picture emerges.

There's no way of putting it except to say that computing is unique among all the professional fields. You can see this most clearly when looking at the "big picture" across the last 40 years and identifying which of the technical professions women opted to enter and when they did so. The first distinction for computing was an early upside in women's participation. Beginning in the mid-1960s, women entered the emerging computing profession and eventually did so in unusually large numbers (Fig. 1.1). In the United States, women went from being roughly one in ten in the undergraduate computing cohort to being nearly four in ten. At the peak in the mid-1980s women earned 37% of all U.S. bachelor degrees in computing, and across these decades women entered the computing workforce in large numbers. In the late 1980s, women constituted fully 38% of the U.S. white-collar computing workforce. This was a significant success for computing and for the women's movement. Chapters in this volume describe why, for roughly two decades, computing attracted so many women.

Figure 1.1. Woman studying linear programming. For recruiting, Honeywell created a positive image of women programmers in 1969. Women, such as Christine Johnson, composed one-third of the opening class of 40 at Honeywell's Wellesley Hills, Massachusetts, education center. (Courtesy of Charles Babbage Institute.)

We need to better understand why women elected to study *computing* in such large numbers. Why not chemistry or physics or engineering or one of the other technical professions? Men through the 1960s soundly dominated all of these fields. In this book we explore why large numbers of women experienced programming and other computer-related jobs to be more congenial than working in science labs or in engineering offices. We show that women worked as programmers, as systems analysts, as managers, and as computer executives. In the mid-1980s, while women flooded into computing education and from there into the computing workforce, there were proportionately more women in computing than anywhere else in the engineering world. Medical school was to a large degree still a boy's club, with sizable increases in women medical students just beginning. (Only psychology and certain of the social sciences had equal numbers of women and men; and, of course, the professions of nursing, teaching, librarianship, and social work were, from their origins earlier in the 20th century, distinctively hospitable to women.) This book tells the stories of women computing professionals, including accounts of their struggles and celebrations of their successes. The chapters also give visibility to the many women who worked in lower-status and lower-pay computer occupations, such as operators and data-entry clerks (Fig. 1.2).

Despite these early successes, something unprecedented in the history of the professions hit computing in the mid-1980s: not merely did women stop entering computing in large numbers, but the proportion of women studying computing actually began falling—and it has continued to fall, steadily, all the way through to the present. No other professional field has ever experienced such a decline in the proportion of women in its ranks. The latest figures from the National Science Foundation (NSF), the Computing Research Association,

Figure 1.2. Women as computer operators. Publicity images often used attractive women models to sell computer systems. But many women actually worked as computer operators, here on an OCR data-entry system, a decided step up from data-entry work (compare Fig. 1.6). (Courtesy of Charles Babbage Institute.)

the Department of Education, and the Bureau of Labor Statistics using various measures and methodologies all tell the same story: women are staying away from computing education and the computing workforce. The most recent NSF figures suggest that women may account for just one in seven undergraduate computing students, or around 15%: a catastrophic drop from the peak of 37%. The Taulbee survey of top-ranked North American computer science and engineering programs puts the recent figures even lower [2]. A minuscule 0.4% of first-year women college students list computer science as a probable major, while as recently as the early 1980s it was fully ten times higher. Even when combining computer science with information science, which has more women students, the trend is unmistakable—and it is down [3].

We initially thought this drop was "only" a problem for academic computer science, but closer inspection of the data indicates there has been a gender-specific tail-off in the computing workforce as well. Recent figures from 2005 indicate that women composed just 29% of the white-collar computing workforce, down nearly 10 percentage points from the 1980s. Clearly, this is not merely an academic problem. Of course, not all practicing programmers have computer science degrees, and indeed only around two-thirds of working programmers and systems analysts have 4-year college degrees of any sort. A large number of computer professionals enter the workforce with associate degrees or other vocational training. (Gender statistics for these vocational programs are not carefully scrutinized by national policymaking bodies; the same goes for proprietary courses offered by Microsoft, Oracle, and other companies.)

A recent report from the Harvard Business School anatomizes the sharp falloff of women in science, engineering, and other technical companies. Most women continue work in these technical fields, including computing, for approximately 10 years—and then fully half of them leave the workforce. This mid-career exodus is not the result of women's "choices" or "preferences" (as some commentators suggest) because, after all, these women actually chose those professions. Rather, "more than half of these women [working in science and technology fields] drop out—pushed and shoved by macho work environments, serious isolation, and extreme job pressures" [4]. This loss of women's talent is alarming. Figures that we obtained from the U.S. Bureau of Labor Statistics indicate that women's presence in the computing workforce is falling off as well. Worse, the falloff in workforce closely follows the downturn in undergraduate computer science graduates—with perhaps as little as a 3-year "lag." If women were leaving the computing workforce after 10 years, that would be bad enough. It appears that the fall in enrollments, number of graduates, and computing workforce numbers are closely related. Indeed, we suspect that the educational and workforce tail-offs together actually reflect some broader, as-yet-unrecognized social or cultural shift. If the employment figures continue to fall as abruptly as the enrollment figures might forecast, then the computing workforce will soon become one of the most gender-segregated professional environments. Computing might return to its gender composition of the 1960s, but the rest of the world has moved forward.

A pressing question that this book addresses, and for the first time with historical data and analysis, is how and when and why women's participation in computing fell so dramatically. This lopsided change in computing's gender balance in the past two decades is entirely without historical precedent. Some of the technical professions appear historically to be resistant to women's entry, such as surgery or civil engineering; yet no other profession has seen the upswing and downturn of women that is strikingly evident in computing. There have been wide swings in the enrollments and employment of varied branches of engineering, as one field or another comes into fashion or falls from favor; these swings are not accompanied by any similar long-term decline in women.

## FRAMING THE GENDER GAP

The dramatic falloff of women in computing is hardly a secret. In 1991 Ellen Spertus, then an MIT graduate student, wrote a paper asking, "Why Are There So Few Female Computer Scientists?" The problem was not so much formal discrimination or overt barriers to women, but rather gender biases encoded in professional culture. Among her findings, Spertus reported a professor introducing robotics to a graduate artificial-intelligence class by telling this would-be joke: "Pretty soon we'll have robots that are sophisticated enough to wander around in shopping malls and pick up girls." Unsurprisingly, the female graduate student who related the episode hardly heard the rest of the lecture. In the years since Spertus's report, the situation has not gotten better. "What Has Driven Women Out of Computer Science?" was one recent headline. "Lack of Women in Computing Has Educators Worried," goes another. The *IEEE Spectrum* [5] warns that the "gender gap is widening."

The gender gap in computing now concerns professionals in the field as well as educators concerned about the composition of their classrooms. Women's absence has contributed to a sharp contraction in U.S. computing enrollments: in 2001 there were 400 majors in each computer science (CS) department, while today there are just over 200. In recent years, the National Science Foundation has put around $20 million annually into various research and demonstration efforts aimed at increasing the participation of women in computing and other science and engineering fields [6]. Educators from K-12 through graduate school encourage young women to study math and science as well as to major in engineering fields, including computer science and electrical engineering. Professional associations mobilize high-level committees of educators and practitioners. Some researchers examine gender as an important variable in designing software and human–computer interfaces, addressing a gender bias broadly similar to medical researchers' past assumption that men's bodies were the normal ones [7]. And science museums, science-fair mentors, Girl Scout leaders, and many others present positive views of science and technical fields as approachable, exciting, and relevant to young women as they plan careers. It's difficult to assess their impact, but it's a safe bet that absent these wide-ranging efforts the worrisome figures on women in computing might be even worse.

We believe that there is some "missing piece" to this picture. Our book is aimed—in three distinct ways—at assisting these reform efforts and, we hope, changing the culture of computing. First, we offer forceful *historical data* documenting the gender gap in computing. It's very clear that smart people have devised many intervention strategies, based on intuitively plausible models of the underlying problem [8]. Yet, surprisingly, not enough is known about how and when and why the gendered culture of computing emerged. This book addresses these very questions. We hope historical insight can improve the outcomes for the wide-ranging efforts at change. Richly textured case studies of women's struggles as well as their own strategies for success, in gaining computing education as well as working for and even running computing companies, can help evaluate and refine these intervention strategies. While we know that women flooded into the computing professions in the 1960s and 1970s, we know all too little about why they did so and what they found there. Women's experiences in the computing workforce are similarly underdocumented and poorly understood [9]. In this book we present fresh evidence of women's striking successes as computer scientists and as entrepreneurs in the computer services industry. This book also documents women's exclusion from high-level computing positions and marginalization within the computing professions. These stories, too, give a more complete picture of the problem.

A second contribution of this book is to offer *tools for grasping the dynamics* of the gender gap. The computing profession changed dramatically across the past three or four decades. We need to record the stories but we also need tools for understanding what was going on, what might have gone wrong, and, for those early decades, what clearly went right with women in computing. Historians, by our disciplinary training, are ideally equipped to understand complexity and change across time. Historians study social processes as well as cultural dynamics; as a profession we deal centrally with language, representations, cultural forms, institutional practices, social and political processes— and power. "The study of computer science education can be seen as a microcosm of how a realm of power can be claimed by one group of people, relegating others to outsiders," as Margolis and Fisher argue in *Unlocking the Clubhouse*. There are "weighty influences that steal women's interest in computer science away from them" [10]. Historians' contributions frequently involve not merely accurately reporting the facts, but also unpacking complex terms at play. Here, it is certain that we need to unpack the terms "women" and "men" and "computing" and to set these into a dynamic framework. Women faced different expectations about gender roles and career paths in the 1960s compared with the 1980s, while computing during these decades was transformed from large mainframe-based installations to the profusion of personal computers. It is worth noting that women flooded into computing during the mainframe era as well as that the sea change in gender occurred during the rise of personal computers in the 1980s.

This book profiles the astonishing diversity of women's experiences in the "computing profession" as well: they worked as highly paid programmers and systems analysts and managers, as well as lower-status operators, data-entry clerks, and maintenance workers. Some of these women, especially ones with managerial or executive responsibilities, are at the upper scale of white-collar work, while the lower-status jobs are squarely blue-collar ones. A key process that we document and analyze is the "feminization" of work as well as the "masculinization" of the professions. This book highlights how computing is understood in gendered terms and how it is represented in popular culture.

Figure 1.3. "Computing = Development" for Ivory Coast women. Ivory Coast stamp from 1972 surrounds a woman with computer images, including an IBM mainframe, punch cards, and core memory. In French, *informatique* can be either computing or the discipline of computer science. (Courtesy of Charles Babbage Institute.)

It is probably happenstance that the movie "Revenge of the Nerds" (1984) appeared just as women's enrollments in computer science were peaking, but there is some relationship between popular culture and the computing culture. We believe it is no coincidence that the sea change in gender of the 1980s closely paralleled the emergence of male nerds in popular culture as well as the rise of distinctly gendered computer gaming, now a multibillion dollar industry (see below). All the same, the mass media's amplified masculine image of computing is clearly a misleading one. Media images of computing are even less gender balanced than the actual practices of computing (see Chapter 12).

Finally, this book frames the problem of gender and computing in *international and comparative terms* (Fig. 1.3). Much thinking about the gender gap so far has taken the United States to be the normative case. Certainly, in the global economy of today, any uniquely national perspective is increasingly irrelevant. A recent CRA-Taulbee survey indicates that students from outside North America make up 59% of entering Ph.D. students in computing at North American universities. Computing professionals increasingly work in thoroughly international and multicultural environments, whether for large multinational companies or even in smaller entrepreneurial start-ups. We need to know how divergent perceptions and expectations regarding gender interact in this multicultural environment: this is the daily work experience for thousands of computing professionals today. This book presents historical cases and contributions that begin a much-needed international and comparative analysis of gender and computing. The chapters include substantial material on Britain, Germany, Greece, Norway, and the United States as well as briefer comparative reflections on other countries. It's a modest step to a more thoroughly global picture [11].

## STRATEGIES FOR REFORM

Before turning to the detailed contributions of this book, we should give an overview of the reform efforts underway today. The favored intervention strategies aim at increasing the number of women in the computing professions, at both the undergraduate and graduate levels as well as in the ranks of faculty and in the wider workforce. The results of reform are not always easy to determine, especially with the persistent, long-term decline of women in computing. Social scientists and educators have identified five "explanatory factors" that underpin most existing interventions and experiments [12]. First, who feels welcome in the computing classroom or workplace—and who feels out of place—is shaped by experiences and even more strongly by entry barriers. When undergraduate computer science programs began requiring prior programming experience for introductory level classes, they did not intend to send a negative message to women but all the same that is exactly what occurred. It so happened that young men interested in computing had frequently done extensive after-hours programming at school or at home, but relatively few young women interested in computing had done so. The requirement of prior programming experience constituted a gender-selecting entry barrier. Indeed, recognizing this problem, some computer science programs have restructured introductory courses to focus less on programming prowess and more on conceptual issues.

Second, the topics treated in a computing curriculum as well as the examples used to illustrate them can be more or less gender-specific. For years, programming assignments did computations with professional football scores or baseball statistics. At one high school a woman student using football statistics in a programming exercise "was ridiculed because she used the name of a baseball team instead of a football team" [13]. (Some have suggested knitting diagrams as an alternate way of studying algorithmic thinking [14].) Some recent research suggests that women as well as men respond positively to course assignments that show how computing can make a difference in the wider world (Fig. 1.4). "Their motivation for learning computer science very much hung on the purpose that computing was going to be used for," suggests Jane Margolis, co-author of *Unlocking the Clubhouse: Women in Computing*, about women computer science students at Carnegie Mellon. "It wasn't just hacking for hacking's sake. There was a real social context that gave them motivation and meaning" [15]. Students transferring into computing majors from other disciplines, such as the sciences, also may require computing programs to offer catch-up courses.

While for years computer science programs were notoriously "hard"—frequently a large lecture class functioned as a wash-out course to thin the ranks [16]—it's become apparent that women were disproportionately hit by such treatment. Computer science programs are now actively looking for ways to

Figure 1.4. Computing as meaningful work in society. Burroughs recruiting in 1980 pictured Toni Sternal, a project manager based in Pasadena, California. After 10 years in field engineering, Sternal directed a team of hardware support specialists in the "center of activity for medium computer systems." (Courtesy of Charles Babbage Institute.)

improve retention and satisfaction of all students, in part because their enrollments are down overall, leading to consideration of the third and fourth "explanatory factors." Positive role models and mentoring in the classroom and at work are crucial institutional supports. The well-regarded "A Study on the Status of Women Faculty in Science at MIT" [17] found that female junior faculty were rarely included in the informal networks and mentoring relationships that assisted male junior faculty in learning the ropes, including how to hire graduate students, submit conference papers, and craft successful grants. Efforts at mentoring, especially with established professionals outside one's own institution such as MentorNet, seem particularly promising [18]. Fourth, peer support seems particularly important to students, whether women, men, or underrepresented minorities, who may have their sense of self-confidence jarred by daily challenges. So-called pair programming is one positive step, where two students together tackle programming assignments instead of working alone. Educational researchers have found that women in such pair-programming classes are substantially more likely to take additional computing classes or, if a computing major, to successfully complete the major.

Finally, all reform efforts need to confront the distinctive culture of computing. If language creates culture, then computing has created its own universe. You start a computer by *booting* it, if it unexpectedly *crashes* or *bombs* an expert might do a *code dump*, you *execute* instructions or programs, or if something goes wrong you *kill* or *abort* them, a *code warrior* dreams of creating

Figure 1.5. Men as self-appointed masters of computing. Computer data punched on paper tape scrutinized by the masculine gaze. (Compare Figures 3.1, 9.5, and 12.6.) (Courtesy of Charles Babbage Institute.)

a *killer app*—all these everyday terms in computing are loaded ones that carry distinctive values. And this is not a woman's world. "Women are obligated to adopt some degree of macho to become part of [the computing world]," suggests Karen Coyle. "To question the masculinity of computers is tantamount to questioning our image of masculinity itself: computers are power" [19]. Popular images in advertisements, movies, computer games, and computer magazines all tend to reinforce the assertive male dominance of the field (Fig. 1.5). "Is it possible that this emphasis on engineering and other masculine activities arise because computing, particularly programming, and software activities are in fact not 'manly' enough?" asks Frances Grundy. "Do these terms to some extent compensate for the absence of the screwdriver, the soldering iron and the oily rag—even maybe the roar of the engines?" [20]. And, it bears saying, garden-variety sexism persists in computing education and work. Female computer-science graduate students recently reported "incidents ranging from differential and demeaning to crude and offensive behaviors" [21].

The "girl gamers" movement in the mid-1990s formed an intentional countermovement aimed at recruiting women into computing. Gender had only recently emerged in computer gaming. The earliest computer games, such as Spacewar and Space Travel, did not themselves feature explicitly gendered content: spaceships and photon torpedoes were the screen images. While the avatar-paddle for the Atari videogame Pong (1972) was also without explicit gender, Ms. PacMan (1980–1981) was the first to feature a gender-specific avatar. In the 1980s damsels-in-distress figured in the video games Donkey Kong and Dragon's Lair and in countless games since [22]. The controversial female avatar Lara Croft anchored the best-selling Tomb Raider video games (first launched in 1996) and the character, played by Angelina Jolie, starred in the subsequent movie. Lara is renowned for her intelligence, good looks, daring, and wit. She is also ogled on screen for her hypersexualized virtual body. Her creator, Toby Gard, once lamented, "I just wish that when she was taken out of my hands they hadn't made her boobs so big" [23].

The "girl gamers" movement was launched with the hope of fostering girls' interest in computers and computer games by encouraging the development of games that toned down the typical gratuitous violence and sexually aggressive imagery. Two edited volumes from MIT Press form something like bookends. The first volume, *From Barbie to Mortal Kombat* (1998), presented programmatic chapters, many written by idealistic young women suggesting a New Jerusalem was at hand. The movement hoped for a "virtuous cycle" where girls playing computer games would lead to women writing game software, and hence more girl-friendly game experiences, and even more girl gamers. There are some signs of success. Women's participation as gamers is certainly up—recent industry statistics indicate 38% of U.S. game players are women, playing an average of 7.4 hours per week (just 0.2 hour less than the average male gamer)—and there are changes in the gaming industry [24]. For instance, in *Tomb Raider: Legend* (2006), Lara Croft was redesigned in part to appeal to girl gamers [25]. And in recent years, the best-selling "Sims" game franchise (launched in 2000) has a solid majority of female players. Women create an estimated 50% of the characters in "Second Life," the popular online role-playing platform.

Even so, many obstacles remain in the gaming world. Women comprise just 11.5% of the game industry workforce according to the International Game Developers Association, and many games as well as many game-industry trade shows persist in using preposterous sexual stereotypes. In "The Future of Games Does Not Include Women" (2006), Nikki Douglas, the long-serving senior editor of Grrlgamer.com, blasted the game industry with a strong critique of its pervasive, blatant, and offensive male bias. She cited a 2006 game advertisement in *Computer Gaming World* where the principal image "is a woman lying in lingerie on a bed in [high heels] with a bullet-hole in her forehead. The tagline is 'Beautifully executed'." The second MIT Press volume, *Beyond Barbie and Mortal Kombat* (2008), presented a much more sober and cautious view of girl gamers [26].

## HISTORY IN THE PRESENT

This book's chapters, taken together, represent a unique examination of the historical evolution of gender and computing. We firmly believe that effective interventions to improve professional practices in computing (and other technical fields) require greater historical awareness and understanding. This is especially important in the field of computing, with its perennial celebration of progress and the belief that the past is gone and done. Yet, as William Faulkner famously observed in *Requiem for a Nun*, "The past is never dead. It's not even past." Effective reform efforts will need to grapple with the somewhat paradoxical fact that the computing profession has at once a compelling recent history as well as a longer institutional and cultural history that stretches back many decades. We need to learn lessons from both of these histories, for they are very much with us today.

This book's first three chapters, including this introductory one, are efforts at specifying the gender-gap problem in computing and introducing historical tools for conceptualizing it. In Chapter 2, Caroline Hayes presents a full set of national statistics to get a better picture of the turning points in the United States. She draws on several existing data sets, including ones from the National Science Foundation and several longitudinal surveys. The result is a long-run and multilevel portrait of women in computing, from the 1960s to the present. Her data anatomizes the upside through the mid-1980s as well as the unprecedented downside since then. Two aspects of her chapter are distinctive. While it is common to treat "computer science" education as a lump entity, Hayes shows that there are distinctive trajectories and dynamics at work at the undergraduate level (bachelor's) as contrasted with the graduate level (master's and doctoral degrees). In brief, while women's participation at the master's and doctoral levels is still low, the figures have been rising slowly across the decades. (There are worrying trends in the ranks of women computer-science faculty, especially at mid-career.) It is at the bachelor's level, with the unprecedented drop in women's participation, that something really unusual is going on. Moreover, she presents striking new data from the Bureau of Labor Statistics that suggest women's participation in the computing workforce is falling off— and possibly even faster than the dire figures for computing enrollments might predict. We believe this unexpected link is one of the undiscovered "missing pieces." If confirmed, her findings suggest that a broad cultural shift—influencing women at universities as well as in the computing work force—may be the chief challenge for reformers to address.

In Chapter 3, Thomas Haigh examines a classic instance in the automation of American industry, as data-processing computers were introduced into offices. He recounts the professionalizing efforts by the industry's managers and supervisors as they confronted data-processing's strongly feminized labor force (Fig. 1.6). The Data Processing Management Association, for years the largest professional organization in computing, improved the professional standing of its members by striving for the "masculinity of the organization man," consciously separating the emerging professional field from feminized office work. He notes that the effort to remake "business computing as men's work occurred because of, not despite of, the presence of women in the field." He concludes that sex typing and status anxiety, far more than any supposed natural talents of women or men, account for gender-segregated work in data processing. He also contextualizes his narrative through a statistical analysis of occupational data, again finding strong evidence of gender marked employment. Moving up the salary ladder—from keypunch workers (at the bottom), through computer operators, programmers, and (at the top) systems analysts—he finds remarkable consistency in that "the proportion of women drops and the average pay rises."

Figure 1.6. Computer automation of female clerical work. Women working on data-entry terminals supplemented the main OCR data-entry system at this installation (compare Fig. 1.2). (Courtesy of Charles Babbage Institute.)

While women's proportion in the job category of computer software developer has been shrinking, Haigh's reading of the statistics indicates some small measure of hope. There seems to be a rise in the aggregate number of women employed in such high-status jobs as information science manager, systems analyst, and computer software engineer.

The unsettled and unstable dynamics of gender and computing are the topics in the two middle sections of the book. Chapters 4–7 (Schlombs, Hicks, Ensmenger, Downey) deal with specific institutional contexts, while Chapters 8 and 9 (Corneliussen and Tympas et al.) deal with popular culture and mass media.

The chapters in Part II: Institutional Life distill lessons from automation or computerization in several distinct sectors—including offices, government, the emerging profession of programming, and those information-centric institutions known as libraries. In Chapter 4, Corinna Schlombs assesses the gender consequences of computerized automation in government and private-sector offices. Even though many proponents of automation believed that electronic computers carried the promise of improving working conditions, the historical record is distinctly mixed. In the early 20th century, following Herman Hollerith's pioneering use of punch cards for the 1890 Census, women became the primary workers in the punch-card industry, a novel development since women were relative newcomers to office work at the time. Schlombs aptly contrasts Germany and the United States, where punch-card work took two quite different paths. Whereas in Germany punch-card work was a male-only domain, dirty and loud, and often physically kept separate from the rest of the office, in the United States women soundly dominated such work, which was also altered through office design and architecture. By 1930 there were more than 30,000 women punch-card machine operators. After the Second World War, the introduction of computers into offices seems to have put many of these women out of work. Computers effectively replaced the legions of punch-card workers, and instead of moving into the higher-status computing jobs, women filled the follow-on occupation of data-entry clerks. One important lesson, especially given the computing field's general enthusiasm about the transformative character of technology, is that while technology induces changes "the outcomes of the change are constrained by the pre-existing organization of work of which gender is an integral part."

In Chapter 5, Marie Hicks presents an example where computing was initially a women's sphere of work and then "very self-consciously re-engineered as a field of masculine endeavor." The shift reflects the emergence and hardening of a "gender line" in computing. Her extended case study is the British governmental sector, as it became increasingly dependent on computing with the postwar expansion of the welfare state and the need to compete in a high-technology economy. British women dominated the prewar mechanical punch-card work, much as Schlombs described for the United States, but in Britain women also dominated the early installations of government computing. "Boys generally prefer laboratory work to computing," as one 1955 government report put it, and computing became a feminized job class. Computer program-mers were recruited from the largely feminized Machine Grades of employment although there was creeping preference for recruits from the male-heavy Executive Grades. In the mid-1960s, with the launch of Prime Minister Harold Wilson's avowed "technological revolution," the government advertised pro-gramming positions as "suitable for women" as well as for men. The door for women's advancement from lower to higher grades was closed in 1970, however, when the government created a new Automatic Data Processing work grade for programmers and systems analysts but explicitly excluded the (femi-nized) grades from either having a favorable review for an upgrade or, for the Machine Grade, from applying at all. Women's computing work in the govern-ment sector thus became "peasant work," literally a dead end. Hicks observes that these "different hiring rubrics for men and women" constituted a potent institutional and cultural form of gender discrimination against women. And, consequently, Britain's economic performance flagged. Once again, the funda-mental point seems to be the notions of gender that undervalued women's contributions to the workforce and consequently overvalued men's. Connecting her history to the present debates on women's underrepresentation, Hicks con-cludes that simply increasing the number of well-qualified women graduates is unlikely to address the underlying problems of gender and culture.

In Chapter 6, "Making Programming Masculine," Nathan Ensmenger outlines how men and women became programmers. In the early days, he reminds us, no one really knew how to select good candidates for training as programmers. A variety of different selection mechanisms were widely dis-cussed in the computing profession as well as in individual companies. The most famous by far was IBM's Programmer Aptitude Test, which was widely used to identify promising recruits (and only years later actually evaluated and found to be a poor predictor of programming talent) [27]. "My smashing grade

Figure 1.7. Emergence of gendered work in office computing. Men and women often worked side-by-side (here at a Honeywell computer center in the late 1960s) but typically did different jobs. Women often tended data storage units. (Courtesy of Charles Babbage Institute.)

on the PAT was like a guardian angel which would hover over my entire career at IBM," noted one programmer hired in the 1960s [28]. In the event, these selection mechanisms were put into place during the years that women first entered the programming profession in large numbers (Fig. 1.7). It's not at all clear that these selection mechanisms actually discriminated against women. All the same, his chapter underscores how such selection mechanisms, including the imperatives of professionalization and anxieties about professional status, shape the culture of computing and elevate certain norms while devaluating others.

In Chapter 7 Greg Downey examines library automation with attention to "the changing social meanings of both femininity and masculinity which we might refer to as 'gender'." His chapter parallels Marie Hicks's in that librarianship too was a firmly feminized profession well before computer automation. Beginning in the 1960s, the library profession showcased the future of electronic catalog records and networked communication systems at the World's Fairs in Seattle and New York while library leaders, primarily males at the most prestigious academic libraries, enthusiastically promoted computing in many forms, including the national efforts that spawned MARC and OCLC. As with office work, however, computerization and computers themselves had specific gendered consequences for the work of librarians (predominantly female and at many diverse sites) as well as the image of the library profession. This chapter examines the ferment raised by library feminism in the 1970s and 1980s, as women sought parity in library professionalism, as well as the subsequent discussions about computerized library catalogs through the 1990s. The library profession came surprisingly late to an understanding of the profound impact of computer automation, Downey finds, and seemed on balance not to properly understand the links between professionalization, computerization, and gender. Overall, by spotlighting the debate on gender and library automation, his chapter suggests that "moments of new technological possibility ... are moments of social reflection and change."

In Part III: Media and Culture, the chapters deal with the images of computing to be found in popular culture and mass media. These images shape practices, although not always in straightforward ways. In Chapter 8 Hilde Corneliussen uses the tools of discourse analysis to understand the construction of gender and computing. Her chapter analyzes a data set of 200 newspaper articles from Norway's largest national newspaper, *Aftenposten*, with the goal of understanding how computing was represented and perceived in the public sphere. The time period, from 1980 to 2007, spans the personal-computer and networked eras of computing. She notes several larger patterns. In a Scandinavian instance of "geek mythology" [29], newspaper reports were most likely to stress men's mastery and competence in using computers while, in contrast, reports about women and computing often focused on their supposed indifference and lack of mastery or skill. These reports simply overlooked the large majority of male computer users who were not technical adepts as well as the sizable number of women who were technically proficient users of computers. Partial fragments of a gendered pattern were inaccurately generalized to be hard evidence about men, women, and computing. A related point was the "intersection rhetoric," where evidence about home uses of computing, or educational experiences with computing, was mobilized as an explanation for work uses, or vice versa. Women who might prefer not to have computers at home were presumed, somewhat illogically, to lack educational experiences and to be in grave danger of being "left behind" in the workplace. There seems to be a big picture of the correct way, aptly termed a hegemonic discourse, of conceptualizing computers and the future [30]. Corneliussen also makes visible the "nonhegemonic groups," including groups of female computer users as well as male nonusers. She also finds that as computers have become more pervasive in society since 2000, there is great attention to the "new" users of computing, often less experienced, and who are inevitably portrayed as female. Such a double standard makes it difficult for women to establish themselves as genuine technical experts about computing in work, education, or business.

In Chapter 9, Aristotle Tympas and co-authors examine the construction of gender and computing through advertising images. They examined and analyzed 1500 advertisements in the leading Greek journal for home computing, *Computing for All*, again beginning with the PC and networking era in the 1980s through to the recent past. In a different manner, they challenge the notion that computing is an exclusively male domain. In these advertisements, there is no shortage of women; but there is a very strong pattern in how women are shown with computers and what they are shown doing with them (Fig. 1.8). Time and again women are working on the screen, hands on the keyboard, or dealing directly with the printer—fully engaged with the routine office work of computing. In sharp contrast, men are rarely shown with hands on the keyboard (more frequently with a phone or coffee cup in their hands) and while they might receive a computer printout, they don't do the actual work of printing. There is a strong normative slant that women are supposed to be doing some computing

Figure 1.8. Women in computing confront a "crowded" field. This "powerful data entry and editing system" from Inforex (1975), while promising to minimize programming effort and save thousands of dollars annually, left this woman precious little room for movement. (Courtesy of Charles Babbage Institute.)

jobs, while men are doing others (compare Fig. 1.7, 5.3, and 12.7). And it's not a surprise how these gender-marked advertisements map onto the higher- or lower-status jobs in computing. These gendered patterns continue straight into the world of computer education. Vocational computer schools aimed at teaching students to be proficient at routine data-entry jobs show women doing this work, hands on keyboards, often with generic computers: a vision of their futures, if you will. By comparison, computer schools teaching students to be programmers typically show men at the job, often with an interesting variety of computers; again a vision of the future. In an important comparative point, Tympas and co-authors note that Greek women—as well as Turkish and Malaysian women—are unusually prominent in university-level computing education, at least compared with the United States, but that despite their higher educational attainments they end up in similar office-level positions just as U.S. women lacking computing degrees. It seems that gender shapes these outcomes as powerfully as educational opportunities, which is an important cautionary tale for reform efforts.

In Part IV, our book's final chapters offer several ways to move forward on the "problem" of gender and computing. (Chapter 12 summarizes the "lessons learned" from the book's chapters and Chapter 13 suggests their consequences for reform efforts.) Janet Abbate's Chapter 10 is based on a wide-ranging set of 52 interviews done with notable women in the computer field. Drawing on this veritable "who's who" of women programmers and computer scientists, Abbate presents compelling interview abstracts documenting what these women found attractive about the field of computing and why they got excited about it. While earlier studies, such as the Margolis–Fisher book, *Unlocking the Clubhouse: Women in Computing* [31], emphasized that men were the ones most often emotionally attracted to computing, Abbate's interviews certainly provide evidence of these notable women's deep and passionate attractions to the field. There is certainly something fresh in a woman computer scientist announcing, "I still think, of all the fields open to women, computer science is the most wonderful one." Genuine enthusiasm about computing animates these voices. Abbate's set of interviews ranges widely across industry, government, and the academic world, and includes women from the United Kingdom as well as the United States They were mostly active during the years that women were flooding into computing, from the 1950s through the 1980s. As Abbate notes, computer programmers were in high demand and, revealingly, "the profession was new enough that they had little awareness of *any* popular image, positive or negative." This combination of high demand, newness, and weak gender stereotypes—positive or negative—help to make clear why so many women chose computing as a profession during these years. Another "missing piece" to the gender gap, however, may be located in Abbate's assessment that the way these women defined success in their careers and experienced pleasure in their work did not match prevailing male and female stereotypes. The sad fact is that the computing profession, as it took form and matured across these same decades (see Chapters 3–6), did not value the accomplishments that these leading women attained.

In Chapter 11, "Programming Enterprise: Women Entrepreneurs in Software and Computer Services," Jeffrey Yost opens with the celebrity cases of HP's Carly Fiorina and eBay's Meg Whitman and other notable women business executives at Oracle and IBM. The chapter surveys the broader environment for IT employment for women, including the opportunities for women working as programmers, systems analysts, computer engineers, and computer operators during the classic mainframe era of computing. The core of his chapter profiles the successful careers of three women active in entrepreneurial companies in the computer services industry as well as the trade associations for that industry. Luanne Johnson, Grace Gentry, and Philiss Murphy each ran successful software and computer services companies, and also took up leadership roles in the Association for Data Processing Services Organizations (ADAPSO) and the National Association of Computer Consultant Businesses (NACCB). These women's notable successes certainly need celebrating. All the same, these brand-new computing fields offered alternatives to the more established career lines where gender discrimination did occur. Early on, "women weren't 'good enough' to be programmers," recalled one woman programmer. "We were hired at 20 percent less than men and only allowed to set up the test cases." Such pay disparities persisted for many years, as Yost's statistics gathered from the trade press demonstrate. Some gender-based slights dogged even these successful women—such as when a bank demanded that Peggy Smith, a long-established businesswoman, have her new husband co-sign for a business loan, despite his having no role in the business. Yet in the main, there were few gender-specific barriers to success in this field and so, as Phyliss Murphy explained her success, it was her ability to deliver results *and* her gender that "stood out."

# REFERENCES

**1.** Information on the Grace Hopper Celebration of Women in Computing is available at www.gracehopper.org (accessed February 2009).

**2.** In the Taulbee report, published in the May 2008 edition of *Computing Research News*, it was stated: "Perhaps even more alarming is the drop in the fraction of Bachelor's degrees awarded to women, from 14.2 percent last year to 11.8 percent this year [data collected academic year 2006–2007]. The fraction of new female students is reported now to be less than 10 percent in many Bachelor's programs"; Stuart Zweben, "Ph.D. Production Exceeds 1,700," *Computing Research News* (Vol. 20, No. 3). In the most recent CRA–Taulbee survey [2008–2009 data] only 11.2% of bachelor's graduates were women. Documents available at www.cra.org/resources/crn/ and www.cra.org/resources/taulbee.

**3.** The National Center for Education Statistics combines "computer" and "information" sciences, but still its statistics indicate a peak in the mid-1980s and a substantial drop since then. See Scott Carlson, "Wanted: Female Computer-Science Students," *Chronicle of Higher Education*, Vol. 52, No. 19 (13 January 2006): A35; available at chronicle.com/free/v52/i19/19a03501.htm.

**4.** Sylvia Ann Hewlett, Carolyn Buck Luce, Lisa J. Servon, Laura Sherbin, Peggy Shiller, Eytan Sosnovich, and Karen Sumberg, *The Athena Factor: Reversing the Brain Drain in Science, Engineering, and Technology* (Harvard Business Review Research Report, May 2008); available at braindrain.hbr.org. Sylvia Ann Hewlett, "Women and Technology," Harvard Business Review Blog, posted 16 May, 2008, discussionleader.hbsp.com/hewlett/2008/05/women_and_technology_the_ugly.html (March 2009).

**5.** Ellen Spertus, "Why Are There So Few Female Computer Scientists?" AI Lab Technical Report 1315 (August 1991); the 1991 report is available at people.mills.edu/spertus/Gender/why.html. Randall Stross, "What Has Driven Women Out of Computer Science?" *New York Times* (15 November 2008), Business section. Anne Brataas, "Lack of Women in Computing Has Educators Worried," *Inside Science News Service* (16 June 2008). Erico Guizzo, "The EE Gender Gap is Widening," *IEEE Spectrum*, Vol. 45, No. 12 (December 2008): 23.

**6.** To take NSF's central initiatives, "ADVANCE: Increasing the Participation and Advancement of Women in Academic Science and Engineering Careers" is funded at $16 million for FY 2009 and FY 2010. A related effort, NSF's "Broadening Participation in Computing," is funded at $14 million; while "Research on Gender in Science and Engineering" is funded at $5 million.

**7.** Laura Beckwith, Margaret Burnett, Valentina Grigoreanu, and Susan Wiedenbeck, "Gender HCI: What About the Software?" *IEEE Computer* (2006): 97–101. Alison Adam, "Constructions of Gender in the History of Artificial Intelligence," *IEEE Annals of the History of Computing*, Vol. 18, No. 3 (1996): 47–53.

**8.** See J. McGrath Cohoon and William Aspray, eds., *Women and Information Technology: Research on Underrepresentation* (Cambridge: MIT Press, 2006), Chapter 5; and Maria Klawe, Telle Whitney, and Caroline Simard, "Women in Computing—Take 2," *Communications of the ACM*, Vol. 52, No. 2 (2009): 68–76. The intervention strategies include changing the culture of computing; altering precollege and college experiences; reducing entry barriers; altering curricula; providing role models and mentoring; and improving student–faculty interactions and peer support.

**9.** See Krista Scott-Dixon, *Doing IT* (Toronto: Sumach Press, 2004).

**10.** Jane Margolis and Allan Fisher, *Unlocking the Clubhouse: Women in Computing* (Cambridge: MIT Press, 2002), quote p. 6. Melanie Stewart Millar, *Cracking the Gender Code: Who Rules the Wired World?* (Toronto: Second Story Press, 1998), pp. 23–27, 46–52.

**11.** A good place to start is the cross-national aggregate data in Maria Charles and Karen Bradley, "A Matter of Degrees: Female Underrepresentation in Computer Science Programs Cross-Nationally," in J. McGrath Cohoon and William Aspray, eds., *Women and Information Technology: Research on Underrepresentation* (Cambridge: MIT Press, 2006), pp. 183–204. See also Vashti Galpin, "Women in Computing Around the World," *ACM SIGCSE Bulletin*, Vol. 34, No. 2 (June 2002): 94–100; and the European Union-funded project "Strategies of Inclusion: Gender and the Information Society (SIGIS)," available at **www.rcss.ed.ac.uk/sigis/index. php** (accessed 30 June 2009). For Africa, an important study is Eva M. Rathgeber and Edith Ofwona Adera, eds., *Gender and the Information Revolution in Africa* (Ottawa: International Development Research Centre, 2000).

**12.** See the analysis in J. McGrath Cohoon and William Aspray, eds., *Women and Information Technology: Research on Underrepresentation* (Cambridge: MIT Press, 2006). For an extended study of Carnegie Mellon, see Jane Margolis and Allan Fisher, *Unlocking the Clubhouse: Women in Computing*. For workforce issues, see Sylvia Ann Hewlett et al., *The Athena Factor: Reversing the Brain Drain in Science, Engineering, and Technology* (Harvard Business Review Research Report, May 2008).

**13.** Jane Margolis and Allan Fisher, *Unlocking the Clubhouse: Women in Computing*, quote p. 36. Tony Greening, "Gender Stereotyping in a Computer Science Course," *ACM SIGCSE Bulletin*, Vol. 31, No. 1 (1999): 203–207.

**14.** Knitting "has an attractive deep structural logic based on geometry and proportion, pattern and shape and iterative processes" according to one self-described geek knitter; see Teresa Nielsen Hayden, "geek knitting," Making Light. Entry posted January 12, 2004; available at **nielsenhayden.com/makinglight/ archives/004347.html** (March 2009).

**15.** Jane Margolis quoted in Scott Carlson, "Wanted: Female Computer-Science Students," *Chronicle of Higher Education*, Vol. 52, No. 19 (13 January 2006): A35.

**16.** At Carnegie Mellon University (CMU), the wash-out course was 15-211, Fundamental Structures of Computer Science. Earlier CS courses at CMU were smaller (with around 25 students) and taught by dedicated, student-friendly instructors. By contrast, 15-211 was taught in a large lecture format by a rotating teaching staff, with little faculty contact. During 1997–1998, "this class became a downhill turning point for many women students" according to Margolis and Fisher, *Unlocking the Clubhouse: Women in Computing* (Cambridge: MIT Press, 2002), p. 83. At Georgia Tech, where "many students run in fear of CS 1321," official policy "forbids its introductory computer science students from seeking any help from other students on their homework"; see Jay Mathews, "Shaping the Learning Curve Through a Code," *Washington Post* (16 April 2002).

**17.** See "A Study on the Status of Women Faculty in Science at MIT," *MIT Faculty Newsletter*, Vol. XI, No. 4 (March 1999); available at **web.mit. edu/fnl/women/women.html**.

**18.** See the role that mentoring played in a successful 2008 job search by FemaleCSGradStudent, "How I Got a Job"; available at **thewayfaringstranger.blogspot.com/ search/label/job%20search**, entry posted April 25, 2008.

**19.** Karen Coyle, "How Hard Can it Be?" *Wired_ Women* (Seattle: Seal Press, 1996) quoted in Gianna LaPin, "Shapeshifters" (6 April 1999); available at **www.fragment.nl/mirror/various/ LaPin_G.1999.Shapeshifters.htm**.

**20.** Frances Grundy, *Women and Computers* (Exeter: Intellect Books, 1996) quoted in Danielle R. Bernstein, "Java, Women and the Culture of Computing," Proceedings of the 12th Annual Conference of the National Advisory Committee on Computing Qualifications, July 1999, Dunedin, New Zealand; available at **turbo.kean.edu/ ~dbernste/naccq.html**.

**21.** J. McGrath Cohoon and Jie Chao, "Sexism— Toxic to Women's Persistence in CSE Doctoral Programs," *Computing Research News*, Vol. 21, No. 1 (January 2009); available at **www.cra.org/ CRN/articles/jan09/cohoon_on_sexism.html**. See also Richard Weber and Bruce Gilchrist, "Discrimination in the Employment of Women in the Computer Industry," *Communications of the ACM*, Vol. 18, No. 7 (1975): 416–418.

**22.** For gender in early computer games, see Geoff King and Tanya Krzywinska, *Tomb Raiders and Space Invaders: Videogame Forms and Contexts* (London/New York: I.B. Tauris & Co., 2006), pp. 178–184; and Chapter 12.

**23.** Mike Leonard, "Closer Look: Lara Croft Tomb Raider: Legend," *AllXbox* (2008); available at **web. archive.org/web/20080101225525/http:// www.allxbox.com/gamewatcher/closerlook/ lara1.asp**. For analysis see Helen W. Kennedy, "Lara Croft: Feminist Icon or Cyberbimbo?" *Game Studies*, Vol. 2, No. 2 (2002); available at **www. gamestudies.org/0202/kennedy/**; Laura Fantone, "Final Fantasies," *Feminist Theory*, Vol. 4, No. 1 (2003): 51–72; and Annika Waern, Anna Larsson, and Carina Nerén, "Hypersexual Avatars: Who Wants Them?" in *Proceedings of the 2005 ACM SIGCHI International Conference on Advances in*

*Computer Entertainment Technology* (Valencia, Spain, 15–17 June 2005). ACE '05 Vol. 265 (New York: ACM, 2005), pp. 238–241.

**24.** For game industry statistics, see Michigan State University's "Research Findings on Gender and Gaming"; available at **www.investigaming.com/index/tag/game_industry.**

**25.** "Lara's curves reduced to appeal to female gamers," *The Sydney Morning Herald* (21 May 2005); available at **www.smh.com.au/news/World/Real-appeal/2005/05/21/1116533572111.html.**

**26.** For the "girl gamer" movement, see Justine Cassell and Henry Jenkins, eds., *From Barbie to Mortal Kombat: Gender and Computer Games* (Cambridge: MIT Press, 1998); and Yasmin Kafai, Carrie Heeter, Jill Denner, and Jen Sun, eds., *Beyond Barbie and Mortal Kombat: New Perspectives on Gender and Gaming* (Cambridge: MIT Press, 2008). Nikki Douglas, "The Future of Games Does Not Include Women" (5 April 2006); available at **www.grrlgamer.com/article.php?t=futureofgames** (accessed August 2009).

**27.** Lawrence J. Mazlack, "Identifying Potential to Acquire Programming Skill," *Communications of the ACM*, Vol. 23, No. 1 (January 1980): 14–17.

**28.** Shayne Nelson, "The 60's—Getting into IBM Through the Side Door"; available at **it.toolbox.com/blogs/tricks-of-the-trade/monthly/9/2004** (entry posted 13 September 2004).

**29.** Jane Margolis and Allan Fisher, in *Unlocking the Clubhouse: Women in Computing* (Cambridge: MIT Press, 2002), p. 68, identify a "geek mythology," noting that fully 69% of female students as well as 32% of male students "perceive themselves as different from the majority of their peers and assert that their lives do not revolve around computers."

**30.** Hegemony and domination are powerful concepts needing careful use, lest they be transformed unwittingly into determinist machines that erase human agency. For helpful framings of "code" as technically mediated forms of domination, see Andrew Feenberg, *Transforming Technology: A Critical Theory Revised* (Oxford: Oxford University Press, 2002); and Lawrence Lessig, *Code and Other Laws of Cyberspace* (New York: Basic Books, 1999).

**31.** In interviews with 100 computer science majors at Carnegie Mellon University "most of the men describe an early, sizzling attraction to the computer," according to Margolis and Fisher, in *Unlocking the Clubhouse: Women in Computing* (Cambridge: MIT Press, 2002), p. 16.

# Computer Science
## The Incredible Shrinking Woman

**2**

CAROLINE CLARKE HAYES

Computer science only recently emerged as a discipline with its own identity during the latter half of the 20th century. In that short time, it has experienced both incredible growth and serious growing pains, particularly with respect to the representation of women. The percentage of women has steadily increased over the last 40 years in almost all science, technology, engineering, and math (STEM) disciplines. However, what is uniquely perplexing about computer science is that the proportion of women undergraduates has been steadily dropping for 20 years. This long-term drop in the proportion of women is counter to the trends in all other STEM disciplines, and the causes have largely been a mystery.

The primary aims of this chapter are to present data from national data sets on the representation of women in multiple STEM fields over time (1966–2006), so as to characterize the extent and depth of this phenomenon, and propose a possible explanation for the recent decline in the proportion of undergraduate women in computer science. Additionally, the chapter will outline continuing research questions important for better understanding the phenomenon, and discuss several approaches for change.

The breadth of data presented in this chapter is intended to provide a numerical "big picture" of the status of women in computer science education over a 40-year time span. The data will be used to show the following:

- The growth of computer science as an educational discipline,

*Gender Codes: Why Women Are Leaving Computing*, Edited by Thomas J. Misa
Copyright © 2010 the IEEE Computer Society

- The changing representation of women at multiple levels of educational achievement (undergraduate, graduate, and faculty), and
- The changing representation of women in the computing workforce, illustrating parallels between computing education and the workforce.

These data reveal a complex and multilayered picture of computer science. It grew rapidly from an esoteric field of study in the mid-1960s to a popular major by the mid-1980s, only 20 years later. However, once established, the proportion of women earning computer science undergraduate degrees started to fall in the mid-1980s and has continued to do so for 20 years. While there are many possible explanations for why this might be so, this chapter proposes that as the popularity of computer science increased, so did the general public awareness of stereotypes depicting computer scientists as male "computer nerds" and "hackers." The increasing prevalence of these stereotypes from the 1980s through the present day may have contributed to a decline in the proportion of women choosing computer science.

Other chapters in this volume provide further insights into this issue through a variety of qualitative data sources. Chapters 8 and 9 suggest that news, advertising, and other media have played a large role in establishing, spreading, and perpetuating images of men as the decision makers, experts, and innovators in computing, and women as "computer phobes" or users who merely execute the instructions of men. Furthermore, Chapters 10 and 11 show that the reality of many women's experiences in computing have been quite different from these stereotypes.

Finally, if an overly masculine image is part of the problem, then an image "makeover" may be just what is needed to bring more gender balance to computer science, as well as to other historically male-dominated disciplines such as engineering (see Chapters 12 and 13).

## UNEXPLAINED DIFFERENCES

Over the last 40 years, there have been great increases in the number of women in many traditionally male-dominated professions such as law and medicine. However, women have not entered all such professions at the same rates. For example, in 2007 medical schools in the United States graduated 49% women [1] while computer science programs graduated only 20% women with bachelor of science degrees and 21% women with doctoral degrees [2]. Literature on women in STEM fields (science, technology, engineering, and math) documents many factors that have made it difficult for women to gain acceptance in traditionally male-dominated professions, including a dearth of female role models [3,4], stereotypes of women and their skills which are often at odds with stereotypes of people working in traditionally male fields [5], implicit gender biases [6], and reluctance, often unconscious, from people in positions of power to include women in their informal networks or to act as their professional allies [7].

However, since these factors apply to *all* historically male-dominated disciplines, they do not adequately explain why fields such as law, medicine, psychology, and biological sciences have achieved higher representation of women than has computer science. Women are still dramatically underrepresented in computer science, as well as in disciplines such as engineering and physics. However, what is most unusual about computer science is that the representation of women undergraduates has been *falling* steadily for 20 years, and this trend shows no signs of reversing. While a few other fields experienced small temporary drops in the percentage of women undergraduates during the late 1980s and early 1990s, none have experienced a decline of this size or duration. If this trend were to continue at the rate experienced from 1986 to 2006, there will be *no* women bachelor degree graduates in computer science by 2032.

Many existing hypotheses for the small proportions of women in computer science do not explain why computer science has followed a trend so different from other STEM disciplines. For example, it is often stated that women avoid computer science because they don't like math. However, statistics show that since 1985 between 45% and 50% of the bachelor degrees in math have been awarded to women (see Fig. 2.2), which certainly does not suggest that women stay away from math intensive curricula. Another explanation offered by Margolis and Fisher is that the male-oriented culture of computer science is not welcoming to women [5]. While this is true, Blum and Frieze report a case study in which the culture within the undergraduate computer science program at Carnegie Mellon University became more equitable as the proportions of men and women students became more balanced [8]. So is the male-oriented culture in computer science a reason for—or a result of—the lack of women? Furthermore, all historically male-dominated fields started out presumably with male-oriented cultures. Yet many have achieved gender parity (if not equity) and none have shown large, long-term declines in the representation of women. There must be additional factors that explain the unprecedented decline in computer science.

A critical step toward understanding and changing a situation is assessment of the past and current situation. Toward this end, this chapter will present and analyze data on the representation of women from several national data sets over time (1966–2006), across multiple STEM fields, and at multiple levels (undergraduate, graduate, and faculty). Data sources used in this work include the National Science Foundation, the National Center for Women and Information Technology, Nelson's data on women and minorities in STEM disciplines at research universities, and the Bureau of Labor Statistics [9–13]. This analysis focuses primarily (but not exclusively) on higher education in the United States because of the ready availability of these data sets, the potential for higher education to impact the career choices of both men and women, and the need to limit the scope of this study to make it manageable.

It is essential that we, as a society, understand and overcome the barriers for women in computing; it is necessary to develop as much potential talent as possible if we are to have a sufficient number of computing professionals to support continuing and future development of the high-tech information technology intensive economy [12]. It is also necessary to have a diverse information technology workforce to maximize the vibrancy and creativity of the ideas it produces. Finally, as Blum and Frieze discovered, strategies for change that can attract highly talented women will likely attract diverse and talented computer scientists of both genders and improve the climate for all [8,14].

# STATUS OF WOMEN IN PROFESSIONAL LIFE

There are several trends that appear to be common across practically all fields. First, the proportion of women has been steadily increasing for 40 or more years. Second, regardless of whether a field is male dominated or not, there are proportionately fewer women holding management and leadership positions relative to other positions. Third, women continue to be promoted more slowly and paid less, even at comparable levels of accomplishment. Thus, while the situation is changing for both men and women, equal numbers may not mean equal status.

From the beginning of the 20th century, women earned degrees at colleges and universities, although the proportion of women graduates earning STEM degrees was relatively small prior to 1960 [4]. However, between the late 1960s and today the participation of women in STEM fields has increased dramatically, with particularly rapid changes occurring during the 1970s and early 1980s. In 1960, slightly more than 40% of bachelor degrees and roughly 8% of doctoral degrees were awarded to women at American educational institutions. Now, more than 60% of all bachelor degrees and almost 50% of all doctoral degrees are awarded to women in the United States [15].

However, even in such fields as law, medicine, and publishing, where women are relatively well represented among the graduates, they are not as well represented in the higher prestige, higher paying subfields. Furthermore, they are rare in leadership roles such as upper management [3,4]. In fields such as computer science, where women are scarce, the number of women in high-level leadership roles is very small. For example, in the author's own science and engineering college, there has never been a woman department head or dean in its 75-year history [16]. Thus, to get a complete picture of the status of women in any field it is necessary to look at more than just the numbers of male and female graduates. Ideally, one must also examine what happens after graduation [15]. What type of positions do women hold? How receptive and supportive is the working environment for women? What salaries do they command? Are there opportunities for them to take leadership roles capable of shaping a field? While it would be difficult to examine *all* of these factors in this chapter, it will examine leadership roles held by women in higher education (faculty positions).

In fields where there are relatively few women, such as computer science and engineering, all of the challenges above can be exacerbated. Evaluation biases favoring men may be particularly strong in fields where there are few women [17]. Evaluation bias is the tendency to judge people's talents more positively when they match the stereotype for a discipline; such biases can differentially impact the rates at which men and women are hired, retained, or promoted in male-dominated fields. Nelson reports that women in science and engineering are tenured at half the rate as men [11]. Other women drop out voluntarily, citing a variety of reasons ranging from an inhospitable climate to overwhelming pressure from a combination of professional and family demands [15]. Those who do stay are paid, on average, less than their male counterparts, even after controlling for variables including institution type, discipline, rank, teaching, and publications [15].

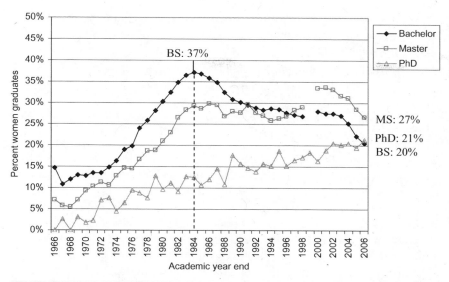

Figure 2.1. Proportions of women receiving BS, MS, and Ph.D. degrees in computer science in the United States [9].

# CHANGING REPRESENTATION OF WOMEN IN COMPUTER SCIENCE

## Women and Computer Science Degrees

Figure 2.1 shows the proportion of women earning bachelor, master, and doctoral degrees in computer science [9]. The interval between 1972 and 1984 was a period of rapid growth in the proportion of women earning *all* types of degrees, including computer science (CS), possibly as a result of the women's movement. However, 1984 marked a turning point and the start of a long and statistically significant period of decline in the proportion of women earning CS bachelor degrees, and this decline has continued through the current day [18,19].

The central question to be explored in the remainder of this chapter is "Why?" While this is too large of a question to answer completely in one chapter or even one book, by exploring numerical trends in education and workforce across multiple STEM fields, this study will identify differences between computer science and other fields. These differences provide clues to why computer science has followed such a different path than other disciplines with respect to gender composition, and may suggest areas in which to focus future investigations.

The following are several numerical "snapshots" at roughly 20-year intervals illustrating the changes in the representation of women over time:

■ **1967:** Only 11% of the people receiving computer science bachelor degrees were women; 24 were awarded to women out of a total of 222 earned that year.

- **1984:** The proportion of women earning CS bachelor degrees peaked; women were earning 37% of all CS bachelor degrees (12,066 out of a total 32,435).

- **2006:** After the turning point in 1984, the proportion of women earning CS bachelor degrees fell over a period of 22 years to only 20% (14,406 out of 57,405). A recent Taulbee survey of North American computer science departments shows this downward trend has continued into 2007 [19].

On a positive note, the HERI/USC freshmen survey, in which freshmen are asked to state their intended major, suggests that this decline may level out over the next few years, but it is not yet clear at what level [20].

These data raise many questions, such as "Why did the proportion of women undergraduates in computer science programs fall after 1984?" and "Is the problem isolated to CS undergraduates, or does it extend to other areas such as the workforce and leadership levels as well?" However, to answer these, one must first ask "Is the situation in computer science unusual relative to other disciplines?" and if so, "How unusual?"

## Women and Undergraduate STEM Degrees

Figure 2.2 shows the National Science Foundation's data on the changing proportions of bachelor degrees awarded to women in a variety of STEM and non-STEM disciplines over the past four decades (1966 to 2006) [9]. Computer science is represented by the solid black line almost at the bottom. (Solid or

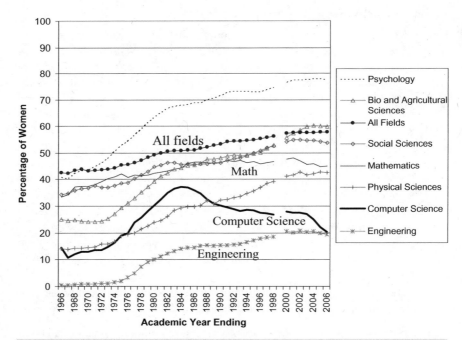

Figure 2.2. Proportions of BS degrees awarded to women in the United States for various disciplines [9].

dotted lines in the figure represent individual disciplines, while lines marked with symbols, squares, triangles, and so on represent aggregates of several disciplines.) As a baseline for comparison, the dark line marked with circles (close to the top of the graph) shows the percentage of bachelor degrees earned by women across *all fields* offered in the United States. Note that this baseline has changed over time; women earned 44% of all bachelor degrees in 1966, but they were earning 58% by 2006.

This graph reveals that computer science is unusual in several respects:

- Between 1972 and 1984, the proportion of women earning bachelor degrees *increased* more rapidly in computer science than in any of the 21 individual STEM disciplines [21] tracked by the National Science Foundation.
- After 1984, computer science was the only one of the 21 STEM disciplines which experienced a marked and prolonged decrease in the participation of women.

Thus, computer science has paradoxically been both a vanguard and a throwback during different time periods.

Looking at overall trends across many fields, the proportion of women has increased in almost all fields at the bachelor's level, due to increasing participation of women in higher education. Their percentage has grown much faster in STEM than in other fields, particularly during the time period roughly between 1972 and 1984. Surprisingly, the fastest changing field during this time was computer science (which increased 24% between 1972 and 1984) followed closely by economics (which increased 22%).

Increased female participation in the 1970s and early 1980s in all professions may have been a reflection of the feminist movement, which increased women's interest in having a professional career. The greater increases in STEM fields may have resulted because the feminist movement additionally raised popular awareness that women could have careers in traditionally male-dominated fields. A woman entering college today is much more likely to choose a STEM major than she would have been in 1966; in 1966, 20% of all women bachelor degree graduates were STEM majors, while in 2006, 28% were. This indicates a significant change in the way women are selecting majors; they are choosing traditional "male" STEM fields far more than in former times. However, the exceptional gains in women's participation in computer science are more difficult to explain. Perhaps, given that computer science was a relatively new and expanding field, women viewed it as a frontier in which the rules had not yet been entirely set; where there were still opportunities to get in on the "ground floor."

Despite the rapid increases in the 1970s and early 1980s, the percentage of women in computer science started to drop rapidly after 1984, falling 17% over the 22 years between 1984 and 2006. Figure 2.2 makes clear just how unusual this drop is when set in the context of other fields, almost all of which show steady growth in the percentage of women receiving bachelor degrees. However, most lines in Figure 2.2 are actually aggregates of several fields, which might possibly obscure similar behavior in the individual fields. Might one find other STEM fields that follow a pattern similar to computer science if one examined them individually? To find out, we examined 21 STEM fields [21] from the NSF data set, but found none that showed such dramatic or prolonged drops as computer science. Six other STEM fields (biological sciences, earth science, economics, electrical engineering, industrial science, and material science) experienced small drops in the proportion of women ranging from 2% to 5%, over periods ranging from 5 to 11 years starting in the mid- to late 1980s, but they have all since rebounded while computer science has not. These small drops may represent temporary backlash reactions to the large changes of the 1970s and early 1980s. Several fields show almost no change since the 1980s, such as mathematics and sociology, but mathematics has reached almost balanced proportions of men and women at the bachelor's level (45% women as of 2006), and sociology now has 70% women (as of 2006). More women would create a greater gender imbalance, and great imbalance in either direction is not necessarily healthy in any field.

When examined in the context of other STEM disciplines, computer science appears to be a field of extremes, being both the fastest growing and declining in different time periods with respect to representation of women. The deep decline that has continued over more than 20 years is an alarming trend distinct from any other STEM field examined, and it appears to be continuing still. Has this trend also occurred in the computing workforce, or is it isolated to undergraduate computer science education? Certainly, it has not impacted growth in the proportion of women earning CS doctoral degrees (see Fig. 2.1). Furthermore, the computing workforce has traditionally been augmented by people who may have bachelor degrees in areas other than computer science, or no college degrees, so it does not necessarily follow that the computing workforce must follow the same pattern as undergraduate education.

## Women in the Computing Workforce

Figure 2.3 estimates the percentage of women holding various types of computing jobs: computer systems analyst, computer software developer, and data processing and equipment repair. These data were collected by the Bureau of Labor Statistics (BLS) through surveys given to a sample of the general population. Survey respondents were asked to self-report their job category from a list supplied by the BLS [13]. The first two are considered "white-collar" professions; the majority of people holding these positions have 4-year degrees. The last one, data processing and equipment repair is considered more of a trade; the majority of workers do not hold 4-year degrees [22]. All three job categories show rapid increases in the proportion of women up through the late 1980s (or even the mid-1990s for data processing and equipment repair) followed by rapid falloffs continuing through 2006. Thus, it appears the computing workforce does indeed follow a pattern similar to that in undergraduate computer science education, particularly the professional segments (systems analysts and software developers).

It is also worth saying a word about each of the two professional computing job categories. In 1987, computer systems analysts comprised 34% women, while computer software developers (e.g., programmers) comprised 42% women. Incidentally, computer systems analysts have also been better paid on average than computer software developers on average, between 1971 and 2006.

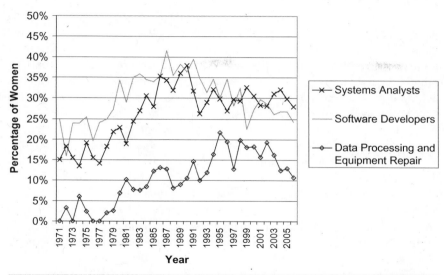

Figure 2.3. Percentage of women in the computing workforce in the United States 1971–2006 [13].

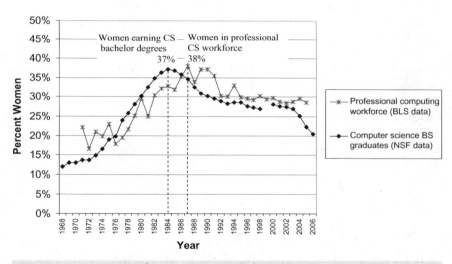

Figure 2.4. Proportion of women in a sample from the computing workforce [13].

In order to assess just how similar the patterns are (or are not), Figure 2.4 juxtapositions educational data from Figure 2.1, with Bureau of Labor Statistics data estimating the proportion of women in the professional "white-collar" computing workforce (a weighted average of systems analysts and software developers). We chose to focus on the professional jobs (excluding managerial positions) because they are the type most likely to be relevant to the new computer science bachelor degree graduates. The two curves for bachelors and professional workforce follow each other closely, with the workforce trailing 3 years behind the bachelor's. Thus, when the proportion of women earning bachelor's degrees rose or fell, the proportion of women in the computing workforce also rose or fell to those same levels three years later.

Similarly, the proportion of women earning CS bachelor degrees reached its peak at 37% in 1984, while the professional computing workforce reached its peak at a very similar level of 38% in 1987, 3 years later. A simple set of correlations verifies that this lag is indeed 3 years (and not 2 years, 4 years, or otherwise); the strongest correlation between education and workforce (0.94) is achieved when the workforce data is shifted backwards by 3 years. At the time of this writing, the author has workforce data for only one other comparison field, electrical engineering; the proportion of women working as electrical engineers is also highly correlated with the proportion earning electrical engineering bachelor degrees (correlation 0.89), but with no obvious lag between the two.

What do these data suggest? They may indicate that computer science graduates comprise most of the workers in professional computing jobs, and after some delay as older workers are replaced by new, the proportion of women in the workforce shifts to match the proportions among the newer graduates. However, given that only around 60% of the computing professionals report having 4 years of college education, it suggests that the people in computing jobs are not necessarily the same people who graduated with computer science degrees some year earlier (although perhaps those without college degrees have come from 2-year technical programs in computing). Alternatively, the data may indicate that both the undergraduate and professional populations are shaped by similar social biases about who can or should be a computer scientist. These biases may impact not only the rate at which both women and men choose computer science as a major, but also the rate at which they choose to enter (or leave) computing jobs, regardless of their college training.

More investigation is needed in order to assess whether these or other hypotheses may be true, and to what degree. Our society must better understand the relationship between the demographics of higher education and the workforce if we are to formulate effective interventions. In particular, it is critical to understand to what degree, if any, educational institutions can shape the future computing workforce by influencing more women to choose computer science as their major.

## GROWTH OF COMPUTER SCIENCE AS A DISCIPLINE

In looking for possible reasons for and influences on the long and significant decline in the proportion of women in undergraduate computing degrees and computing professions, it is important to understand the larger context. This section examines changes in the overall numbers of people taking computer science degrees and employed in computing professions. While overall numbers without regard to gender do not directly tell the story of women in computer science, they set the stage and provide the context in which it happened.

### Growth and Decline as a Field of Undergraduate Study

**Early Growth (1966–1986).** In the 1960s, computer science was a tiny field of study. The first U.S. computer science department was established at Purdue

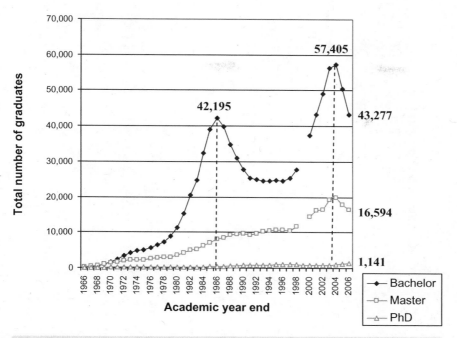

Figure 2.5. Total number of computer science bachelor, master, and doctoral degrees awarded in the United States [9].

University in 1962 [23]. By 1966, there were still only a handful of colleges and universities that offered computer science degrees; only 89 graduates earned bachelor degrees in computer science, and 19 earned doctoral degrees that year. However, computer science BS programs expanded explosively from the mid-1960s through the mid-1980s, peaking at 42,195 bachelor degree graduates in 1986, as shown in Figure 2.5. This represents a 474-fold increase in only 20 years. This rate of growth is not only unusual relative to other disciplines, it is perhaps unprecedented.

**A Slump (1986–1996).** For the 10 years between 1986 and 1996, the number of bachelor degrees awarded in CS fell sharply from a peak of 42,195 in 1986 down to 24,545 in 1996, a drop of 41%. Interestingly, this slump in bachelor degrees was not accompanied by a corresponding drop in graduates from computer science MS or Ph.D. programs (see Fig. 2.1), nor in the workforce, which kept right on growing (see Fig. 2.2). We will return to this point later.

**Later Growth and Decline (1996–2006).** A second growth period of roughly 8 years peaked at 57,405 bachelor degree graduates in 2004, surpassing the 1986 peak and more than doubling the 1996 numbers. This later period of growth and decline may reflect the "dot.com bubble," which lasted roughly from 1995 to 2001 [24]. Two years after the end of the dot.com bubble, the number of bachelor degrees granted started to drop again; growth in the workforce also leveled out. This educational trend shows no signs of turning around in the near future. The Taulbee Survey indicates that numbers continued to drop

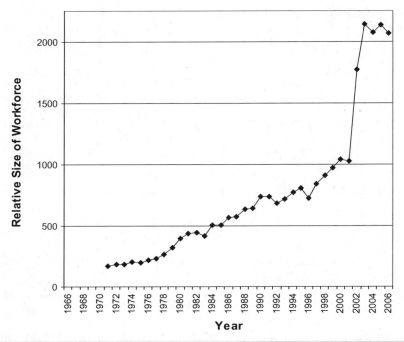

Figure 2.6. Growth in the computing workforce in the United States [13].

in 2007, and the HERI/USC freshman survey indicates that they are likely to drop further still, down to 1% of all U.S. bachelor degree graduates by 2010, compared with 3% in 2006 (see Fig. 2.3) [19,25]. Historically, this survey has been an accurate predictor. Computer science MS degrees have also dropped off, but doctoral degrees have continued to grow, suggesting that the factors that influence students to earn doctoral degrees may be quite different from those that influence them to earn bachelor and master degrees.

## Growth of the Computing Workforce

Figure 2.6 shows that the computing workforce grew rapidly and continually from 1971 through 2003, experiencing a 12-fold expansion during this time period. The computing workforce only recently leveled off after 2003. The data in Figure 2.2 starts at 1971 because the Bureau of Labor Statistics only started tracking computing related professions in 1971, although their database goes back to 1968 for other job titles. The computing workforce expanded more slowly than computer science bachelor degrees, which increased 24-fold in the same time period, but it was a significant expansion relative to professions such as electrical engineering, which remained comparatively level during the same time period [26]. Interestingly, the largest gains ever in the computing workforce occurred immediately after the end of the dot.com bubble, in 2002 and 2003. While dot.coms may have offered some of the most glamorous computing jobs for a time, they did not necessarily represent the majority of computing jobs, given that information technology has become a necessity in most organizations and software is an essential part of many products. Thus, the dot.com crash may have had less impact on computing jobs opportunities than it did on public perceptions of opportunities.

Since the proportion of men and women in the white-collar computing workforce closely follows the proportion of men and women earning computer science bachelor degrees, one might also expect total growth in the computing workforce to parallel or in some way mirror total growth in computer science bachelor degrees, but they are only roughly related to each other. Both expanded rapidly in the latter half of the 20th century but the workforce did not experience the large fluctuations seen in education. There are many possible reasons for this; for example, students may use different criteria in choosing majors than jobs; not all computing jobs are filled by people with computer science degrees ("I graduated in English, but now I have to make a living somehow"), and not all computer science majors go on to work in computing jobs ("I graduated in CS but I am burned out on programming now. I prefer technical management.")

However, this insight impacts interpretation of the previous figure, Figure 2.4. Why did the percentage of women in the computing workforce follow the percentage of women CS bachelor degree graduates, with a 3-year lag? Were these graduates going out and filling these programming and computer analyst jobs, with turnover occurring over a period of 3 years? To some extent this may be true, but Figures 2.5 and 2.6 indicate that the people in the computing workforce do not all come from computer science backgrounds: how else could the computing workforce grow while bachelor degrees stagnate? Social forces may also be independently shaping who chooses to study computer science, as well as who chooses to take computing jobs (regardless of their undergraduate training), and stay.

## Growth Relative to Other Disciplines

Computer science has undergone many ups and downs over the past 40 years. Undergraduate degrees in CS grew from almost nothing to 4% of all bachelor degree graduates in the United States in only 20 years (1966 to 1986), which is more than twice the graduates in all the physical sciences put together in 1986. Since then, CS bachelor degree graduates have fluctuated between 4% and 2%. Are these fluctuations meaningful? In other words, are they unusual (and therefore possible factors in the drop in female CS representation), or are they typical of other fields? To help answer these questions, Figure 2.7 shows the proportion of bachelor degrees awarded in computer science and other STEM fields, out of all bachelor degrees awarded in the United States. Most of the comparison lines in Figure 2.7 are aggregates of several fields; aggregates are shown as lines augmented with symbols—squares, triangles, and so on— while individual disciplines are shown as unadorned solid or dotted lines (e.g., computer science, psychology, and mathematics).

These data suggest the following.

1. The rapid growth in CS bachelor degrees awarded before 1986 is unusual, reflecting the "start-up" status and subsequent success of computer science as a professional field. All other disciplines shown in Figure 2.7 were established prior to 1960. This is not to say that there were not plenty of other disciplines establishing themselves

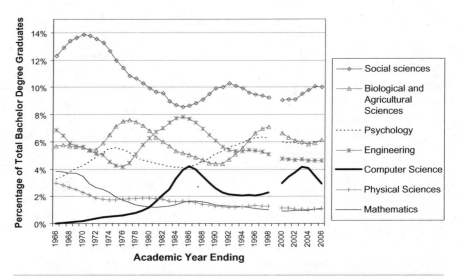

Figure 2.7. Fluctuations in bachelor degrees earned across many fields.

during the last 40 years (e.g., robotics); however, they did not reach the size or receive the national attention that computer science did. Computer science appears unique among STEM fields during this time period in that it was a start-up that became sufficiently sizable and economically important to receive broad public attention.

2. The fluctuations occurring in computer science after 1986 are typical of many established fields. Engineering experienced proportionately similar swings, rising from 4% up to 8% of all U.S. bachelor degrees graduates in only 9 years (1976–1985) and down again to 5% by 2000; the social sciences have fluctuated between 14% and 8% (1970–1985); and mathematics has experienced a long decline over 40 years, falling from 4% in 1966 down to only 1% in 2006.

## Development of a Public Identity

The first point is important because one outcome of professionalization (the process of declaring oneself to be a discipline and formalization of training) is the emergence and solidification of internal and external (public) identities for the discipline. Internal identities reflect how people within a discipline see the discipline and themselves; public identities reflect how people outside a discipline view it and the people who work within it, and these two viewpoints are not always in alignment. Of particular concern in this discussion are the public identities that emerged for computer science as it grew, including public attitudes and the images and stereotypes of computer scientists, such as the geek and the hacker.

It is relevant to bring stereotypes into a discussion that is otherwise primarily about numbers, because before computer science became prevalent, few people had opinions about what computer scientists were like, if they even knew what it was. However, as the profession grew and its social and economic impact became apparent, the general public was exposed more and more frequently to images of computer scientists. Numbers provide indictors of growing public awareness of the discipline. We will return later to discussion of how stereotypes of computer scientists may have begun to turn women away in disproportionate numbers as those stereotypes began to take hold in the public consciousness, starting in the mid-1980s and continuing through the current day.

The second point is important because some have suggested that the drop in total computer science graduates after 1986 may have *caused* the drop in the representation of women in computer science. However, this does not seem likely since the fluctuations in computer science post-1986 are proportionately no bigger or smaller than those seen in other disciplines, yet the representation of women has been growing steadily in most other disciplines. The changing popularity of an established discipline appears to have little impact on the representation of women in that discipline.

# LEADERSHIP: WOMEN AT HIGHER LEVELS

The previous sections have focused mainly on women at the bachelor degree level and on computing jobs held primarily by people with bachelor degrees. However, phenomena that occur at one "level" may or may not be common to all levels; ideally one would like to know if the dramatic drop in the representation of women among computer science undergraduates also occurred at other levels—faculty, administration, and management. This section will examine the percentage of women attaining doctoral degrees in CS and faculty positions.

## Increasing Rank, Shrinking Representation

Across almost all disciplines, the representation of women shrinks as the educational level and prestige of the position increases, as is illustrated in Figure 2.8.

The disciplines in Figure 2.8 are sorted from the largest to smallest percentage of women undergraduate degrees. With few exceptions, *all* disciplines

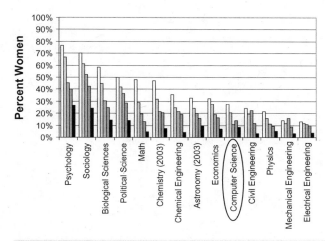

Figure 2.8. Women students and faculty in various disciplines at American colleges and universities, 2002; sorted from highest to lowest percentage of women undergraduates.

follow a very similar pattern in which the percentage of women shrinks (and the percentage of men grows) as rank increases. This is true even in disciplines dominated by women at the undergraduate *and* doctoral level, such as psychology, where men still comprise the majority of faculty in all ranks. Other studies indicate that this phenomenon is not isolated to faculty positions: it is also true for management positions.

This suggests that general societal impedances cutting across all disciplines have made it difficult for women to attain high status positions [3]. This has resulted in a "layering" effect, seen in Figure 2.8, in which the lower levels of any discipline are relatively "richer" in women, while the upper levels exist in an atmosphere rarified of women. Many have suggested that there are fewer women at the higher levels primarily because there were fewer women in the "pipeline" at the time at which these people entered the profession. While this is true to an extent, in most disciplines the percentage of women faculty is significantly smaller than the historical pipeline of women with doctoral degrees. This is true for computer science, and it is also true for disciplines such as psychology that have been female dominated at the graduate level for many years. Interestingly, the primary exceptions are many of the engineering disciplines that have very few women either historically or currently. It is not clear why this is so.

## Women and Computer Science Doctoral Degrees

The percentage of women earning computer science doctoral degrees has risen continually from 1966 through 2006 at an average rate of about 0.5% a year as shown in Figure 2.9; women with CS doctoral degrees have continued to

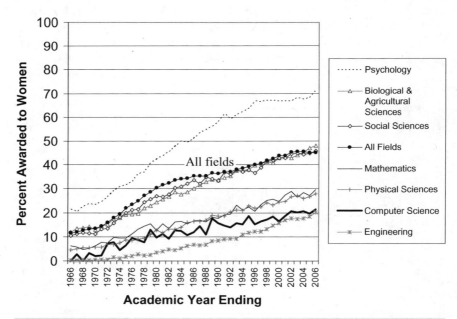

Figure 2.9. Percentage of women with doctoral degrees in computer science relative to other fields, United States 1966–2006 [9].

increase even while the proportion of women with CS bachelor degrees has been shrinking over the past 20 years. But does this mean that women's representation in computer science Ph.D. programs has been unaffected? Figure 2.9 puts this question into a larger context by showing the National Science Foundation data on the proportion of women receiving doctoral degrees in a variety of disciplines. Computer science is shown as the solid dark line near the bottom of the graph, with only engineering and mathematics below it. As in Figure 2.2, individual disciplines are shown as simple lines, and aggregates of several disciplines are shown as lines marked with symbols (circles, triangles, etc.)

The percentage of women earning doctoral degrees has increased greatly in *all* fields since 1966, growing from 12% in 1966 to 45% in 2006. This is an enormous increase of 33%, with the most rapid growth occurring in the 1970s and early 1980s during the women's movement. In contrast, the percentage of women earning bachelor degrees has grown more slowly, increasing by a relatively modest 14% over the last 40 years (from 44% in 1966 to 58% in 2006). Computer science, the physical sciences, mathematics, and engineering grew more slowly than average, while psychology grew much faster, increasing its percentage of women with doctoral degrees by an amazing 50% over 40 years.

What is notable about doctoral degrees in computer science is that in the 1970s through the early 1980s, the percentage of women with doctoral degrees in CS closely followed that of the physical sciences and mathematics. But after the mid-1980s it started to move toward engineering, converging in 2005 at the same levels of approximately 20% women.

This could be interpreted several ways. It could mean that the factors causing the decline in women CS undergrads may also have slowed growth in the percentage of women earning CS doctorates. It may also reflect a cultural shift in computer science, from alignment with one set of disciplines, such as mathematics and the physical sciences, toward engineering influences. At the undergraduate level in computer science, the percentage of women has also recently converged with that of engineering at approximately 20% (as shown in Figure 2.2).

While having similar percentages of women does not necessarily imply any relationship between computer science and another discipline, it is worth examining how the relationships between computer science, mathematics, and engineering programs have changed over time as computer science has become professionalized and educational programs have been established. In particular, educational programs in new areas (such as computer science) often exist in some related department long before that area is identified formally as a "discipline" with its own department. Anecdotal reports indicate that many undergraduate computer science programs started out life under the wing of mathematics and other departments, housed in either liberal arts or physical sciences colleges, but later moved into computer science departments, which are often housed in engineering colleges. This is relevant because organizational shifts that occurred in the processes of becoming an established discipline may have had a strong cultural impact on computer science, causing it to shift from a discipline influenced by the cultures of mathematics and, to some extent, the physical sciences or liberal arts, to one that is more strongly aligned with engineering. Furthermore, of all the engineering disciplines, computer science is possibly most strongly aligned with electrical engineering.

A quick examination of the five top-ranked U.S. computer science departments [27] reveals that at least two of these undergraduate programs started out as programs within mathematics departments, which were housed in a college of liberal arts and a college of physical sciences, respectively. (It is not clear in what departments the other three programs began.) Currently, three of these five programs reside in departments of computer science and two in departments of electrical engineering and computer science. Four of these departments are housed in engineering colleges, and one, at Carnegie Mellon University, is housed in a separate school of computer science. If these top five departments are representative of the evolution of computer science departments more broadly, it lends weight to the hypothesis that shifts in the disciplinary "homes" of computer science programs may have contributed to shifts in the disciplinary culture and the percentage of women.

## Women as Computer Science Faculty

While both male and female faculty can be role models and inspirations to all students, the presence of women faculty in a discipline where they are under-represented may be particularly important to prospective women students. Figure 2.10 shows the data from the National Center for Women and Information Technology (NCWIT) on the percentages of women faculty at American colleges and universities holding assistant, associate, and full professor positions over the decade from 1995 to 2005 [10].

As a baseline for comparison, in 2002 women comprised 39% of all full-time faculty across all ranks and fields in the United States but only 11% of the computer science faculty [11,15]. Furthermore, women comprised 24% of all full professors across all fields, but only 8% in computer science [15]. When compared to other STEM fields, computer science falls somewhere in the middle, in terms of the proportion of women faculty: National Science

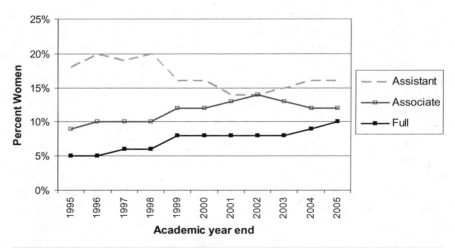

Figure 2.10. Percentage of women computer science faculty in American colleges and universities, 1995–2005.

Foundation data show it below psychology, social, and life sciences, but above mathematics, the physical sciences, and engineering fields [28].

It is worth noting that the proportion of assistant professors has recently dropped from 20% in 1998 to 16% in 2005. This is relevant because assistant professors are drawn from the CS Ph.D. pool, where the proportion of women has continued to rise. This may imply that fewer women Ph.D. graduates are seeking or attaining new faculty positions in computer science than in past years.

On the positive side, the proportion of women attaining the rank of associate and full professor in computer science has slowly but steadily risen over the course of a decade from 5% in 1995 to 10% in 2005. Thus, at first glance, it would not appear that a shrinking proportion of female faculty role models is responsible for the shrinking proportion of female undergraduates.

## SUMMARY

A substantial and persistent drop has occurred over the last 20 years in the representation of women among computer science undergraduates and computing professionals at a time when the proportion of women has been steadily rising in all other STEM fields. This trend is all the more worrying because it comes at a time when overall interest in computing for both men and women is down, yet a strong and creative information technology workforce is needed for competition in the global economy. If computer science continues to become increasingly skewed, its appeal for *all* students choosing careers may sink even further. However, it is not clear how the situation in computer science arose, nor how to turn it around.

In order to gain insights into these phenomena, this chapter has examined national trends in the representation of women in STEM disciplines over a 40-year time period, and at multiple levels of achievement, in order to identify differences between the patterns followed in computer science and in other disciplines. These differences can provide clues as to possible causes and influences, and directions for further investigations.

Computer science is different from other STEM disciplines in the following ways.

1. It is the only STEM discipline in the United States to have experienced such a long and dramatic drop in the representation of undergraduate women over the past 40 years—falling 17% over 22 years between 1984 and 2006. There has also been a similar drop in the percentage of women in the computing workforce. However, at this time the author does not have the comparative workforce data to know if this drop is unique to the computing workforce, or whether the proportion of women in the workforce typically closely follows the proportion graduating several years prior. This would be important to know in order to assess to what degree it may be possible to change the demographics of the computing workforce by changing the demographics of the new CS graduates.

2. It is the only newly established STEM discipline in the last 40 years to grow so rapidly or achieve such prominence, increasing from just

above 0% in 1966 to slightly over 4% of all undergraduate degrees granted in the United States only 20 years later. During this time, computer science oriented degree programs were being established, often initially in "host" departments like mathematics and other disciplines, and moving into separate departments established in colleges and universities across the country.

3. The proportion of women in computer science appears to be heading toward levels very close to those in engineering, as of 2006. This is true at both the undergraduate and graduate levels.

4. Large rates of change are possible. During the late 1970s, the percentage of women graduating with computer science bachelor degrees increased by 4% in a single year.

5. The percentage of women at some level in computer science has continued to grow, even while in other segments their proportion has been shrinking.

The current shrinking representation of women has primarily impacted undergraduate education and the computing workforce including programmers, systems analysts, and data processing and equipment repair. However, the proportions of women at higher levels—doctorates and faculty, have continued to grow overall. This analysis has not yet looked at trends in managerial positions in the workforce, but it is also an important segment to examine. The upper levels of computing, such as people with doctorates, faculty, and computing managers, may be particularly important in implementing change. While they represent only a small fraction of all people in computing, people in these roles can have a great deal of influence.

## SOME POSSIBLE EXPLANATIONS

Two hypotheses that may explain factors contributing to the shrinking percentage of women in computer science are the following:

- As the discipline of computer science became established and known to the general public during the 1970s and 1980s, unappealing stereotypes of computer scientists as nerds and hackers also became established in the general consciousness. These stereotypes were probably unappealing to both men and women, but disproportionally so to women.

- As computer science professionalized, computer science programs were established in a range of departments, such as mathematics, physics, or electrical engineering and housed in a variety of colleges ranging from liberal arts to physical sciences and engineering. Gradually these programs became independent computer science departments, which are now often located predominantly in engineering colleges. Thus, computer science likely started out with a wide variety of disciplinary cultural influences, and it has gradually moved closer to a culture reminiscent of engineering, with similar proportions of women.

One or both of these hypotheses may be true. Both are consistent with the numerical trends presented in this chapter, but both will require further investigation before it is possible to assess their likelihood. The next section outlines some possible future directions that may help to clarify the current downward trend in computer science, and how to rectify it in order to create a healthier climate for all.

## FUTURE RESEARCH QUESTIONS

1. *When did images or stereotypes of computer scientists become prevalent in the public consciousness, and through what vehicles?* Few news articles about "computer nerds" appear before the mid-1980s, but many appear after that date; likewise for movies featuring computer nerds. However, the public can hold multiple images, both positive and negative, simultaneously; for example, the "computer geek" and the "computer start-up entrepreneur/billionaire."

2. *How do images and stereotypes impact the career choices of both men and women?* The stereotype that women "don't like math" does not appear to have greatly deterred them from becoming math majors, as almost 50% of undergraduate mathematics bachelor degrees are awarded to women. Similarly, to what degree do "computer geek" stereotypes actually impact students' choices when selecting a major?

3. *Where did computer science programs find their first homes: in what departments and colleges? And where are the bulk of these programs now?* These questions require some fairly deep digging at individual institutions to find the answers; many computer science departments' histories state when the department was founded, and when graduate and undergraduate programs were established within their own units. However, even if earlier versions of these computer science programs were housed initially in other departments, the institutional memory of these predecessors may be seriously faded.

4. *Are there models of the professionalization of disciplines to help explain the phenomena in computer science?* Many other disciplines were established as fields of study in the last 100 to 150 years, including psychology and many of the engineering fields. Are there general patterns of growth and change that mirror some of those seen more recently in computer science that can help us to better understand its changes?

5. *Can changing the demographics of computer science undergraduates alter the demographics of the computing workforce?* More study of the relationships between the demographics of the two is needed across all STEM fields. The ultimate goal is to alter the workforce by changing education.

6. *How important are female role models?* It is strongly believed that it is important to have female role models, but to what degree do they matter? Are some role models more important than others? Mathematics departments have large numbers of women undergraduates

despite the fact that most have very few women faculty. This raises the question, how critical are female faculty for attracting and retaining female students? Alternatively, are role models experienced in childhood, such as mothers, fathers, or favorite aunts, more important? Do media images provide early role models (or anti-role models) for children and young adults that impact their future career choices?

7. *How important are female leaders?* Leaders may also be role models, but additionally leaders are in positions to make systemic changes. In general, there are very few women leaders in STEM disciplines who have the roles of upper level managers, CEOs, department heads, deans, and so on. A lack of female leaders may mean that gender inequities are less likely to be seen as priorities, or changes implemented. Furthermore, it may turn ambitious women away from a discipline if they desire leadership opportunities.

## STRATEGIES FOR CHANGE

Successful strategies for change are not well understood at this time. However, if indeed public perceptions and images of computer science are part of the problem, public perceptions can be changed through advertising, media, and examples. Furthermore, while existing stereotypes, such as the computer geek, may be remarkably hard to erase, multiple images and possibly contradictory stereotypes can coexist. For example, the computer geek stereotype coexisted with the hip 20-something entrepreneur during the dot.com bubble of the 1990s. These images were likely joint influences on students' choices of discipline during the 1990s and may explain both the upsurge of (mostly male) computer science bachelor degree graduates in the 1990s and the following downswing shortly after the bubble burst (see Figure 2.5).

If a variety of male images, both positive and negative, can be created for computer scientists, presumably positive female images can be created as well. In recent discussions with a group of women computer science undergraduate and Ph.D. students, they described plans to create their own web-distributed drama/movie featuring a female computer scientist hero. They felt the need to do it themselves because Hollywood didn't seem likely to do it any time soon.

Some strategies for improving gender balance do not focus on accounting for gender differences, but on encouraging diversity of background and ideas. Margolis and Fisher and later Blum and Frieze performed some very interesting studies of men and women in the Computer Science Department at Carnegie Mellon University, which may provide important insights [5,8]. Margolis and Fisher performed their study in the mid-1990s when the Carnegie Mellon Computer Science Department had a very gender-imbalanced environment. They interviewed approximately 100 students and found many differences between the male and female students in background, prior computer experience, computer programming skills, and feelings of satisfaction and inclusion in their program of study.

In the late 1990s the department made some changes to its admission standards with the goal of attracting more women. They kept high standards for

GREs and grades, but added an emphasis on leadership qualities and dropped requirements for prior programming experience. Additionally, they added a few "catch-up" courses to the curriculum to level out background differences. None of these changes were inherently gender specific, but after implementing them the department increased the percentage of women students from somewhat less than 10% to more than 30%, and greatly changed the culture.

Another Blum–Frieze finding, discovered by interviewing students during and after these changes, was that as the environment became more gender balanced, many of the apparent differences observed earlier by Margolis and Fisher began to fade. The background of both male and female students became more diverse, and the level of satisfaction of both had increased. Since the time of that study, the proportion of female undergraduates has sagged again, but Frieze reports that the department has managed to keep the more diverse culture among the undergraduates [29]. If measures can be taken to improve the gender balance and culture of undergraduate computer science at Carnegie Mellon University, it may be possible to transfer these approaches to other undergraduate organizations so as to change its appeal not only for women but for men too.

## CLOSING THOUGHTS

While the field of computer science has changed greatly over the past 40 years, women are still greatly underrepresented. Paradoxically, computer science changed more rapidly than most STEM disciplines during the late 1970s and early 1980s in the number of women represented; then, in a complete turnaround, it has been regressing since the mid-1980s while most other disciplines continued to increase their representation of women. The challenge ahead is to understand why representation has been falling and to identify approaches that may remedy the situation. Further change will likely require a sustained effort, simultaneously addressing multiple factors at multiple levels, from the ideas and examples taught to our children to the very highest levels of leadership.

It is likely that attaining and maintaining gender equity in computer science (or any discipline) will *not* be like maintaining the position of a rock once placed in a field. An analogy to a school of fish in a stream may be more appropriate. Keeping those fish in the center of the stream may be difficult. The school's position will always be shifting somewhat from side to side, and smaller groups may break off and go their own way. There may be a constant current against which the fish must always swim; as well as dangerous eddies in the backwaters in which the fish may get caught. However, change is necessary if we are to have a diverse, fully productive, and creative computing workforce. Furthermore, if the Blum–Frieze study is any indicator, continued change will likely improve the climate and appeal of computer science for *all*.

## ACKNOWLEDGMENTS

I would like to extend heartfelt thanks to Peter Meyer for donating his time to extract workforce data from Bureau of Labor Statistics databases.

# REFERENCES

**1.** Association of American Medical Colleges, *AAMC Data Book: Medical Schools and Teaching Hospitals by the Numbers 2008* (Washington, DC: Association of American Medical Colleges, May 2008), Table B-9. Web version: "U.S. Medical School Applicants and Students 1982–83 to 2007–08"; available at www.aamc.org/data/facts/charts1982to2007.pdf.

**2.** National Science Foundation, Division of Science Resources Statistics, *Science and Engineering Degrees: 1966–2006*; detailed statistical tables NSF 08-321 (Arlington, VA: National Science Foundation, 2008); available at www.nsf.gov/statistics/nsf08321/.

**3.** Virginia Valian, *Why So Slow? The Advancement of Women* (Cambridge: MIT Press, 1998).

**4.** Mary Ann Mason and Eve Mason Ekman, *Mothers on the Fast Track: How a New Generation Can Balance Family and Careers* (New York: Oxford University Press, 2007).

**5.** Jane Margolis and Allan Fisher, *Unlocking the Clubhouse: Women in Computing* (Cambridge: MIT Press, 2002).

**6.** Readers can test themselves by taking the Implicit Association Test (IAT) online at implicit.harvard.edu/implicit/. Mahzarin R. Banaji and Anthony G. Greenwald, "Implicit Gender Stereotyping in Judgments of Fame," *Journal of Personality and Social Psychology*, Vol. 68, No. 2 (1995): 181–198.

**7.** Henry Etzkowitz, Carol Kemelgor, and Brian Uzzi, *Athena Unbound: The Advancement of Women in Science and Technology* (Cambridge, UK: Cambridge University Press, 2000). Pat Griffin, "Introductory Module for the Single Issue Courses," in Maurianne Adams, Lee Anne Bell, and Pat Griffin, eds., *Teaching for Diversity and Social Justice: A Sourcebook* (New York: Routledge, 1997), pp. 61–109.

**8.** Lenore Blum and Carol Frieze, "The Evolving Culture of Computing: Similarity Is the Difference," *Frontiers: A Journal of Women Studies*, Vol. 26, No. 1 (2005): 110–125.

**9.** National Science Foundation, *Science and Engineering Degrees: 1966–2006*.

**10.** National Center for Women and Information Technology, *NCWIT Scorecard 2007: A Report on the Status of Women in Information Technology* (University of Colorado, Boulder, 2007); available at ncwit.org/pdf/2007_Scorecard_Web.pdf (accessed March 2007).

**11.** Donna J. Nelson, "A National Analysis of Diversity in Science and Engineering Faculties at Research Universities," 15 January 2004; available at cheminfo.chem.ou.edu/~djn/diversity/briefings/Diversity%20Report%20Final.pdf.

**12.** Donna J. Nelson, "A National Analysis of Minorities in Science and Engineering Faculties at Research Universities," October 31, 2007; available at cheminfo.ou.edu/~djn/diversity/Faculty_Tables_FY07/FinalReport07.html.

**13.** Bureau of Labor Statistics Database, accessed May 2008, courtesy of Peter Meyer.

**14.** Mary C. Murphy, Claude M. Steele, and James J. Gross, "Signaling Threat," *Psychological Science*, Vol. 3, No. 10 (2007): 879–885.

**15.** Martha S. West and John W. Curtis, "AAUP Faculty Gender Equity Indicators 2006," American Society of University Professors, Washington, DC, 2006.

**16.** However, there have been two female associate deans of the Institute of Technology at the University of Minnesota, which is the college of science and engineering, founded in 1935.

**17.** Andrea M. Atkin, Ruth Green, and Laura McLaughlin, "Patching the Leaky Pipeline," *Journal of College Science Teaching*, Vol. 32, No. 2 (2002): 102–108.

**18.** Jay Vegso, "Female CS/CE Students and Faculty," *Computing Research Association Bulletin* (18 June, 2008); available at www.cra.org/wp/index.php?p=147.

**19.** Stuart Zweben, "2006–2007 Taulbee Survey: Ph.D. Production Exceeds 1,700, Undergraduate Enrollment Trends Still Unclear," *Computing Research News*, Computing Research Association, May 2008.

**20.** Randall Stross, "What Has Driven Women Out of Computer Science?" *New York Times* (15 November 2008), Business section; available at www.nytimes.com/2008/11/16/business/16digi.html. Higher Education Research Institute at UCLA databases, available at www.gseis.ucla.edu/heri/gainaccess.php.

**21.** These 21 individual STEM disciplines (as defined by the National Science Foundation) are:

Agricultural, Biological, Atmospheric, Earth, Ocean, and Computer Sciences; Mathematics, Astronomy, Chemistry, Physics, Psychology, Economics, Political Science, and Sociology; Aeronautical, Chemical, Civil, Chemical, Industrial, Materials and Metallurgy, and Mechanical Engineering.

**22.** Having at least 4 years of higher education was reported by 60% of the people who held software developer positions between 1971 and 2006, 63% of the systems analysts, and 13% of the data processing and equipment repair workers.

**23.** John R. Rice and Saul Rosen, "The History of the Computer Sciences Department at Purdue University," in Richard DeMillo and John Rice, eds. *Studies in Computer Science: In Honor of Samuel D. Conte* (New York: Plenum Press, 1994), pp. 45–72.

**24.** Roger Lowenstein, *Origins of the Crash* (New York: Penguin Books, 2004).

**25.** Jay Vegso, "Freshman Interest in CS and Degree Production Trends," *Computing Research Association Bulletin* (1 October 2007); available at **www.cra.org/wp/index.php?cat=33**.

**26.** Relative size of the electrical engineering workforce was estimated by the BLS job category "electrical engineer"; Bureau of Labor Statistics database, accessed May 2008, courtesy of Peter Meyer.

**27.** The top five computer science departments as ranked by *U.S. News and World Report* for 2008 are in order: Stanford, MIT, Berkeley, Carnegie Mellon, University of Illinois Champaign-Urbana.

**28.** Joan Burrelli, *Thirty-Three Years of Women in S&E Faculty Positions*, June 2008, NSF 08-308; available at **www.nsf.gov/statistics/infbrief/nsf08308/**.

**29.** Carol Frieze, phone conversation, March 2008.

# Masculinity and the Machine Man

## Gender in the History of Data Processing

**3**

THOMAS HAIGH

Historian David Noble has characterized science as "A World Without Women," arguing that this is a result of the patterning of universities on a medieval monastic model [1]. While this phrase may describe academic computer science, it was never true of data processing, as the administrative use of computers and punched card machines was known until the 1980s. Corporate computing departments were full of women from the very beginning, but men and women were clustered in different occupations. My aim here is to explain why this occurred and how this sexual segregation has evolved over time.

I chart the role of gender in the history of data processing from the 1950s to the 1970s, with an epilogue exploring census data evidence to the present day. The chapter begins with a look at the gendering of work in the punched card installations and the influence this exerted on early administrative computing work. It explores the status of women as data-entry workers and looks at the relationship between this form of feminized labor and the emerging professionalization agenda of data processing supervisors. Efforts by the Data Processing Management Association, a professional association of data processing managers and supervisors, to upgrade the standing of its members reflected aspirations toward a particular vision of masculinity, called here the "masculinity of the organization man," and an equally important desire to separate the new field from the feminized world of office work. In this case, the push to position business computing as men's work occurred because of, not despite, the presence of women in the field. The conclusion sketches the relevance of this historical perspective for understanding gender in computing today.

## THE SEX TYPING OF DATA PROCESSING WORK

In 1954 General Electric's appliance plant in Louisville, Kentucky, became the first site in America to use an electronic computer for regularly scheduled administrative tasks. Within 5 years it had been joined by thousands of other companies, in a sudden wave of computerization. Computers seemed revolutionary, and computer departments received generous budgets, modern facilities, and nice furniture. Within a few years administrative applications such as payroll processing, billing, and accounting had replaced scientific and technical computation as the dominant tasks for which organizations ordered computers and staffed computing installations.

But when firms first computerized they frequently carried over the personnel and culture of the existing tabulating machine department into their new "electronic data processing" department [2]. During the 1950s punched card data processing and administrative computing were inseparable, and both were growing rapidly. The computer industry grew out of the earlier office machine industry and, in particular, from the two suppliers of electromechanical punched card machines: IBM and Remington Rand [3]. Likewise, work practices and occupational identities in data processing evolved from those already established for administrative work rather than being transplanted from the scientific laboratory. Punched card work was renamed "data processing" to emphasize its close relationship with electronic data processing. Companies used their computers to do the same kind of tasks, in the same kind of way, as their punched card machines [4]. The most common applications for each were payroll, accounting, billing, and inventory control.

To understand the gendered identities of corporate computing, we must therefore begin with those of punched card work. A typical punched card operation employed roughly equal numbers of men and women. But the women were mostly to be found sitting at keypunch machines, using a keyboard to code data from paper onto punched cards. When people spoke of "punched card machine operators," they meant people controlling other machines that processed data already punched onto cards. This work involved a great deal of hands on configuration and operation of specialized machines such as sorters, collators, multipliers, and tabulators. The machines were not programmable, so to run a single job machine staff had to repeatedly feed decks of cards through different machines in an elaborate sequence of operations. Machine operators were usually men with a high school education, who learned their craft on the job beginning with simple routine tasks and gradually progressing to complex work such as control board writing and the development of new procedures (not always documented in writing) [5, pp. 152–173]. Little formal training was available in this field. Many were hired as clerical workers before shifting to the machine room, and aptitude tests were sometimes used to identify potential operators [6]. The career path led upward to supervisory positions and eventually to department head.

The tabulating room was a noisy, stuffy place often consigned to a basement or other out of the way location. Punched card departments hosted a masculine craft culture side by side with feminine clerical work. As one veteran of a Bureau of Public Debt tabulating center in Chicago recalled, "When the weather got too hot (and after the women secretaries, control clerks left), we men would strip down to our shorts" [7].

In 1958 a doctoral student gathered data from most (42) of the punched card installations operating in Oklahoma City, then one of the 50 largest cities in America. Melvin Edwards documented a consistent trend from women to men ascending the ladder of pay and prestige within data processing. At the bottom, keypunch workers accounted for around 37% of the workforce in the punched card installations. They were all women. Then 24% of the punched card machine operators were women, and 10% of the supervisors. Keypunch work was a dead-end job. Although the average keypunch operator had more experience in punched card work than the average machine operator, she could hold little hope of advancement within the department. Only 3% of the punched card machine operators had originally been hired as keypunch operators [8]. No department supervisor had worked as a keypunch operator.

Edwards concluded that:

> The job classifications in numerous machine-accounting units at first appear to provide a natural promotional sequence from clerk to key-punch operator and finally to supervisor. However, the statements of machine supervisors indicated that in most instances promotions occur only within job classifications rather than from one classification to another. The basic reason for this is the preference for men in machine operator positions, and women in key-punch operator positions. [8, p. 145]

This preference is an example of what labor historians call "occupational sex typing." One of the most relevant insights from the body of work on labor and gender is that the gender segregation of different kinds of work has usually been presented as based on the natural aptitudes of men and women. But closer analysis reveals that definitions of these aptitudes shift and that a particular activity can be described in different ways to emphasize characteristics associated with either sex [9].

In the 1950s sex discrimination was legal and commonplace. Job descriptions specified sex and age requirements for many positions, and newspapers grouped their classified ads into separate areas for men and women. Some occupations, such as keypunch operation or auto mechanic, were rigidly sex typed. Others were mixed but skewed to one sex or another. Punched card machine operation fell into this category. This did not necessarily reflect a mix within most individual workplaces. The gender allocation of particular jobs might vary from one firm to another, or reflect the desirability of particular jobs. For example, waiters and waitresses were both common, but they rarely did the same job.

Whether a specific company would hire women to operate punched card equipment, computers, or peripherals depended on its corporate culture, human resources policies, the preferences of the department supervisor, and its size. Punched card installations varied greatly in size. By 1951 Prudential Insurance had thirteen separate punched card centers, which between them employed six hundred people and more than a thousand machines [10]. In contrast, the detailed survey of the punched card installations of Oklahoma City found that the median staff size was just seven people [8]. In very small departments keypunch operators might have found it easier to gain experience operating other equipment such as sorters or tabulators. When the Terre Haute Brewing Company established its punched card center, it employed a male supervisor, one female assistant to help operate its handful of machines, and a number of keypunch women [7].

The most successful computer models of the 1950s and early 1960s (IBM's 650 and 1401 machines) were sold as complements to, and extensions of, its existing lines of punched card machines. Staff for administrative computing installations came from two main sources: existing punched card machine installations within the company and midlevel staff from the departments being computerized. As *Computing News* advised its readers in 1957: "As a rule, your good tab operators will make good [electronic data processing machine] operators. ... Your operators know their present jobs—a paycheck is still a paycheck, even when processed by EDPM. Through experience, they know the pitfalls and exceptions" [11].

In larger companies, planning for new administrative procedures and the design of new punched card applications was carried out by specialists in "systems and procedures" work, a field that boomed after World War II. These specialists called themselves the "systems men," which gives you a fair idea of their gender composition [12]. With computerization, the systems men spent more and more of their time working on the design of data processing applications, and their groups were often merged into data processing departments. Their work on computer applications was called systems analysis, a term still used today.

The one big change with computerization was the addition of a new job: programming. The packaged application software business only started to develop during the 1970s, so almost all applications were written within user companies (sometimes with assistance from consulting firms or using sample code from manufacturers). Programming was constructed very differently in data processing from its conception in early scientific computing as a kind of routine mathematical labor. It was seen instead as a hybrid of aspects of the work previously carried out by operators and by systems analysts. Whereas instructions created by the analyst were previously interpreted directly by punched card machine operators, they now had to be translated into the enormously pedantic language of the computer before they could be given to computer operators. The programmer's perceived job was to take detailed flow charts created by the analyst and turn them into program code. So in the transition from punched card work, some skill and control were transferred from the operator to the programmer [5, pp. 291–319].

The trade magazine *Business Automation* published a regular survey of data processing salaries and employment patterns. Its 1960 survey covered almost five hundred companies and revealed that "the computer department is still a man's world ... Only two firms reported a female manager, and only one company reported a woman as supervisor of the programming section. Less than 15 percent of the programmers reported were women" [13]. (See Figure 3.1.) This should not be a surprise. Punched card machine operators were

Figure 3.1. "Computer department is a man's world." Console of the Army's Ballistic Research Laboratories computer (c. 1962): Lou Moeller (center) and Horace Burkintere (left). (Source: U.S. Army Photo, **ftp.arl.army.mil/ftp/ historic-computers/**.)

mostly men. Systems analysts were overwhelmingly male. Administrative programming was constructed as an intermediate occupation between these two existing kinds of work. It inherited the existing gendered division of work.

## DATA PROCESSING: BETWEEN OFFICE WORK AND MANAGEMENT

Edwards attributed this sex typing of data processing jobs to the "preferences" of machine supervisors. Supervisors did not work in isolation from broader cultural ideas and social trends. But with discretion to hire, fire, and promote within their departments, they played a vital role in reproducing the work culture of data processing. So why were the (predominantly male) data processing supervisors so keen to keep women corralled in the keypunching side of the department? I argue that the intersection of two powerful social mechanisms, sex typing and status anxiety, gave ambitious data processing supervisors making the transition into the computer age a powerful motivation to ensure that women remained in their place. In *Beyond the Typewriter*, Sharon Strom [14] has written persuasively about the gender dimensions of professionalization efforts in the accounting field. Strom shows that much of the impetus for accountants to create legal barriers to entry and demarcate an exclusive area of professional knowledge came from an influx of women into the bookkeeping field. There is no inherent point of separation between the work of the accountant and the work of the bookkeeper. But constructing an impermeable professional barrier protected the authority and earnings of male accountants.

A similar process was at work in data processing in the 1950s. Punched card machine operation was still men's work in most companies. But it was a tiny island of male craft work in a sea of low-status female office labor. Operation of other administrative machinery such as typewriters, bookkeeping machines, dictating machines, addressing machines, copiers, and of course keypunches was already women's work. Beginning with new occupations, such as typist, one clerical job category after another had flipped from male to female. Historians have a rich literature on this topic from the 1870s, when clerical work was an overwhelmingly male activity seen as a good starting point for the apprentice businessman, to the 1920s when most clerical jobs were low-paid dead-end positions filled with women. These jobs had no prospect for advancement beyond the supervision of other clerical workers and were seen as work a woman would do for a few years before marriage. Pay differentials, policies such as the firing of women upon marriage, and the explicit statement of gender requirements for open positions maintained a strict segregation of gendered occupations [15].

The realities of the clerical labor market put pressure on punched card supervisors to maintain a firm gender divide between keypunch operation and other kinds of punched card work and to stress the masculine nature of their craft. If a rigid separation from keypunching was not preserved, then the masculine identity of punched card work could suffer a precipitous collapse.

Data processing supervisors were not content merely to defend the status quo. The arrival of the computer and the ever increasing importance of data processing promised ambitious men the chance to elevate their positions within the corporate hierarchy. They associated this with the embrace of a new, and more managerial, form of masculinity. One of their main vehicles for collective mobility was the National Machine Accountants Association (NMAA), founded in 1951. It was intended for the supervisors of punched card machine departments. As Figure 3.2 suggests, its founders were almost entirely male (one woman is glimpsed in the back row). The association grew rapidly, reaching 10,000 members by 1957. During the late-1950s it became the main association for senior staff within administrative computing installations, leading to a name change in 1963 to the Data Processing Management Association [16]. Until the 1970s it was by far the largest computing association [17].

In 1958 the association invited James P. Moore, the Vice President and Comptroller of the Mutual Benefit Life Insurance Company, to address its meeting. He challenged their aspirations to class mobility, reminding those he termed the "machine men" that "in the recent past such men were regarded by management in very much the same way as management regarded factory workers or automobile mechanics. In other words, they have been thought of in large part … as blue collar workers or at the very least as having blue piping on their white collars." He conceded that thanks to the "electronic boom" they "seem to have a new hairdo, and some mighty attractive clothes which virtually obliterate any of the blue hues" but suggested that to succeed in "up-grading their own status and realizing their own aspirations to management" they would

Figure 3.2. National Machine Accounting Association annual meeting (1951). One unidentified woman is in the back row at far left. (Courtesy of the Charles Babbage Institute.)

have to "divest themselves extensively of the aura of technical mystery with which they seem to like to surround themselves" [18].

The problem was not that the "machine men" were not masculine enough. The problem was that they were identified with the wrong kind of masculinity. Historians have found it useful to distinguish between the biological sexes of male and female and particular cultural identities of masculinity and femininity. These identities are socially constructed and change over time, interacting with other aspects of identity such as class and race. With respect to gender and work, the best starting point remains the seminal anthology *Work Engendered* edited by Ava Baron [19]. As Roger Horowitz has written, the book showed "how gender was embedded in daily work practices and class relations. … Baron firmly established among social historians that gender was about men as well as women" [20].

We see in Moore's comments a distinction between two different kinds of masculine identity, fissured along class lines. Moore acknowledges the masculinity of his audience but brands them mere machine men, blue-collar tinkerers in love with machinery as an end in itself. He claims for management a different kind of masculinity. Following the title of William H. Whyte's hugely popular book, published just 2 years earlier, this might be termed the masculinity of the "organization man." As Whyte wrote, the organization man is proud and ambitious but thoroughly vested in the culture of the organization, a contradiction resolved only by using "the language of individualism to describe the collective" [21].

This new kind of masculinity evolved along with big business. The rise of big business and corporate capitalism from the 1880s onward created many new kinds of jobs, but none of them fitted well with traditional masculinity. There were different varieties of masculine identity in the late 19th century, including the rough working class masculinity of unskilled workers, the refined working class mobility of the upwardly mobile skilled worker, the capitalist masculinity of the successful businessman, and the genteel masculinity of the traditional middle class. The most obvious uniting factor here is the crucial importance of autonomy to masculine identity. But the career manager's power came not from owning a business but from a particular position on an organization chart. He exerted power over those below him, but only when acting in the name of those above.

In *Company Men*, Clark Davis gives an elegant explanation of the gender identity shifts necessary to legitimate corporate white-collar work as manly and the resulting problem of masculine status anxiety.

> Business men attempted to demonstrate white-collar work's masculine nature by careful [sic] excluding women from most middle- and upper-level positions. … While Americans came to view management as distinctly masculine, most firms recruited all new hires into lower-level positions. Companies thus had to convince these young men that entry-level posts offered manly opportunities. The very fact that some women held these jobs, however, called into question the acceptability of such work for men. … Seeking to combat such gender-related anxieties, companies physically separated men and women and often retitled positions based on the holders' sex. [22, p. 145]

Davis adds that companies

> constructed within their corporate cultures a distinct new vision of white-collar manhood. … The corporation provided a ladder, they argued. There were high rungs and low rungs, but they were all part of the same ascension toward a noble, manly identity. [22, p. 146]

The struggle of ambitious men to rise up the organizational pyramid becomes a matter not just of seeking money or power but of affirming one's masculine worth. Likewise, as data processing supervisors struggled to elevate the position of their occupation, they associated this with an affirmation of its masculine character.

The interest of data processing supervisors in upward mobility required them to distinguish the putatively managerial, high-level aspects of the department's work from its less exalted technical and clerical activities. Lester E. Hill, the chief of tabulating for Ryan Aeronautical and one of the leaders of the national association, was not afraid of hyperbole. "The machine accountant in the punched card field," he told its members in 1957, "is a combination of an industrial management engineer, an industrial accountant, and industrial engineer, general accountant, cost accountant, office manager, and executive administrator, as well as being a first rate technician. Believe me, this is some man!" [23]. All of the diverse occupational identities to which Hill appealed were strongly masculine.

Punched card departments and early electronic data processing departments tended to languish under the purview of a corporation's financial staff, with the departmental manager buried in the organization chart three or four levels below the corporate controller. The men above a data processing supervisor were usually accountants, and so the immediate challenge facing members of the association in their quest to win more respect and higher status was to convince corporate accountants that they deserved more autonomy. In the early 1960s this effort produced the ill-fated Certificate in Data Processing, intended as a professional certification for data processing supervisors to prove command of a body of knowledge including management, computer technology and punched card techniques [24]. It was explicitly inspired by the CPA.

Article after article in the association's journals and newsletters hammered home the message that data processing supervisors must become more professional and managerially oriented if they were to deserve advancement [5, pp. 174–188, 239–246]. The tension between the tinkering, craft-based masculinity of the computer room and the bottom-line focus of the organization man is a recurring theme in the history of business computer use. From the punched card era to the present day the same message has endlessly been repeated: the day of the technical specialist is over and to thrive in administrative computing in the future you will need to adopt the viewpoint and culture of management rather than indulging a passion for playing with the latest technologies [25]. The advice, given by experts, trade journalists, columnists, association speakers, and consultants has always seemed reasonable, and administrative computing has always granted greater pay and prestige as one moves away from programming or machine operation and into systems analysis or management. Indeed, the imminent replacement of the rank-and-file corporate applications programmer by some new technique or other was confidently predicted from the 1950s to the 1990s [5, pp. 534–543]. Yet no such abrupt shift in the orientation of administrative computing staff or the balance of employment away from technical positions ever took place. To this day, the cultural gulf between IT staff and normal corporate people remains a subject of constant anguish in the business computing trade press.

## THE GENDER POLITICS OF DATA PROCESSING

A 1953 membership roster from the NMAA's Kansas City Chapter suggests that around 10% of its early members were female, including its publicity and publications officer [26]. This is in keeping with Edwards's findings on the gender breakdown of punched card supervisors. The shift to computing technology may have been accompanied by a further shift toward men. A 1964 national survey found that 73% of its members identified themselves with the job category "manager, supervisor, or director of data processing" and just 2% were female [27].

The first few issues of The Hopper, the newsletter of the NMAA, contained studio publicity photographs of minor Hollywood starlets scattered to fill in blank space throughout the publication as a kind of pin-up. But there were women present at the association's functions, just as there were women in the data processing department. In seeking to emulate managerial culture, the association enlisted members' wives to entertain and display social graces. The main activity entrusted to women within the NMAA/DPMA was organizing the "Ladies Program" for its annual meeting. According to executive committee minutes from December 7, 1957, plans "include a Hospitality Room with a local girl in attendance to advise the women on the things to see in Atlantic City. ... [O]n Wednesday there will be a luncheon and fashion show and Thursday will include a brunch and an interior decorating talk at the 500 Club." A session entitled "Women and Automation" was also promised. The ladies program was still running strong for the 1966 meeting in Chicago, where three and a half days of busy programming included a visit to the Sara Lee bakeries, a "lecture on gourmet dining and living," and an excursion to the Arlington Race Track.

The need of ambitious data processing managers to distance themselves from the feminized world of office work is seen most clearly in depictions of keypunch women. Keypunch workers were most definitely not welcome as members of the National Machine Accountants Association. The first issue of *The Hopper*, published in 1950, included a questions and answers section. This defined "machine accountants" as "those men who are directly connected with the operation and supervision of punched card accounting machines in a supervisory capacity." It did not even bother to pose the question of membership for keypunch operators. The question "Are tabulating machine operators eligible for membership?" met with the reply, "The association has restricted membership to applicants in the supervisory capacity. It was thought that this would enable the Association to have a better selection of men who are experienced in tabulating methods and procedures and who have closer contact with top management" [28]. In later years the association's leaders were unsure as to whether the supervisors of keypunch workers should be eligible for membership. As with other kinds of first-line clerical management jobs, the position of keypunch supervisor was often filled by women who had advanced from clerical positions. In 1962 one spoke of the need to "upgrade the Association ... and get a better caliber of person interested. I think we could well lose some key punch supervisors and pick up systems analysts" [29]. This "upgrade" would have displaced many of the association's already small band of female members.

The presence of keypunch women in data processing departments lowered the status of the field in the eyes of academic computer specialists already leery of the world of business. Walter M. Carlson, later chair of the Association for Computing Machinery, recalls the reaction from members of the ACM Council when in 1960 he presented a proposal that the association create a system of interest groups. "Insofar as business data processing was concerned, many of the ACM leaders I talked to spoke of 'super bookkeepers,' and some of them even reflected on joint Chapter meetings with punched-card people, where the managers usually brought along their best looking keypunch operator" [30].

The data processing trade literature served to codify and reinforce these gender divisions. Publications such as *Business Automation* and *Office Executive* were full of well illustrated reports on data processing work within particular companies and advertisements for data processing products. Office machines such as copying machines, filing systems, and dictating machines were usually shown with attractive young women in fashionable clothes [31]. Women were also pictured next to printers, data-entry devices, and tape reels in advertisements for products of a basically clerical nature (see Chapter 9). On the other hand, when computers were advertised or if exemplary computer installations were profiled, they were usually accompanied by pictures of white men in dark suits. Occasionally, these depictions were explicitly sexualized. Far more often, they passed without explicit reference to the gender of the subjects. This kind of endless symbolic repetition naturalized the gendered segregation of the data processing workplace, reflecting and reinforcing the taken-for-granted associations of certain jobs and machines with men and other jobs and machines with women.

Association with keypunch work remained a threat to masculinity into the 1960s and beyond. Standard Register, a venerable supplier of office forms and related equipment, had come up with a new kind of punch that produced both a paper form and a punched card for electronic processing. This was a small step in the direction of today's world, where users key or capture data directly rather than passing paper copies to keypunch women. But since keypunch operation was a low-status, feminized job, one can imagine user resistance to the idea. So Standard Register tried to use humor to defuse the threat to masculinity, showing that proximity to the punch had not rendered this collection of smoking, tattooed, overweight, and unsmiling blue-collar workers any less cartoonishly manly (Fig. 3.3). The new system was "not for sissies. … With this machine any red-blooded guy can simultaneously punch and print." The machine, it concluded, would "fit in just like one of the boys." This depiction of blue-collar masculinity was very rare in the data processing press, prompted here only by its diametric contrast with feminized clerical work.

This routine denigration of women resulted in some advertisements shocking to modern sensibilities. Terminal firm Entrex ran a series of advertisements informing data processing managers that their new data-entry systems were so easy to use it was no longer necessary to hire intelligent women. One advertisement in the series boasted that a data-entry clerk could now be selected on her "looks alone." Another consisted of a huge bright red pair of plump red lips parted for a kiss. The headline read: "We taught our data entry system to speak a new language: Dumb Blond." In small print it continued "To her it's a typewriter and a nifty little tv screen. (She can be the dumbest blond you can find.) To you it's a CRT-to-disk data entry validate/verify system with mag tape output" [32].

Perceived ties to keypunch work sometimes delegitimized women from administrative programming work, turning the woman programmer into a freakish figure of fun. A humorous 1962 article in *Datamation*, "How to Hire a Programmer," presented the misadventures of the fictional Ball-of-Wax Manufacturing Company as it launched on a comically ill-considered automation drive. Three job candidates represent the era's archetypal inept programmers. One is an arrogant, inexperienced male student in need of "a haircut and a bath." Another has terrible academic qualifications but invents experience. The final candidate is female:

> Miss Sallyann Bunch from East Passerk, New Jersey. Sallyann has had a lot of computer-related experience: two years in the key punch pool of the Unforgivable Assurance Association of North America, Newark, and seven months in charge of tab board wire storage. …
>     Sallyann wears flat shoes, and she is a little cross-eyed. Her figure resembles a full potato sack. Her dress and makeup indicate that she is a solid, plain-thinking

# The key-punch girls

There's a new system for controlling material, production, inventory, or whatever. But it's not for sissies.

It's called the Source Record Punch System. And it was developed and field-tested by Standard Register especially for use by guys in general industry.

The heart of The System is an inexpensive electric data collection machine that records information at the point of origin.

With the machine, any red-blooded guy can simultaneously punch and print constant, semi-variable and variable information on a compact form set. In both man and machine language. He'll have paper copies to serve as documents for action. And a tab card suitable for immediate data processing.

The machine reads a prepunched card to pick up fixed information. Semi-variable data such as date, department number, etc., is set up by means of easily reached slides inside the machine. Variable data is entered through the keyboard.

The result? Improved communication and control both in the plant and the office. With clean, accurate input for data processing. Audit trail copies. And, low-cost record preparation.

Contact The Standard Register Company, Dayton, Ohio 45401, and find out how economically the Source Record Punch System will adapt to your operation.

Why, it'll fit in just like one of the boys.

**Source Record Punch by Standard Register**

Figure 3.3. "The keypunch girls"—advertisement for Source Register punch from *Data Processing Magazine*, Vol. 8, No. 1 (September 1966). (Courtesy of Standard Register.)

person with no frills at all. Miss Bunch is the spitting (she chews Copenhagen) image of a lady programmer.

An offer is made to Sallyann, and she goes home to ask her mother about it. [33]

Even those who favored expanding the opportunities available to women continued to work within the framework of sex typing and its appeals to the inherent characteristics of men and women. A 1963 *Datamation* article used beliefs about the gendered nature of abilities and personality to argue for the desirability of hiring women, noting that "a few" companies favored women, having found them "less aggressive and more content to remain in one position. Many women chose not to advance in position ... others feel that promotion is a threat to their femininity." As a result, "there is a considerably lower turnover

Figure 3.4. Grace Hopper as DPMA's "Man of the Year." Grace Hopper received the DPMA's inaugural Computer Sciences Man of the Year award at its 1970 annual meeting in Seattle. She is hugged by Cal Elliot, its executive director. (Courtesy Charles Babbage Institute.)

rate in women programmers." She also noted that "women have greater patience than men and are better at details ... it is also felt that women have a humanizing influence, making working conditions more pleasant" [34].

Not until around 1970 does any explicit discussion of sexism or the need to examine and redefine gender assumptions appear in the data processing literature. Within the Data Processing Management Association, the shift was dramatic. In 1970 it awarded its very first "Computer Sciences Man of the Year" award to Grace Hopper (Fig. 3.4) [35]. In 1971 its magazine ran a positive feature on "Women in EDP Management" [36]. A smattering of women even served in elected offices within the national association during the 1970s.

Some within the field were actively hostile to what was then called "women's liberation." Arnold E. Keller, longtime publisher of *Business Automation*, repeatedly criticized it in his editorials and in the features his magazine ran. The emergence of this explicit debate does not necessarily indicate any fundamental shift in the experiences of the data processing workforce, but it does indicate a shift in the prevalent rhetoric toward regretting the low participation of women in the field's higher status jobs. More research is necessary to determine the extent to which the women's movement of the 1970s can explain the significant increase in women's work as data processing programmers and systems analysts over this decade.

## DATA PROCESSING LABOR IN THE 1970S

Into the 1970s the organization of work inside corporate computing departments continued to mirror that of punched card departments decades earlier. Keypunch work remained the largest single occupation (almost one-third of all data processing workers) [37]. The shift from punched card machines to computers did little to change the position of keypunch work, though it did trigger a major expansion of the occupation as the changeover to computer operations generally required a huge amount of new data-entry work (see Figs 4.5 and 7.1). Keypunch work remained part of the data processing department, often taking place in an annex to the computer room. Until the 1970s this was how almost all administrative information made its way into computer systems.

The relative pay and prestige of data processing jobs remained constant over time. In increasing order of pay and prestige they ran: keypunch operator, computer/punched card machine operator, computer programmer, systems analyst, and manager/supervisor. The less well paid the job, the more likely it was to be filled by a woman. *Business Automation*'s 1971 salary survey, based on data concerning more than 600,000 workers in 1443 data processing installations, found that women made up 14% of systems analysts and 21% of computer programmers [37].

Based on her personal experience as a programmer and community college teacher, Joan Greenbaum reported that the data processing hierarchy of the mid-1970s offered diminishing opportunities for personal advancement. Data processing job distinctions, she argued, were reflected in the ethnic, gender, and class positions of those recruited to fill each job:

> In general, computer operators are men and the set-up and support functions are performed by women. ... Applications programming titles are divided by rungs in the ladder. Today the lower rungs within the applications ladders are increasingly being filled by women; the higher one goes up the ladder, the more the positions are held by college educated males. Systems programmers, the "elite" among programming ranks, are most often men from middle-class and professional families. Systems analysts generally are selected from the same backgrounds. [38]

The United States Census Bureau added several data processing occupations to its occupation classifications for the 1970 census. This data provides access to gender breakdowns for programmer, analyst, operations and systems research, computer operator, tabulating machine operator, and keypunch operator. Here too, as one ascends the data processing hierarchy from keypunch worker (89% female) to computer and peripheral equipment operator (29% female), to programmer (23% female), to systems analyst (14% female), the proportion of women drops and the average pay rises. Even within job classifications, men earned more than women. For example, male analysts earned 42% more than their female colleagues [39].

From 1971 onward the same classifications were used in the monthly Current Population Survey. Figure 3.5 shows that data processing was by no means a world without women during the 1970s. Overall employment of women in these job categories was only about one-sixth lower than that of men in the early 1970s. From 1979 onward women outnumbered men. But, as before, women were doing different kinds of work.

The vast majority of female data processing workers in the early 1970s were performing data-entry work. Women accounted for 85% of keypunch operators in 1971, rising to 95% a decade later [40]. As the decade goes on we see an influx of women into the job category "Computer and peripheral equipment operators." In 1971 more than two-thirds of these workers were men, little changed from tabulating work in the 1950s. By 1982 this breakdown had been reversed, with two-thirds of a vastly expanded pool of operator jobs held by women.

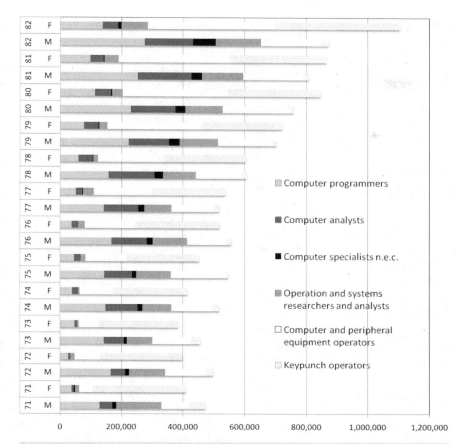

Figure 3.5. Estimates of employment in computing occupations 1971–1982 from the Current Population Survey (for clarity the sparsely populated category of tabulating machine operator is excluded). Bars are plotted left-to-right in same order as legends top-to-bottom.

Changes were less dramatic in the other categories. The numbers bounce around from year to year, with a trend of increasing women's representation in most jobs. Women made up 23% of the programming workforce in 1971 and 34% in 1982. Thirteen percent of analysts were women in 1971, rising to 24% in 1982. Of course, women's share of the overall labor force also increased during this period, by about 6%.

I suspect that the statistical flip of operations work from male to female reflects the increasing use of minicomputer and personal computer systems for administrative work. The adoption of word processing technology during the late 1970s led to the creation of many new jobs for word processing operators [41]. This presumably led to the reclassification of women who had formerly been typists or clerks as the operators of computer and peripheral equipment.

The published tabulations of the 1980 census provide consistent data (programmers 31% female, analysts 22%, operators 59%). Only 7% of women working as operators had completed 4 years of college, compared with 46% of those working as programmers. Work was also segregated by race—African

Americans were overrepresented among keypunch operators but underrepresented among programmers and analysts [42].

While there were some shifts in data processing labor from the 1950s to the 1970s, the most striking finding is how little changed. Women were still concentrated in the lowest paid, lowest status jobs with the worst prospects for career advancement. But one key lesson from labor history is that it takes constant effort to keep things the way that they are. Stasis is equally in need of historical explanation as is change.

## AFTER DATA PROCESSING: THE 1980S AND BEYOND

By the 1980s "data processing" was starting to sound old fashioned. Computer departments received new names, such as information systems. The Vice President of Data Processing gave way to the Chief Information Officer. This reflected a technological transformation, in which the proliferation of personal computers, minicomputers, and video terminals was decentralizing computing work, creating many new kinds of computer jobs, and allowing many more people to directly use and even create computer applications.

Changes in the computing workforce remained incremental. Space does not permit a thorough presentation of the Current Population Survey data from the 1980s to the present day, the interpretation of which demands careful analysis because of several discontinuities in the categories and coding schemes [40]. Through 1992 the total number of women reported in computer-related occupations continued to exceed the number of men. As in the late-1970s, women were clustered in the lowest status work categories of operator (which remained about two-thirds female) and data-entry keyer. (For consistency, I am continuing to count data-entry work as a computer-related occupation, even though the shift away from mainframes means that from the 1980s on this work was increasingly moved out of computer departments.) About 37% of programmers were female from 1982 to 1992, with no clear trend up or down. Because of the rapid growth of the category, this still meant a two-thirds increase in the actual number of women programmers reported.

Since 1992, when a new set of occupational classifications was introduced, the overall number of women reported in computer-related occupations has been fairly constant at around 1.5 million, while the number of men has doubled to just under 3 million. This might suggest a stagnation for women's career prospects in computing. But a closer look at the data presents a different and more encouraging picture. The number of women working as data-entry clerks and computer operators has dropped dramatically. This has been counterbalanced by a rapid increase in the number of women classified as systems analysts and computer managers.

Women's percentage share of the job categories most closely related with programming has fluctuated over time, in part with changes in the categorization method. But stasis in percentage terms can still mean rapid growth in the employment of women. For example, a "computer analyst and scientist" classification was used in the Current Population Survey from 1992 to 2002. Women made up around 29% of this category throughout the period. But looking at numbers, rather than percentages, shows that the number of women reported in this category almost tripled in 10 years. Likewise, from 1992 to 2002, aggregate female employment within the categories of software developer and systems analyst/computer scientist increased by 83%.

The most recent data, from 2002 to 2006, shows no exodus of women from high-status computing positions even as female computer operator and data-entry jobs continue to vanish. Women's share of the computer programmer classification was around 25% in recent years (down from 35% of "computer software developers" in 1991 and 1992). But the importance of this category has been shrinking with the move to packaged software. In fact, the aggregate number of women reported across the high-status categories of computer and information science manager, computer scientist/systems analyst, computer programmer, and computer software engineer rose by 9% from 2003 to 2006.

The historical pattern of women's concentration in the least desirable computing jobs has been partially reversed. As one looks from programming to the higher status work of analyst or manager, women's representation actually increases. In recent years, women held around a 30% share of the new "computer and information science manager" job category. And the job of systems analyst, held by a relatively large and growing number of women, remains higher level and better paid than that of programmer. This trend seems likely to continue—according to the *Occupational Outlook Handbook*, the number of programmers will decline in coming years while the number of systems analysts will rise [43].

## IMPLICATIONS FOR WOMEN IN COMPUTING

What are the implications of this historical story for the underrepresentation of women in computing? Its relevance lies not just in uncovering factual nuggets but, as work in the humanities is supposed to, challenging the implicit assumptions underlying current thought. One challenge is conceptual. Much current discussion concerns gender problems within "the profession of computing." No such profession exists, making it a unit of analysis that obscures much more than it reveals. Consider two facts.

First, computing is not a single kind of work but a collection of hugely diverse jobs across many industries, from help desk worker to CIO and from genome database expert to hardware salesperson. The rhetoric of computing as a single profession first surfaced in the 1960s. It never became reality, but when relatively few people worked directly with computer technology, this was at least a coherent concept. Today, a huge proportion of the U.S. workforce spends most of its time interacting with computers, but only a small and arbitrarily chosen proportion of this activity is considered "computing." (Estimates of the "IT worker" population from different bodies range from 3 to 10 million, though no one seems to consider financial analysts or bloggers to be part of the IT workforce.) While IT jobs all involve computers, their differences are more profound than their similarities. Each has its own gender dynamics. We see, for example, that women were always overrepresented in data-entry work but have now made up ground in systems analysis and computer management, while losing it in programming.

Second, not one of these many IT occupations has actually professionalized. We saw that data processing supervisors attempted this in the 1960s, and a comparable effort is underway today in software engineering. Professional fields have various characteristics, traditionally including a professional graduate degree, legal monopoly on practice in a certain area, continuing education requirements, strong professional associations, accreditation of degree programs, and self-regulation. These are conspicuous by their absence in computing. (The ACM and IEEE serve effectively as scientific societies but represent only a tiny fraction of the IT workers in the United States.) Recent years have seen an influx of women into well-paid professional fields such as law and medicine. Perhaps the failure of IT occupations to professionalize is more off-putting to women than men.

This perspective offered here of the gender dynamics in administrative computing work as an evolution of earlier punched card labor practices gives an interesting contrast with the tendency in discussion of women and computing to begin with ENIAC and other experimental scientific electronic computers. We should follow the advice of the late Mike Mahoney to look at the "histories of computing(s)" rather than a single "history of computing" [44]. Thinking of computing as a single area of activity makes it hard to understand why women were inventing programming in the 1940s but made up only a small proportion of the corporate computing workforce a decade later. This situation looks very different if we conceptualize programming as a task carried out in many different social contexts, or in Mahoney's terms, in multiple computings each with its own history. Why would we expect the accountant in charge of an insurance company's project to staff its electronic data processing department in the mid-1950s to be guided by the fact that participants in the experimental military/academic ENIAC project believed female mathematicians to have an aptitude for translating mathematical methods into switch and wire configurations?

History broadens our perspectives. The literature on women in computing is dominated by discussion of computer science education. Fixing computer science is equated with fixing computing. This is justified by the metaphor of the "pipeline" carrying women from specialist education into IT work. Yet we saw that the gender dynamics of data processing were well formed by the 1960s, before undergraduate computer science education was an appreciable factor. Gender dynamics were shaped instead by the specific historical legacy of data processing work and the broader gender politics of corporate society. So to understand gender segmentation in the workforce, we must study the workplace as well as the classroom. It's encouraging that women's participation in the more prestigious and better paid of the computing occupations, particularly in management and systems analysis, has not suffered anything like the catastrophic drop in absolute numbers faced by computer science degree programs.

Of course, the world has changed since the 1960s. Computer science became a popular major, and many more people hold degrees. Computer science degrees are now expected in some occupations, most notably systems programming. But most IT jobs have remained open to workers with training in many fields. Computer science is only one of several IT fields, alongside management information systems and informatics. Even so, the National Science Foundation found that only one-third of undergraduate degrees held by workers in "computer-related occupations" were in "computer and information science." For programmers the figure was 42%, and for analysts 34% [45]. Historically, the use of computers in business has always been seen as a hybrid of technical and business knowledge, and today an ambitious analyst would still be more likely to seek out a graduate degree in business than in computer science. Furthermore, 4-year degrees remain far from universal in computing occupations. The number of computer science degrees ever granted in the United States is much smaller than the number of people holding vendor-issued technical certifications, such as those granted by Microsoft and Cisco. Today, around two-thirds of programmers hold bachelor degrees (which still suggests that less than 30% hold computing degrees) but operator and help desk positions are held mostly by the high school educated. There are issues of social class at work here that deserve more attention.

To understand the experiences of women in computing, we must look at gender identities, including both masculinities and femininities, and their relationships to specific occupational cultures and broader historical trends. Computing was never a world without women, and the analysis of gender in computing can never be a world without masculinity.

# REFERENCES

**1.** David F. Noble, *A World Without Women: The Christian Clerical Culture of Western Science* (New York: Knopf, 1992).

**2.** Thomas Haigh, "The Chromium-Plated Tabulator," *IEEE Annals of the History of Computing*, Vol. 23, No. 4 (2001): 75–104.

**3.** The transition is explored in James Cortada, *Before the Computer: IBM, Burroughs and Remington Rand and the Industry They Created, 1865–1956* (Princeton, NJ: Princeton University Press, 1993).

**4.** JoAnne Yates, *Structuring the Information Age: Life Insurance and Technology in the Twentieth Century* (Baltimore: Johns Hopkins University Press, 2005).

**5.** Thomas Haigh, "Technology, Information and Power" (Ph.D. thesis, University of Pennsylvania, 2003).

**6.** Ernest J. McCormick and Robert H. Finn, "Tests for Use in Selecting IBM Operators," *Journal of Machine Accounting*, Vol. 6, No. 2 (February 1955): 12–13, 17.

**7.** John J. McCaffrey, *From Punched Cards to Personal Computers* (manuscript memoir 1989), Charles Babbage Institute (CBI 47), University of Minnesota, Minneapolis.

**8.** Melvin Lloyd Edwards, "The Effect of Automation on Accounting Jobs" (Doctor of Education, University of Oklahoma, 1959).

**9.** See Ruth Milkman, *Gender at Work: The Dynamics of Job Segregation by Sex During World War II* (Urbana: University of Illinois Press, 1987).

**10.** F. M. Johnson, "Control of Machine Accounting Equipment," *Systems and Procedures Quarterly*, Vol. 4, No. 2 (May 1953): 18–22, 26.

**11.** Anonymous, "Staff Organization and their Training," *Computing News*, Vol. 5, No. 95 (15 February 1957): 8–11.

**12.** The "systems men" are discussed in Thomas Haigh, "Inventing Information Systems," *Business History Review*, Vol. 75, No. 1 (Spring 2001): 15–61, and in more detail in Ref. 5, Chapter 3.

**13.** Anonymous, "National Survey of Computer Department Statistics," *Management and Business Automation* (June 1960): 22. Unfortunately, gender breakdowns were not reported for the other job types.

**14.** Sharon Strom, *Beyond the Typewriter: Gender, Class, and the Origins of Modern American Office Work, 1900–1930* (Urbana: University of Illinois Press, 1992).

**15.** The literature on women's office labor to 1930 is voluminous. Its initial questions were set by Harry Braverman, *Labor and Monopoly Capital: The Degradation of Work in the Twentieth Century* (New York: Monthly Review Press, 1974) and articulated most programmatically in Margery W. Davies, *Woman's Place Is at the Typewriter:*

Office Work and Office Workers, 1870–1930 (Philadelphia, PA: Temple University Press, 1982).

**16.** The history of the NMAA/DPMA is summarized by a participant in Sonya Lee Anderson, "*The Data Processing Management Association*" (Ph.D. thesis, Claremont Graduate University, 1987). A more critical look is given in Ref. 5, pp. 558–734.

**17.** In 1969 the DPMA had almost 27,000 members, still several thousand more than the (faster-growing) Association for Computing Machinery.

**18.** James P. Moore, Jr., "Management Viewpoints on Men, Machines and Methods," in Charles H. Johnson (ed.), *Data Processing: 1958 Proceedings* (Atlantic City, NJ: National Machine Accountants Association, 1958), pp. 26–31.

**19.** Ava Baron, ed., *Work Engendered: Towards a New History of American Labor* (Ithaca, NY: Cornell University Press, 1991).

**20.** Roger Horowitz, "Introduction," in Roger Horowitz, ed., *Boys and Their Toys? Masculinity, Class, and Technology in America* (New York: Routledge, 2001), p. 1.

**21.** William Hollingsworth Whyte, *The Organization Man* (New York: Simon and Schuster, 1956).

**22.** Clark Davis, *Company Men: White-collar Life and Corporate Cultures in Los Angeles, 1892–1941* (Baltimore: Johns Hopkins University Press, 2000).

**23.** Lester E. Hill, "The Machine Accountant and His 'Electronic' Opportunity," *Journal of Machine Accounting*, Vol. 8, No. 1 (January 1957): 12–14, 23–25.

**24.** The history of the DPMA's Certificate in Data Processing is given in Ref. 5, pp. 567–610, 663–667, 689–706; and Sonya Lee Anderson, "The Data Processing Management Association" (Ph.D. thesis, Clasemont Graduate University, 1987), Chapters 5 and 6.

**25.** This stream of rhetoric culminated in the Chief Information Officer movement of the 1980s and 1990s. See Ref. 5, Chapter 14.

**26.** NMAA Kansas City Chapter, *Membership Roster and Program of Meetings, 1953–54*, contained in Data Processing Management Association Records (CBI 88), Charles Babbage Institute, University of Minnesota, Minneapolis.

**27.** Data Processing Management Association, *Membership Profile, April 1964*, contained in DPMA Records (CBI 88).

**28.** Anonymous, "Questions and Answers," *The Hopper*, Vol. 1, No. 1 (September 1950): 2.

**29.** National Machine Accountants Association, *Executive Committee Meeting Minutes, 21 Feb—Verbatim*, 1962, p. 59; contained in DPMA Records (CBI 88).

**30.** Walter Carlson, "ACM and Special Interest Groups," *Data Base*, Vol. 25, No. 2 (1994): 9–12.

**31.** A similar conclusion was reached in William Aspray and Donald B. Beaver, "Marketing the Monster: Advertising Computer Technology," *Annals of the History of Computing*, Vol. 8, No. 2 (1986): 127–143.

**32.** Advertisement for Entrex terminals, *Business Automation*, Vol. 17, No. 7 (July 1970): 49. The image can be viewed online at **www. tomandmaria.com/dumbblond.htm**.

**33.** Jackson W. Granholm, "How to Hire a Programmer," *Datamation*, Vol. 8, No. 8 (August 1962): 31–32.

**34.** Valerie Rockmael, "The Woman Programmer," *Datamation*, Vol. 9, No. 1 (January 1963): 41.

**35.** Anonymous, "On the Scene," *Journal of Data Management*, Vol. 8, No. 8 (August 1970): 36–37.

**36.** Helen M. Milecki, "Women in EDP Management," *Data Management*, Vol. 9, No. 2 (February 1971): 18–23.

**37.** Anonymous, "Data Processing Salaries Report—1971," *Business Automation*, Vol. 18, No. 8 (1 June 1971): 18–29.

**38.** Joan Greenbaum, *In the Name of Efficiency: Management Theory and Shopfloor Practice in Data-Processing Work* (Philadelphia: Temple University Press, 1979), p. 99.

**39.** United States Census Bureau, *1970 Census of Population, Subject Reports: Occupational Characteristics* (Washington, DC: US GPO, 1973), table 1.

**40.** Miriam King , Steven Ruggles, Trent Alexander, Donna Leicach, Matthew Sobek, *Integrated Public Use Microdata Series, Current Population Survey: Version 2.0.* (Minneapolis, MN: Minnesota Population Center, 2004).

**41.** Thomas Haigh, "Remembering the Office of the Future," *IEEE Annals of the History of Computing*, Vol. 28, No. 4 (October-December 2006): 6–31.

**42.** United States Census Bureau, *1980 Census of Population, Vol. 2: Subject Reports, Occupation by Industry* (Washington, DC: US GPO, 1984), tables 1 and 2.

**43.** Bureau of Labor Statistics, *Occupational Outlook Handbook, 2008–9 edition* (2008); available at **www.bls.gov/OCO/**.

**44.** Michael S. Mahoney, "The Histories of Computing(s)," *Interdisciplinary Science Review*, Vol. 30, No. 2 (2005): 119–135.

**45.** Roger Moncarz, "Training for Techies," *Occupational Outlook Quarterly*, Vol. 46, No. 3 (Fall 2002): 38–45.

# Institutional Life

# A Gendered Job Carousel

## Employment Effects of Computer Automation

**4**

CORINNA SCHLOMBS

It is often observed that women are underrepresented in computing and computer science. However, a closer look at computer-related occupations reveals a more complex picture: high numbers of women in some computing areas counterbalance low numbers in others. While few women work in computer specialist occupations such as software engineering and programming, many work in the occupations that make intensive use of computers, in particular, in the office and secretarial occupations. Although in 2004 women constituted only 27% of IT specialists in the United States, for example, women represented almost 50% of the overall workforce using information and communication technologies, and almost 90% of the clerical workforce using information and communication technologies [1]. While these numbers prove that women are adept computer users, they also reveal that few women obtain advanced positions in computing. Historical roots explain this persistent pattern of female (non) participation in computing.

When electronic computers were introduced to shop floors and offices in the 1950s, they carried the promise of improving working conditions. Automation proponents such as John Diebold claimed that computers would relieve workers from arduous routine jobs and create more skilled positions. "The computer techniques make possible an entirely new approach to many of the information-handling problems of business," he wrote in 1952 in *Automation* [2]. Since women operated most of the punch card machines that were to be

Figure 4.1. Computer automation of data entry in the insurance industry. Computerization with Inforex data-entry system: "Data is displayed progressively as it is keyed to build full records for visual inspection." Screen reads "ERROR," but "operators easily make on-the-spot correction." (Courtesy of Charles Babbage Institute.)

replaced by computers, contemporaries might have expected that women would benefit from computer automation. Also, since computers made office work physically easier—no more piles of punch cards and noisy machines—the new computer-centered data processing work should have become a more suitable occupation for women.

However, these expectations were not fulfilled. Automation in the insurance industry did indeed create some highly paid and highly skilled positions, but men mostly filled them with only a small number of women in supervisory positions. At the same time, computer technology in insurance and elsewhere required a new set of tedious tasks—data entry—to which many women found themselves relegated (Fig. 4.1). In the decades following the introduction of electronic computers, thousands of women took on data-entry positions that were even more onerous and demanding than earlier punch-card work. Rather than relieve women, computer automation created more routine and stressful work for them.

Historical analysis of gender and technology helps clarify these occupational patterns. Feminist historians of technology have shown that although new technologies such as electronic computers do indeed induce change, "the outcomes of the change are constrained by the pre-existing organization of work of which gender is an integral part" [3, p. 28]. The gender division in clerical work was established in the late 19th and early 20th century when punch-card machines and other mechanical data processing machines came into use. Late Victorian ideals about women as respectable housewives limited the professional goals women could aspire to and helped relegate them to low-paid, dead-end jobs at the time. With the introduction of new electronic computing technologies in the 1950s, this gender division of data processing work was transferred to the new computing work. Again, women were relegated to subservient positions without career prospects. This pattern persisted when word processing technologies were introduced into corporate offices in the 1980s.

Social and cultural ideas—not the technologies—shaped which kind of data processing work was done by women or by men, and under which conditions. In as far as these ideas still persist, the historical analysis reveals stumbling blocks that must be addressed by any effort to increase the participation of women in computing today.

## AN UNLIKELY ALLIANCE: WOMEN AND PUNCH-CARD MACHINES

At the turn of the 20th century, the expansion of the federal government and the emergence of large multidivisional corporations in the United States rapidly increased the need to process ever growing amounts of data, requiring a variety of clerical work from copying letters to tallying accounts. At the same time, clerical labor was scarce and expensive. These conditions strongly favored the mechanization of data processing tasks. The federal government, railroads, and other big corporations acquired new machinery ranging from typewriters, phonographs, duplicating presses, and vertical filing cabinets, to mechanical calculators and punch-card machines, in order to perform data processing tasks faster and more economically [4]. As mechanical office machinery entered late Victorian offices, ideas about appropriate work for men and women shaped occupational patterns that continued throughout most of the 20th century.

At the time, women were newcomers to the clerical workforce, and special social and cultural arrangements were necessary to secure their position in governmental and corporate offices. The U.S. federal government first hired significant numbers of women during the Civil War. Not only was this one of the first places of clerical employment for women, it also foreshadowed the emergence, during times of war, of women's entry into other male-dominated workplaces, including Rosie the Riveter during Word War II. In the four decades to 1893, the federal government expanded more than 12-fold, to over 17,000 employees, more than a third of whom were women. These women often sought employment to support their families in times of need, for example, when a father or husband died.

Taking up gainful employment as clerks moved these young middle class women squarely into the public sphere and required Americans to reconsider what it meant to be a respectable woman. Earlier, only daughters from farming families or immigrant families had worked in textile mills or other manufacturing industries, while native-born daughters of urban middle class families remained restricted to their domestic roles as housewives. Clerical work was well paid and provided good working conditions, comparable to teaching positions, and much better than employment as saleswomen in department stores or as workers in factories. It required high school or college education, and women clerks mostly originated from native middle class families or from working class families who aspired to upward social mobility for their daughters through education and a white-collar occupation [5]. To make federal offices appropriate for the employment of these women, male clerks had to learn not to smoke, spit, swear, or be drunk, at least at work. Although female employment seemed to violate the Victorian ideals of domesticity and leisured women, federal employment became acceptable for them. The federal administration served as an experimental space in which women found their place in the office. Under the watchful public eye, men and women worked side by side in federal offices without either losing their respectability [6, p. 5].

Private corporations followed suit, employing sizable numbers of women in the last two decades of the century. Unlike the federal government, however, many corporations sought to keep male and female employees strictly separated from each other. At the New York headquarters office of the Metropolitan Life Insurance Company, for example, men and women used separate entrances, separate doorways, separate staircases, and separate elevators. Departments were clearly gender segregated; most stenographers were female, and only women worked in the filing room. Women and men also ate in separate dining rooms, and women were not allowed to leave the premises during lunch hour. MetLife organized dance lessons which—although only women were allowed to practice together—might prepare them for less virtuous encounters on weekend trips to Coney Island and elsewhere. Also, young men and women occasionally mingled on the roof of the MetLife skyscraper for fun and leisure activities. Despite these and other contacts between men and women required in daily office routines—such as when men supervised all-female departments, or when female stenographers took dictation from mostly male managers—the carefully cultivated image of clean and cloistered offices allowed corporations to maintain the respectability of their employees [7].

In the midst of these social changes women benefited from the oppor-tunities created when punch-card machines entered federal and corporate offices. Developed by Herman Hollerith for the 1890 U.S. Census, punch-card machines came to be used for counting, sorting, computing, and tabulating many types of data. In the Census Bureau, the first to employ punch-card machines, women came to operate the new office machines. As ever larger numbers of tabulating machines were installed in federal and corporate offices, punch-card machine operations evolved into large departments. Employing women for its punch-card operations, the Census Bureau seems to have set a widely followed precedent for information processing work for the next half century.

How was it that women became the machine operators for the 1890 census? The Census Bureau initially conducted a pilot study with a female day shift and a male night shift. Their work comprised two steps: first, keypunch operators punched the census interview data onto cards (one card for each of the 62 million U.S. residents), and then tabulating operators sorted and counted the cards on specially designed machines to tally the census results. While some men and women left these demanding jobs after a short time, women operators overall proved to be 50% faster than their male counterparts. Whether this outcome stemmed from the women's innate manual dexterity—as census super-intendent Robert Porter claimed—or from their motivation to be admitted to the new, promising field of office work, is not easy to answer. Other factors may also have played a role in this decision. For example, passing the tabulating work between shifts was especially difficult to do, since it frequently entailed multistep procedures that ran for hours. More troubling, at least for the time, men and women working on the same machines were found to be passing romantic notes to each other [8]. At the end of the trial period, the male night shift was abandoned and additional machines were ordered for daytime operations by women. Despite the abolition of the male night shift, the census work was never completely segregated. A workforce composing 527 female and 137 male "computers" tallied the 1890 census, with both working on punching as well as tabulating equipment. Women thus became Hollerith machine operators.

Operating punch-card machinery would seem at first sight not particularly appropriate for women. Women were primarily employed in occupations considered "light," or physically easy, work [9]. Hollerith's creations were huge, bulky machines that measured 3 to 5 feet in width, 2 feet in depth, and 4 feet in height. They were far too heavy to be moved by a single person, man or woman. Furthermore, they required regular maintenance such as oiling and greasing to operate smoothly. Most importantly, tabulating machines were noisy; in addition to the persistent noise from the mechanical parts, the early Hollerith machines continually rang bells to signal the correct processing of each punch card. The constant din of the machines was noisy enough that it troubled the keypunch operators and even increased their rate of mistakes. It is somewhat puzzling that such heavy, dirty, and noisy machines became part of the female domain in the office; after all, among the clerical occupations, operating a punch-card machine probably was one of the most physically taxing occupations.

Special spatial arrangements helped to turn punch-card operation into a woman's job in the United States. In Germany, for example, Hollerith machines were located in separate rooms that were extremely noisy and dominated by heavy machinery—with the rationale of protecting other departments from the noise. In such an environment, tabulating rooms became male-dominated technical dungeons, and punch-card operations turned into a male-only profession. A German insurance manager noted with evident surprise during a visit to the United States in the 1950s that women operated punch-card machines there. He observed that tabulating machines were installed in open areas, with wall paneling and other architectural features that reduced noise levels in the punch-card area as well as in the surrounding departments, turning American punch-card departments into environments suitable for their female employees [10]. Punch-card operations thus became an integral physical part of office operations.

In the United States, women clearly benefited from the technological opportunity when mechanical punch-card machines were introduced in the late 19th century. Against all odds, they became punch-card operators (Fig. 4.2). Feminist historians of technology have shown that while women rarely broke into established male domains, they sometimes entered new jobs that required new skills [3, p. 37]. The introduction of punch-card machines was one of these rare opportunities; data processing indeed became a female occupation in the United States.

## PUNCH-CARD OPERATIONS—A TYPICAL FEMALE JOB

Yet, what initially seemed like a glorious technological opportunity soon turned into its opposite. Punch-card work became gender segregated, low skill, and low paid. While this was typical for women's work, it was not an automatic

Figure 4.2. Keypunching computer cards as prototypical women's work. In 1971 Sperry-Rand Univac publicized keypunching by cloistered Carmelite nuns in the Bronx, New York. "The nuns, whose life is devoted to silence and isolation from the world, enter data on punched cards during the periods allotted to manual labor in their daily schedules." (Courtesy of Charles Babbage Institute.)

process. Social ideas about the role of women in society determined that either men or women were assigned to a particular task. Women and men rarely worked side by side in the gender-segregated workforce of the first half of the 20th century. Regardless of their class or ethnic background, women were usually given work that was considered "light," although what counted as "light work" varied regionally and changed over time; for example, "Rosie the Riveter" and her colleagues took over jobs on factory shop floors that were previously assigned to men only [11]. This indicates that what became women's work or men's work was a social agreement rather than based on qualities inherent in the technology or in women's or men's natures.

Starting with the pioneering punch-card operations at the Census Bureau, punch-card operations in the United States were mostly performed by women. By 1930, over 80% of the 38,100 machine operators were women. Punch-card operations thus constituted a typical gender-segregated occupation. Some historians, causally linking feminization and mechanization of office work, argue that administrations and corporations divided complex tasks into single steps that could be performed either by machines or by low-skilled workers. These changes in the work process helped increase the efficiency of the burgeoning paperwork by hiring less skilled workers—mostly women—in the new positions. In this view, the feminization of office work went hand in hand with its routinization and mechanization; both helped organizations to decrease their labor costs [12]. These observations may hold true for many women in private corporations; however, the feminization of office work overall was a complex process, and it did not necessarily lead to routinization and mechanization for all women at all places.

In the federal bureaucracy, for example, strategies for women's employment differed from department to department. Some departments employed women for routine tasks only, while others gave them the full range of skilled tasks at hand; some departments relegated women to separate work areas, and in other offices, women worked side by side with men. The Patent Office, for example, instituted a strict division of labor with separate copying offices more than two decades before the office began hiring women in the 1870s and created a women-only copying office. In the Bureau of Statistics, by contrast, labor was not divided by gender and women typically performed all tasks, like their male colleagues. Clearly, in late Victorian offices, women were not yet necessarily relegated to routine tasks in segregated spaces [6, p. 5].

Unfortunately, little is documented about the work of women or men in the operations of tabulating rooms. In some ways tabulating work resembled a craft that required the learning of particular skills, the operation of a varied number of machines—sorters, collators, tabulators, calculators—and the performance of a number of processes. Some tabulating machine operators learned to operate different kinds of punch-card machines. In at least one installation, operated by young women, the work atmosphere was friendly and collegial, and the women helped each other if one was finished with her assigned task, to the degree that occasionally all women might be occupied with the same task [13]. Men in the punch-card department often originated from the mail department or other lower clerical occupations, with technical savvy or tinkering spirit recommending them for their new work [14]. As in manufacturing, the gender allocation of work may have changed from place to place, but any given installation was most likely either male or female. Most commonly, punch-card tabulations were broken down into small, routinized steps; punch-card operation was thus a routinized low-skill occupation.

Punch-card operation was everywhere a low-paid occupation. Punch machine operators earned less than most male-dominated clerical occupations such as chief clerks, bookkeepers, cost and shipping clerks, and junior clerks, and they earned more than only two male occupations, ledger clerks and mail clerks. Compared to other predominantly female clerical occupations, the 12% of women clerks working as machine operators were paid medium salaries of $15 to $30 per week in 1926; this was less than secretarial stenographers and senior stenographers—$25 to $55 and $20 to $35, respectively—but slightly more than typists, switchboard operators, junior stenographers, file clerks, and inexperienced typists, whose salaries started as low as $10 per week and did not exceed $27 per week [15, pp. 49, 208]. Women machine operators thus were generally paid less than men in clerical occupations, but received medium wages compared to other female clerical occupations. The pay scales suggest that machine operation was considered more like the work of stenographers and typists—whose work was routine and supervised.

The pay scale for punch-card operators was likely depressed for two reasons. The job was routine and required low-skilled workers, and it was a female-dominated occupation. Women often received lower pay for their work, even if they performed the same tasks as their male colleagues. For example, in the federal Treasury Department in 1871, 96% of the women employed earned $900 or less, whereas 89% of the men earned $1200 or more. This pay differential decreased as men and women worked in similar positions and male salaries began declining; by 1901, 81% of women earned $900 or more, while 23% of men earned $1000 or less [6, pp. 82–86]. Up to the mid-20th century, the gendered pay differential was legitimized by the widely held idea of the "family wage." A man, regardless of his personal situation, was considered entitled to a family wage that allowed him to provide for a family as the sole wage earner. A woman was thought of as part of a family where a wage earner— her father or her husband—provided for her. A woman's wage therefore was to be a living wage that would barely allow her to subsist on her own [16, pp. 8–9]. Although claiming punch-card operations as their domain had seemed like a victory for women in the early 20th century, by the mid-20th century, punch-card operations displayed the typical characteristics of a female occupation: segregated, routinized, low skilled, and low paid.

## A GENDERED JOB CAROUSEL: THE INTRODUCTION OF ELECTRONIC COMPUTERS

The gendered patterns of clerical work established in the early 20th century strongly influenced the introduction of electronic computers in the 1950s. Electronic computers were a wartime development, initially devised for top-secret code breaking and for large-scale calculations. One of the first electronic calculators, the ENIAC, was built with U.S. Army funding at the University of Pennsylvania to calculate ballistic firing tables, but was then first used to solve mathematical problems for the Manhattan Project. The two designers of the ENIAC, John Mauchly and John Presper Eckert, soon realized that electronic computers were also suited to perform large-scale data processing tasks. They left the university over a patent dispute, and they founded a start-up company to develop a successor model of the ENIAC for large-scale data processing tasks. Their successor machine, the Univac computer, was acquired by corporations with large data processing needs such as railroads, public utilities, large manufacturing companies, and insurance companies, among them the Metropolitan Life Insurance Company in New York.

The transition from punch-card operations to an electronic computer had major ramifications for the clerical workforce. For the large number of women who provided between one-third and one-half of the clerical workforce in the United States during the first half of the 20th century, it radically changed their working conditions. Recognizing the magnitude of the changes, the U.S. Department of Labor extensively documented the effects of MetLife's computerization on the company's clerical workforce [17]. MetLife used its first Univac for statistical analysis in the actuarial department. This department was separated from daily data processing requirements such as payroll or billing, and so the computer installation did not interrupt regular operations. Without direct customer service obligations, plagued by constant concerns about labor shortages, and characterized by routinized feminized jobs, the actuarial department provided an excellent field to try the new and unproven computer technology.

The computer brought drastic changes for the workforce at MetLife's actuarial statistics department. By September 1955, a bit more than a year after the installation of the computer, 106 persons had been released from the department; of these 97 were women and only 9 were men. As the Bureau of Labor Statistics observed, "women workers in this industry were among those most affected by the electronic computer" [18, pp. vi, 7]. The nine men were transferred to other jobs. Of the 97 women, 78 were transferred to other jobs, 1 retired, and 18 outright resigned. In addition, six supervisors lost their positions. Four of them became part of the computer team—three for computer operations and one for computer development—one transferred to another staff position, and one accepted a higher paying, nonsupervisory position. Unfortunately, we cannot say whether the affected supervisors were male or female. Regardless, the 97 women who lost their jobs represented the (vast) majority of those affected by the computer installation.

In the new computer department, the gender composition of the operating staff differed significantly from the punch-card division. While 189 women and 9 men had worked in the punch-card division, the new 20-person computer staff comprised 12 men and 8 women. The introduction of the computer thus reversed the gender ratio from 1:21 to 3:2. About half of the new computer staff came from the defunct punch-card division and the rest from other divisions in the company. The head of MetLife's computer operating team, an electronics engineer, was hired from Remington Rand, the office machine company that had acquired Eckert and Mauchly's start-up company and that sold the Univac to MetLife.

A comparison of the payscale between the former punch-card and the new computer groups provides more concrete insights into the gendered effects for the workforce. In the former punch-card division, the five highest-paid positions, at $7200 and more, were all held by men; similarly, six men in the new computer division earned $7200 and more—very likely the supervisor, the operators, and the machine room distributor. Women had dominated the medium payscale in the punch-card division, with 52 women earning between $3700 and $5000, and four women forming the female punch-card elite with earnings between $5400 and $6700. Some women in the new computer division occupied the same medium-level payscale: seven of the eight women in the computer division earned between $4000 and $5800. Finally, in the former punch-card operation, the vast majority of the women—132—earned the lowest wages, between $2500 and $3400 (Figs. 4.3 and 4.4). This section of the workforce is entirely missing from the newly created jobs in computer operation. The technical transition preserved the better-paying jobs and eliminated the lowest-paying—mostly female—ones. Very clearly, the women performing routine punch-card operations were the ones released or reassigned. The women in the better-paid positions and the men in the highest-paid positions had better chances to transfer to the new computer division [20].

In MetLife's new computer operation division, men comprised the majority of the staff, and they also occupied the top ranks. The head electrical engineer and the other four computer operators and assistant operators were all men, as was the machine room distributor. Two supporting teams were mixed, with women heading these teams. Notably, the auxiliary equipment team was headed by a woman, as was the converter team where four male clerks converted punch-card data to magnetic tape. Similarly, the female tape librarian oversaw a male tape filing clerk. Finally, there was a team of four female control captains and control clerks. Not only was the gender ratio reversed in the new computer division, but additionally, all central positions in computer operation were male, while women were relegated to the auxiliary teams.

In addition to holding the majority of the new computer staff and occupying the best-paid positions, men soundly dominated the computer development

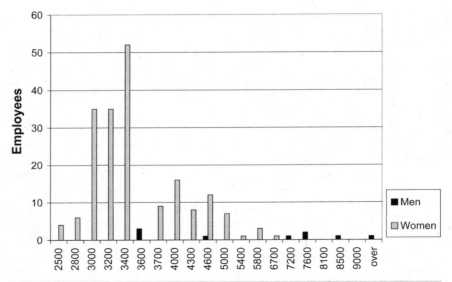

Figure 4.3. MetLife salaries before computerization (punch-card division). Approximate annual salary range of punch-card employees in MetLife's actuarial department (before installation of computer in 1954). Data from Reference 19.

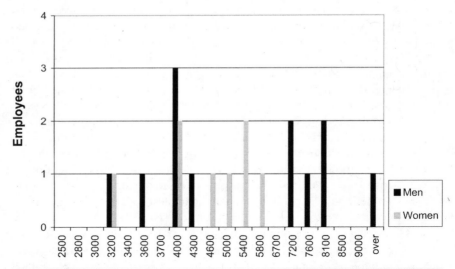

Figure 4.4. MetLife salaries after computerization (computer division). Approximate annual salary range of new computer employees in MetLife's actuarial department (one year after installation of computer in 1954). Data from Reference 19.

group that prepared the installation of MetLife's Univac computer. With five men holding the lead analyst positions, a male and a female in programmer positions, and two women in lower-level flow chart and coding clerk positions, men comprised the majority of the group and occupied the highest-ranking positions. But the real "electronic elite" was to be found in the newly created Electronic Installations Division that was responsible for MetLife's long-term computer strategy. The head of this division—the vice president who headed the Univac studies—and the first eight members were all men. Over 250 employees applied to join the team, and they took up to three exams to qualify. Within a year, the division had grown to about 60 employees who were selected on the basis of their company experience, seniority, and aptitude ranking—criteria that worked against the transitory workforce of women [18, p. 10; 21]. Few women found positions in the new electronic computing field, and even fewer managed to obtain leading positions. The majority of the women who had performed punch-card operations were either retrained or dismissed.

MetLife was certainly not the only company where this was the case. In *Automation in the Office* [14], Ida Hoos found a strongly gendered pattern of replacement in 19 Bay Area (California) companies. The fate of Mrs. Marvis Roberts and her "girls" at the British Overseas Airways Corporation, a predecessor of today's British Airways, provides additional detail [22]. Mrs. Roberts oversaw the company's punch-card department, holding a strict reign over the hundreds of young women who operated the punch-card machines, scolding them for tardiness and placing a strong emphasis on appropriate attire and comportment. The punch-card department under Mrs. Roberts ran like a finely tuned machine—until September 1958, when the airline installed its first electronic computer. While information processing technology evolved gradually, the operating personnel did not. Mrs. Roberts chose early retirement over adjusting to the new computer environment, and many of the women left the department with her. Men took over the data processing operations of the British airline. Charles Baker, the former representative of Remington Rand's British subsidiary from which the airline had acquired its punch-card machines and now its first computer, became the airline's first electronic data processing manager, and the airline also hired its first two programmers from the same source. As at MetLife, many women did not transition to the electronic data processing department, and men—some of them hired from the computer manufacturing company—took over the leading positions in the new department.

## NEW DRUDGE WORK IN THE ELECTRONIC AGE

With the introduction of electronic computers, data processing was redefined from a task that required (female) manual dexterity to a task that boosted (male) intellectual analysis and planning. As men took over the control of electronic computers, one electronic data processing task became a female domain: data entry. The advent of electronic computers turned data entry, always a routine task, into a tightly controlled, physically taxing chore. The human operators assigned this chore came to be seen as both the bottleneck of information processing and the source of mistakes. Information to be processed existed in different forms in the real world, often recorded on paper. For example, clock times were stamped on time cards for payroll applications; payee names and balances on checks for banking applications; and monthly payments for insurance applications. None of this information was readable by a computer in the form in which it was recorded in daily life. Turning it into a computer-legible form became a female task; in other words, women became the computer's eyes.

It is likely that many of the women replaced by MetLife's computer eventually found themselves in data-entry positions for the new computer. A highly monotonous task, data entry was easily controllable. Often, the output of keypunch operators was measured in inches of cards punched, and even if supervisors did not keep exact production counts, they could easily assess a keypunch operator's work by her output; some companies went so far as to consider introducing piece work for keypunch operators. Constant pressure to work quickly turned the women operating keypunches into "nervous wrecks." Supervisors reported that "[i]f you happen to speak to an operator while she is working, she will jump a mile" or "[i]f you just tap one of them [keypunch operator] on the shoulder when she is working, she'll fly through the ceiling." When women did not alleviate their stress with tranquilizers, they often opted out with their feet; absenteeism among keypunch operators was high, and keypunch departments had annual turnover rates as high as 75%. Many women dreaded their new assignments, and they felt they were "working for the machine now" [14, p. 67]. If anything, the work of these women had become even more physically taxing and repetitious with the introduction of electronic computers. As in so many other historical examples, new computing technology created more (drudge) work for women [23].

The technologies for entering data into a computer-legible form changed over the three decades. Initially, data was most often punched onto punch cards that could be fed into a computer and either directly stored in the computer memory or converted into a magnetic tape, which allowed faster data access by the computer. Alternatively, data could be entered directly into machines that recorded it onto magnetic tape. By the late 1960s, women entered data on workstations, which stored information on floppy disks. While the recording medium changed, and the work became less physically taxing with improving designs for keyboards, the tasks of the women working in data-entry positions changed little (Fig. 4.5). Data entry remained routine work in a high-pressure environment that still necessitated high concentration and accuracy under tight time pressure.

Over time, the women's data-entry work came to be seen as an annoying bottleneck in electronic data processing. Before electronic computers, the accuracy of manual data processing had been a major concern among managers and supervisors. During the punch-card era, control systems were in place to identify mistakes by checking data entries against each other. Computers promised to remedy the problem of accuracy because machines were not prone to making "human" mistakes, regardless of how routine and boring the task would be for a human operator. The need for data entry, however, reintroduced the human element through the backdoor: the accuracy of an electronic computer was only as good as the accuracy of the data fed into it. Thus, through data-entry operations, women were not only subjugated to routine work, but the data processing executives also placed the burden of suspicion on the female data-entry clerks.

In the 1970s, Carl Hammer, a prominent computer scientist and computer proselytizer who worked for Remington Rand, addressed the problem of

Figure 4.5. Women's work in transition between punch cards and computers. At a Houston insurance company, computerized data entry (background) replaced conventional keypunching (foreground), resulting in a reported 20% cost saving—but little change in women's work. (Courtesy of Charles Babbage Institute.)

data-entry errors. Taking one particular data-entry job as an example, he showed that the error rate could be calculated in different ways. If one counted the number of *cards* with mistakes in relation to the total number of cards, the error rate for a particular job was as high as 17.5%; if instead, one counted the number of wrong *digits* in relation to all the positions the operator had to enter, the error rate was as low as 0.3%. Hammer identified ways in which the operator's psychological response to tedious work, the keyboard design, and the layout of the input document each affected her errors—all potential points of efficiency improvements. In the article, Hammer developed sympathy for the operator, who turned from an "unknown keypunch operator" into "our girl"—now more emphatically thought of but designated (and denigrated) by her gender. Hammer concluded with a plea to pay more attention to "(wo)man–machine interfaces" and to ease the work of the thousands of "really unsung heroines in our age of automation" [24]. Computer manufacturers and corporations tried to find technical solutions to the data-entry problem, but for many years suitable optical character recognition technologies to automatically scan and enter data remained elusive. Data entry remained a thorn in the sides of executives, and women bore the brunt of their suspicion, in addition to being subjected to unskilled, routine work under deplorable conditions.

## POSTWAR IDEAS ABOUT THE WORK OF WOMEN

Electronic computers and a small group of well-paid men and somewhat lesser-paid women took over corporate data processing, performing tasks that had hitherto been performed by punch-card machines and legions of low-paid women. Women continued to work in offices and in data processing. Relegated to data entry, they became the eyes of the new machines, while for the most part men took over the control—or brains—of the prestigious new machines and departments.

Given the arrangements necessary for punch-card operations to become a female domain, women might have been able to benefit from electronic computers. After all, electronic computers made the task of information processing physically easier; electronic computers were much quieter than punch-card machines. Their cooling fans and other parts still generated some background noise but their electronic elements no longer required dirty grease; while computers and peripherals such as printers and card readers still required maintenance and some oiling, it was not nearly as dirty or demanding as punch-card machines. One IBM machine of the mid-1960s actually required lubrication with spray oil, which evaporated and disseminated a distinct machine smell, reminding one of the mechanical origins of the computer in the supposedly clean office environment. Also, electronic data processing eliminated the physically demanding task of carrying heavy piles of punch cards from one tabulating machine to another. In addition, electronic computers replaced the punch-card machines that had previously been operated by women. Yet, as we have seen, the faithful punch-card women were released or retrained, while their male colleagues claimed the computer for themselves and reaped the main benefits associated with the new corporate prestige object. Gendered ideas and structures such as the marriage bar and the lack of union representation—rather than anything inherent in the nature of men and women or the technology—shaped the new computer occupations. They helped relegate women to the low-paid routine data entry positions that carried the typical characteristics of female work (Fig. 4.6).

Even if wartime changes began to weaken the stereotypes about the work of men and women, many still remained and continued to shape the data processing occupations. One of them concerned women's right to work and to earn equal salaries. In the 1920s, women's advocates had raised the demand for "equal pay for equal work" to claim women's right to be paid according to their skill level, and to protest the idea of the family wage. In the postwar years, the new ideology of consumerism, popular Keynesian ideas legitimizing women's work, and the idea of a higher standard of living all served to uphold women's right to work. The demand for equal pay now came to delineate women's capacity to help their families and to help their nation. At the same time, the labor movement, family-oriented conservatives, and the Bureau of Labor Statistics Women's Bureau all seized on the slogan to protect the wages of men against the threat of cheap female labor. In their interpretation, the right to "equal pay" served to consolidate the segregation of work that protected male wages in the areas where women were excluded. These ideas also played out in the data processing field, preventing women from benefiting from the historical opportunities in electronic computing.

Business representatives agreed that women and men should work in different jobs and that men could be paid more than women. Siding with the labor movement and family-oriented conservatives, they expected that women worked during the 5 to 10 years between graduation and marriage. The ideal of this so-called marriage bar was upheld, even though increasing numbers of

Figure 4.6. Electronic data entry as women's computing work. Digital Equipment Corporation's smart terminal in 1972 featured BASIC programming and tape storage as well as "character string manipulation" for data editing. (Courtesy of Charles Babbage Institute.)

women remained employed beyond their mid-twenties, either not marrying or working despite being married. In addition, business executives argued, the amenities necessary for women such as extra bathrooms and a dining hall added extra costs that ought to be deducted from women's wages. By contrast, men were being trained for future positions and therefore needed to be retained for the company; thus, they were to be paid more [16, pp. 84, 92, 110].

MetLife was one of the companies that upheld the marriage bar in the 1950s, and used it to expel women from data processing positions. MetLife executives expected that women worked only for a short period, and there was no expectation for women to seek continuous employment. They saw women as follows:

> A high proportion of the company's office employees are girls recently graduated from high school. Company experience with these unskilled clerical workers has led to the rule-of-thumb that a new graduate will stay with the company on the average about 3 years and that there will be an almost complete turnover of all female clerks every 5 years. This results from the fact that most young women in this age group are not seeking careers but rather are filling in time until marriage or in some cases until other employment opportunities come their way [18, p. 3].

Women were seen as not interested in a career that would promise a more qualified position [25]; they seemed content to work for just a couple of years in an unskilled, low-paid job. Women thus are presented as compliant in their position in the labor force.

Most certainly, this viewpoint was not an accurate description of the workforce within MetLife's tabulating division. There, almost one-third of the women occupied positions of medium pay that they were unlikely to reach within a short career of only 3–5 years. As their pay suggests, a sizable number of women continued to work beyond their mid-twenties, staying on in their jobs after marriage or not marrying at all. These women often advanced into more responsible, better-paid positions such as secretary, employment manager, or office manager. However, the widespread expectation that women would not seek continuous employment—as expressed in MetLife's statement—justified employers denying promotions and better payscales to women. The social expectation of women serving as a transitory workforce before marriage effectively prevented them from achieving more responsible and challenging career options.

Another reason for women's disadvantage was the lack of union representation. As a transitory workforce, women were difficult to organize. In addition, two demographic characteristics led to the exclusion of female office workers from union representation, first as clerks and second as women. Craft unions—the dominant form of labor organization until the 1930s—largely excluded nonwhite, nonmale laborers. Only with the rise of industrial unions in the 1930s were women organized more frequently and allowed some leadership roles in the labor movement. In addition, salaried employment in offices was traditionally seen as a transitory stage toward management or ownership, excluding clerks from blue-color labor organizations. When these social aspirations waned in the early 20th century, some male clerks began organizing unions for "professional" clerks to prevent the undermining of their position by mechanization, feminization, and rationalization; many others left clerical positions for professional positions in sales and management. Those female office workers who organized in mutual associations usually agitated for higher wages and equal pay. This led to a bifurcation in the organization of male and female clerical labor [15, p. 204; 26]. Women lacked the union support that may have helped them stay in data processing positions.

Women thus had several reasons for concern about the negative impact of electronic computer technology. It even found expression in the 1957 Hollywood movie *Desk Set*, starring Spencer Tracy and Katherine Hepburn. In the movie, Richard Sumner (Tracy) was hired to install an electronic computer in a TV station's research department headed by Bunny Watson (Hepburn). As a "methods engineer"—a euphemism for the infamous efficiency expert—Sumner mentions in his first conversation with Watson that "people seem to go into a panic" when they hear what he does. Even with his mission supposedly kept secret, Watson and the three women on her staff—alerted by the mere appearance of the measuring Sumner—gloomily predict that it means "the end of us all" and begin seeking legal support from union headquarters.

The women grow increasingly sarcastic. When the company's president asks Watson during a presentation whether the computer has already been of help, she caustically remarks that it hadn't "started to give [back] yet" since the staff had been busy feeding information into it. But, she continues, one "could safely say that it will provide more leisure for more people." After a dramatic buildup, the film comes to a truly Hollywood-style end, even without support from the union. It turns out that the pink dismissal slips—which everyone from the messenger boy to the company president received with their weekly pay-checks—were printed by mistake by the payroll computer; the research depart-ment's computer helps Watson to swiftly answer a request that earns her a promotion; and, in the end, she chooses to marry the methods engineer Sumner over her long-time vice-president lover [27]. Unfortunately, real-life experiences often did not live up to the happy ending of this Hollywood romance.

For women, the pattern of female occupation in the industries using computers continued into the 1980s. As the use of electronic computers increased, so did the number of women working in data-entry positions. The number of keypunch operators—a mostly female occupation—quintupled over three decades, from 75,091 in 1950 to 382,118 in 1980. By contrast, the number of tabulating machine operators—most likely a mixed occupation—suffered an overall decline during the same time period. They peaked in 1960 at 26,937 and declined to 3345 in 1980 (Fig. 4.7) [28].

During the 1980s, a second wave of computer automation swept over the clerical occupations with the introduction of word processors. By this time, with the women's movement in full swing, feminist scholars eagerly studied and recorded the changes. Barbara Baran [29] argued in her quantitative study of the insurance industry that the tasks of insurance underwriting and rating under-went automation, which restructured employment in the insurance industry. The process integrated tasks that had previously been fragmented and created highly skilled positions for women with college degrees. Baran noted that the increased emphasis on college education narrowed opportunities for less-educated black and white working class women. More importantly, even the new, highly skilled clerical positions offered little opportunity for career

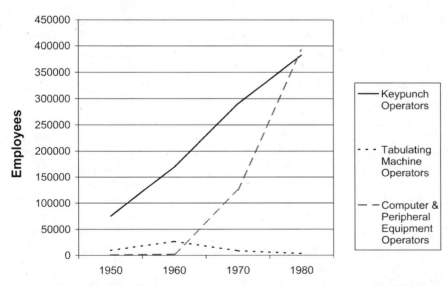

Figure 4.7. U.S. employment in clerical occupations (1950–1980). Data from Reference 28.

advancement. While Baran argues that the work process in the insurance industry was radically restructured and created new jobs, the social and institutional structures that women's work was subjected to did not change; women still found themselves in dead-end positions that were paid lower than the jobs that men had advanced to [29].

## CONCLUSION

This chapter analyzes two contingent moments in the history of computing. At the turn of the 20th century, women seized upon the new punch-card technology, but their jobs were soon relegated to the typical conditions of female clerical work. In the 1950s, data processing changed its gender association, turning from a female occupation into a male profession. Women were relegated to data-entry positions that, on top of being tedious and routine work, were subjected to the usual conditions of female work. The pattern established by the mid-20th century continued to operate well into the late 20th century.

These social repercussions of automation were not inscribed in data processing technologies or computers. The design of information technology defined only what kind of tasks needed to be done for electronic information processing. For instance, the design of punch-card machines, and later the design of electronic computers, determined that data needed to be entered onto punch cards or another medium to be readable by the machines. But the technical designs did not determine who would perform the tasks of data entry and processing, and under what conditions, as the comparison of German and American offices makes plain. Social ideas about the work of men and women determined who did which job, how it was supervised, and how it was paid. Based on widely accepted ideas about women's work in the United States, women were repeatedly relegated to low-paid, dead-end positions, no matter what kind of work they did.

Gender divisions remain a reality to the present day, even within computer specialist occupations. In 2005, fewer than one-quarter of software engineers and programmers were women in the United States, and among computer hardware engineers, as well as telecommunication, electrical, and electronic engineers, fewer than 15% were women [30]. While the "marriage bar" may no longer hold sway, it has been replaced by the expectation that women devote themselves to their family and children. This kind of segregation easily makes female positions vulnerable for lower payment and more constricted career options. Historical analysis suggests that it is unlikely that any technological change will alter this pattern; it is up to us to change the social and institutional conditions of the wide range of computing occupations. As long as the conditions remain the same, young women make very rational choices when they decide not to go into computing. They understand what the distribution of work in computing is telling them—often more subtly than the optimistic promises of educators, boosters, and others. The computer positions that are primarily open to women do not require any special qualification from years of study; only if the structure of computer-related occupations is changed to accommodate women will a degree in computer science open a more compelling future perspective to them.

# REFERENCES

**1.** Organisation for Economic Co-operation and Development, Directorate for Science, Technology and Industry, Committee for Information, Computer and Communications Policy. *ICTs and Gender* (March 2007), Vol. 4, p. 42. Available at www.oecd.org/dataoecd/16/33/38332121.pdf (accessed 18 November 2008).

**2.** John Diebold, *Automation: The Advent of the Automatic Factory* (New York: Van Nostrand, 1952), p. 110.

**3.** Judy Wajcman, *Feminism Confronts Technology* (University Park: Pennsylvania State University Press, 1991).

**4.** JoAnne Yates, *Control Through Communication: The Rise of System in American Management* (Baltimore: Johns Hopkins University Press, 1989). By contrast, given the abundance of cheap clerical labor there, administrations and corporations in Britain continued to process data manually.

**5.** African-American women were generally barred from clerical occupations, unless in corporations owned by African-Americans. For comparison, see Susan Porter-Benson, *Counter Cultures: Saleswomen, Managers, and Customers in American Department Stores, 1890–1940* (Urbana: University of Illinois Press, 1986), pp. 177–216. For the heterogeneity in the female workforce, see Sharon Hartman Strom, *Beyond the Typewriter: Gender, Class, and the Origins of Modern American Office Work, 1900–1930* (Urbana: University of Illinois Press, 1992), pp. 273–314.

**6.** Cindy Sondik Aron, *Ladies and Gentlemen of the Civil Service: Middle-Class Workers in Victorian American* (New York: Oxford University Press, 1987).

**7.** Olivier Zunz, *Making America Corporate 1870–1920* (Chicago: University of Chicago Press, 1990), pp. 117–120.

**8.** Geoffrey D. Austrian, *Hermann Hollerith: Forgotten Giant of Information Processing* (New York: Columbia University Press, 1982), pp. 60, 72.

**9.** Sharon Hartman Strom, " 'Light Manufacturing': The Feminization of American Office Work, 1900–1930," *Industrial and Labor Relations Review*, Vol. 43, No. 1 (1989): 53–70.

**10.** Müller-Lutz of the German Allianz insurance company commented on this difference with surprise in one of his travel reports. Heinz L. Müller-Lutz, *Bericht über eine Reise nach USA*. 1954. Entwicklung EDV (Müller-Lutz), Box 1, Allianz Firmenarchiv, Munich, Germany.

**11.** After the war, many of the women who had worked during the war years voiced concerns about taking away jobs from their male colleagues, and they returned to their prewar roles as housewives. Ruth Milkman, *Gender at Work: The Dynamics of Job Segregation by Sex During World War II* (Urbana: University of Illinois Press, 1987).

**12.** Margery W. Davies, *Woman's Place Is at the Typewriter: Office Work and Office Workers, 1870–1930* (Philadelphia: Temple University Press, 1982), p. 55; Harry Braverman, *Labor and Monopoly Capital: The Degradation of Work in the Twentieth Century* (New York: Monthly Review Press, 1974), pp. 293–358.

**13.** Harold Farlow Craig, *Administering a Conversion to Electronic Accounting: A Case Study of a Large Office* (Boston: Harvard University Graduate School of Business Administration, 1955), p. 87.

**14.** Ida R. Hoos, *Automation in the Office* (Washington, DC: Public Affairs Press, 1961).

**15.** Sharon Hartman Strom, *Beyond the Typewriter: Gender, Class, and the Origins of Modern American Office Work, 1900–1930* (Urbana: University of Illinois Press, 1992).

**16.** Alice Kessler-Harris, *A Woman's Wage: Historical Meanings and Social Consequences* (Lexington: University of Kentucky Press, 1990).

**17.** This study does not identify Metropolitan Life Insurance Company by name, but comparison of Univac delivery dates identifies MetLife as the company studied. Ironically, Remington Rand reprinted and distributed the BLS report as Remington Rand, *Electronic Data-Processing: Techniques—Methods—Applications*. Reprint of U.S. Department of Labor, Bureau of Labor Statistics, *The Introduction of an Electronic Computer in a Large Insurance Company* (Philadelphia, Remington Rand Univac, 1956). Box 345, Sperry Corporation, Univac Division, Hagley Museum and Library, Wilmington, Delaware.

**18.** Remington Rand, *Electronic Data-Processing: Techniques—Methods—Applications* (Philadelphia: Remington Rand Univac, 1956).

**19.** Bureau of Labor Statistics, *Introduction of an Electronic Computer in a Large Insurance Company* (Philadelphia: Remington Rand Univac, 1956).

**20.** It remains an open question whether MetLife's transition was exceptional or representative among U.S. companies; unfortunately, most statistical data lacks the gender and fine-grained job classifications needed to identify the effects of office automation on female clerks. A study of office automation in 19 Bay Area (California) companies, however, shows a similarly gendered pattern of replacement; see Ref. 14.

**21.** Unfortunately, the gender composition of the Electronic Installations Division is not clear.

**22.** Brian Harris, *BABS, BEACON and BOADICEA: A History of Computing in British Airways and Its Predecessor Airlines* (London: Speedwing Press, 1993).

**23.** See the seminal study of household technology by Ruth Schwartz Cowan, *More Work for Mother: The Ironies of Household Technology from the Open Health to the Microwave* (New York: Basic Books, 1983).

**24.** Carl Hammer, "Watch Your Statistics," *Journal of Systems Management*, Vol. 21 (1970): 40–41.

**25.** Characteristically, this description ignores the women in the medium payscale—almost one-third of the women in the affected punch-card division alone—which must have been working for a much longer time.

**26.** For white-collar workers, see also Elizabeth Faulkner Baker, *Technology and Woman's Work* (New York: Columbia University Press, 1964).

**27.** For the movie's representation of computers as unthreatening machines that were "suitable to take over repetitive tasks that human workers found boring," see Cheryl Knott Malone, "Imagining Information Retrieval in the Library: *Desk Set* in Historical Context," *IEEE Annals of the History of Computing*, Vol. 24, No. 3 (2002): 14–22.

**28.** H. Allan Hunt and Timothy L. Hunt, "Recent Trends in Clerical Employment," in Heidi H. Hartmann, Robert E. Kraut, and Louise A. Tilly, eds. *Computer Chips and Paper Clips*, Volume II. (Washington, DC: National Academy Press, 1986), pp. 223–267.

**29.** Barbara Baran, *Technological Innovation and Deregulation* (Washington DC: U.S. Congress, Office of Technology Assessment, 1985). For a personal reflection on this change, see Linda Stepulevage, "Computer-Based Office Work," *IEEE Annals of the History of Computing*, Vol. 25, No. 4 (2003): 67–72.

**30.** Organisation for Economic Co-operation and Development, *ICTs and Gender* (March 2007), Vol. 4, p. 14.

# Meritocracy and Feminization in Conflict

## Computerization in the British Government

5

MARIE HICKS

In 1992, the Commission of the European Communities tackled the issue of women's underrepresentation in jobs created by the proliferation of new digital information technologies. The University of Wales researcher who produced the report was especially concerned with the dearth of women in positions of power and responsibility, but not simply because of the negative effect this state of affairs had on women. Her report showed how culturally constructed gender roles in Britain, and European society more broadly, tended to focus only on men's technical competence. As a result, a powerful popular image—sometimes accurate and sometimes not—of technically incompetent or maladept women workers both fed a cycle of perpetual skill shortage and encouraged low technical achievement for women as a group [1]. In attempting to offer solutions to the problem of skill shortages in information technology fields like business computing management, programming, and systems analysis, the report postulated an important connection between skilled labor shortfalls in the technology sector and the underutilization of female labor in those fields.

By the time this report was commissioned, the field of computing had already acquired a distinctly masculine image within British society. So much so that, as Cynthia Cockburn, an influential labor researcher, noted, "for a woman

*Gender Codes: Why Women Are Leaving Computing*, Edited by Thomas J. Misa
Copyright © 2010 the IEEE Computer Society

95

to aspire to technical competence is, in a very real sense, to transgress the rules of gender" [2, p. 185]. Despite decades of equal pay and significant investment in educational strategies designed to change this situation on both sides of the Atlantic, patterns of female underachievement and the perception of female technical maladroitness persist within Anglo-American culture, business, and higher education.

Yet, however seemingly timeless and enormously powerful, the idea that the history of computing is a defeminized realm is belied by multiple, important historical examples. British computing labor in the sprawling public sector, for instance, contradicts this image, while offering insight into why this perception took hold. The history of computing in the British civil service and nationalized industries reveals how computing was first institutionalized as a feminized sphere of work, and then very self-consciously re-engineered as a field of masculine endeavor. The reasons for this change, while historically specific, shed light on many of the widespread biases and processes of institutionalized discrimination that still influence hiring and industrial policy on a macro level.

## GENDER AND HISTORICAL ANALYSIS

Queer theorists like Judith Butler have convincingly argued that gender, as a category of social difference that structures society, is not a static category but a performative one; one that by its very nature requires change and reinterpretation in order to retain its analytical and cultural utility. Gendered mores have the ability to help construct and order social relations as historical circumstances change. Yet, as a set of relational categories made real by social performance, gender can neither be understood as something natural and unconflicted, nor as something consciously assumed by individuals choosing freely between identities. Rather, gendered categories are an aggregate of constantly changing cultural understandings and social negotiations, which, far from being purely descriptive, strongly tend to produce the phenomena they set out to describe.

This discursive model of gender analysis—wherein description and reiteration of categories, standards, and ideals tend to produce their own subjects—also means that "power is not only imposed externally but works as the regulatory and normative means by which subjects are formed" [3]. One need only recall the furor over the remarks made by the previous president of Harvard regarding women's lack of technical and scientific ability for a recent example. Addressing a National Board of Economic Research conference convened to discuss the underrepresentation of women and minorities in the sciences and engineering, Larry Summers theorized that innate differences between the sexes could be a major factor behind women's underachievement. The fear that his comments, however unsupported, might help reinvigorate a powerful discourse of women's scientific incompetence by virtue of his prominent position, shows how discourse is widely understood to be not merely descriptive but in fact generative. Gendered discourses have the power to create categories that structure society, and often determine how people navigate a wide range of social, legal, and economic interactions.

The perception of a masculine ideal for computer workers is, in and of itself, an issue that researchers, educators, and even businesses have recognized as a critical stumbling block for women's entry and advancement in high technology fields. Even when women enter and advance, such ideals can suppress full recognition of their contributions. As a result, a historical period in which computing was not yet a "man's job" can offer important insights into how and why this masculine ideal was self-consciously constructed. In the case of the British public sector, management believed that undoing the longstanding feminization of the data processing workforce was critical to the success of the government's computing projects (Fig. 5.1).

Figure 5.1. Gendered practices and the structure of society. At a Day, Inc., sportswear factory in 1972, man with computer-output microfilm equipment (above) controls women production workers (below) "on a projected-requirement basis." (Courtesy of Charles Babbage Institute.)

# THE BRITISH EXAMPLE

With its sprawling civil service, nationalized industries, National Health Service, and many other far-reaching social insurance and welfare programs, the British government required ever greater data processing power throughout the 20th century, both in terms of computing machinery and human labor. By the 1970s, Britain expended more than 40% of its gross domestic product on the public sector and created data-intensive services as part of the cradle-to-grave welfare state that could not have existed without early and brisk integration of electronic computing [2, p. 136]. The size, scale, and importance of computing to the British state makes the public sector a critical historical laboratory for analyzing computing labor patterns. Computing took many forms under the auspices of the government, and, as a result, the similarities in gender discrimination across the British public sector are instructive.

These patterns are all the more relevant to current experience because of the British government's longstanding commitment to equality of pay and opportunity in the civil service. Since the 1950s, women who worked in the public sector had received equal pay. The government's employment practices were the apogee of meritocracy in a nation that did not adopt equal pay industrywide until 1975. Yet, the "fair field with no favor" of the civil service and nationalized industries was an ideal that could not translate directly into reality [4]. The conflict between meritocratic ideals and the reality of hiring practices and workers' lives created a situation where seemingly equitable policies had very different effects on men and women. The history of this computing labor force therefore holds applicable lessons for other high technology workforces constructed within the varied, but often broadly similar, institutional and cultural molds of Anglo-American tradition.

# FROM PREELECTRONIC TO ELECTRONIC COMPUTING

The preelectronic history of data processing in Britain represented a firmly feminized field of endeavor in the early and mid-20th century. Perceived as rote, deskilled work, women trainees were hired exclusively to operate and program the machines that performed payroll, accounting, and even scientific computations. This association of women workers with technical machine work might seem to fly in the face of cultural stereotypes. Yet, by constructing technical work as being at odds with the intellectual work of government officers, managers' association of women with this work did not break down any barriers. Instead, it served to strengthen them, limiting women to lower level jobs with little responsibility over others and little room to advance.

These "machine grades" were so dominated by women workers that, prior to 1954, when the government granted equal pay to its own employees, the machine grades were explicitly labeled a "women's grade." Hiring focused exclusively on female recruits. After 1954, the grade remained feminized, but the women's grades instead became known as the "excluded grades," because they were excluded from the provisions of the Equal Pay Act. Arguing that the wages of the very few men working in these jobs were erroneously high, the government determined, with an eye to their own economic advantage, that

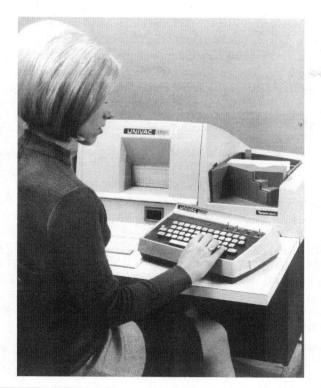

Figure 5.2. Office machines and feminized labor. Data entry on punch cards was gendered as female labor. In 1971, Univac's verifying punch combined keypunching and verifying of data. (Courtesy of Charles Babbage Institute.)

the lower, women's rate for machine operation was the fair market price for the labor. Only women in the higher classes of the civil service, where men worked in equal or higher numbers, were entitled to pay equalization. Yet, the wages of the men within the excluded grades were not lowered to the women's rate. Instead, their job titles changed. As a result of this inequitable equal pay plan, a large proportion of women working in the public sector did not benefit from the change. Rather, the association of women with deskilled, low-paid, and usually dead-ended machine work became institutionalized (Fig. 5.2).

Located firmly below clerical workers, those whose jobs depended on office machines formed a subclerical, feminized underclass of liminally white-collar labor. Although performed in an office, the association of these jobs with machinery meant that they were often seen as more aligned with the manual work of a factory than the intellectual work of an office. Many managers viewed the work as relatively unskilled, even though some recognized that this was not the case. Only as more expensive and complex electronic computers began to creep into government offices did this negative perception slowly began to shift.

For instance, women doing computation in the Aeronautical Research Department as Scientific Assistants in the 1950s used a variety of specialized tools, including electromechanical and digital computers for which they coded complex mathematical problems. Yet, these jobs were considered low level and led to a career dead end. When considering the idea of making a long-term career for computing workers in 1955, the department reported: "Boys generally prefer laboratory work to computing ... this might be due in part to the absence of any recognized career in computing and of any suitable specialist courses or qualifications; if this be true it may be possible to make computing into an attractive career for some boys if current plans come to fruition." Simultaneously, the report noted that "a high proportion of the [Scientific] Assistants are girls; this appears to be because they like the routine work. The resignation of a large proportion on marriage certainly eases the problem of careers in computing" [5]. As a result, the young men working in the department were put on laboratory work instead of computing, since there was room to advance there. Meanwhile, the young women remained on computing.

The issue at stake was not one of technical skill, or differences in men's and women's abilities to perform the work at hand, but rather the improbability of keeping young men in a field with no career progression or opportunity for advancement. Women's and men's technical aptitudes did not direct hiring policy; rather, social expectations about men's and women's proper roles in society tended to enforce different job opportunities. This tended to create different career outcomes along gendered lines, even within the civil service's "meritocracy." Feminization of computation work preceded, and helped devalue, early electronic computing jobs in the public sector. The deskilled, devalued perception of the work in turn limited career opportunities and pay, ensuring that the field remained feminized.

In 1955, it was not surprising that young men were regularly considered for different work and better career opportunities than young women. The government had granted equal pay, however imperfectly, to its female employees just one year earlier, and it was less than a decade since the government-wide ban on employing married women had been lifted. What was surprising, however, were the far-reaching and transformative effects of institutional discrimination that coded certain types of opportunities "male" and others "female." In some cases, identical work could be considered different in terms of difficulty and importance depending on whether men or women were performing it, or expected to perform it.

By the late 1950s, departmental managers expressed concerns that more complex and powerful computing equipment would require a different type of worker: one who would be suitable to manage workers and work flow, not simply deal with machines. Whereas office machine operators and programmers had once been considered low level, electronic computers had begun to change data processing from an easily circumscribed endeavor into one whose borders threatened to bleed into administrative, managerial, and long-term planning work. As office computers increasingly became perceived as management tools, management-aspirant staff would be required to function within the data processing system, working with the machines.

## ELECTRONIC COMPUTING WORK GETS AN UPGRADE

In 1959, the government's Central Tabulating Installation (later renamed the Central Computing Bureau) endeavored to hire operators and programmers from the managerial "executive class" of the civil service to run its new computer. Instead of utilizing the women already present in operator jobs, young men were brought in, because department heads perceived computing work to be increasing in importance and scope. The problem, however, was that none of these executives had any familiarity with computer programming, or even operation. Each of the hires was "new and inexperienced" and would "require a long period of training and 'running in'" for the first six to nine months [6].

Undeterred, the head of the tabulating installation hired several executive class programmer trainees to run the computing section. The programming work, however, would continue to be done by a senior machine operator already in charge of programming and orchestrating work flow for the electronic computer. Described by her superiors as having "a good brain and a special flair for this type of work," she would be responsible for training the new male, executive-level programmers, as well as doing all the programming and testing of programs [6].

Yet instead of gaining a promotion, she would only receive a temporary bonus in pay. Eventually, she would be demoted to an assistantship position under her former trainees: "We can leave the senior machine operator on programming until the supervisory executive officer recommended for [programming] in our report is fully trained, say, 9 months, and then replace her with an executive officer … [she] will eventually become an assistant to the executive officer on programming work," reported the department heads' meeting minutes [6]. This senior machine operator was not allowed to take up a supervisory post, despite holding all of the requisite technical skills. As a woman, and as a machine-grade operative, she was seen as not suited for higher responsibility, nor capable of supervising men. These perceptions of her nontechnical potential scuttled her chances of ever being on an equal footing with her new trainees.

By 1961, government hiring managers administered specially designed aptitude tests for machine operator hiring, with an eye to finding not just good operators but potentially good programmers as well. Departmental managers initially felt that "the operation of computers was expected to be similar to that of punched card equipment and thus proper to SMOs [senior machine operators]" [7], but soon this gave way to the idea that computing jobs were too complex and required too much training to warrant the continued use of the feminized labor in the senior machine operator class [8]. Technical skill and aptitude, once again, were not the main concern; the primary issue at stake was wasting training for more complex automatic data processing machines on a workforce expected to have high turnover and short working lives.

## PROGRAMMING AS A MANAGEMENT TOOL

As operator work increasingly became separable from programming work, the central government began to develop more specific hiring standards for programmers. A 1962 overview of government computing policy reported that the government aimed to recruit most programmers from the ranks of the 70,000 workers within the executive class. Over 90% of executive class workers were male. By contrast, there were roughly a quarter of a million workers in the largely female clerical and machine-grade classes. In 1963, 70% of the workers in the machine grades worked in computing installations, making computing operation a firmly feminized job class [9].

Workers in the executive class were middle managers who dealt with long-term departmental goals and developed more efficient work processes. In general, they had more advanced secondary school training, but they did not have university educations nor any particular skill set commonly associated with programming expertise or aptitude. Explained one organization specialist in the Treasury who helped design the new hiring rubrics: "It was early decided that for most programming of clerical operations one did not need graduates in mathematics or other knowledge of professional standard, but a reasonable level of intelligence and certain aptitudes" [10]. Management potential and a broad understanding of the workings of government agencies were the key qualities that hiring managers sought in the new computing workers (Fig. 5.3).

Not surprisingly, the decision to recruit programmer trainees only from the higher-powered and more prestigious executive grades quickly ran into difficulties. Implementing the policy was easier said than done because, in general, it was women from the machine operator class who had the experience for these posts. While aptitude testing for programming jobs proved an unreliable measure of recruits' future success, familiarity with the departmental computing installations tended to produce programming trainees more easily [11]. As the

Figure 5.3. Computerization and masculine management. In 1971, Honeywell's Keyplex Data Entry System seemed to promise tidy masculine management over female clerical workers. (Courtesy of Charles Babbage Institute.)

government struggled to computerize as quickly as possible, the management abilities of executive class recruits could only go so far in preparing them for the technical aspects of the work, which required a different set of skills and training. As the amount of time that it took to find and train suitable executives for technical jobs became an increasingly precious commodity, these deficiencies proved to be a major stumbling block.

Popular perception had also begun to shift slightly by the mid-1960s. More and more women were joining the workforce, and many married women were staying at work longer than before. The idea that women were unsuitable for careers or any kind of serious work responsibility had begun to be contested by many working women, as well as by journalists, political commentators, and authors of popular literature aimed at the young. (Women trade unionists had long agitated for single and married women workers' rights, but their power to change institutional frameworks and the popular discourse on women's roles in society remained limited in the decades following World War II.) Increasingly, Britain had begun to realize, from the highest levels of government down, that high technology and the reskilling of their entire available workforce would be necessary to maintain superpower status as their geographic and economic empire shrank. The "technological revolution" proclaimed by Labor Prime Minister Harold Wilson in 1964 promised to usher in a new, more meritocratic society by leveraging the latest technologies for the good of the country as a whole. Technology in general and computing in particular were to save Britain from its seemingly inexorable slide toward second-rate world power status.

## SHIFTING IDEALS IN A CRISIS-DRIVEN STATE

Despite the institutionalization of a growing preference for young, career-oriented men for public-sector computing work, the 1960s did not, for the most part, witness a hemorrhaging of women from computer operation and programming jobs. During the mid-1960s, intense high tech labor shortages and economic turmoil in the country at large pushed broader concerns about shaping a professional, career computing class to the back burner. Although women in the government's employ had been nominally given the same rate for the job as men, inequality of opportunity meant that women civil servants generally clustered in lower level and less well-paid positions, meaning that they were often less expensive to employ. Even well into the 1960s, many government departments still regarded programming as appropriate work for higher machine operator posts, a logical progression from lower level machine operator work [12].

From the 1950s on, Britain's gross national product had grown slowly, outpaced by the economic growth of continental rivals. At the same time, former colonies and commonwealth trading partners increasingly turned to the United States. Successive British governments attempted to reverse the poor trading situation through technological modernization geared to increase production for both domestic and export markets. These measures, however, could not produce a quick or dramatic enough change in the nation's economic outlook, and Britain's power on the world stage continued to decline.

By the summer of 1965, an economic crisis had sharpened enough to necessitate a government pay freeze and an expenditure reduction policy. This policy required deferring computer purchases unless they effected major reductions in civil service labor costs [13]. Government cost–benefit projections nearly always claimed that savings would accrue from new computer installations, despite the fact that these expected savings had repeatedly failed to materialize. Nonetheless, the idea that large computing installations were somehow economical influenced government purchasing during economic downturns. Since there was little room for savings on the cost of machines, labor cost was the only fungible aspect. Throughout the mid-1960s, a period when the British government was buying ever greater numbers of computers, economic crisis consistently shadowed the government. By November 1967, the pound had to be devalued against the dollar for the second time within two decades, a move that failed to quell inflation or give British exports the necessary boost. Dockyard strikes in 1966 and 1970 frustrated Britain's already flagging export position.

In the face of these difficulties, government computing installations altered their recruiting and training tactics. The pay-scales offered, hindered by the government pay freeze, were not competitive with industry. The most desirable candidates—bright young men with career promise—would be unlikely to gravitate to civil service computing jobs. In 1964 and 1965, as public sector computing projects ramped up, the programmer shortage became so acute that hiring managers were ordered to make recruiting concessions, while still confining job calls for programming trainees to the higher grades of the civil service.

After one call for applications met with little success, it was reissued with assurances that applicants who "did not make the grade as programmers" would be allowed to return to their previous posts [14]. While this was a procedural nightmare, and a plan that would potentially waste an enormous amount of money training unsuitable candidates, it was also an apparent necessity in coaxing people to apply. In addition, hiring managers had to add a paragraph to the job listing describing what a programmer actually did: workers outside the machine grades were not expected to know even the most basic information about the job for which they were applying. Finally, they lowered the minimum age for promotion to the executive class from 28 to 25, changing the fundamental promotion structure of the entire civil service in order to cast a wider net for a specific kind of programmer trainee [15].

Yet, as one executive in charge of finding programmers pointed out, suitable candidates were likely not to be forthcoming because of apprehension among higher civil servants that volunteering for such work would stall their careers: "There is a fear among staff … of getting in a 'backwater,'" he pointed out. "Could we say," he hedged, "that once on programming an officer is not likely to remain in this work for the rest of his career?" [16]. The gender and class intimations of machine work, combined with the uncertain career prospects of computing jobs, frightened away higher-level workers throughout much of the 1960s [17].

As a result, recruitment literature and job postings began by saying explicitly that these positions were "suitable for women" as well as for men [18]. Unfortunately, the lack of a programmer career ladder in the civil service tended to scare the few executive-level women in the service away from the jobs just as effectively as it had men [19]. Women who had risen above the traditionally female-coded work of machine operation were, if anything, even less likely to risk their careers in a potentially feminized, deskilled job category. As such, their inclusion in these job postings did little to enhance the pool of potential recruits. The emphasis on "equality of opportunity" for women in this case, when little attention was paid to women's low representation in higher civil service jobs in general, speaks volumes about the continuing stigma of machine work in the British civil service through the mid-1960s.

In a somewhat ironic twist, the government even considered "a proposal to widen the eligibility of senior machine operators for promotion to the executive class, and hence for [higher level] ADP [automatic data processing] work," instead of simply recruiting and training members of the machine class for programming and systems analysis work from their current positions [15]. At first glance, this may seem forward-thinking, but in fact it did little to combat the inequality of opportunity faced by workers in these feminized grades. While such a plan would have been beneficial for the few female recruits elevated to executive status so they could continue working in computing at higher levels, it would have again confirmed the low status of the machine class: only workers who could be promoted out of the class were considered good enough for computing jobs. This tactic, had it been employed, might also have cemented the perception of computing as a feminized endeavor and ultimately scared away many other recruits. Realizing that such a plan was not viable in the long term as a way to create a cadre of mostly male, management-grade programmers, the government quickly discarded the idea.

Instead, managers redoubled their efforts to recruit young men *and* young women into computing jobs in accordance with central hiring policies. Still, the available applicants within the civil service were not enough, so hiring calls went out in the major London newspapers. One advertisement for work in the new post office computing center showed an increasing willingness to hire and train an entry-level, gender-diverse workforce. This had become a necessity in overcoming the labor shortage born out of the government's inability to compete with the pay rates in industry. The job call made no secret of the fact that experience in related fields was of no import: "Know Nothing About Computers? Then We'll Teach You (and pay you while doing so)" read the advertisement, promising that "Here at the GPO London Computer Center ... you can take your first steps into the fascinating world of computers—into a fascinating future as well!" [20].

## INDIVIDUAL OPPORTUNITIES ... INSTITUTIONAL CRISIS

This advertisement immediately appealed to several thousand young men and women. Asking explicitly for both male and female applicants was a rarity at the time for jobs of this nature. Often jobs that were presented as career opportunities confined their applications to men, while the routine office jobs, with potentially high starting pay but little upward mobility, sought only female applicants. Those who applied had a chance at a life-long post in the civil service and, perhaps more importantly, paid training in the highly lucrative skill sets required for computing jobs.

While many advertisements that pitched a job to one gender or the other did so by openly asking for either men or women, even greater numbers of advertisements employed subtler language or fine print. Some limited applications by asking applicants to direct inquiries to the company's "Women's Officer." Others warned that night work would be required, intimating that men were preferred. A variety of code words having to do with career opportunity, pension plans, and the possibility for advancement to salaries over £1500 were often used to convey that young men, rather than young women, were the target demographic for a staff wanted advertisement. Pension plans, when mentioned in an advertisement seeking young employees, were almost exclusively targeted toward young men. Young women generally lost pension rights upon marriage, and therefore, if they opted or were allowed to contribute to a pension plan at all, they would take a lump-sum payout of their contributions in the form of a "marriage bonus" upon finding a husband to help them set up a married household. Women, on the other hand, were targeted with promises of part-time work flexibility, marriage bonuses, sociable outlets at the workplace, and workplaces in districts of London described as exciting, fun, and fashionable—the shopping area of Kensington or the West End theater district were perennial favorites.

The post office computing job advertisement uniquely combined elements that were meant to appeal to young men and also young women. The thousands caught in the wide net cast by this job listing came from diverse backgrounds, but all were relatively young, since the job call was confined to those under 25 years of age. One of these applicants, an 18-year-old named Cathy Gillespie, was working in a shoe shop when she applied, having dropped out of secretarial college. Another applicant, Anne Sayce, applied for the position from within the civil service where she was already employed in accounting, but she still had to compete along with all the external applicants. At 24, she barely squeaked in under the age limit. Gillespie's and Sayce's experiences show the enormous promise and upward mobility possible for early computing workers. Women and other nonideal recruits benefited from a situation of institutional crisis that unseated some of the ingrained sexism and classism pervading nominally equitable and gender-blind government hiring and promotion practices.

In the fall of 1965, both women started work at the London post office's LEO III/26 installation, joining roughly 60 other operators spread across three shifts. LEO, short for Lyons Electronic Office, was the brainchild of managers at the Lyons tea shop and bakery company, who parlayed an in-house inventory and payroll automation project into one of the most successful early British computer companies. The original LEO was based on the Cambridge EDSAC [21]. After 2 weeks of dedicated training, during which time they memorized the functions and machine code in the thick LEO operator's manual, the new operators began work. Roughly half were female, but all were overseen by male supervisors. For the most part, each of them recalled the atmosphere of the job as pleasant, fun, and exciting. It was, Gillespie recalled, "great to be young in a new industry, earning good money and being on a par with the men regarding wages and opportunities" [22].

To many, computers seemed like a fascinating new field. A cut above the other jobs available, located neither in the dull world of the office nor in the realm of the service industry or factory labor, computing work seemed to represent the remarkable new social and economic future that Labour, and the nation, had begun aligning itself with by the mid-1960s. Nor did the reality of the job disappoint. Recalled Sayce, "operating a computer at that time was quite interesting and exciting," a sentiment echoed by Gillespie: "the atmosphere was fantastic and the best bit was that no one knew what I did as it was so new" [23]. In addition to being interesting and relatively well paid, the work had a particular caché and a level of prestige associated with it. Cutting edge technology elevated both the work performed and the workers who performed it.

Yet, gendered proscriptions intersected with class-specific social mores in a variety of ways, and female workers sometimes inhabited confusing social identities at the crossroads. Intangible factors strongly contributed to Gillespie's and Sayce's perceptions of themselves and their jobs. Both recalled that the married engineers who were on site to fix the computers thought female operators were "a bit dodgy" and shied away from them, seeing them as "man eaters." A similar view was held of the women in the all-female punching pool, who were seen as loud and sexually aggressive. Trousers were not allowed attire for machine operators despite the physicality of the job, even though protective attire, like a long "overall" coat, was sometimes supplied. The only exception was that women on shifts commencing after seven in the evening could wear trousers, hinting at the breakdown of gendered norms that night work implied for women. Indeed, Sayce had even been banned from Woolworth's a few years earlier for wearing trousers. At the same time, hemlines were rising, and women were wearing more and more revealing fashions to work.

Even workers doing the same job in the same installation could see their social roles quite differently. Gillespie remembered that women who worked on required night shifts with men were sometimes looked at in a suspicious light: "'What sort of a woman would want to do that?' was the idea," she recalled, adding, "there was also this idea that you didn't indulge in sexual things before marriage." Her former co-worker Anne Sayce agreed with her first statement, but not the latter, asking incredulously: "What sixties were *you* in?" [23]. Women's real or imagined sexual availability could be perceived very negatively and potentially damage their careers, even while proscriptions against sexual experimentation seemed to be crumbling.

As female co-workers left to have children, the gender balance of operators shifted, and new female hires did not replace the old. Both Gillespie and Sayce saw married colleagues come back to work after having had children in different, less desirable jobs, and at lower pay. From her own experience applying for the job, Sayce recalled that some workers were more equal than others. In addition to passing the required math and writing tests for the post office job, she had to convince the hiring officers that she would not have children in the near future: "You would never get the job until you swore up and down that you wouldn't have children" [23]. Male applicants had to offer no such assurances of loyalty. In fact, one government department had all of its new programmer trainees resign their posts upon completion of their training. They had all found higher-paying positions in industry with their brand new skills [24].

The gradual phasing out of female operators in many government installations through turnover comported with the government's concerns about finding the most appropriate workers for their professionalizing cadre of management-oriented technocrats. Two years on, with no room to advance, Gillespie and Sayce both left their post office jobs for positions at the Central Electricity Generating Board, where there was more potential for promotion. Gillespie later used her experience to make the leap to the private sector, while Sayce soon left the workforce to have children. Even as working women became more numerous, and working wives more accepted, employers and British society in general withheld full tolerance. Women often faced significant stresses and institutional discrimination associated with the continuing belief that their paid work was incidental, and that the work most appropriate to them was unpaid labor in the domestic sphere [25].

## REVIVAL OF THE MANAGEMENT COMPUTER MEN

The dire high tech labor shortages and the economic crises of the mid-1960s, paired with the rubric of Labour's "technological revolution," gave women a temporary opportunity to join the newly professionalizing computing workforce on a nearly equal basis with men. This equality, however, would be shallow and short-lived. As economic conditions stabilized and high tech labor shortages lessened, women in computing would find themselves consigned to less desirable positions or kept from entering and training in the field at all. The resurgence of subtle and not-so-subtle institutional proscriptions against women holding career-oriented and management-aspirant jobs meant that women in computing jobs soon became subject to the larger cultural trends acting upon women workers in general. As a result, many women made choices against their own best professional interests, while many others had those choices made for them.

The Royal Air Force's computing installation, struggling to keep its staff as young women computer operators resigned en masse due to "low rates of pay" and "dissatisfaction with the job" soon decided that they needed to hire a different kind of worker—rather than improve the conditions of the job. "Machine operators are required who have no career ambitions and who simply want to earn a bit of money," stated an RAF report. Therefore, "the best bet is the middle-aged married woman" [26, pp. 3, 49]. Women were perceived to be technically proficient but they were not, in general, considered the best or most likely candidates for computing careers. As a result, the RAF focused on hiring women who had no expectation of career progression, rather than improving pay and promotion prospects to hold onto their young, female workforce.

Conversely, young men were never expected to take professional jobs in which there was no guarantee of career progression. Most organizations in the private sector "recruit young men as machine operators," the RAF noted, "because they offer a complete career to such people, and partly, as was said earlier, because it is felt that the computer field is generally a young man's domain. ... The young man seems to represent the 'best bet' if career opportunities and financial rewards are satisfactory" [26, pp. 48–49].

That young men represented the "best bet" for computing careers did not always mean that they were the first chosen; indeed, in times of economic crisis or uncertainty, the government simply could not compete with private industry for these workers. It did mean, however, that once the financial crisis had been averted, departments focused on hiring young men and groomed them for promotion to management and more complex, responsible work. Relatedly, once economic conditions permitted the hiring of these "best bet" candidates, existing women workers could be phased out through turnover, or kept in the lowest echelons of the computing-work hierarchy with little opportunity for further training or promotion. By the late 1960s and early 1970s, exactly such a movement was underway in the British public sector.

As economic conditions improved to the point where the government could afford these more desirable candidates, women who had been seen as performing well as computer operators and programmers were often seen as no longer worth the money being paid to them. As late as 1967, the government's Central Computing Bureau noted that they were "pleased to see that the quality" of their "girl trainees" was "still very high" and had begun to send larger and larger complements of machine-grade operators for training in the programming language NICOL (Nineteen Hundred Commercial Language). NICOL, a subset of the imperative programming language PL/1, was developed by the British computing company International Computers and Tabulators (ICT) for programming the 1900 series of large mainframe computers upon which the British public sector relied heavily [27].

Yet just two years later in 1969, when the government was no longer as constrained by the lean computing labor market of the middle part of the decade, Central Computing Bureau management did an about-face, balking at paying these workers the appropriate rate for their labor on the grounds that they were "unqualified" in comparison to higher-level, nontechnical staff who earned similar salaries. The operators at the Central Computing Bureau from 1966 to 1970 made roughly £800 per year, at a time when £1000 per year was a good salary even for professional young men. Extra allowances for speed, specialized skills, shift work, and overtime further enhanced salaries. Some senior operators could make as much as, or more than, managerial civil servants who did not do computing work. Nonetheless, the government payscales attached to these computing jobs were only at or below fair market rate when compared with the private sector.

Some of the highest-level managers within the government felt that these "girls" were getting too much money for their jobs. In addition, these managers wanted to stem, rather than encourage, the flow of machine operators into higher civil service posts. In the process of setting up the new Central Computing Bureau, the government had to hire many new, young, female operators. By 1969, there were already 17 full-time, pensioned senior machine operators there below the age of 25, and dozens of lower-level computer workers, with more needed. One manager stated that although he was "quite satisfied that the machine operators being promoted are fully capable of doing senior machine operator work, we are not happy with the size of the group we are building up receiving pay on a scale starting at £814 per annum. It is out of proportion that these girls, academically unqualified compared with clerical staff, should so quickly be able to reach salary levels above those of clerical officers and even executive officers" [28].

With no further promotion outlets in the machine operator class, these young women could theoretically take examinations to move into the firmly white-collar and career-oriented clerical or executive classes and from there attain positions of much greater responsibility and influence. In practice, such promotions rarely, if ever, occurred. But even the small chance that these workers might be promoted into general management and supervision duties alarmed some. The Central Computing Bureau's hiring manager suggested that "a fundamental and searching examination of the grading and pay of the machine class is badly needed," if such young recruits were rising so quickly through the ranks and earning so much [28]. Meanwhile, young men of the same age, earning the same amounts, were not subjected to such scrutiny.

These workers were not only young, but still slightly stained by a perception that machine work was only liminally professional. The fact that they were mostly single women exacerbated the situation further. At a time when male Clerical Officers wrote angry letters to civil service union newsletters complaining about how their low salaries meant they could not "afford to keep a wife" or support a family, many civil servants believed that market forces had pushed hiring in an unsavory direction [29].

In response to these fewer than 200 computer operators perceived as somehow undeserving of their pay and position, officials actually suggested that all new hires, irrespective of merit, should be subject to new decremented payscales with a slower promotion track and lower top-level earnings. This unprecedented action went against decades of government agreements with clerical unions, and after severe union backlash, the idea ultimately fizzled. Nonetheless, many promotions were intentionally deferred in an attempt to throttle back the flow of young women into high computing operation and programming positions at the Central Computing Bureau. "Where it is not absolutely essential that we fill posts now, we will defer appointments," wrote the Bureau's manager in early 1969 [28].

## THE PUBLIC FACE OF GOVERNMENT MERITOCRACY

That same year, the Department of Employment released an animated public service film called "Job for Girls" that implored young women and their parents to take careers for women seriously [30]. Between 1961 and 1971, the proportion of women in the workforce had rocketed up by 18%, even as men's workforce participation slightly declined by 2% [31]. The short film presented the cautionary tale of a woman left to fend for herself after her husband and children were gone. It depicts her rise and fall, beginning when she takes a job in a factory as a young person, earns good money, and has an active social life. She leaves her job when she gets married and has children, but after raising her children she is left on her own and has to return to the same low-level factory work that she did all those years ago when she had just entered the workforce.

The film's message, addressed as much to parents as to young women, was clear: society was changing and women had to adapt. It was no longer the best option for a young woman to get a job that paid well in the short term if it lacked room for lifelong advancement. The film attempted to persuade viewers of the wisdom of this course of action, rather than offering much material insight into how girls might go about getting careers rather than jobs, or what sort of work might fit the bill—and with good reason. Embarking on a career was still not as socially respectable an option as leaving the workforce to care for children, and women who attempted such would encounter both obvious and subtle disincentives and discrimination. While well-meaning, the film highlights the schizophrenic paradigm professional women were advised to enact by carefully maintaining (limited) career prospects while spending equal or greater effort maintaining a home or raising a family.

Despite the government's propaganda, the idea of equal job opportunities for women still had yet to gain significant traction in British society. National equal opportunity laws would not be enacted until 1975, and in the 1980s Britain was admonished by the European Court for failing to properly institute the equal pay and equal opportunity measures required by the EEC. Even in new fields of endeavor like computing, which might have been expected to offer escape from old stereotypes, well-established patterns molded work processes and workers' responsibilities. Actions taken by the highest-level ministers in the civil service in regard to new high technology jobs perpetuated the position of men and women in jobs with different prestige, remuneration, and opportunities. Informal segregation of jobs and tasks continued despite long-held ideals of meritocracy within the government service's self-described "fair field with no favor" [32]. Young women continued to inhabit an uneasy place in the modern British economy given the conflicting dictates of their roles within society and the family.

In 1970, the government set up a new Automatic Data Processing work grade in the civil service to cater to the pay and career needs of programmers and systems analysts. The decision to exclude the machine operator class from the list of grades whose work would be reviewed and upgraded as part of the process, and also to exclude the machine grades from putting forward candidates for the new jobs in this grade, drew objection from the now largely female union, but the plans moved ahead unchanged [33]. One leader of the Society of Civil Servants went so far as to tell her superiors that "peasant work" was all that was left to the majority of civil servants working in data processing. Her attempts to lobby the government on behalf of her union for changes in how programmer training was doled out, and how certain higher-level computing work was organized, however, went nowhere [34].

## CONCLUSION

Within machine operation and early computing jobs in the British public sector, women initially held a clear majority. As office computing work gained structure and prestige, government hiring policies began to systematically exclude the majority of the applicable workforce from consideration for the most responsible and difficult-to-staff computing positions. In so doing, the government seriously undermined not only the long-term position of women in Britain's high technology economy but also the health of the nation's technological projects themselves.

The period in which government computing faced economic crisis and labor shortage provided the most opportunities for women in the nascent field, but this did not produce a long-term institutional change, only a short-term situation that benefited certain, young individuals within a very limited time frame. In some sense, this is not surprising. The exigencies of war, for instance, have brought women workers into myriad positions in industry that were not considered ideally suited to them—including many of the earliest computer operation and programming jobs (see Figs. 6.3 and 6.4) [35]. Yet, the ends of such crises usually mark a self-conscious return to previous staffing models, regardless of whether or not women performed the work successfully.

As the economic crisis and high tech labor shortage lessened, a reversion to hiring and promotion best practices that favored young men and management-level operatives, where available, took hold in public sector computing, forcing women applicants to the back of the queue for the most desirable jobs. As Barbara Reskin and Patricia Roos have discussed in their research on feminized and male-dominated fields of paid work, in order to understand why women lose out in the labor market—particularly in well-remunerated or traditionally male fields—we must redirect our inquiry away from the "characteristics of female workers, to the structural properties of labor markets." These labor markets are, for the most part, "shaped by the preferences of employers and male workers" who have the most power in establishing the institutional shape of current and future workforces in the most desirable fields [36].

The association of computing, then as now, with some of the most lucrative and powerful positions in industry will undoubtedly work to exclude women, in the aggregate, from the field; the most desirable workers and managers are still, in general, perceived to be men. Stereotypes about women's technical incompetence, however, seem not to have been an issue in this historical case, proving that women can nonetheless lose out in a technical field even when their technical competence is not at issue. In order to change this bias in the computing labor market, a fresh analysis of the underlying factors that make women seem to be less valuable candidates must occur alongside any increase in the numbers of trained female computing professionals. Then, as now, career interruption or termination due to the demands of family present a major reason for women's downgraded image, in the aggregate, as valuable and reliable workers. In addition, there is the less tangible issue of women's perceived inability to manage personnel, especially male personnel, as effectively as male managers.

Going forward, it is critical to dispense with the idea that individual bias and individual culpability, on the part of either workers or managers, hold the key to solving intractable problems of underrepresentation. As this history shows, management acted as a bloc to create different hiring rubrics for men and women, on the assumption that this was necessary for institutional preservation in different economic circumstances. Meanwhile, women's failure to excel in computing jobs was not an issue of individual women not being technically proficient or not wanting to perform technical work; rather, it was due to the fact that their work was undervalued as a result of expectations about women's and men's work patterns in the aggregate. In order to change institutional patterns of bias and underrepresentation in computing, as in any field, the solution requires altering the very gendered ideals on which men's and women's contributions throughout paid and unpaid work are predicated, and how these contributions are measured. For this reason, the problem of women's underrepresentation in computing is first and foremost a social problem, rather than an educational, economic, or technical one.

# REFERENCES

**1.** Teresa Rees, *Skill Shortages, Woman and the New Information Technologies* (Luxembourg: Office for Official Publications of the European Communities, 1992), pp. 26–27. Far from being confined to the European context, similar processes have constructed technical skills in other large industrialized, Western nations. See Ruth Oldenziel, *Making Technology Masculine* (Amsterdam: Amsterdam University Press, 1999).

**2.** Cynthia Cockburn, "Women and Technology," in Kate Purcell, Stephen Wood, Alan Waton, and Sheila Allen, eds., *The Changing Experience of Employment: Restructuring and Recession* (London: Macmillan, 1986).

**3.** Judith Butler, *Bodies that Matter* (New York: Routledge, 1993), p. 22.

**4.** *The Marriage Bar in the Civil Service: Report of the Civil Service National Whitley Council Committee* (London: HMSO, 1946), p. 4.

**5.** Aeronautical Research Council, *Training and Careers for Computers* (London: Aeronautical Research Council, 1955), DSIR 23/23112, National Archives, Surrey.

**6.** Minutes, 20 April 1959 and 20 May 1959, STAT 14/2320 Accounts Division: Combined Tabulating Installation Staff Inspection Report 1958–1959.

**7.** "Computer Operations Staffing: Note by the London Office," 28 September 1966, AB 46/16 Authority-wide Computer Operations Staffing, 1965–1969.

**8.** Treasury Report, "Government Statistical Services Advisory Committee on Computers," pp. 1–3, 31 August 1967, HN 1/16 ADP Staffing Problems Other than Shift Working 1956–67.

**9.** Confidential letter from D. W. G. Wass in Treasury to P. W. Buckerfield in HMSO, 14 June 1963, STAT 14/2765 Review of Machine Operator Grades 1961–1970.

**10.** "Electronic Computers 'Oil' the Wheels of Government," J. D. W. Janes, Organization and Methods Department, Treasury, p. 11, June 1962, T 216/710 Redundancy Owing to the Introduction of Computers.

**11.** July 1968, ADP Staffing and Projects, HN 1/67 Consultation with Civil Service Staff Association About Automated Data Processing (ADP) 1968–1971.

**12.** Machine Grades—notes of an interdepartmental meeting held in the Treasury, 8 May 1964, STAT 14/2765 Review of Machine Operator Grades 1961–1970.

**13.** T 224/900 Economic Situation 1965: Deferment of Expenditure on Capital Projects, Application to Computers.

**14.** Memo from Drake to Shipton, 20 May 1965, LAB 12/1471 Policy Considerations on Recruitment of Programmers and Computer Operators.

**15.** T. H. Caulcott, Treasury Circular, 12 March 1965, LAB 12/1471.

**16.** Minutes, 30 June 1965, LAB 12/1471.

**17.** In this round of calls for programmers, recruits were accepted from Clerical Grades 3, 4, and 5. By decade's end, only pensioned recruits from Grade 6 were accepted. LAB 12/1553 Shift Working of Computer Operators: Applications for Vacancies and Other Papers 1966–1969.

**18.** Note from J. Bruce, 25 May 1965, LAB 12/1471.

**19.** Women made up only 8% of the executive classes in 1970. "Career Prospects for Women Civil Servants," *Civil Service Opinion Magazine: Down Among the Datacrats Issue* (February 1970): 52. HN 1/67 Consultation with Civil Service Staff Association about Automated Data Processing (ADP) 1968–71.

**20.** *Evening Standard*, "Know Nothing About Computers?" Staff Wanted Ad (21 July 1965): 20; (23 July 1965): 18.

**21.** See Peter Bird, *Leo* (Wokingham: Hasler Publishing Ltd., 1994).

**22.** Cathy Gillespie, author's interview regarding her work as a computer operator (1965–1968), London, 5 January 2006.

**23.** Cathy Gillespie and Ann Sayce, author's interview regarding their work as computer operators (1965–1968), London, 5 January 2006.

**24.** Roger Watts, "Down Among the Datacrats," *Civil Service Opinion Magazine: Down Among the Datacrats Issue* (February 1970): 42. HN 1/67 Consultation with Civil Service Staff Association About Automated Data Processing (ADP) 1968–71.

**25.** Dolly Smith Wilson, "A New Look at the Affluent Worker," *Twentieth Century British History*, Vol. 17, No. 2 (2006): 206–229.

**26.** P. R. Bixby, *Report on Recruitment and Retention of Machine Operators* (London: Royal Air Force, 1967), AIR 77/384 National Archives, Surrey.

**27.** CCB Steering Committee Meeting Report, 8 June 1967 and 5 June 1968, STAT 14/3303 Shift Working of Computer Operators: Applications for Vacancies and Other Papers 1966–1969.

**28.** Letter from C. W. Blundell in HMSO (Norwich Computing Installation) to F. G. Burrett in Civil Service Department, 25 February 1969, STAT 14/2765, Review of Machine Operator Grades 1961–1970.

**29.** Roger Mortensen, "Economic Nightmare," Letter to Editor, *Civil Service Opinion Magazine: Down Among the Datacrats Issue* (February 1970): 54. HN 1/67 Consultation with Civil Service Staff Association about Automated Data Processing (ADP) 1968–71.

**30.** From www.nationalarchives.gov.uk/films/1964to1979/filmpage_jobs.htm.

**31.** *Census 1961, Summary Tables*, p. 64; *Census 1971, Part I*, p. 1.

**32.** Civil Service National Whitley Council Committee, *The Marriage Bar in the Civil Service* (London: HMSO, 1946), p. 4.

**33.** "Computers in Government Ten Years Ahead: Notes of an Informal Meeting with the National Staff Side," 21 September 1970, HN 1/22 Report on Development of Computers in Government: Forecast for Next Ten Years 1969–1971.

**34.** CCA memo, "Staff in Confidence," 25 October 1972, HN 1/72 Interdepartmental Working Party on Computer Personnel: Implementation of Recommendations, 1972–1973.

**35.** Both the Colossus and ENIAC projects heavily utilized women's labor. For ENIAC, see Jennifer Light, "When Computers Were Women," *Technology and Culture*, Vol. 40, No. 3 (1999): 455–483.

**36.** Barbara Reskin and Patricia Roos, *Job Queues, Gender Queues* (Philadelphia: Temple University Press, 1990), pp. 108–109.

# Making Programming Masculine

# 6

NATHAN ENSMENGER

In the April 1967 issue of *Cosmopolitan* magazine, sandwiched between "The Bachelor Girls of Japan" and "A Dog Speaks: Why a Girl Should Own a Pooch," there appeared a curious little essay entitled simply "The Computer Girls." As the article explained, these were the female "computer programmers" who taught the dazzling new "miracle machines" called computers "what to do and how to do it." There were already more than 20,000 women working as computer programmers in the United States, argued the article's author, Lois Mandel, and there was an immediate demand for 20,000 more. Not only could a talented "computer girl" command as much $20,000 a year, but the opportunities for women in computing were effectively "unlimited." The rapid expansion of the computer industry meant that "sex discrimination in hiring" was unheard of, Mandel confidently declared, and anyone with aptitude—male or female, college educated or not—could succeed in the field. And not only were women in computing treated as equals, but they actually had many advantages over their male colleagues. Programming was "just like planning a dinner," Mandel quoted the noted computer scientist Dr. Grace Hopper as saying, "You have to plan ahead and schedule everything so it's ready when you need it. Programming requires patience and the ability to handle detail. Women are 'naturals' at computer programming" [1].

It would be easy to dismiss "The Computer Girls" as a fluff piece, a half-hearted attempt by *Cosmopolitan* to capitalize on contemporary interest in the computer revolution. To modern readers the very language of the "computer girl" appears condescending and sexist. The analogy between computer programming and recipe creation seems forced and superficial (see Fig. 8.3). At times the article descends into what seems almost a parody of formulaic *Cosmopolitanism*, such as when Sally Brown, "a redhead from South Bend,

*Gender Codes: Why Women Are Leaving Computing*, Edited by Thomas J. Misa
Copyright © 2010 the IEEE Computer Society

Indiana," confesses that she doesn't mind working late because there is often "a nice male programmer to take a girl home...." At one point the author speculates, seemingly without irony, about the "the chances of meeting men in computer work." (The conclusion she comes to is that these are "very good," as the field was currently "overrun" with men.) The last word of the article text comes from a patronizing male programmer: of course "we like having the girls around," he declares, "they're prettier than the rest of us." And, in true *Cosmopolitan* style, the article concludes with a "Cosmo Quiz"—by answering a few simple questions, any *Cosmo* girl could see whether she too had what it took to be a professional computer programmer making "$15,000 after five years" [1].

But underneath its seemingly frivolous exterior, "The Computer Girls" article gives insight into the gender dynamics of computer work at one of the most critical periods in its history. It reflects very accurately the confusing—and often contradictory—messages about the proper role of women in the computing fields. On the one hand, women did play a critical role in early computing, particularly in computer programming. Compared to most technical professions, computer programming was unusually open to females (see Figs. 1.1, 10.1, 10.3, and 12.4). But on the other hand, in the late 1960s the computer programming community was also actively making itself masculine, pursuing a strategy of professional development that would eventually make it one of the most stereotypically male professions, inhospitable to all but the most adventurous and unconventional women.

Let's begin with what the *Cosmopolitan* article gets right.

First, it is true that in the late 1960s there were an exceptionally large number of women working in computer programming. In fact, if anything the *Cosmo* article *underestimates* the percentage of women programmers. Mandel suggests that one out of every nine working programmers was female. This is probably overly conservative. The exact percentage of female programmers is difficult to pin down with any accuracy—even figuring out the total number of programmers in this period is difficult—but other reliable contemporary observers suggest that it was closer to 30% [2]. The first government statistics on the programming profession do not appear until 1970, when it was calculated that 22.5% of all programmers were women—an estimate more than twice Mandel's estimate [3].

Of course, computing itself is a very broad term covering a multitude of occupational categories, including high-status jobs like computer programming and systems analysis as well as low-status jobs such as keypunch operator. Women tended to congregate in the lower end of the occupational pool in computing. Even within computer programming there were different roles differentially available to men and women. But as the *Cosmopolitan* article rightly points out, compared to most of the traditional professions, computer programming was remarkably receptive to females (see Chapters 10 and 11). One of the programmers it profiled, Helene Carson, had previously earned an MA degree in astrophysics at Harvard. Although Carlson had discovered that "there wasn't much a woman could do in astronomy," in computing she felt that she had been "fully accepted as a professional" [1].

Again, there is evidence that Carlson (and *Cosmo*) was absolutely spot-on in regard to the vertical mobility available to women in computer programming. Compared to other technical disciplines, computer programming was not highly stratified along gender lines. Not only were women able to break into the entry levels of the profession, but some were able to climb to its highest pinnacles. In 1969, for example, the Data Processing Management Association recognized Grace Hopper with its very first "man of the year" award in the computer sciences. That an emerging professional society with grand aspirations for technical and managerial leadership would even consider giving its *first* major award to a woman is really quite remarkable. Although Hopper was unusual in that she possessed both a Ph.D. and a commission in the United States Navy (at that time as a Lieutenant Commander), she was not entirely *sui generis*: other women, including Betty Snyder Holberton, Jean Sammet, and Beatrice Helen Worsley, all came to occupy influential positions within the computing community (see Figs. 3.4, 6.3, 12.2, and 12.3) [4].

In addition to accurately representing the state of the contemporary labor market in programming, the *Cosmopolitan* article also does a reasonable job of explaining its unique characteristics. In large part, the unusual freedom of opportunity available to women in computing was simply an outgrowth of the rapid growth of the commercial computer industry. An industry that was doubling in size every year or two simply could not afford to discriminate against women (Fig. 6.1). "*Every* company that makes or uses computers hires women to program them," the article noted matter-of-factly: "If a girl is qualified, she's got the job." And since the meaning of "qualified" in this period was still being

Dear Girl Graduate,          Dear Mom and Dad,

Figure 6.1. Control Data appeals to "girl graduate" and her parents. "The world of opportunity lies before you … be part of the data processing, computers, and orbiting space vehicle intrigue," suggested Control Data to the "girl graduate." To her parents, "You're not losing a daughter—you're gaining a career girl. … Let her give Control Data a try." (Courtesy of Charles Babbage Institute.)

negotiated (more on this point later), there was no particular reason for firms to privilege men over women [1].

It would be difficult to overemphasize the degree to which the programmer labor shortage of the 1960s dominated contemporary discussions of the health and future of the computer industry. For years, industry employers had been warning of an imminent shortage of computer programmers. The "gap in programming support" threatened to wreak havoc with the industry [5]. In 1962 the editors of the powerful industry journal *Datamation* declared that "first on anyone's checklist of professional problems is the manpower shortage of both trained and even untrained programmers, operators, logical designers and engineers" [6]. In 1966 the "personnel crisis" had developed into a full blown "software crisis," according to *Business Week* magazine [7]. An informal 1967 survey of MIS (management information systems) managers identified as the primary hurdle "handicapping the progress of MIS" to be "the shortage of good, experienced people" [8]. One widely quoted study released that same year noted that although there were already 100,000 programmers working in the United States, there was an immediate need for at least 50,000 more [9]. Estimates of the number of programmers that would be required by 1970 ranged as high as 650,000 [10]. "Competition for programmers has driven salaries up so fast," warned *Fortune* in 1967, "that programming has become probably the country's highest paid technological occupation. ... Even so, some companies can't find experienced programmers at any price" [11]. The ongoing "shortage of capable programmers," argued *Datamation*, "had profound implications, not only for the computer industry as it is now, but for how it can be in the future" [10].

In the face of this perpetual shortage of programmers, employers turned to extraordinary measures. Recruitment companies scoured local community centers and YMCA facilities for potential programmer trainees, administering programming aptitude tests to almost every warm body they could find [12]. In 1968 one computer service bureau in New York City even began testing inmates at the nearby Sing Sing prison, promising them permanent positions on their release [13]. Given that employers were willing to hire prisoners as programmers, their appeal to *Cosmopolitan* readers is unexceptional. As in the case of other severe labor shortages—wartime, for example—women were able to move into fields from which they might otherwise have been excluded.

The combination of low barriers to entry and subsidized technical education made programming powerfully appealing to many women who might otherwise be trapped in traditionally female occupations. But it was not only the desperate need for programmers that allowed women unique opportunities within the profession. Although in the late 1960s programming was generally considered highly skilled labor—as one observer declared, "generating software is 'brain business,' often an agonizingly difficult intellectual effort"—the exact nature of that intellectual effort was not yet clearly defined [11]. Programming was "not yet a science," argued the same observer, "but an art that lacks standards, definitions, agreement on theories and approaches" [11]. The lack of a fully established scientific or engineering identity left space open for women. Although the possession of a college degree in mathematics was still considered a necessity in scientific computing (which tipped the scales demographically in favor of males), business computing—the most rapidly growing segment of the commercial computer programming industry—required an entirely different set of skills. What these skills were no one quite knew, and so many firms relied on aptitude tests to determine which employees had the most potential for programming. Aptitude was everything; you either had it or you didn't. And since there was no particular reason that these aptitude tests were gender specific (again, more on this later), there was also no reason that men would be more likely than women to be selected as programmer trainees. In addition, as the *Cosmopolitan* article also correctly noted, since most firms preferred to train programmers from within, and therefore often tested *all* of their employees for programming aptitude, even women working in such highly feminized (and low-status) occupations as stenography had a chance at becoming a programmer. The trick was getting some initial experience: as one employment counselor cited by Mandel argued, "a girl's best bet is to get a spot *anywhere* in the computer department, using skills like filing or typing or accounting, with the plan in mind to get on the firm's programmer-trainee list from the inside." There were outside vocational schools that claimed to prepare people for careers in programming, but as one of the "girls" quoted in the article declared, "I'd never consider paying for my own training when I can get someone else to pay for it." [1, p. 56].

It is worth noting as well that, given this context, the quiz provided at the end of "The Computer Girls" article was no superfluous or silly afterthought. The quiz included real questions from the aptitude test developed by NCR to test for programming aptitude. Similar tests, most notably the IBM Programmer Aptitude Test (PAT), were used by 80% of all employers to select for programmer trainees [14]. In 1967 alone, the PAT was administered to more than 700,000 individuals [15].

In any case, after noting a few other reasons why programming might be an appealing profession for women—including that at least some programming work could be done at home (while children were napping)—the *Cosmopolitan* article concluded by suggesting that it was largely a lack of knowledge about the field that kept women from entering it in greater numbers. Since programming was thought to be vaguely mathematical in nature (incorrectly, the article concludes), and since female students were often discouraged from pursuing any fields involving science or mathematics, they too often missed out on the exciting opportunities available in programming. This was unfortunate. "I don't know of any other field, outside of teaching, where there's as much opportunity for a woman," the article quoted the director of education for the Association for Computing Machinery, James Adams, as saying. "Soon, mothers will be telling their daughters: 'Now study your arithmetic so you can become a computer girl.'" (See Figure 6.2.)

What makes the vision of widespread female participation in the computer industry portrayed in "The Computer Girls" so intriguing today, of course, is that it is so unfamiliar. From a contemporary perspective, the computing professions appear egregiously male dominated. The problem of female participation in computer science programs—declining since the mid-1980s—is of particular concern and is generally explained in terms of "opening up" the discipline to women. The idea that many of the computing professions were

Figure 6.2. Evelyn Murphy, a "computer girl," at the control console of the National Bureau of Standards pilot computer (c.1960). (National Bureau of Standards image number 30062–3.)

not only historically unusually accepting of women, but were in fact once considered "feminized" occupations, seems extraordinary, if not unbelievable. And yet a historical understanding of how the computing professions acquired their gendered identity, how they were "made masculine," is critical to any attempt to address the current gender imbalance in computing. The historical perspective, in this case, is not only relevant but essential.

Beginning in the 1990s, historians of computing began to recognize the crucial contributions that women made to the development of electronic computing. Like many such (re)discoveries of the previously unrecognized contributions of women, this one had both historical and contemporary significance. Given that computing was generally considered to be particularly masculine (even when compared to the traditionally male-dominated engineering disciplines), the surprisingly large presence of women in early computing seemed to turn on its head conventional assumptions about the lack of female participation in contemporary computing. It wasn't that women were uninterested in computing, or unprepared or constitutionally disinclined to participate, the historical evidence seemed to suggest, but rather that their participation had been systematically ignored or underreported [16]. In light of contemporary debates about low (and declining) female enrollments in departments of computer science, this seemed a significant and empowering discovery [17]. The focus of most of this literature has been, understandably enough, on what Judy Wacjman, among others, has called the "hidden history" of women in technology [18]. The goal was to explore what the history of women in computing had to say about women—about their contributions, experiences, and abilities [19].

This chapter will address instead the flip side of this question: namely, what the history of women in computing has to say about *computing*. Because of the modern association of computer work—particularly computer programming—with high-status males, we tend to assume that such work has always been masculine, and that the presence of women is therefore exceptional. My argument is that most computer work—again, particularly computer programming—*began* as women's work. It had to be *made* masculine. This process of masculinization was closely associated with the development of the professional structures of the discipline: formal programs in computer science, professional journals and societies, certification programs, and standardized development methodologies. Seen from the perspective of aspiring computer professionals (primarily male), "The Computer Girls" article represented not a celebration of the openness and opportunity inherent in their industry, but an indictment of everything that was wrong with it.

In terms of the larger questions addressed in this volume, this chapter provides important insights into the way in which the *structures* of a profession both reflect and replicate the *culture* of its practitioners. One of the most significant barriers to female participation in computing is the culture of computing, a culture that is perceived to be inherently (and excessively) masculine. The roots of this culture reach back into the early history of electronic computing and can only be understood, and addressed, in the context of a full historical understanding of its origins.

## IN THE BEGINNING WERE THE WOMEN ...

The most prominent case study in the history of women in early computing is, in fact, the earliest. In the early 1940s a group of six women—Kathleen McNulty, Frances Bilas, Betty Jean Jennings, Betty Holberton, Ruth Lichterman, and Marlyn Wescoff—were recruited to assist with the development and operation of the University of Pennsylvania's ENIAC machine (Fig. 6.3). The ENIAC (Electronic Numerical Integrator And Computer) was one of the first, and certainly most famous, early electronic computers, and the "ENIAC girls" (as they were often referred to by contemporaries) were the female "human computers" recruited by the male ENIAC engineers/managers to "set up" the general-purpose ENIAC machine to perform the specific "plans of computation" required to solve real-world problems. Although the idea of the computer "program" had not yet been developed, the women of ENIAC are nevertheless widely celebrated as the world's first computer programmers. And not only was the pioneering work that they did on the ENIAC historically significant, many went on to subsequent careers—often at the highest levels—in electronic computing.

The expectation was that the work of "setting up" the ENIAC would be relatively trivial. But in his 1996 article based on interviews with the ENIAC

Figure 6.3. Frances (Betty) Holberton (right) and Glen Beck (left) with ENIAC at the U.S. Army Ballistic Research Laboratory (BRL) at Aberdeen Proving Ground, Maryland. (U.S. Army Photo, http://ftp.arl.army.mil/~mike/comphist/.)

programmers, Barkley Fritz highlights the substantial contributions that these women made to the operation—and particularly the troubleshooting—of the ENIAC. According to Betty Jean Jennings, for example, the ENIAC women learned to understand the internal wiring diagrams of the ENIAC machine, and "as a result we could diagnose troubles almost down to the individual vacuum tube. Since we knew both the application and the machine, we learned to diagnose troubles as well as, if not better than, the engineer" [20, p. 20]. In a few cases these female programmers significantly affected the design of the ENIAC and subsequent computers. ENIAC programmer Betty Holberton recalled one particularly significant episode when she convinced John von Neumann to include a "stop instruction" in the machine: although initially dismissive, von Neumann eventually recognized the programmer's legitimate need for such an instruction. Other accounts by participants and observers echo the critically important—but generally unanticipated—role that the ENIAC programmers played in facilitating the successful launch of one of the world's most famous early electronic computers. Yet, as Jennifer Light has convincingly demonstrated, the contributions of these women were subsequently systematically eliminated from the historical record [16].

There is no question that the work of the ENIAC women was disregarded in large part simply because they were women. But almost as significant as their gender was their subordinate position as "software" workers in a hardware-oriented development project. Obviously, the two are closely related. Of course, use of the word "software" in this context is anachronistic—the word itself would not be introduced until 1958—but the hierarchical distinctions and gender connotations it embodies—between "hard" technical mastery and the "softer," more social (and implicitly, of secondary importance) aspects of computer work—are applicable [21]. In the status hierarchy of the ENIAC project, it was clearly the male computer engineers who were significant. The ENIAC women were expected to simply adapt the "plans of computation" already widely used in human computing projects to the new technology of the electronic computer. These "plans of computation" were themselves highly gendered, having been traditionally developed by women for women (human computing had been largely feminized by the 1940s). The ENIAC women would simply "set up" the machine to perform these predetermined plans: that this work would, in fact, be difficult and require radically innovative thinking was completely unanticipated [22, p. 53]. The telephone switchboard-like appearance of the ENIAC programming cable-and-plug panels reinforced the notion that programmers were mere machine operators, that programming was more handicraft than science, more feminine than masculine, more mechanical than intellectual (Fig. 6.4).

The idea that the development of hardware was the real business of computing, and that software was at best secondary, persisted for many years. In the first textbook on computing published in the United States, for example, Herman Goldstine and John von Neumann outlined a clear division of labor in computing—presumably based on their experience with the ENIAC project—that clearly distinguished between the "head-work" of the (male) scientist, or "planner," and "hand-work" of the (largely female) "coder" [23]. In the

Figure 6.4. Programming ENIAC as telephone switching. Betty Jean Jennings Bartik (left) and Frances Bilas Spence (right) setting up the ENIAC at the Moore School. (U.S. Army Photo, http://ftp.arl.army.mil/~mike/comphist/.)

Goldstine–von Neumann schema, the "planner" did the intellectual work of analysis, and the "coder" simply translated this work into a form that a computer could understand. "Coding" was a "static" process that could be performed by a low-level clerical worker. "Coding" implied mechanical translation or rote transcription; "coders" were obviously low on the intellectual and professional status hierarchy. It was not unreasonable to expect that, as was the case in the ENIAC project, that most of these "coders" would be women.

An early manuscript version of the UNIVAC "Introduction to Programming" manual mirrored this distinction between "planner" and "coder." In this instance the term "programmer" was used, somewhat unconventionally, in place of "planner," but the distinction between the analytical "programmer" (the person who "studies the problem, determines the appropriate method of solution, and prepares the flow chart") and the clerical "coder" (who "need only be familiar with the technique of reducing the flow chart to the specific instructions, or coding, required by the UNIVAC to solve the problem") remains the same [24]. In the UNIVAC manual, like the Goldstine–von Neumann textbook, the real business of programming was analysis: the actual coding aspect of programming was trivial and mechanical.

It was not until the early 1950s that the term "programmer" was widely adopted within the computing community. As David Grier has suggested, the verb "to program," with its military connotations of "to assemble" or "to organize," suggested a more thoughtful and system-oriented activity [22, p. 52]. But even as "programmer" was increasingly adopted within the computing community, software workers would struggle to distance themselves from the status (and gender) connotations suggested by the older designation "coder." The accusation that programmers were "mere coders" was used throughout the 1950s and 1960s by those who wanted to counter the influence of "uppity" software workers. The noted computer scientist John Backus, for example, argued that the adoption of the title "programmer" by former "coders" happened "for the same reason that janitors are now called 'custodians'. ... Programmer was considered a higher class enterprise than 'coder,' and things have a tendency to move in that direction" [25].

The conflation of programming and coding, and the association of both with low-status clerical labor, suggested the ways in which early software workers were gendered female. In the ENIAC project, of course, the programmers actually were women. But the suggestion that "coding" was low-status clerical work also implied an additional association with female labor. As Margery Davies [26], Sharon Hartman Strom [27], and Elyce Rotella [28] have described, clerical work had, by the second decade of the 20th century, become largely feminized. This was particularly true of clerical occupations that were characterized by the rigid division of labor and the introduction of new technologies. Some of these occupations carried over directly into the computer era: the job of keypunch operator, for example, had been thoroughly feminized long before it became associated with electronic data processing [29]. And although today we do not associate the work of keypunchers with the work of the computer programmer, in the 1950s and 1960s the differentiation between keypunch operator and other forms of computer work was not always clear. The *Cosmopolitan* article, for example, lumped keypunch operators in among the "computer girls," and other contemporary sources identified keypunch operators as an obvious source of programmer trainees [30, 31]. In any case, the historical pattern has been that low-status occupations, with the exception of those requiring certain forms of physical strength, have often become feminized.

## THE "BAD BOYS" OF PROGRAMMING

In the 1950s, however, computer programming was beginning to acquire new status and a new gender identity. The experience of the ENIAC girls had shown that electronic computing was anything but an "automated form of hand computation." The neat distinction made by Goldstine and von Neumann between analysis and implementation quickly broke down in practice. To begin with, since the primary purpose of the earliest computers was to produce solutions to complex mathematical functions that could not be solved analytically, the programmers of these computers necessarily required skill in numerical analysis. This process of analysis was itself something of an art form: numerical solutions always involved a compromise between speed and accuracy—even when using the fastest computers. Choosing the right approximation involved balancing acceptable error against the specific limitations of a given machine—a process that required daring, creativity, and mathematical intuition.

Perhaps even more significantly, the performance and memory constraints of the first generation of electronic computers demanded that programmers cultivate a series of idiosyncratic craft techniques to overcome the limitations of primitive hardware. For example, contemporary memory devices were so slow and had such little capacity that programmers had to develop ingenious techniques to fit their programs into the available memory space. In order to coax every bit of speed out of a relatively slow storage device such as a rotating memory drum, programmers would carefully organize their coded instructions in such a way as to assure that each instruction passed by the magnetic read head in the right order and at just the right execution time. Only the best programmers could hope to develop applications that worked at acceptable levels of usability and performance.

For all of these reasons, programming began to acquire a reputation for being incomprehensible to all but a small set of extremely talented insiders. As John Backus would later describe it, "programming in the 1950s was a black art, a private arcane matter ... each problem required a unique beginning at square one, and the success of a program depended primarily on the programmer's private techniques and invention." Techniques developed for one application or installation could not be easily adapted for other purposes. There were few useful or widely applicable tools available to programmers, and certainly no "science" of programming. Programmers often worked in relative isolation and had few opportunities for formal or even informal education. They generally perceived little value in the work going on at other firms or laboratories, as it was equally haphazard and idiosyncratic. They placed great emphasis on local knowledge and individual ability.

The heady combination of mathematics, engineering "tinkering," and arcane technique attracted a certain kind of male to computer programming. Some had abandoned careers in more established scientific disciplines to pursue the emerging field of electronic computing. Others drifted in from mathematics or electrical engineering, or from careers in business or data processing. A few, such as the physicist-turned-programmer Edsger Dijkstra, worried about the lack of a "sound body of knowledge that could support it [programming] as an intellectually respectable discipline" [32]. The popular notion that programmers were idiosyncratic geniuses and that "a really competent programmer should be puzzle-minded and very fond of clever tricks" was a pernicious anachronism, Dijkstra would later argue, that encouraged a short-sighted, "tinkering" approach to software development. Academically minded programmers like Dijkstra felt that too many of their colleagues regarded their work as temporary solutions to local problems, rather than as an opportunity to develop a more permanent body of knowledge and technique. What computing needed to realize its true revolutionary potential, Dijkstra argued, was a more rigorous approach to programming, one modeled after the science of applied mathematics [33]. But most programmers accepted—and many reveled in—the conventional belief that, at least for the conceivable future, programming would remain the exclusive domain of the select few who possessed the "right stuff." Either way, this new occupational and professional identity, whether based on the academic prestige of the emerging discipline of computer science or the exclusivity of the "lone gun" tinkerer, was essentially masculine.

This perception of programming as an idiosyncratic arcane discipline—and, by extension, its practitioners a "long-haired programming priesthood" [34, p. 201]—was reinforced by a series of aptitude tests and personality profiles that focused on innate abilities. By the mid-1960s the majority of companies (80%) were using such tests and profiles as their primary tool for identifying programmer trainees. "Creativity is a major attribute of technically oriented people," suggested one representative profile: "Look for those who like intellectual challenge rather than interpersonal relations or managerial decision-making. Look for the chess player, the solver of mathematical puzzles" [35]. Many of the advertisements for programmers in this period specifically referenced chess playing, musical ability, and mathematics [36]. In 1956 IBM launched an advertisement for programmers that led to the hiring of such notable chessmen as Arthur Bisguier, the U.S. Open Chess champion, Alex Bernstein, a U.S. collegiate champion, and Sid Noble, the self-proclaimed "chess champion of the French Riviera" [37]. (It should be noted, however, that the same campaign also netted an Oxford trained crystallographer, an English Ph.D. candidate from Columbia University, an ex-fashion model (female), and a "proto-hippie," so obviously chess-playing ability was not the sole criterion.) In any case, good programming was believed to be dependent on unique qualified individuals, and that what defined these unique individuals was some indescribable, impalpable quality—a "twinkle in the eye," an "indefinable enthusiasm," or what one interviewer described as "the programming bug that meant ... we're going to take a chance on him despite his background" [38].

In addition, great disparities were discovered between the productivity of individual programmers, with one widely cited IBM study suggesting that a truly excellent programmer was 26 times more efficient than his merely average colleagues [39]. Despite the serious methodological flaws that compromised this particular study (including a sample population of only 12 individuals), the

26:1 performance ratio quickly became part of the standard lore of the industry. "When a programmer is good, he is very, very good. But when he is bad, he is horrid," the study declared, reinforcing the notion that skilled programmers were thought to be effectively irreplaceable and were to be treated and compensated accordingly. Programmers were to be selected for their intellectual gifts and aptitudes, rather than their business knowledge or managerial savvy.

The notion that programming was a "black art" pervades the literature from the early decades of computing. Even today, more than half a century after the invention of the first electronic computers, the notion that computer programming still retains an essentially "artistic" character is still widely accepted [40, 41]. Whether or not this is true or desirable is an entirely different question— a subject of considerable and contentious debate. What is important is that by characterizing the work that they did as "artistic," programmers could lay claim to the autonomy and authority that came with being an artist. Note that the appeal here is to the tradition of the artisan, or craftsman, which is a masculine identity, not the potentially effeminate "artsy" type.

The widespread perception that programming ability was an innate ability, rather than an acquired skill or the product of a particular form of technical education, could be seen as gender neutral or even female friendly. After all, the aptitude tests for programming ability were widely distributed among female employees, including clerical workers and secretaries. And, according to one 1968 study, it was found that a successful team of computer specialists included an "ex-farmer, a former tabulating machine operator, an ex-key punch operator, a girl who had done secretarial work, a musician and a graduate in mathematics." Of these, the mathematician "was considered the least competent" [31]. As hiring practices went, aptitude testing at least had the virtue of being impersonal and seemingly objective. Being a member of the "old boys club" does not do much for one's scores on a standardized exam. (Fraternities and other male social organizations did serve as clearinghouses for stolen copies of popular aptitude tests such as the IBM PAT. Such theft and other forms of cheating were rampant in the industry, and taking the test more than once was almost certain to lead to a passing grade.)

But the aptitude tests and personality profiles did embody and privilege masculine characteristics. For example, despite the growing consensus within the industry (particularly in business data processing) that mathematical training was irrelevant to most commercial programming, popular aptitude tests such as the IBM PAT still emphasized mathematical ability [42, 43]. Some of the mathematical questions tested only logical thinking and pattern recognition, but others required formal training in mathematics—a fact that *Cosmopolitan* noted as discriminating against women.

Even worse were the personality profiles. The use of personality profiles to identify programmers began, as with other industry-standard recruiting practices, at the System Development Corporation (SDC), the Rand Corporation spin-off charged with the development of the software for the SAGE air-defense system. Faced with the need to train computer programmers in unprecedented numbers—in 1956 SDC employed 700 programmers, almost three-fifths of the total number of programmers available worldwide, and by the beginning of the 1960s had trained 7000 more—SDC relied extensively on aptitude testing and personality profiling. By the beginning of the 1960s, however, SDC psychologists had developed more sophisticated models based on the extensive employment data the company had collected over the previous decade, as well as surveys of members of the Association for Computing Machinery and the Data Processing Management Association. In a series of papers published in serious academic journals such as the *Journal of Applied Psychology* and *Personnel Psychology*, SDC psychologists Dallis Perry and William Cannon provided a detailed profile of the "vocational interests of computer programmers" [44]. The scientific basis for their profile was the Strong Vocational Interest Bank (SVIB), which had been widely used in vocational testing since the late 1920s.

The basic SVIB in this period consisted of 400 questions aimed at eliciting an emotional response ("like," "dislike," or "indifferent") to specific occupations, work and recreational activities, types of people, and personality types. By the 1960s, more than 50 statistically significant collections of preferences ("keys") had been developed for such occupations as artist, mathematician, policeman, and airplane pilot. The assumption behind the use of such profiles was that candidates who had interests in common with those individuals who were successful in a given occupation were themselves also likely to achieve similar success.

Many of the traits that Perry and Cannon attributed to successful programmers were unremarkable: for the most part programmers enjoyed their work, disliked routine and regimentation, and were especially interested in problem and puzzle-solving activities [44]. The programmer key they developed bore some resemblance to the existing keys for engineering and chemistry, but not to those of physics or mathematics, which Perry and Cannon interpreted as a refutation of the traditional focus on mathematics training in programmer recruitment. Otherwise, programmers resembled other white-collar professionals in such diverse fields as optometry, public administration, accounting, and personnel management.

In fact, there was only one really "striking characteristic" about programmers that the Perry and Cannon study identified. This was "their disinterest in people." Compared with other professional men, "programmers dislike activities involving close personal interaction. They prefer to work with things rather than people" [44]. In a subsequent study, Perry and Cannon demonstrated this to be true of female programmers as well [45].

The idea that computer programmers lacked "people skills" quickly became part of the lore of the computer industry. The influential industry analyst Richard Brandon argued that this was in part a reflection of the selection process itself, with its emphasis on mathematics and logic. The "Darwinian selection" mechanism of personnel profiling, Brandon suggested, selected for personality traits that performed well in the artificial isolation of the testing environment, but which proved dysfunctional in the more complex social environment of a corporate development project. Programmers were "excessively independent," argued Brandon, often to the point of mild paranoia. The programmer type is "often egocentric, slightly neurotic, and he borders upon a limited schizophrenia. The incidence of beards, sandals, and other symptoms of rugged individualism or nonconformity are notably greater among this demographic group. Stories about programmers and their attitudes and peculiarities are legion, and do not bear repeating here" [46].

Needless to say, these psychological profiles embodied a preference for stereotypically masculine characteristics. A 1970 review of the psychometric literature noted that computer programmers received unusually high masculinity and low femininity scores. In fact, only four occupational groups received higher masculinity scores (unfortunately, the review does not mention which four). "These consistent results [high masculinity scores] define one characteristic of the people in data processing jobs," the review concluded—namely, their masculine self-identity [47].

The idea that "detached" (read male) individuals made good programmers was embodied, in the form of the psychological profile, into the hiring practices of the industry [43]. Possibly this was a legacy of the murky origins of programming in the early 1950s; perhaps it was a self-fulfilling prophecy. Nevertheless, the idea of the programmer as being particularly ill-equipped for or uninterested in social interaction did become part of the conventional wisdom of the industry. The association of masculine personality characteristics with inherent programming ability helped create an occupational culture in which female programmers were seen as exceptional or marginal. Only by behaving less "female" could they be perceived as being acceptable. Many women still did continue to be hired as programmers and other computer specialists, but they did so in an environment that was becoming increasingly normalized as masculine.

One interpretation of the male bias embedded in these aptitude tests and personality profiles is that such tests are, in fact, an accurate reflection of the mental or emotional characteristics that make for a good programmer—logical, detached, antisocial—and that these traits just happen to be more predominant in males. This is the essentialist argument: gender discrimination as a function of biology. Even in the 1960s and 1970s there seemed little evidence for such reductionist explanations [48].

A second interpretation is that the tests were developed deliberately to exclude women from an increasingly high-status, lucrative, and therefore male-dominated profession. This is the conspiratorial argument.

Another interpretation is that programming ability has no correlation at all with biologically determined predispositions, but that the widespread use of gender-biased testing regimes by industry employers nevertheless did create a feedback cycle that ultimately selected for programmers with stereotypically masculine characteristics. The primary selection mechanism used by the industry selected for antisocial, mathematically inclined males, and therefore antisocial, mathematically inclined males were overrepresented in the programmer population; this in turn reinforced the popular perception that programmers *ought* to be antisocial and mathematically inclined (and male), and so on ad infinitum. This would be a historically continent argument: gender discrimination as a function of historical accident.

It is this last explanation that seems most plausible. In the case of aptitude testing and personality profiling, at least, it appears that the privileging of masculine characteristics is the result of some combination of laziness, ambiguity, and traditional male privilege. There was widespread evidence, even in the late 1960s, that psychometric testing was inaccurate, was unscientific, had been widely compromised, and was a poor predictor of future performance. Nevertheless, these methods continued to be used simply because they were convenient. The rapid expansion of the commercial computer industry in the early 1960s demanded the recruitment of large armies of new professional programmers. At the same time, the general lack of consensus about what constituted relevant knowledge or experience in the computer fields undermined attempts to systematize the production of programmers. Commercial programming schools were seen as being too lax in their standards; the emerging academic discipline of computer science was seen as too stringent. Neither offered a reliable short-term solution to the burgeoning labor shortage in programming. In the face of such uncertainty and ambiguity, aptitude testing and personality profiling promised at least the illusion of managerial control. To borrow a phrase from contemporary computer industry parlance, aptitude testing was a solution that *scaled efficiently*. That is to say, the costs of aptitude testing grew in a predictable, linear relationship to the number of applicants (as opposed to other recruitment methods such as personal interviews, whose costs in time and money grew rapidly). Put even more simply, it was possible to administer aptitude tests quickly and inexpensively to thousands of aspiring programmers. Compared to its time-consuming and expensive alternatives, aptitude testing was a cheap and easy solution. And since the contemporary emphasis on individual genius over experience or education meant that a star programmer was as likely to come from the secretarial pool as the engineering department, the ability to screen large numbers of potential trainees was preeminent.

But the kinds of questions that could easily be tested using multiple choice aptitude tests and mass-administered personality profiles necessarily focused on mathematical trivia, logic puzzles, and word games. The test format simply did not allow for any more nuanced or meaningful or context-specific problem solving. And, in the 1950s and 1960s at least, such questions did privilege the typical male educational experience. Again, this bias toward male programmers was not so much deliberate as it was convenient. The fact that the use of lazy screening practices inadvertently excluded large numbers of potential *female* trainees was simply never considered. But the increasing assumption that the average programmer was also male did play a key role in the establishment of a highly masculine programming subculture.

There has been much written in recent years about the distinctively masculine culture of computing and the way in which this culture discourages women from entering the computing professions [49–51]. Of all the explanations given for the deplorably low rates of female participation in computing (or at least in academic computer science), cultural arguments are the most convincing. It is important to note, therefore, that the origins of this culture lie not in the early 1940s, with the invention of computing, but in subsequent decades. This culture was not inherent in electronic computing, or even adopted directly from related disciplines; it had to be created, and recreated, over the course of decades. One of the essential ways in which this culture was replicated was through the development of practices and institutions.

## PROFESSIONALIZATION = MASCULINIZATION

The process of making programming masculine did not begin—or end—with the transformation of the feminized clerical work of "coding" into the highly masculine, seat-of-the-pants "black art" of programming of the 1950s, not even with the embodiment of certain masculine values into the hiring procedures of the industry. To begin with, this transformation was never fully complete. Aspects of programming remained rote, mechanical, and low status. It was also not clear that the frontier mentality of programming culture in the 1950s was anything but a function of the immaturity of the industry. The influx of new programmer trainees and vocational school graduates into the software labor market exacerbated an already bad labor situation. The market was flooded with aspiring programmers with little training and no practical experience. As one study by the Association for Computing Machinery's Special Interest Group on Computer Personnel Research (SIGCPR) warned, by 1968 there was a growing *oversupply* of a certain undesirable species of software specialist. "The ranks of the computer world are being swelled by growing hordes of program-mers, systems analysts and related personnel," the SIGCPR argued. "Educational, performance and professional standards are virtually nonexistent and confusion grows rampant in selecting, training, and assigning people to do jobs" [52]. At the same time that the demand for skilled programmers was increasing dramati-cally (and seemingly without limit), when salaries and opportunities for occu-pational mobility were at their peak, many programmers were plagued with uncertainty about the status and future of their discipline.

There were tangible reasons for this uncertainty. The increasing capabili-ties and reliability of second generation hardware meant that the baroque "work arounds" and optimizations so prized by programmer-tinkerers were no longer necessary. In addition, the development of "automatic programming systems" threatened to make programmers obsolete altogether, and to return responsibil-ity for the "head work" involved in problem analysis back to the scientists and managers. The persistent lack of programmers to develop a "scientific" basis for their discipline suggested that they were at best artisans or technicians, the last vestiges of a "pre industrial" approach to software development. (The most damning critique of the "black art" of programming came from Douglas McIroy at the 1968 NATO Conference on Software Engineering: "We undoubtedly produce software by backward techniques. We undoubtedly get the short end of the stick in confrontations with hardware people because they are the indus-trialists and we are the crofters. Software production today appears in the scale of industrialization somewhere below the more backward construction agen-cies. I think that its proper place is considerable higher, and would like to investigate the prospects for mass-production techniques in software.") The organizational tensions provoked by the increasing use of computerized systems for managerial purposes created resentment against the perceived "abdication" of management imperatives to whiz-kid "computer boys" [53]. These tensions reflected themselves in active attempts by managers to reassert their traditional authority over computer programmers by redefining their work as "merely" technical. Finally, the rising cost of software relative to hardware meant that firms began looking for ways to reduce costs by "rationalizing" their develop-ment practices (Fig. 6.5). Such "rationalization" often meant the incorporation of a less expensive, lower skill (read feminized) workforce.

Certainly corporations, academics, and other reformers tried to ratio-nalize the practices of computer programmers in response to the emerging

Figure 6.5. At Tulane University, systems analyst William Cahill and computer programmer Dorothy J. King provided time-sharing services for computer-assisted menu planning (c. 1964). (Courtesy Charles Babbage Institute.)

"software crisis" of the late 1960s. In *Programmers and Managers: The Routinization of Computer Programming in the United States*, the historian Philip Kraft argued that managers had, in fact, been successful in "degrading" the work of computer specialists. "Programmers, systems analysts, and other software workers," he argued, were the victims of efforts to "break down, simplify, routinize, and standardize" their work practices. Kraft suggested that corporate managers had generally been successful in imposing structures on programmers that have eliminated their creativity and autonomy. His analysis was remarkably comprehensive, covering such issues as training and education, structured programming techniques ("the software manager's answer to the conveyor belt"), the social organization of the workplace (aimed at reinforcing the fragmentation between "head" planning and "hand" labor), and careers, pay, and professionalism (encouraged by managers as a means of discouraging unions). In 1979 Joan Greenbaum echoed Kraft's conclusions, arguing that "if we strip away the spin words used today like 'knowledge' worker, 'flexible' work, and 'high tech' work, and if we insert the word 'information system' for 'machinery,' we are still talking about management attempts to control and coordinate labor processes" [54]. More recently, Greg Downey has suggested a connection between routinization, feminization, and the increasing use of foreign labor in software development ("outsourcing") [55].

It is questionable how successful corporate managers and other "rationalizers" were in their quest to transform software development into a controlled, industrial manufacturing process. Computer programmers are, on the whole, well paid, highly valued, and largely autonomous professionals. But it is clear that many programmers in the 1960s were worried about the *possibility* of having their work routinized and degraded. Certainly the management literature from this period is full of confident claims about the ability of new performance metrics, development methodologies, and automatic programming languages to reduce corporate dependence on individual programmers [56]. As Michael Cusumano has described, the vision of the "software factory"—in which hordes of low-paid, low-skill programmers cranked out mass-produced software products—was a persistent theme in this literature [57].

One of the time-honored strategies for dealing with labor "problems" in the United States has been the use of female workers. There is a vast historical literature on this topic: from the very origins of the American industrial system women have been seen as a source of cheap, compliant, and undemanding labor [58, 59].

The same dynamic was a work in computer programming. In a 1963 *Datamation* article lauding the virtues of the female computer programmer, for example, Valerie Rockmael focused specifically on her stability, reliability, and relative docility: "Women are less aggressive and more content in one position. ... Women consider fringe benefits of more importance than their male peers and are more prone to stay on the job if they are content, regardless of a lack of advancement. They also maintain their original geographic roots and are less willing to travel or change job locations, particularly if they are married or engaged" [60]. In an era in which turnover rates for programmers *averaged* 20% annually, this was a compelling argument for employers. Note that this was something of a backhanded compliment, aimed more at the needs of employers than female programmers. In fact, the "most undesirable category of programmers," Rockmael argued, was "the female about 21 years old and unmarried," because "when she would start thinking about her social commitments for the weekend, her work suffered proportionately" [60].

Women were often used in advertisements from this period as a visual proxy for low-skill, low-wage labor. For example, in its 1968 "Meet Susie Meyers" advertisements, the IBM Corporation suggested that even a "young girl" with "no previous programming experience" could program a computer using its new PL/1 programming language. The two-page, full-color advertisements showed a pretty blond in a colorful miniskirt dancing circles around her computer. If the problem with programming was that it was overly expensive ("Let's face it," the ad copy confided, "the cost of programming just keeps going up"), then the solution was the combination of mechanization and feminization. Although the advertisement promised "a brighter future for your programmers," the obvious subtext was that these programmers were becoming increasingly replaceable. If pretty little Susie Meyers, with her spunky miniskirt and utter lack of programming experience, could develop software effectively in PL/1, so could just about anyone.

These attempts to mobilize gendered rhetoric and visuals in the service of what one contemporary described as the "the domestication of this once proud, wild animal" (the computer programmer) did not go unnoticed by programmers [61]. "The Computer Girls" article, for example, prompted an almost immediate response from the Computer Sciences Corporation. Although the overlying tone of the advertisement was light-hearted—"In a recent issue of *Cosmopolitan*, Helen Gurley Brown exhorted her girl readers to become programmers and make 15,000 after five years ..."—the underlying concern it expressed was also quite apparent: the suggestion that "Cosmo girls" could make for good programmers was implicitly demeaning, and threatening to the status and future of the discipline [62].

I have written extensively elsewhere about the "Question of Professionalism" as it emerged in the computer fields during the late 1960s [63, 64]. For the purposes of this chapter it is enough to note that the development of the structures of a programming profession—including formal programs in academic computer science, professional journals and societies, and professional certification programs—became the goal of many computer programmers, and their corporate employers, as a means of addressing the perceived "software crisis" of the late 1960s.

The professionalization of programming and other computer specialties was appealing to a number of constituencies. For practitioners, professionalism offered increased social status, greater autonomy, improved opportunities for advancement, and better pay. It provided individuals with a "monopoly of competence"—the control over a valuable skill that was readily transferable from organization to organization—that provided leverage in the labor market [65]. Professionalism provided a means of excluding undesirables and competitors; it assured basic standards of quality and reliability; it provided a certain degree of protection from the fluctuations of the labor market; and it was seen by many workers as a means of advancement into the middle class [66]. The 1960s were a period when many white-collar occupations were pursuing professional agendas, and the sociological literature of the period seemed to provide a clear road map to the benefits of professionalism. These benefits seemed available to almost any occupation. (The sociologist Harold Wilensky describes numerous case studies of occupations attempting to professionalize in this period, among them librarians, pharmacists, funeral directors, and high school teachers [67].)

The professionalization efforts of computer specialists were, to a certain extent, encouraged by their corporate employers. Professionalism provided a familiar solution to the increasingly complex problems of programmer management. "The concept of professionalism," argued one personnel research journal from the early 1970s, "affords a business-like answer to the existing and future computer skills market. ... The professional's rewards are full utilization of his talents, the continuing challenge and stimulus of new EDP situations, and an invaluable broadening of his experience base" [68]. Insofar as it encouraged good corporate citizenship, professionalism had the potential to solve a number of pressing management problems: it might motivate staff members to improve their capabilities; it could bring about more commonality of approaches; it could be used for hiring, promotions, and raises; and it could help solve the perennial question of "who is qualified" [69]. At the very least, allowing programmers to *think* that they were professionals would go a long way toward reducing turnover and maintaining the stability of the data processing staff [70].

The desire to develop professional standards is an understandable, and indeed laudable, agenda for programmers to pursue. But it does carry with it certain implications for the gender dynamics of the discipline. As Margaret Rossiter and others have suggested, professionalization implies masculinization [71–73]. The imposition of formal educational requirements, such as a college degree, can make it difficult for women—particularly women who have taken time off to raise children—to enter the profession. Similarly, certification programs or licensing requirements—such as the Data Processing Management Association's Certificate in Data Processing Program—also erected barriers to entry that disproportionately affected women. In 1965, for example, the Association for Computing Machinery imposed a 4-year degree requirement for membership, which, in an era when the gender ratio of male to female college undergraduates was close to 2 : 1, excluded significantly more women than men [74]. A survey from the late 1970s showed that fewer than 10% of ACM members were women [75]. Professionalism also suggests a certain degree of managerial authority and competence—skills and characteristics that were often seen as being masculine rather than feminine (see Chapter 5, this volume). The CDP examinations explicitly required candidates to have at least 3 years of experience, and the majority of CDP holders worked in middle management [76]. And in his 1971 book *The Psychology of Computer Programming*, Gerald Weinberg notes the commonly held belief that female programmers were incapable of leading a group or supervising their male colleagues [43]. The more programmers were seen as potential managers (a new development that came with professionalization), the more women were excluded.

There were other, more subtle ways in which professionalization implied masculinization. Perhaps most significantly, professionalization requires segmentation and stratification. In order to elevate the overall status of their discipline, aspiring professionals had to distance themselves from those aspects of their work that were seen as low status and routine. This work did not just disappear—it was just done by *other* people. The job category of "programmer" had been used as a blanket term to describe a broad range of computer workers, but it was increasingly replaced by a complicated hierarchy of job titles: junior programmer, senior programmer, lead programmer, junior analyst, senior analysts, program manager, and so on. Again, it is difficult to gather accurate statistics on who occupied what categories, but there is some evidence to suggest that women were generally confined to the lower levels of the professional pyramid [77]. This calls into question the more optimistic claims about the participation of women in computing: without knowing exactly what *kinds* of work these women were doing, it is difficult to draw any firm conclusions about the true nature of the opportunities available to women in computing [78].

## CONCLUSION

Contemporary discussions about the underrepresentation of women in computing often center around the precipitous decline in female enrollments in academic computer science programs that started in the mid-1980s. But this sudden decline was only relative to an earlier and equally dramatic *increase* in female enrollments that occurred over the previous decades. In many ways it is this remarkable bulge in female enrollments that most deserves explanation. Compared to other scientific and engineering disciplines in this period, computer science—or at least computer programming, which was its closest analog prior to the institutionalization of the discipline in the late 1960s—was unusually welcoming to women. As "The Computer Girls" article in *Cosmopolitan* illustrates, and many other sources confirm, computing in its early years was seen as not only being unusually open to women, but also as having unique advantages for women (e.g., the ability to work from home) [79]. It is only more recently that computer programming acquired its characteristically masculine identity. Unlike other technical or academic disciplines, which had been traditionally male dominated and had to be opened up to female participation, computer programming started out with an ambiguous gender identity. An activity originally intended to be performed by low-status clerical staff—and more often than not female—computer programming was gradually and deliberately transformed into a high-status, scientific, and masculine discipline.

The "masculinization" of computing was not universal or linear. Even as the computing fields were beginning to professionalize, women were continuing to work in computing in substantial numbers—as the continuing increase in computer science enrollments throughout the early 1980s indicates. To suggest that a discipline has been made masculine, however, is not to claim that all of its practitioners are male, but rather that the ideals of the discipline are masculine ideals. It is entirely possible, for example, to talk about science being gendered male without arguing that there are no female scientists [71, 80]. To the degree that women succeed in masculinized disciplines, however, it is by suppressing their femininity: to act female in such contexts is to act "unprofessionally" [81]. There is a large literature on the ways in which women in such fields are forced to accommodate themselves to the dominant gender dynamics of the discipline. The masculinization of a profession erects barriers to female participation, but it does not eliminate it altogether.

The history of the "computer girls" suggests at least two explanations for the remarkable occupational sex change that occurred in computing over the course of the mid-20th century. The first is a structural argument and suggests that masculinization is characteristic of any discipline that is actively professionalizing. In any case, seen through the lens of the history of the professionalization of the computing disciplines, the unusual pattern of female enrollments in computer science is slightly more explicable. In the early decades of computing, before the discipline was effectively professionalized, the field was much more open to female participation. The additional opportunities promised by the emergence of the personal computer might explain the final surge of the late 1970s. But eventually the development of the structures of a profession—a slow but steady process that had started decades earlier—brought to an end the era of unprecedented openness in computing, and brought enrollments in computer science programs back in line with other scientific, mathematical, and engineering disciplines. In this sense, while enrollments in computer science programs are an extremely inadequate measure of female participation in computing overall, it is a reasonable measure of the professionalization and masculinization of the discipline. In fact, if we interpret the formation of academic computer science programs as a crucial contributor to the masculinization of programming, rather than as a measure of its degree, then the focus of the conversation changes fundamentally. Instead of asking why there are so few women in computer science, we might ask instead why a particular vision of the discipline—one based on masculine ideals and values—came to dominate the academic study of computer programming.

This structural explanation is not entirely sufficient, however. Although patterns in computer science enrollments do resemble those of other scientific disciplines (and perhaps even more those of engineering programs), it also has its own, distinctively masculine culture. Many observers have identified this culture as being particularly unappealing to women. The popular association of computing culture with the "nerd" stereotype is perhaps the most common explanation for low rates of participation among females. In recent decades the "computer nerd" has become a staple of modern American culture and is invariably represented as eccentric, unkempt, antisocial—and male.

The story of the computer "nerd" is often associated with the personal computer. A powerful mythology has developed around the role of the nerdy loner in the "accidental" creation of the personal computer industry [82]. The presence of white, adolescent, male nerds is often represented as the essential characteristic of any successful technological start-up company. Nerd culture supposedly dominates most modern computer science departments.

As we have seen, however, the social construction of the computer programmer as a nerdy eccentric predates the personal computer by several decades. It originated in the early association of programming ability with chess playing and mathematics puzzles, was reinforced by scientifically dubious aptitude tests and personality profiles, and by the early 1960s had become embodied in the hiring practices of the growing commercial computer industry. The institutionalization of gender norms in this period highlights the ways in which structure and culture are mutually constitutive, and ultimately self-replicating. Even as underlying structural explanations disappear, the cultural superstructure remains intact.

One simple but powerful example of this relationship has to do with the development of the "nocturnal" culture of computing. In an era when computers were large, expensive machines that ran in batch-production mode, computer programmers often had unfettered access to the computer only during off-hours, which often meant overnight. In some cases, this represented a tangible structural barrier to female participation: some corporations specifically prohibited women from remaining on-premises after business hours (ostensibly for safety reasons), which effectively prevented these women from working as programmers [43, p. 85]. But even after the technical requirements for such nocturnal programming activities disappeared, the culture of staying up all night and ignoring the normal conventions of 24-hour time continued to persist and, in fact, be celebrated, within certain computing communities [83–85]. The degree to which these practices are unappealing or impractical for women reflects the close interaction between culture and structure in the replication of gender norms and identity. What seems to contemporaries like the "natural" way in which things have "always" been done is historically contingent.

It is this relationship between structure and culture that reveals most clearly the value of the history of computing to the contemporary practice of computing. Ideas about *how* computing should be done corresponded closely with perceptions of *who* should be doing the computing. In the case of computer programming, these ideas and perceptions changed dramatically over the course of the mid-20th century, often in ways that were invisible to practitioners. The widespread adoption of aptitude testing by corporate employers, for example, was not deliberately aimed at excluding women and, in fact, might in other circumstances have served to expand opportunities for female participation. But the particular ways in which aptitude tests and personality profiles were developed, and the ways in which these tests and profiles were used in the context of other efforts to define what computer programming was and who should be doing it, had unintended consequences. These consequences became embodied in the structures of the industry. The gender identity and culture of computing became fixed, and ultimately self-perpetuating, as these structures became normalized.

# REFERENCES

**1.** Lois Mandel, "The Computer Girls," *Cosmopolitan* (April 1967): 52–56.

**2.** Richard Canning, "Issues in Programming Management," *EDP Analyzer*, Vol. 12, No. 4 (1974): 1–14.

**3.** Bruce Gilchrist and Richard Weber, "Enumerating Full-Time Programmers," *Communications of the ACM*, Vol. 17, No. 10 (1974): 592–593.

**4.** Adele Mildred Koss, "Programming on the Univac 1," *IEEE Annals of the History of Computing*, Vol. 25, No. 1 (2003): 48–59; Scott M. Campbell, "Beatrice Helen Worsley," *IEEE Annals of the History of Computing*, Vol. 25, No. 4 (2003): 51–62.

**5.** Robert Patrick, "The Gap in Programming Support," *Datamation*, Vol. 7, No. 5 (1961): 37; Don Madden, "The Population Problem," *Datamation*, Vol. 8, No. 1 (1962): 26.

**6.** "Careers in Computers" [advertisement], *Datamation*, Vol. 8, No. 1 (1962): 80, 21.

**7.** "Software Gap—A Growing Crisis for Computers," *Business Week* (5 November 1966): 127.

**8.** "Not Quite All About MIS," *Datamation*, Vol. 13, No. 5 (1967): 21.

**9.** Edward Markham, "EDP Schools—An Inside View," *Datamation*, Vol. 14, No. 4 (1968): 22–27.

**10.** Richard Tanaka, "Fee or Free Software," *Datamation*, Vol. 13, No. 10 (1967): 205–206.

**11.** Gene Bylinsky, "Help Wanted," *Fortune*, Vol. 75, No. 3 (1967): 141.

**12.** Jean P. Gilbert and David B. Mayer, "Experiences in Self-selection of Disadvantaged People into a Computer Operator Training Program," in *SIGCPR '69: Proceedings of the Seventh Annual Conference on SIGCPR* (New York: ACM Press, 1969), pp. 79–90.

**13.** "First Programmer Class at Sing Sing Graduates," *Datamation*, Vol. 14, No. 6 (1968): 97–98.

**14.** Charles Lawson, "A Survey of Computer Facility Management," *Datamation*, Vol. 8, No. 7 (1962): 29–32.

**15.** Walter J. McNamara, "The Selection of Computer Personnel," in *SIGCPR '67: Proceedings of the Fifth SIGCPR Conference on Computer Personnel Research* (New York: ACM Press, 1967), pp. 52–56.

**16.** Jennifer Light, "When Computers Were Women," *Technology & Culture*, Vol. 40, No. 3 (1999): 455–483.

**17.** Amita Goyal, "Women in Computing," *IEEE Annals of the History of Computing*, Vol. 18, No. 3 (1996): 36–42.

**18.** Judy Wajcman, "Reflections on Gender and Technology," *Social Studies of Science*, Vol. 30, No. 3 (2000): 447–464.

**19.** Janet Abbate, "How Did You First Get into Computing?" *IEEE Annals of the History of Computing*, Vol. 25, No. 4 (2003): 4–8.

**20.** W. Barkley Fritz, "The Women of ENIAC," *Annals of the History of Computing*, Vol. 18, No. 3 (1996): 13–23.

**21.** John Tukey, "The Teaching of Concrete Mathematics," *American Mathematical Monthly*, Vol. 65, No. 1 (1958): 1–9.

**22.** David Alan Grier, "The ENIAC, the Verb to Program, and the Emergence of Digital Computers," *IEEE Annals of the History of Computing*, Vol. 18, No. 1 (1996): 51–55.

**23.** Herman Goldstine and John von Neumann, *Planning and Coding of Problems for an Electronic Computing Instrument* (Princeton, NJ: Institute for Advanced Study, 1947).

**24.** "Introduction to Programming," typewritten manuscript, dated 11 June 1949. Hagley Archives, Sperry Rand Corporation: Univac Division (Accession 1825), Box 372.

**25.** Richard Wexelblat, ed., *History of Programming Languages* (New York: Academic Press, 1981), p. 69.

**26.** Margery Davies, *Woman's Place Is at the Typewriter: Office Work and Office Workers, 1870–1930* (Philadelphia: Temple University Press, 1982).

**27.** Sharon Hartman Strom, *Beyond the Typewriter: Gender, Class, and the Origins of Modern American Office Work, 1900–1930* (Urbana: University of Illinois Press, 1992).

**28.** Elyce J. Rotella. *From Home to Office: U.S. Women at Work, 1870–1930* (Ann Arbor: UMI Research Press, 1981).

**29.** Thomas Haigh, "The Chromium-Plated Tabulator," *IEEE Annals of the History of Computing*, Vol. 23, No. 4 (2001): 75–104.

**30.** Jackson Granholm, "How to Hire a Programmer," *Datamation*, Vol. 8, No. 8 (1962): 31–32.

**31.** Hans Albert Rhee, *Office Automation in Social Perspective: The Progress and Social Implications of Electronic Data Processing* (Oxford: Basil Blackwell, 1968).

**32.** Edsger Dijkstra, "The Humble Programmer," *Communications of the ACM*, Vol. 15, No. 10 (1972): 859–866.

**33.** Edsger Dijkstra, "Programming as a Discipline of Mathematical Nature," *American Mathematical Monthly*, Vol. 81, No. 6 (1974): 608–612.

**34.** Martin Campbell-Kelly and William Aspray, *Computer: A History of the Information Machine* (New York: Basic Books, 1996).

**35.** Joseph O'Shields, "Selection of EDP Personnel," *Personnel Journal*, Vol. 44, No. 9 (1965): 472–474.

**36.** Nathan Ensmenger, *The Computer Boys Take Over: Computers, Programmers, and the Politics of Technical Expertise* (Cambridge: MIT Press, 2010).

**37.** Mark Halpern, "Memoirs (Part 1)," *Annals of the History of Computing*, Vol. 13, No. 1 (1991): 101–111.

**38.** "The Computer Personnel Research Group," *Datamation*, Vol. 9, No. 1 (1963): 38–39.

**39.** Hal Sackman, Warren J. Erickson, and E. E. Grant, "Exploratory Experimental Studies Comparing Online and Offline Programming Performance," *Communications of the ACM*, Vol. 11, No. 1 (1968): 3–11.

**40.** Rustom P. Mody, "Is Programming an Art?" *Software Engineering Notes*, Vol. 17, No. 4 (1992): 19–21.

**41.** Maurice Black, *The Art of Code* (Ph.D. thesis, University of Pennsylvania, 2002).

**42.** William Paschell, *Automation and Employment Opportunities for Office Workers: A Report on the Effect of Electronic Computers on Employment of Clerical Workers* (Washington, DC: Bureau of Labor Statistics, 1958).

**43.** Gerald Weinberg, *The Psychology of Computer Programming* (New York: Van Nostrand Rheinhold, 1971).

**44.** Dallis Perry and William Cannon, "Vocational Interests of Computer Programmers," *Journal of Applied Psychology*, Vol. 51, No. 1 (1967): 28–34.

**45.** Dallis Perry and William Cannon, "Vocational Interests of Female Computer Programmers," *Journal of Applied Psychology*, Vol. 52, No. 1 (1968): 31.

**46.** Richard Brandon, "The Problem in Perspective," in *Proceedings of the 1968 23rd ACM National Conference* (New York: ACM Press, 1968), pp. 332–334.

**47.** Theodore Willoughby, "Needs, Interests, and Reinforcer Preferences of Data Processing Personnel," in *Proceedings of the Eighth Annual SIGCPR Conference* (New York: ACM Press, 1970), pp. 119–143.

**48.** William Ledbetter, "Programming Aptitude: How Significant Is It?" *Personnel Journal*, Vol. 54, No. 3 (1975): 165–166, 175.

**49.** Jane Margolis and Allan Fisher, *Unlocking the Clubhouse* (Cambridge: MIT Press, 2002).

**50.** Jennifer Taylor, "The Decline of Women in Computer Science, 1940–1982" (MA thesis, Harvard University Graduate School of Education, 2005).

**51.** J. McGrath Cohoon and William Aspray, *Women and Information Technology: Research on Underrepresentation* (Cambridge: MIT Press, 2006).

**52.** Hal Sackman, "Conference on Personnel Research," *Datamation*, Vol. 14, No. 7 (1968): 74–76, 81.

**53.** John Golda, "The Effects of Computer Technology on the Traditional Role of Management" (MA thesis, Wharton School of Business, University of Pennsylvania, 1965).

**54.** Joan Greenbaum, "On Twenty-five Years with Braverman's 'Labor and Monopoly Capital'," *Monthly Review*, Vol. 50, No. 8 (1999): 28–42.

**55.** Greg Downey, "Commentary," *International Review of Social History*, Vol. 48, No. 11 (2003): 225–261.

**56.** Nathan Ensmenger, "From 'Black Art' to Industrial Discipline" (Ph.D. thesis, University of Pennsylvania, 2001).

**57.** Michael Cusumano, "Factory Concepts and Practices in Software Development," *IEEE Annals of the History of Computing*, Vol. 13, No. 1 (1991): 3–32.

**58.** Ruth Milkman, *Gender at Work: The Dynamics of Job Segregation by Sex During World War II* (Urbana: University of Illinois Press, 1987).

**59.** Alice Kessler-Harris, *Out to Work: A History of Wage Earning Women in the United States* (New York: Oxford University Press, 1982).

**60.** Valerie Rockmael, "The Woman Programmer," *Datamation*, Vol. 9, No. 1 (1963): 41.

**61.** Datamation Editorial, "Of Maturity and Meatballs," *Datamation*, Vol. 9, No. 8 (1963): 23.

**62.** Computer Sciences Corporation, "In case you missed our first test …" *Datamation*, Vol. 13, No. 9 (1967): 149.

**63.** Nathan Ensmenger, "The 'Question of Professionalism' in the Computer Fields," *IEEE Annals of the History of Computing*, Vol. 23, No. 4 (2001): 56–73.

**64.** Nathan Ensmenger and William Aspray, "Software as a Labor Process," in Ulf Hashagen, Reinhard Keil-Slawik, and Arthur L. Norberg, eds., *History of Computing: Software Issues* (New York: Springer-Verlag, 2002), pp. 139–166.

**65.** Magali Sarfatti Larson, *The Rise of Professionalism: A Sociological Analysis* (Berkeley: University of California Press, 1977).

**66.** Robert Zussman, *Mechanics of the Middle Class: Work and Politics Among American Engineers* (Berkeley: University of California Press, 1985).

**67.** Harold Wilensky, "The Professionalization of Everyone?" *American Journal of Sociology*, Vol. 70, No. 2 (1964): 137–158.

**68.** *Personnel Journal* Editorial, "Professionalism Termed Key to Computer Personnel Situation," *Personnel Journal*, Vol. 51, No. 2 (1971): 156–157.

**69.** Richard Canning, "Professionalism: Coming or Not?" *EDP Analyzer*, Vol. 14, No. 3 (1976): 1–12.

**70.** Robert Gordon, "Personnel Selection," in Fred Gruenberger and Stanley Naftaly, eds., *Data Processing … Practically Speaking* (Los Angeles: Data Processing Digest, 1967), pp. 87–88.

**71.** Margaret Rossiter, *Women Scientists in America: Struggles and Strategies to 1940* (Baltimore: Johns Hopkins University Press, 1982).

**72.** Jeffrey Hearn, "Notes on Patriarchy, Professionalization and the Semi-Professions," *Sociology*, Vol. 16, No. 2 (1982): 184–202.

**73.** Ruth Oldenziel, *Making Technology Masculine: Men, Women, and Modern Machines in America, 1870–1945* (Amsterdam: Amsterdam University Press, 1999).

**74.** Claudia Goldin, Lawrence Katz, and Ilyana Kuziemko, "The Homecoming of American College Women," *Journal of Economic Perspectives*, Vol. 20, No. 4 (2006): 133–156.

**75.** Thomas D'Auria, "ACM Membership Profile Report," *Communications of the ACM*, Vol. 20, No. 10 (1977): 688–692.

**76.** Theodore Willoughby, "Psychometric Characteristics of the CDP Examination," in *Proceedings* of the *Thirteenth Annual SIGCPR Conference* (New York: ACM Press, 1975), pp. 152–160.

**77.** Richard Weber and Bruce Gilchrist, "Discrimination in the Employment of Women in the Computer Industry," *Communications of the ACM*, Vol. 18, No. 7 (1975): 416–418.

**78.** Beverly H. Burris, "Technocracy and Gender in the Workplace," *Social Problems*, Vol. 36, No. 2 (1989): 165–180.

**79.** Adele Mildred Koss, "Programming at Burroughs and Philco in the 1950s," *IEEE Annals of the History of Computing*, Vol. 25, No. 4 (2003): 40–50.

**80.** Evelyn Fox Keller, "Gender and Science: Origin, History, and Politics," *Osiris*, Vol. 10 (1995): 27–38.

**81.** Carol Cohn, "War, Wimps and Women," in M. Cooke and A. Woolcott, eds., *Gendering War Talk* (Princeton, NJ: Princeton University Press, 1993), pp. 227–246.

**82.** Robert Cringely, *Accidental Empires: How the Boys of Silicon Valley Make Their Millions, Battle Foreign Competition, and Still Can't Get a Date* (New York: Addison-Wesley, 1992).

**83.** Joseph Weizenbaum, *Computer Power and Human Reason: From Judgment of Calculation* (San Francisco: W.H. Freeman, 1976).

**84.** Steven Levy, *Hackers: Heroes of the Computer Revolution* (Garden City, NY: Anchor Press/ Doubleday, 1984).

**85.** Sherry Turkle, *The Second Self: Computers and the Human Spirit* (New York: Simon and Schuster, 1984).

# Gender and Computing in the Push-Button Library  7

GREG DOWNEY

Historians of computing enjoy great freedom of choice in the sites they investigate, since digital devices from mainframes to microcontrollers over the last half-century have entered nearly every domain of human economic and cultural production, from the factory floor to the artist's studio. One recent history of computing took three volumes to track the introduction of computer technology to U.S. manufacturing, transportation, retail, financial, telecommunications, media, entertainment, and public sector industries. But even this encyclopedic work of over 1500 pages devoted only 10 of those pages to the history of computing in U.S. libraries [1]. Such a proportion might be reasonable if one is attempting to investigate the economic impact or business management of computerization. But in order to begin to understand the recent history of women's engagement with computing—part of the larger project of analyzing technological change together with the changing social meanings of both femininity and masculinity, which we might refer to as "gender"—we must explore a whole range of sites where women actively encountered, employed, and challenged computer technology [2]. Since librarianship was numerically dominated by women all through the development of the general-purpose programmable computer, looking for connections between women and computing in the library seems like a good place to start.

But investigating "the library" is no simple task. Historians of librarianship might focus on large research and academic libraries, on urban and suburban public libraries, on primary and secondary school libraries, or on a myriad of corporate and government libraries and archives [3]. No matter what the size or audience, all libraries are technological spaces, suffused with individual artifacts for information storage and access (from printed books and periodicals to magnetic audiovisual and digital media) and also networked systems for information organization and retrieval (from the drawer-filed catalog cards of a century ago to the microfilm and digital catalogs of today). In a very real sense, the library, at all of its various scales and sites, acts as an internet-worked information technology made up of both human and material components [4].

The early 1960s represented a turning point for this technology in the United States, when decades-old dreams of "library automation" based on various combinations of punched-card sorting equipment and microphotography storage techniques shifted both rapidly and publicly to dreams of "library computerization" based on electronic catalog records and networked communication systems (Fig. 7.1). For example, at the 1962 World's Fair in Seattle, the American Library Association (ALA) secured a spot at a global exposition for the first time. Its fairground library space was literally split into past and future—while one side of the exhibit made room for traditional books and the (largely female) librarians who organized them, the other side showcased a Univac computer and its (also largely female) data-entry technicians. This space-age, computer-based "LIBRARY 21," reprised two years later at the 1964 World's Fair in New York as "Library/USA," was meant to send a signal not only to the

Figure 7.1. The "push-button library" promised relief from mountains of punch cards. Punch card keypunching and verifying was "hardly outmoded" in 1971, Sperry-Rand insisted, since its new equipment could verify the stack of 20,000 cards (left) in "an eight hour day" compared to earlier throughput on right. (Courtesy of Charles Babbage Institute.)

fair-going public, but to legions of library workers across the nation as well: the library of the future was the "push-button" library of the computer [5].

This library of the future, though, was still very much trapped in the gender assumptions of the present. Shortly after these computer library exhibitions, the well-known library historian Jesse Shera, Dean of the School of Library Science at Case Western Reserve University, prepared "a kind of *Intelligent Woman's Guide to Automation in the Library*" for the May 1964 *Wilson Library Bulletin*. He aimed "to set forth in as uncomplicated a fashion as possible the contributions that automation can make to the services the library could and should be offering" [6]. His own contribution to this issue characterized librarian resistance to automation as rooted in "fear" and "anxiety," arguing that "being traditionally humanistic, librarians doubt their capacity even to utilize anything that is scientifically derived" [7]. Indeed, addressing such "doubt" was a main reason the ALA had flown in dozens of librarians from across the United States to work at the World's Fair exhibits, benefiting from their free labor but also training them in a crash course on library automation. Such "fear" and "anxiety" did not affect the special issue's authors, however, whom Shera described as "librarians rather than engineers or experts in computing machinery" [6, p. 742]. But these librarians (including Shera himself) were of a very special sort: all had technological knowledge or experience, all held positions of power, leadership, or consultancy in major academic or corporate libraries (as opposed to public or school libraries), and all, not coincidentally, were men.

The fact that a professional publication touting the benefits of computerization might be authored entirely by men and described in highly gendered language in the early 1960s is not surprising, given the long history of discrimination against (and discouragement of) women in U.S. government, education, and industry [8]. It had only been a year, after all, since the Equal Pay Act of 1963 first dealt with questions of sex-based wage discrimination [9]. What was surprising, however, was the fact that librarianship was (and still is) disproportionately staffed by women. Ever since the late 19th century, when Melvil Dewey (originator of the eponymous Dewey decimal subject classification system) began systematically and publicly recruiting women into librarianship—based on then-current stereotypes of women's supposed greater attention to detail and nurturing moral role, as well as the fact that women could be paid less than men—librarianship in the United States has been demographically dominated by women [10, p. xiv].

But while librarianship was agreed to be an "intelligent woman's" profession in a numerical sense, it was also a gendered profession in an analytical sense, in three ways. Across the main divisions of academic, public, school, and corporate libraries, a *wage* division of labor persisted: women working at the same jobs or performing the same tasks as men received lower remuneration regardless of age, education, or experience. Similarly, in a *vertical* division of labor, men held disproportionately more positions of power—directorships, management positions, or library school professorships—than women. And in a *horizontal* division of labor, men and women tended to be segregated into different kinds of tasks, with women more likely to perform both the most meticulous of back-office "technical services" work (cataloging and circulation) and the most nurturing of front-desk "public services" work (running children's storytime and literacy groups). Through the 1960s and 1970s, "survey after survey reported lower median salaries for women, fewer professional perquisites, and a clouded view of the career ladder, which disclosed men at the top and a preponderance of women at the bottom of the library hierarchy" [11].

Across the profession as a whole, the very institution of the library had long been represented in the public eye as a proper domain for women workers (and women patrons). Popular culture demonstrated a broad range of such gender stereotypes—from the strict yet meek "Marian the librarian" who guarded the moral fiber of River City's youth in *The Music Man* (1962, played by Shirley Jones) to the self-assured and streetwise corporate librarian "Bunny" who stood up to the installation of a mainframe computer in *Desk Set* (1957, played by Katharine Hepburn)—but in nearly all cases an essentialist opposition between the (feminine) traditions of the library and the (masculine) notion of technological progress was assumed [12]. Within the professional library press, advertisements at the dawn of library computerization for paper, photographic, or electromagnetic information technologies often included illustrations of female librarians using these products at the front desk to speed up routine information processing for male patrons, rather than using such tools for information-seeking themselves. During this period of computerization, even some in the library profession itself (often but not always men) advocated the view that librarianship should "guard well its feminine qualities" as supposedly embodied by its women workers, because "until libraries consist of a computer wall which the user plugs into at home, the librarian must continue to deal with people" [13].

At the very same time that librarianship was facing a new computerized future, it was also beginning to grapple with its own gender dynamics and disparities. In 1963, Betty Friedan had published *The Feminine Mystique*; 3 years later, the National Organization for Women was established. By 1969, the computerization dreams of the early 1960s World's Fairs were beginning to make their way into U.S. research libraries through the Library of Congress's new "MAchine Readable Cataloging" (MARC) standardization project (headed by female librarian Henriette Avram) [14]. At the same time, University of Illinois library science professor Anita Schiller had begun to both quantify and popularize the extent of salary and status discrimination within librarianship. Schiller reported that the median and mean salaries of men were, respectively, $8990 and $9598 compared to $7455 and $7746 for women [15]. A year later, at the ALA annual meeting in Detroit, librarians Pat Schuman and Ellen Gay Detlefsen of the ALA Social Responsibility Round Table—sporting wry buttons combining the women's liberation symbol and the words "American Ladies Association"—convinced 500 of their fellow members to support a new Task Force on the Status of Women to address such disparity and discrimination [16,17, p. i]. As both library computerization and the "second wave feminism" of the women's movement gained momentum through the 1970s, the field of librarianship seemed poised for an intertwined technological and social revolution.

Yet the historical record concerning sex discrimination and computer innovation in libraries through the 1970s and 1980s tells not one integrated story, but two separate ones. Library activists, educators, and historians published a wide range of materials on the gender question through this period, from scholarly theses to underground newsletters, special issues of professional journals and special sessions of annual conferences. These writers tracked the (modest) gains in wage and status disparities, revealed the presence of gender-stereotyped language in the library catalog itself, and advocated for the Equal Rights Amendment. Similarly, in the more technical literature, experts and novices alike discussed and debated the merits of computerization, especially in new forums like the *Journal of Library Automation* (founded in 1968). The late-1960s MARC project to create a standard format for electronic catalog records quickly led to efforts to produce those catalog records through networked cooperation online. The most successful of these efforts was the 1970s Ohio College Library Center (OCLC) project to connect participating library workers' cataloging computers together over space and time [18]. A dramatic increase in the number and quality of electronic catalog records led directly to a series of both nonprofit and for-profit Online Public Access Catalog (OPAC) projects in the 1980s, to make those networked electronic catalogs directly available to patrons. Press releases announcing the "closing of the card catalog" were commonplace through the 1980s, serving as indicators that one's public or university library was poised to enter the electronic future. Thus, from the late 1960s to the mid-1980s, both the back-office division of labor in cataloging and the front-desk face that the library presented to the public changed dramatically. But throughout this fervent period of professional activism, neither the feminist writers nor the technical writers connected issues of sex and gender in the library occupation to issues of technology in the library infrastructure.

This chapter considers the question of women's participation in computing through the historical case study of library computerization. But this is a different sort of history than is usually told of women and information technology in the workplace [19]. It is neither a story of librarians programming computers in an engineering sense, nor a story of librarians using computers in a clerical sense (though both did happen). Instead, it is a story of librarians organizing for increased status and wages in a highly technological environment, but using arguments that largely ignored the technological changes taking place in that environment, only coming to a sense of their role within the digital management of library resources years after a computerized division of labor was introduced.

The first part of the chapter briefly describes the most active period of library feminism in the 1970s and 1980s, to demonstrate that female librarians were indeed aware that the most blatant vertical discrimination took place in those libraries most likely to be investing in computer technology, even though these activists rarely connected arguments dealing with gender to those dealing with technology. The second part considers a set of claims that grew through the 1980s into the 1990s about the way that one of the most controversial aspects of the push-button library, the computer-aided production and reproduction of the library catalog, started to be seen in terms of gendered technological change. Finally, I offer some suggestions for understanding gender, computing, and labor within fields such as librarianship, which are intended at their core to produce, organize, and distribute both information itself and the "meta" information—or metadata—that is essential for others to find, use, and value such information. Too often the history of computing focuses only on hardware innovations or software applications. The case of library computing reminds us that computer hardware and software both manipulate computer *data*, and that the production of this data—and the *metadata* that defines and organizes it—might reveal a different kind of computer history than we are used to telling.

## GENDER AND STATUS DIVISIONS WITHIN LIBRARIANSHIP, 1950–1980

To understand the "push-button" library of the 1960s as a gendered vision of the future, we must first describe the gendered division of labor within librarianship at the time. The crucial point is that in the very libraries most likely to have both the financial resources and the scientific user base to motivate experimentation with computerization—that is, large academic and corporate libraries—most of the directors and chief librarians were men. One 1950 study revealed that 84% of the directors of the largest academic libraries in the United States were men, finding "not a single woman is in charge of a library in a school with more than 10,000 students" [20]. Similarly, in the massive midcentury Public Library Inquiry, where librarians turned to social scientists to assess the state of the library as a crucial "public information agency," library science professor Alice Bryan found that although 92% of all librarians surveyed were women, "men held higher positions, were more likely to be married, did less domestic work [in the home], brought home higher salaries, and were more satisfied than women" [10, p. xviii]. In all of the sampled libraries serving populations of 250,000 or more, "all the top administrators [were] men" [21].

By 1962, participants at a special University of Chicago conference on libraries and women concluded that "women depress the status" of librarianship, recommending the recruitment of even more men to positions of power and authority in libraries [22]. In 1971, an assistant librarian from Princeton University, Helen Tuttle, pointed out that the main academic and corporate library professional association, the Association of College and Research Libraries (ACRL), was clearly a male-dominated group: "Since the ALA reorganization in 1957, ACRL has had five different executive secretaries. All have been men. Its journal, *College and Research Libraries*, has never had a female editor. In fact, of the present nine editors and editorial board members who guide the destinies of that periodical, nine are males" [23]. The early 1970s saw the first published "sex and salary surveys" in the *Library Journal*, demonstrating this disparity in stark economic terms: libraries directed by men paid higher starting salaries and had greater per capita support. And the median salary for male library directors was 30% higher than that of female library directors [24].

Even the structure of library education and research publication, which might have been mustered to produce more female directors, was suspect. In 1974 Anita Schiller revealed that the proportion of accredited library schools directed by men had increased from 50% in 1950 to 81% in 1970. Library journals showed the same pattern: roughly half had been edited by women in 1950, but only one-third were by 1971. One explanation? The many new library journals, edited by men, which were wholly tied to computer technology—for example, the *Journal of Library Automation* and *Library Technology Reports*

[25]. Contemporary librarians expressed dismay that the main foundation-based funding organization for library technology projects, the Council on Library Resources, gave relatively few grants to women [17, p. 45]. And library historian Mary Niles Maack later found that, from 1960 to 1980, women faculty in accredited U.S. library school programs decreased from 55% to 41% [26]. This was precisely the period of digital technological change in the curriculum.

Enthusiasm within librarianship for adopting computers during the 1960s resulted in countless pilot projects and system proposals—most of them located within the same large academic and corporate sites where men held the greatest positions of power in librarianship. While few of these computer experiments proved to be long-lasting successes, they did serve to popularize a particular set of meanings for the push-button library which were linked to the gendered division of library labor. For example, one of the articles in Shera's 1964 "woman's guide to automation" claimed that while "what a librarian does is complex enough to defy a quick and simple resort to mechanization," nevertheless this only applied to "the intellectual and not to the clerical processes of librarianship" [27]. Here the "intellectual" processes of librarianship were assumed to be (mostly male, mostly high wage) reference services, management, and administration, while the "clerical" processes of librarianship were assumed to be (mostly female, mostly low wage) cataloging and circulation. Another author in the same issue, University of Missouri librarian and punched-card pioneer Ralph H. Parker, argued that with automation in the library, "the greatest effect is upon routine clerical jobs such as typing, [the] use of calculating and adding machines, and filing. The things machines do best are usually those most boring to people." Thus, in an argument similar to those made by many advocates of automation in other industries around midcentury, Parker assured his librarian readers that "in the actual situation, no one is likely to lose a job; he [sic] will rather be put to more fruitful work" [28]. Computers would automate away the (feminine) clerical and augment the (masculine) creative work—a root argument in almost every theory of the "new information society" from the 1960s onward [29].

What made this upskilling/deskilling argument unique in librarianship was the idea that the two efforts—automating the clerical and augmenting the conceptual—were tied procedurally and almost teleologically together, since the library automators of the 1960s firmly believed that "the success of [automated information retrieval] will in the long run depend on the successful automation of routine library records" [28, p. 753]. Producing new systems for information retrieval, and training the new librarians who would master these systems, was the key goal that both depended on and justified the automation of library clerical processes. And it was indeed a goal that could only be fulfilled, so the argument went, through cooperation by traditional (female) librarians with outside (male) experts—often from the defense industry where new mechanized systems of "documentation" had first been prototyped for organizing scientific and technical report literature. Or as the original designers of the World's Fair "library of the future" exhibits, Joseph Becker and Robert Hayes, put it in the first-ever automation textbook for librarians in 1963, "librarians, documentalists, mathematicians, system designers, equipment manufacturers, operations researchers, and computer programmers" all needed to understand "how interwoven are their interests and how overlapping their responsibilities" [30].

This gendered split in the character of computerized library work could best be seen in one of the most salient metaphors in the literature of the time: that of clerical library work as "housekeeping." For example, in 1970 Janet Freedman (a librarian at the Salem State College Library in Salem, Massachusetts) wrote in the *Library Journal*: "With most of the creative posts dominated by men, women are likely to be utilized for their 'housekeeping' talents in serials, acquisitions, and cataloging work, or for their 'patience and warmth' in school libraries and children's departments" [31]. A year later, librarian Helen Lowenthal wrote in the same trade publication that "women are recruited for the bottom and men for the top" in librarianship, where "those of us in public services play mother to our patrons and those in technical services 'keep house' within our institutions" [32]. Such metaphors and stereotypes were increasingly operationalized through the 1960s and 1970s into gender-based personality tests used for both admissions to library schools and hiring in library jobs. On one such personality test, the California Psychological Inventory, one of the questions that purported to indicate femininity if answered "True" was itself "I think I would like the work of a librarian" [33]. And there were plenty of librarians—even women librarians—who held essentialist views of women as being biologically better suited to so-called technical services work (like cataloging). Librarian F. Bernice Field argued in the 1971 compilation *Women in the Library Profession* that women were preferable as managers of technical services departments because "generally women have more aptitude than men for the kind of detail" needed for technical services operations and also because "men ... tend to move into general administration and are, therefore, not dependable for long-range assignments" in technical services [34].

As a vocal part of the "second wave feminism" movement, female librarians who did not hold such essentialist views did much to publicize and rectify their disproportionate power position and disadvantaged salary position through the 1970s. But few of these efforts focused on technology, even though this was precisely the period when computer terminals were initially introduced to research and public libraries on a large scale (first behind the circulation desk for cooperative cataloging ventures, and later in front of the circulation desk for patrons to use as a new electronic catalog). Such technology received hardly a mention at the 1974 ALA preconference on the status of women in librarianship, where a keynote presentation on discrimination statistics by Anita Schiller was followed by panels on self-image, education, affirmative action, career development, unions, organizing, and tactics [17, p. ii]. Most of the agenda was focused on either achieving pay equity for rank-and-file librarians (through unionization if necessary) or moving librarians up the career ladder to management positions. Now and then an observer might call for women to improve their wage situation by learning new technical skills, as when Philadelphia library director Herman Greenberg argued in the 1975 "Melvil's Rib" symposium on women in librarianship that women should "apply for education and training in computer sciences, a relatively new field in most libraries, so that when information sciences begin to be utilized by a majority of libraries, they will be in a position where their skills are required by the employer" [35]. But such calls were rare (and often fell into a rather simplistic "human factors" analysis of gender discrimination as based on differing skill sets). The situation had not changed much by 1984, when a radical bibliography of library labor and gender issues, *On Account of Sex*, listed not a single work dealing with library computerization or technology from 1977 to 1981 [36]. By the late 1980s the history of feminism within librarianship was itself a topic of academic research, with a content analysis of some 250 articles on women and librarianship from 1965 to 1985 revealing almost no connection to the literature on library technology [37].

## LIBRARY TECHNOLOGY AND LIBRARY LABOR, 1980–1990

Librarians concerned with gender eventually began to talk about library technology in cataloging. The library catalog often served as a touchpoint connecting debates over the future of the library, as it was the one concrete tool shared by library staff and library patrons. In a way it served as a "boundary object" between these two communities of practice. The catalog was a constant point of translation between a patron's view of an information space and a librarian's view of that same domain of knowledge. But even within librarianship, front-desk reference librarians who used the catalog on a daily basis to help patrons locate materials might lament the rushed work of the back-office catalogers who built the finding aid in the first place (just as catalogers might complain that reference librarians rarely made use of the careful cross-referencing and controlled languages they provided to them). And through all of its technological changes—from typewritten cards in drawers to glowing ASCII characters displayed on computer monitors—the library catalog has tended to stand as a concrete symbolic example of the state of technological sophistication in a library (Fig. 7.2). After 1981, when the Library of Congress closed its own card catalog, a library using card drawers might be seen as "behind the times," while

Figure 7.2. Librarians (and others) saw the future in "glowing ASCII characters." A 1971 vision of the future includes "a solid-state keyboard and cathode ray tube (CRT) display," with up to four lines of 32 characters. (Courtesy of Charles Babbage Institute.)

a library using a CRT-based catalog network might be celebrated for being on the "cutting edge." Even though this cataloging technology debate didn't begin as a critical response to gender disparities, it ended up that way.

In the early 1980s, university library director Ruth Hafter argued in her doctoral dissertation that the computer-based, networked cataloging technology of agencies like OCLC could *potentially* deskill catalogers, since more cataloging was performed remotely (and anonymously) than ever before. Still, she didn't specifically link this deskilling to gender. Hafter's original cataloging study was based on 68 interviews with catalogers and managers at six academic libraries on the West Coast [38, p. 6]. Published in 1986, her book pointed out that while the catalog was regularly praised as "the most valuable and unique resource of each library," catalogers themselves were often feared to be the least capable of library professionals, with cataloging departments stereotyped as "a quiet haven for those unable to make it in other areas of the library and/or academic world" [38, pp. 3, 12]. The availability of electronic catalog records through OCLC seemed to exacerbate this contradiction. At the same time that expensive technology was being installed to facilitate cataloging in times of tight library budgets during the recessions and tax revolts of the late 1970s and early 1980s, catalogers themselves seemed to be devalued, since the "routine and standardized records available in the data base" could now "be manipulated by library assistants and clerks, rather than catalogers" [38, p. 125]. This was the deskilling of the "housekeeping" work that many outside library computing advocates had long hoped for, and that many librarians themselves had long feared.

But Hafter's analysis of the changes wrought by computerized cataloging was more complicated than simple deskilling. At the same time that "deprofessionalization" might be occurring in cataloging, Hafter suggested that "the collegial structure of the network tends to mitigate the impact of the controls placed upon catalogers and, in many instances, restores lost authority to them," especially in "self-monitoring of cataloging by accepted leaders of the profession" [38, p. 127]. In other words, catalogers could now peer-review each others' work. Or as she put it in a 1986 article in *College & Research Libraries*, "while the network has sowed the seeds for the deprofessionalization of cataloging, it has also reaped the crop of the new breed of born-again catalogers" [39]. Notably, Hafter's conclusion entirely omitted any kind of gender analysis. For Hafter, neither the threat of deprofessionalization nor the promise of reprofessionalization were driven by the well-known gender disparities within librarianship. Instead, they were driven by a longstanding library management argument about what kind of cataloging to perform, at what cost, and within what kind of spatial, technical, skill, and wage division of labor—and contextualized within a very particular tight economic environment, where shrinking budgets and inflationary pressures motivated those library managers to see computer networking as a key labor-saving measure.

Hafter's study might never have been brought to bear on the questions of gender in librarianship had it not been for SUNY library science professor Suzanne Hildenbrand. A few years after Hafter's book was published, at a 1989 Simmons College symposium on recruiting, educating, and training cataloging librarians, most of the speakers argued that cataloging was in a "crisis" because it was seemingly unable to attract either the career interest of library students or the budget attention of library administrators. Given the profession's very public focus on OCLC as a supposed technological fix to the perennial problem of cataloging backlogs during the early 1980s, it was arguably not surprising that the cataloging subfield took a downturn a few years later. But rather than see the cataloging crisis through the logic of labor and technology, Hildenbrand— herself a feminist historian of librarianship—connected the crisis first and foremost to gender. She argued that "the crisis in cataloging today is linked to a largely unexplored aspect of sexual stratification within librarianship," and that the problems faced by catalogers, such as low wages and low status, "reflect the fact that it is an even more female-intensive occupation than librarianship as a whole" [40, p. 207].

Hildenbrand admitted that evidence to back up her arguments was scarce. Survey data indicated that catalogers' salaries trailed reference librarians' by approximately $550 [40, p. 212]. But most of her claims were rooted in vivid anecdotal evidence of the working conditions within the cataloging departments of the same large academic and corporate libraries that were the original focus of the automation experts: "Every time I go into the cataloging department at one major university I am struck by its similarity to the old time typing pools in the insurance companies. It is a big open area with all these people at their desks filing cards and papers. I think it is significant that only two people in this large department have offices they can go into and close a door to have privacy. Only two people have their own telephone line" [41]. Besides such particular but decontextualized evidence, Hildenbrand cited Hafter's 1986 study in what Hildenbrand called "a decline in the status of catalogers since the introduction of network cataloging," saying that by now "everyone is familiar with descriptions of contemporary cataloging departments that sound like institutional backwaters where outdated modes of management prevail in a kind of white collar sweatshop" [40, p. 213].

Hildenbrand's anecdotal evidence may have pointed to a deprofessionalizing crisis, but where was the gender link? Hildenbrand found this through library education, where she claimed cataloging has been pushed to the periphery even though demand for catalogers was still strong. This argument invoked gender in two ways: first, Hildenbrand pointed out that, even after the feminist agitation of the 1970s, "library educators are predominantly men, while practitioners are predominantly women," citing 1988 survey data still listing library school faculties as 55% male and 45% female [40, p. 215]. Second, Hildenbrand argued that at accredited U.S. library schools in 1983, cataloging was listed as a teaching specialty of 12% of female faculty, but only 5% of male faculty [40, p. 211]. Thus, it was up to a minority of female faculty to teach a minority of classes on cataloging for a minority of (presumably disproportionately female) students.

Absent solid evidence, as Hildenbrand herself admitted, "one must rely on impressions" [42]. Drawing on a very active history of liberal feminism within librarianship, where the stark disparities in comparative salaries, management positions, and library school professorships had been carefully and powerfully documented, Hildenbrand fit the newest "crisis in cataloging" into these same arguments. But just as Hafter's arguments about cataloging being polarized into a deprofessionalized clerical mass and a reprofessionalized management elite really weren't rooted in any systematic gender analysis, Hildenbrand's arguments about cataloging being gendered really weren't rooted in any systematic technology analysis.

It took a third library labor researcher, University of Western Ontario library science professor Roma Harris, to connect the arguments about gender discrimination and computer automation in 1992—a quarter century after the twin discussions about technology and gender began in the late 1960s. Both in her influential monograph *Librarianship: The Erosion of a Woman's Profession* and in a companion article in the journal *Computers in Libraries*, Harris put forth a two-part hypothesis about how technology and gender worked together in librarianship [43,44]. First, Harris argued that the more "masculine" tasks within librarianship—"those involving technology and management"—were more highly valued than the more "feminine" tasks like children's services and cataloging [43, p. 1]. Second, Harris claimed that after decades of library auto-mation and networking, especially the development of OCLC, the largely female specialization of cataloging was "undergoing a process of 'deprofessionaliza-tion' or 'deskilling'" (selectively drawing from Hafter's arguments) [43, p. 121]. Harris recommended that "librarians must give themselves credit for what they know and put a stop to the process of shunning the female-intensive aspects of their work," instead "acknowledging that tasks, such as children's librarianship and cataloging, are central to this field and as worthy of status and financial reward (if not more so) as computing expertise" [43, p. 164]. These 1992 argu-ments continued to exert influence in the library literature into the 21st century, taking on the status of a "standard narrative" about the way technology and gender interacted in librarianship through the 1970s and 1980s.

But as I have tried to demonstrate in this chapter, this narrative is not exactly accurate. In fact, the Harris thesis contains a rather subtle contradiction. On the one hand, the weaving of computer technology into librarianship is cast both as an essentially masculine project (pitted against what are cast as essen-tially feminine projects of serving users, especially children, to address their literacy and information-seeking needs), and as a project that brings men them-selves into librarianship—in key positions of power and authority over women—from the outside fields of information science, computer science, and business management. But on the other hand, this development of library computer technology is cast as a project mostly affecting women, meant to create a "pink-collar sweatshop" of low-paid workers pinned to networked computer terminals in highly rationalized and contingent back-office data management jobs within librarianship (Fig. 7.3). Harris herself expressed this contradiction when she revisited her thesis in 2000, arguing that "in librarianship, where technological change dominates the workplace, we find that men are more likely than women to be seen as the keepers of technology. They derive status from their associa-tion with technology. On the other hand, women's jobs, most of which now also require an intensive use of technology, are nevertheless seen to be easier, to involve less advanced knowledge, and somehow carry a lesser weight" [45]. So in this view, computers are "upskilling" when applied to the male division of labor, and "deskilling" when applied to the female division of labor. As we have seen, this understanding of computer technology as polarizing within the library division of labor actually has a long history.

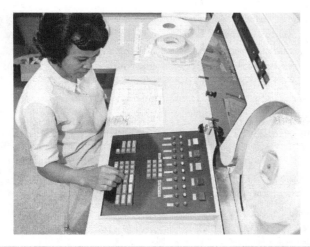

Figure 7.3. Information automation or "pink-collar sweatshop." NCR tag printer as "integral part" of information system. While "unit automatically produces a wide variety" of labels, woman's labor remained. (Courtesy of Charles Babbage Institute.)

Harris's first argument, that the interests of (mostly male) technologists from outside the profession of librarianship were firmly oriented toward restructuring the technical and skill division of labor within the (mostly female) profession of librarianship was indeed accurate; but it was also unsurprising. Such a project had been underway quite openly for at least three decades before Harris articulated it in 1992, wrapped so far into the core assumptions of library systems development in the large academic and corporate research libraries that it ceased to be discussed. Harris's second argument that the computer-based, networked cataloging technology, which originated in the 1970s with OCLC, specifically deskills women catalogers in the library drew directly on the work of Hafter and Hildenbrand from the 1980s. Harris's insight was to combine these two arguments together to claim that the alleged deskilling changes wrought by computerized cataloging technology were disproportionately concentrated on women within librarianship. In other words, the original polarized dream of computerization—both automation of clerical drudgery and augmentation of conceptual creativity—had succeeded for male library workers but failed for female library workers.

Neither Harris, Hildenbrand, nor Hafter contextualized their concerns about cataloging in the broader history of library technology and labor. But the drive to rationalize cataloging into what became known as "technical services," splitting out the lower-paid, lower-status, and lower-skill clerical work of catalog material production from the higher-paid, higher-status, and higher-skill creative work of defining the actual bibliographic metadata that would be stored in catalog materials, began long before computerization and was motivated by more than patriarchal power relations. As early as 1901, in fact, when the Library of Congress began selling complete printed copies of its own 3 × 5 catalog cards to subscribing libraries, librarians had argued over whether cataloging involved clerical transcription or creative production. As Mary Salome Cutler Fairchild, a librarian who taught cataloging in Dewey's own library school, wrote in the *Library Journal* in 1904, "women are as well fitted as men for technical work, even the higher grades of cataloging," because of their "greater conscientiousness, patience, and accuracy in details"; but they were "generally preferred to men or boys in the routine work of a library," because they were "more faithful and on the whole more adaptable" [46].

Gender relations have been an active if unrecognized force within librarianship for over a century [47]. But we still need to understand *how* this history of labor and technology has been intertwined with the production and reproduction of gender relations. The uses of technologies within librarianship do affect social relations, and social relations within librarianship do affect the uses of technologies. This basic insight—a fundamental understanding of current history of technology research—can help us reconstruct a more historically grounded narrative of computers, libraries, and gender that weaves the questions concerning cataloging into the larger labor processes within libraries—and into the larger meaning of the library itself.

## CONCLUSION: FROM CATALOGING TO METADATA

Critiquing the earnest arguments of scholars and practitioners regarding computers, gender, and librarianship for lacking theoretical grounding or historical contextualization is useful only if it can point to a more productive way of conceptualizing this complicated relationship between social change (second-wave feminism in librarianship), technological change (networked computerization in library catalog production), and political-economic change (organizational and labor restructuring in library administration and budgeting). In the final section of this chapter, I want to suggest four ways that a broader, more gender- and labor-aware history of technology can be used to reinterpret this debate.

**1.** *Consider all of librarianship as a "technology," not just the computerized parts.*

From the 1960s to the 1980s, networked computer technology has been the main kind of "technology" under debate within librarianship. Thus, technology and gender were only analyzed together within librarianship once cataloging labor moved to the networked and computerized system of OCLC. But cataloging, in all of its historical forms, is a technology in its own right. The technological innovation (and subsequent standardization) of the unit-card catalog system of the late 19th century, together with preexisting technological systems of print production and postal transport, was what enabled the Library of Congress to turn the "technological fix" of the card catalog into the "spatial fix" of centrally producing catalog records and then shipping them out to subscribing libraries. This publicly funded, nonprofit catalog production network, as well as the privately owned, for-profit competitors that followed it, represented the first "information revolution" in cataloging. It set into motion a whole series of debates, involving both men and women, over the proper place of cataloging practice within library science, leading in midcentury to a redefinition of cataloging from a humanistic, conceptual activity requiring classically trained subject experts in academic settings, to a routinized, manual activity requiring only minimally trained clerical workers of the new "technical services" department.

And even after the computerization projects of MARC in the 1960s and OCLC in the 1970s—combining the "technological fix" of machine-readable catalog records with the "spatial fix" of decentralized cooperative cataloging labor— libraries initially sought *virtual* catalog records on magnetic tape specifically so they could produce new *material* catalog products, on analog media such as microfiche cards or bound paper volumes. In a way, all library processes—from circulation management to reference service to literacy instruction—are "technologies" of a particular sociotechnical sort, as they involve complex combinations of material artifacts, human agents, and codified systems of thought. Thus, a longer-term historical investigation that crosses all of these boundaries is called for, rather than an exclusive focus on computation.

**2.** *Consider the object of library technology not as "data" but as "metadata."*

If the various processes taking place within a library (like cataloging) can be considered as sociotechnical information systems, then the library as a whole might be considered as a sociotechnical information network. We might even scale this idea up to consider the whole of librarianship, whether academic, public, school, or corporate, as part of a sociotechnical information internetwork—an idea not too far from the current claims of digital library advocates that their organizations represent crucial components of "cyberinfrastructure" [48]. But systems, networks, and internetworks suggest some object of interaction, some unit of circulation. What moves through such library infrastructures? In the late 19th century, an observer might respond that the object of circulation was, quite obviously, the book. Today, it has become more commonplace to imagine a general unit of "information" (an article, an image, a fact) moving between library staffers and library patrons. But as the historical example of cataloging illustrates, the true resource of the library cyberinfrastructure is not data, but *metadata*—information *about* the myriad books and magazines, reports and theses, music and video, multimedia and hypermedia of all sorts, which libraries collect, organize, store, and circulate. For example, in cataloging, as Hafter pointed out in the early 1980s, "rules and procedures change" over time in a myriad of ways: subject headings may need to be adjusted for modern terminology, the latest scientific thought, or innovative search practices; user populations for individual libraries may evolve in their needs and sophistication; budgets available to cataloging fluctuate over time; the status conferred by having a "complete" or "detailed" catalog may vary; and, of course, the very technology for entering, storing, and accessing the catalog metadata may change, affecting labor costs, turnaround times, and production techniques [38, pp. 11–12]. Following the metadata through such processes—how it is made visible and invisible, valued and devalued, rendered in both physical and virtual forms—allows the historian of technology to analytically connect practices of librarianship across vastly different institutional, functional, social, and technological contexts.

**3.** *Recognize that it takes human labor to produce, reproduce, and use metadata.*

Metadata is only a useful historical unit of analysis if it can help illuminate the human practices and human decisions underpinning the library mission.

These are questions of *metadata labor*—the work and expertise required to create, organize, store, and use metadata, but also to recreate, reorganize, restore, and reuse it (as the social, organizational, or technological conditions of librarianship change over time). In other words, metadata helps link the labor of the cataloger in the back office to the labor of the reference librarian in the front office. Thinking about metadata as requiring constant labor through all of these moments of production, reproduction, and use points not only to the necessary costs of that labor (in time and money) but also to the unrecognized value of that labor (in skill and experience) when it is put to work helping library patrons navigate a perpetual "information crisis" of abundant materials, which are themselves of little value if they can never be located when needed. Such information labor may even shift, with the passage of time and the development of technology, from producer to user, as patrons navigate computerized search screens and digital databases, which once would have demanded high-paid, high-skilled expert assistance [49]. Again, particularly in the history of cataloging and computation, such a focus can help us understand how librarians of the 1960s through the 1980s, both male and female, often saw (and split) themselves more as new-economy "information intermediaries" with high levels of skill (e.g., doing pay-per-minute or pay-per-record private database searches for patrons) rather than old-style "technical assistants" working with rote online systems to download and adapt centrally produced, clerical cataloging data.

**4.** *Question gendered meanings around the different moments of meta-data labor.*

Finally, these three assumptions—that the library is itself a technology, that the object of that technology is metadata, and that profound labor is required to manage that metadata—can lead us back to the original questions of gender and computing within library history. But it is not enough to simply assert that "computing was masculine" and "librarianship was feminine" because of the demography of the participants (more males in computing, more females in librarianship). We should say something about the cultural assumptions around the social contexts in which those participants worked: to explain how these hegemonic genderings are produced, reproduced, and resisted. Are computer centers and computer programming gendered masculine? Are humanities libraries and reference services gendered feminine?

From the 1960s onward, library computing projects were structured by both an *institutional* and a *spatial* division of labor in librarianship, with digital systems first prototyped by a few large academic and corporate libraries, and only later consumed by a much larger number of smaller public and school libraries. But as the feminist librarians of the 1970s so conclusively demonstrated, the *gender* division of library labor has been structured by this same institutional and spatial division of labor, with proportionately more men in academic and corporate libraries than in public and school libraries. Within the library, the gendering of the computer may link more to the administrative imbalance within librarianship—with technology seen as a rationalizing management strategy—than to the masculine nature or origin of that technology itself.

Ideas of masculinity and femininity still have power within the library internetwork, especially in terms of gendered labor roles. Not just in the 1980s, but all through library history, the application of technology to so-called housekeeping work in the library was often targeted to eliminate or restructure (deskill, devalue, or deprofessionalize) the lowest-status, lowest-wage, most material kinds of library tasks—tasks that were indeed disproportionately performed by women (often by design). In the same way, while automation of "knowledge" work was often imagined as augmenting and uplifting the highest-status, highest-wage, and most conceptual work within librarianship, in this as in other fields, such upgraded work was disproportionately performed by men (again by design). But librarianship adds another wrinkle to this standard story. Just as back-office "housekeeping" clerical labor has long been gendered feminine in myriad occupations, so has its opposite—front-desk "nurturing" service and education labor—long been assumed to be the proper domain of women. If the basic promise of clerical computer automation was to open up more space and time for conceptual computer augmentation, how has the service-oriented work of librarianship negotiated a gender dynamic that might be both masculine and feminine? By connecting the back-office moment of metadata production to the front-desk moment of metadata use, perhaps a new relationship between technological change and gender construction in computing can be seen.

The overall story of libraries, computers, and women is important precisely because it demonstrates that simply adding information technology to an occupation doesn't produce predictable, deterministic results. The way computers were understood and ended up being used within librarianship was quite clearly tied to contemporary notions of the proper gender roles of male and female library professionals. From the 1960s to the 1980s, both ideas about the proper place of women and ideas about the proper use of technology were changing at the same time. Exploring the intertwined history of women, computers, and libraries illustrates how moments of new technological possibility are often moments of social reflection and change as well, precisely because our produced technological environments and our worlds of social meaning are so tied up in each other. And this less-well-known history of gender and computing might be especially relevant today, with printed books rapidly converging with computer interfaces through corporate ventures like Amazon Kindle and Google Print. I doubt that the library is doomed to irrelevance in the new networked computing environment. But I suspect that the fate of the library in this digital future of reading will once again hinge, as it always did, on the labor of women.

# REFERENCES

**1.** James Cortada, *The Digital Hand*, Volume III (New York: Oxford University Press, 2008).

**2.** See, for example, Paul N. Edwards, "The Army and the Microworld," *Signs*, Vol. 16, No. 1 (1990): 102–127; Jennifer Light, "When Computers Were Women," *Technology and Culture*, Vol. 40, No. 3 (1999): 455–483; Nathan L. Ensmenger, "Letting the 'Computer Boys' Take Over: Technology and the Politics of Organizational *Transformation*," in Aad Blok and Greg Downey, eds., *Uncovering Labour in Information Revolutions* (Cambridge, UK: Cambridge University Press, 2004).

**3.** See, for example, Thomas Augst and Wayne A. Wiegand, eds., *The Library as an Agency of Culture* (Madison: University of Wisconsin Press, 2003); Michael H. Harris, *History of Libraries in the Western World*, 4th ed. (Metuchen, NJ: Scarecrow Press, 1995); Wayne A. Wiegand and Donald G. Davis, Jr., eds., *The Encyclopedia of Library History* (New York: Garland, 1994).

**4.** Greg Downey, "Virtual Webs, Physical Technologies, and Hidden Workers," *Technology and Culture*, Vol. 42, No. 2 (2001): 209–235.

**5.** Greg Downey, "The Librarian and the Univac: Automation and Labor at the 1962 Seattle World's Fair" in Catherine McKercher and Vincent Mosco, eds., *Knowledge Workers in the Information Society* (Lanham, MD: Lexington Books, 2007).

**6.** Jesse Shera, (Introduction to special issue on library automation) *Wilson Library Bulletin*, Vol. 38 (May 1964): 741–742.

**7.** Jesse Shera, "Without Reserve," *Wilson Library Bulletin*, Vol. 38 (May 1964): 781.

**8.** See, for example, Anne Witz and Mike Savage, "The Gender of Organizations," in Mike Savage and Anne Witz, eds., *Gender and Bureaucracy* (Cambridge, UK: Blackwell, 1992); Joan Acker, "From Sex Roles to Gendered Institutions," *Contemporary Sociology*, Vol. 21, No. 5 (1992): 565–569.

**9.** Katherine Murphy Dickson, *Sexism and Reentry: Job Realities for Women Librarians* (Lanham, MD: University Press of America, 1997).

**10.** Hope A. Olson and Amber Ritchie, "Gentility, Technicality, and Salary: Women in the Literature of Librarianship" in Betsy Kruger and Catherine Larson, eds., *On Account of Sex: An Annotated Bibliography on the Status of Women in Librarianship, 1998–2002* (Lanham, MD: Scarecrow Press, 2006).

**11.** Katharine Phenix, "Women Predominate, Men Dominate," *Bowker Annual*, Vol. 29 (1984): 83.

**12.** See, for example, Marie L. Radford and Gary P. Radford, "Power, Knowledge, and Fear," *Library Quarterly*, Vol. 67, No. 3 (1997): 250–266; Cheryl Knott Malone, "Imagining Information Retrieval in the Library," *IEEE Annals of the History of Computing*, Vol. 24, No. 3 (2002): 14–22.

**13.** Arnold P. Sable, "The Sexuality of the Library Profession," *Wilson Library Bulletin*, Vol. 43 (April 1969): 751.

**14.** Sally H. McCallum, "MARC," *IEEE Annals of the History of Computing*, Vol. 24, No. 2 (2002): 34–49.

**15.** Anita R. Schiller, with James W. Grimm and Margo C. Trumpeter, *Characteristics of Professional Personnel in College and University Libraries* (Springfield: Illinois State Library, 1969), p. 2.

**16.** Pat Schuman, "Status of Women in Libraries," *Library Journal* (August 1970): 2635.

**17.** Betty-Carol Sellen and Joan K. Marshall, eds., *Women in a Woman's Profession: Strategies*, proceedings, American Library Association Preconference on the Status of Women in Librarianship (July 1974).

**18.** Kathleen L. Maciuszko, *OCLC* (Littleton: Libraries Unlimited, 1984).

**19.** See, for example, Nina E. Lerman, Arwen Palmer Mohun, and Ruth Oldenziel, "The Shoulders We Stand on and the View from Here," *Technology and Culture*, Vol. 38, No. 1 (1997): 9–30; Judy Wajcman, "The Feminization of Work in the Information Age," in Mary Frank Fox, Deborah G. Johnson, and Sue V. Rosser, eds., *Women, Gender, and Technology* (Urbana: University of Illinois, 2006), pp. 80–97.

**20.** Betty Jo Irvine, *Sex Segregation in Librarianship: Demographic and Career Patterns of Academic Library Administrators* (Westport: Greenwood Press, 1985), p. 9.

**21.** Alice Bryan, *The Public Librarian* (New York: Columbia University Press, 1952).

**22.** Suzanne Hildenbrand, "Library Feminism and Library Women's History," *Libraries & Culture*, Vol. 35, No. 1 (2000): 51–67.

**23.** Helen W. Tuttle, "Women in Academic Libraries," *Library Journal* (September 1971): 2594–2596.

**24.** Raymond L. Carpenter and Kenneth D. Shearer, "Sex and Salary Survey," *Library Journal* (15 November 1972): 3682–3685.

**25.** Anita Schiller, "Women in Librarianship," *Advances in Librarianship*, Vol. 4 (1974): 104–147.

**26.** Mary Niles Maack, "Women as Visionaries, Mentors, and Agents of Change," in Joanne E. Passet, ed., *Women's Work: Vision and Change in Librarianship* (Urbana: University of Illinois at Urbana-Champaign GLIS, 1994), p. 111.

**27.** Alan Rees, "New Bottles for Old Wine: Retrieval and Librarianship," *Wilson Library Bulletin* Vol. 38, No. 9 (May 1964): 773.

**28.** Ralph H. Parker, "What Every Librarian Should Know About Automation," *Wilson Library Bulletin*, Vol. 38, No. 9 (May 1964): 754.

**29.** Nick Dyer-Witheford, *Cyber-Marx: Cycles and Circuits of Struggle in High-Technology Capitalism* (Urbana: University of Illinois Press, 1999).

**30.** Joseph Becker and Robert M. Hayes, *Information Storage and Retrieval: Tools, Elements, and Theories* (Hoboken, NJ: John Wiley & Sons, 1963), p. x.

**31.** Janet Freedman, "The Liberated Librarian?" *Library Journal* (1 May 1970): 1709–1711.

**32.** Helen Lowenthal, "A Healthy Anger," *Library Journal* (1 September 1971): 2597–2599.

**33.** Jody Newmyer, "The Image Problem of the Librarian," *Journal of Library History* (1976): 44–67.

**34.** F. Bernice Field, "Technical Services and Women," in Russell E. Bidlack, ed., *Women in the Library Profession: Leadership Roles and Contributions* (Ann Arbor: University of Michigan, 1971), p. 15.

**35.** Herman Greenberg, "Sex Discrimination Against Women in Libraries," in Margaret Myers and Mayra Scarborough, eds., *Women in Librarianship: Melvil's Rib Symposium* (New Brunswick, NJ: Rutgers University Graduate School of Library Service, 1975), p. 52.

**36.** Kathleen Heim and Katharine Phenix, "The Women's Movement Within Librarianship, 1977–1981," in Kathleen Heim and Katharine Phenix, eds., *On Account of Sex: An Annotated Bibliography on the Status of Women in Librarianship, 1977–1981* (Chicago: American Library Association, 1984).

**37.** Christina D. Baum, *Feminist Thought in American Librarianship* (Jefferson, NC: McFarland, 1992).

**38.** Ruth Hafter, *Academic Librarians and Cataloguing Networks: Visibility, Quality Control, and Professional Status* (New York: Greenwood Press, 1986).

**39.** Ruth Hafter, "Born-again Cataloging in the Online Networks," *College & Research Libraries*, Vol. 47 (July 1986): 360–364.

**40.** Suzanne Hildenbrand, "The Crisis in Cataloging: A Feminist Hypothesis" in Sheila S. Intner and Janet Swan Hill, eds., *Recruiting, Educating and Training Cataloging Librarians* (New York: Greenwood Press, 1989).

**41.** Sheila S. Intner and Janet Swan Hill, eds., *Cataloging: The Professional Development Cycle* (New York: Greenwood Press, 1991), p. 71.

**42.** Suzanne Hildenbrand, "Women's Work Within Librarianship," *Library Journal*, Vol. 114 (1 September 1989): 153–155.

**43.** Roma Harris, *Librarianship: The Erosion of a Woman's Profession* (Norwood, NJ: Ablex, 1992).

**44.** Roma Harris, "Information Technology and the De-skilling of Librarians," *Computers in Libraries*, Vol. 12, No. 1 (January 1992): 8.

**45.** Roma M. Harris, "Understanding Gender Relations in the Librarianship of the 1990s," in Betsy Kruger and Catherine A. Larson, eds., *On Account of Sex: An Annotated Bibliography on the Status of Women in Librarianship, 1993–1999* (Lanham, MD: Scarecrow Press, 2000), pp. xix–xx.

**46.** Mary Salome Cutler Fairchild, "Women in American Libraries," *Library Journal* (December 1904): 157–162.

**47.** Mary Niles Maack, "Gender Issues in Librarianship," in Wayne A. Wiegand and Donald G. Davis, eds., *Encyclopedia of Library History* (New York: Garland Publishing, 1994).

**48.** Paul N. Edwards, Steven J. Jackson, Geoffrey C. Bowker, and Cory P. Knobel, *Understanding Infrastructure* (Arlington, VA: National Science Foundation, 2007).

**49.** Bryan Pfaffenberger, *Democratizing Information: Online Databases and the Rise of End-User Searching* (Boston: G.K. Hall & Co., 1990).

# Media and Culture

# Cultural Perceptions of Computers in Norway 1980–2007

## From "Anybody" Via "Male Experts" to "Everybody"

**8**

HILDE G. CORNELIUSSEN

Even though Norway is a country with a strong sense and impression of gender equality and tops the World Economic Forum's gender equality ranking, the labor market is still strongly divided by gender. More women than men attend higher education [1], but computer education is heavily male dominated. Observers in many countries are concerned about computers and computing causing a gender gap, in particular, in relation to computing education and the computing professions, where the number of women, never very high, has decreased during the last decade. These concerns are evident in Norway. In discussions about gender and ICT (information and communication technology) there are often underlying assumptions of gender as a stable structure and the result of "nature." However, unless we believe that men really do have certain masculine qualities that make them more suitable than women in relation to computers, we need to examine the development of ideas about gender and computers. How was the image of men's close relationship to computers, along with ideas about women's indifference, constructed and maintained? How has the computer been perceived, and to whom and what was it considered helpful or necessary?

*Gender Codes: Why Women Are Leaving Computing*, Edited by Thomas J. Misa
Copyright © 2010 the IEEE Computer Society

This chapter explores how the computer was *culturally appropriated* in Norway since the 1980s. We will explore how the relationship between gender and computers was perceived and presented in Norway's largest newspaper, *Aftenposten*. *Aftenposten* is Oslo based, but read by people in all regions of the country, and is Norway's version of the *New York Times*, a mainstream newspaper of record that is widely respected. Thus, this is not "computer history" in a traditional sense. It is not the history about what "really" happened, but rather about how the development was *perceived* in the public sphere.

Gender researchers have shown how gender works as a social construction, providing formal and informal rules, social guidelines, and expectations and assumptions about the proper behaviors and roles of men and women [2]. Gender also gives meaning to other entities and social practices, such as technology. Technology is sometimes conceptualized as physical artifacts, but it also involves knowledge and skills, practices, symbols, and cultural meanings, all of which also express ideas about gender [3,4]. Notions about gender also shape the development and use of diverse technologies, such as bicycles, shavers, medical devices—and computers (see Chapters 1, 6, and 9 in this volume). A keyword in the analysis below is "discourse," referring to socially constructed meanings around a limited area, such as the computer. Discourse theory provides a useful tool to understand and analyze how meanings are constructed, preserved, passed along to others, and, not the least, changed—in continual negotiation (this analysis is inspired by Laclau and Mouffe's discourse theory (1985)). In this chapter we will investigate discourses about computing and gender as a cultural frame of reference. Discourses often appear to be fixed or stable, but when scrutinized we will find that they are unstable, socially constructed structures, continually changing over time and from place to place. The aim of this chapter is to analyze how the discourse of computer technology developed since the 1980s, focusing on the public sphere in Norway—that is, on debates that were available to and concerned "people in general." The empirical material is gathered from *Aftenposten* [5,6] and focuses on 200 news articles that in some way discussed or examined computer technology *and* gender [7]. Below we will explore how these discussions of gender and computer technology helped construct the discourse about computers in a particular way, through a "discursive logic" that resulted in a homogeneous and hegemonic discourse in the period up until 2000, creating different expectations about men's and women's relations to the computer. Despite the seeming stability, there are notable discursive changes since the year 2000 that will be discussed in the second part of the chapter.

## THE PERSONAL COMPUTER

Cheap computers became available on the Norwegian market beginning in the late 1970s. The newness of "personal computers" in this period was not primarily the technology, but the opportunity for "anyone" to acquire a computer, even though it was still not common to own one. In 1985 only 9% of the population between 9 and 79 years old had access to a home computer, and the computer-using population grew steadily to 50% in 1997. The Internet entered the scene in the 1990s, with access increasing rapidly from 13% in 1997 to 52% in 2000. By 2007, access to computers and the Internet had increased to 87% and 83%, respectively.

The computer entered Norwegian culture as a heterogeneous technology, at the intersections between work, home, school, and society at large, promising dramatic changes in all these fields. Claims about the computer entering homes at "full speed" were numerous in the 1980s, and 1995 was described as "the year we connected to the Internet." Thus, the cultural importance of the new computer technology seems to have anticipated its actual diffusion. The early 1980s was envisioned as a time of change that would affect everything and everyone, from the nation to individuals, regardless of gender [8]. Labels like "computer," "information," and "technology" were used as futuristic prefixes to "society," describing the entire society in light of the new technology, where computers made *the* difference [9]: "Our society is about to change—and the 'driving force' is the computer" [10]. The computer constituted "the language of the future," it was claimed, and "those who do not learn the language of the computer today will be the illiterates of tomorrow." In numerous media reports, women were explicitly included in these visions, assumed to be using the computer in the home for typical household tasks (Fig. 8.1) [11]. However, women were soon labeled at risk of becoming "the illiterates of tomorrow."

Figure 8.1. Computers and the information society at home, work, and shopping. Bar-coding systems, such as NCR's model 280 at Montgomery Ward (1970), launched "point of sale" retailing. (Courtesy of Charles Babbage Institute.)

# DISCURSIVE LOGICS BEFORE 2000

## A Pattern of Inclusion and Exclusion

The most common focus on girls and women in *Aftenposten* concerned their lack of interest, experience, and skills, while by contrast the dominant focus on boys and men was their fascination and extraordinary computer skills. This trend contributes to making computer skills both visible and invisible in a certain gendered discursive pattern.

*Aftenposten* writers anatomized women's lack of interest in computers and their low level of participation at work, in education, in the private sphere, and in society in general. Statistics showed a gender gap in access and use, choice of education, as well as references to situations where girls and women were less engaged than boys and men (in the classroom, at computer parties, at home, in school, at work, on the Internet) or in general as a problem for society [12]. All pointed to women's low level of participation. Boys and men were often mentioned in these entries, representing the "norm" against which girls and women were measured and found wanting [13]. These entries increased the visibility and discursive importance of female nonusers, and women's low interest in computers had become "common knowledge" by the late 1990s [3,14]. Not merely the large number of such news reports but also the descriptions, comments, and evaluations in many of the reports focusing on women's lack of interest increased the discursive importance of female nonusers. A typical entry was titled, bluntly, "Women do not give a toss about computer technology." Norway was presented as unique since "nearly all Norwegian homes have a PC" (surely an exaggeration of the real situation) and since a larger proportion of the Norwegian population than in other countries had access to the Internet. However, a 1997 survey found that only 1% of women who had access to the Internet actually did use it, against 12% of men; and similarly, only 1 in 5 women against 1 in 3 men used the PC at home [15]. The survey obviously documented a lower level of use among women. This focus on the difference *between* men and women strengthened the impression of women as nonusers, not only by ignoring the female *users*, who—although not representing a large proportion at that time—still existed, but also by disregarding that a *dominant majority* of men also were nonusers, with two-thirds of men not using the PC and 88% not using the Internet at home. The male nonusers were simply not discussed at all—not in this or any other news report presenting statistics. Women were identified as the future losers, while a similar threat toward male nonusers was overlooked. But why would it be more interesting that women were lagging behind compared to male Internet users rather than the fact that the majority of men were also not users? And why would only *female* nonusers face the threat of becoming "the losers of the future"?

This episode illustrates how relations between gender and technology were made visible and invisible in a certain pattern. Women's nonuse and men's embrace of technology—even though it did not include a majority of men—were made visible. Simultaneously, male nonusers and female users were ignored or made discursively invisible, contributing to an overall homogenization of a masculine discourse of computers.

Not only were women labeled as indifferent to computers, but they were also associated with technophobia. A researcher who described technophobia as something that had always existed was asked by a journalist [16]: "Isn't this [fear of technology] something that in particular applies to women?" The researcher answered the question without responding to the gender part. Although the question about women does not seem to have a meaningful part in the interview, the journalist decided to let the question—more precisely, the assumption about women—remain in the published text. Even though the question was not reflected in the following dialogue, it did *create* meaning in the text by connecting women and fear of technology, illustrating and reinforcing the readily available connection between women and technophobia. And, it was allowed to stay there unchallenged (imagine the journalist asking the same question about men and the interviewee not responding!). Thus, the reports focusing on women's lack of interest in the computer greatly enhanced the impression of women as nonusers, making them the discursively visible ones, at the cost of female users, who remained discursively invisible.

In sharp contrast to the treatment of girls and women, the dominant focus on boys and men was rather their exceptional interest, extraordinary skills, and even love for the computer [17,18]. Two recurring themes operated side by side. First, the reports obviously admired the boys' and young men's skills. They were described as self-educated computer "wizards." Young men in computer companies were "dragged out of the boy's room," to work in a business "where the geniuses are so young they barely escape the penal code against child labor." They belonged to the "hacker generation" and their only education was what they had taught themselves in "the boy's room" [19]. They "lived for their work" and had "the fiddling in their fingers and the computer technology in their heads," talking in a technical language far beyond what even the friendliest mother could possibly understand. These young boys were the masters of the language of the future, as well as the future leaders of society (Fig. 8.2) [20].

The second recurring theme concerned the negative aspects of these male-dominated computer activities: illegal copying of computer programs, in particular, games, violence and sex in computer games, as well as negative effects of playing the games [21]. With the advent of the Internet, online activities generated further worries in the shape of computer viruses "starting as an innocent boy's game," online hacking of computer systems, and violence, sex, and pornography on the Internet [22]. Criticism of the boys' activities did not, however, change their image as highly skilled computer wizards. In most of these reports "the boy's room" was an important metaphor for the computer-skilled boys and young men—even in the computer industry, where offices resembled a boy's room more than a working place [23]. The metaphor became so important as a norm for computer skills that one of the universities even offered a special "boy's room competence course" [24] for female computer students, "in the things we assumed that the boys knew about computers before they attended the program" [25].

There are striking differences between the news reports focusing on women and those focusing on men. First, reports discussing women often involved a comparison of women with men, while entries about men most often remained focused on men alone. Second, women's attitudes toward computers

Figure 8.2. Male "computer wizards". Achievement test evaluation "prescribed by computer" was developed in 1971 by Gary Pleger (left) and Karsten Engh-Kittlesen (right), who "developed the sophisticated evaluation system." (Courtesy of Charles Babbage Institute.)

were often explained through analyzing them "as gender," while gender rarely figured as an explanation in articles about men [26]. Third, the reports about women frequently encouraged female nonusers to acquire computer skills, while not a single report encouraged the same for male nonusers. Finally, while the focus on women's lack of interest made female computer users invisible, the focus on computer-skilled males made unskilled boys and men invisible. The atypical self-made computer wizards from "the boy's room" were deemed to represent the "typical" male relationship with the computer [27].

This discursive construction also seems to have made it easier to "remember," and consequently to repeat, gender as a feature assumed to make a difference. Several news articles presented statistics showing a difference between users and nonusers related to gender, age, education, income, or geography. Sometimes all of these features were involved, sometimes only a few of them, and occasionally gender was explicitly mentioned *not* to be one of them [28]. However, gender and to some degree age are the only markers that were commonly discussed as important. Thus, the hegemonic discourse made certain meanings suitable and others unsuitable, and it was apparently easier to rely on gender as the primary difference rather than other social characteristics like class or education. An entry discussing use and nonuse of different media in Norway quoted a survey showing that "technophobia" was mostly found among women, the elderly, and the poorly educated. The (male) author added a postscript: "Age is not an important factor" [29]. The rejection of age as important illustrates a homogenization of the discourse by neglecting the "unsuitable" differences, making the remaining differences even more important.

The near exclusive focus on girls' and women's lack of interest compared to boys and men as highly skilled computer users produced a particular discursive effect. Male users and female nonusers were made visible and included as "self-evident" in the hegemonic discourse, whereas male nonusers and female users remained invisible and were in effect excluded from the discourse. This pattern of inclusion and exclusion—based on making computer skills and gender visible and invisible—is perhaps the most important construction in this discourse, and it also forms an important basis for the next discursive construction: the "intersection rhetoric."

## The "Intersection Rhetoric"

The dominant perspective assuming the computer would have revolutionary impact on all different societal spheres fostered a distinctive "intersection rhetoric." It featured a tendency to use one context, such as home or work, to "explain" a completely different context. One example is found in a report discussing "computer phobia" in working life [30]. Although computer phobia was found among both men and women, it was more widespread among women, or so it was claimed, illustrated by a woman describing her difficulties in using a computer at work. This report went on to explain the differences between men's and women's relations to the computer by referring to a study of computers in Norwegian households, where many women seemingly resisted the computer because of their husbands' intense and time-consuming use of it. Thus, women's resistance was explained as a protest against men's extensive use. However, in the context of this news report, research about women's resistance to computers in the *home* was used to shed light on women's computer phobia in *working life*. The computer's position at an intersection between different fields of society developed into a particular "intersection rhetoric," making observations or arguments from one sphere appear to be valid for another sphere.

Another example of this intersection rhetoric starts with an "expert" from a computer company who worried about women's inability to keep up with the technological development. "Many women see the PC as a boy thing for men who are a bit childish," he claimed, and too many women are spectators to, instead of participants in, the rapid development [31]. In consequence, women were facing the risk of becoming "the losers of the future" who would miss out on exciting jobs and might even "have to go back to the kitchen sink or low paid professions." They would also "experience a greater distance to children's everyday life because they do not understand what children are doing" [32]. The "intersection rhetoric" in this report involves education, working life, and the home, as well as different levels of computer skills. One university lecturer claimed that it was often "required that you can handle a PC when you apply for a job," then moved on to talk about the small number of women in computer science, again illustrating the "intersection rhetoric" by conflating two fundamentally different types or levels of computer knowledge.

The fact that the computer entered the culture at an intersection between different spheres and different levels of users, from the hobby user to the secretary to the expert, apparently made it easy—and even natural—to use an

Figure 8.3. Honeywell's "kitchen computer" at the office. "If she can only cook as well as Honeywell can compute." In 1969 Honeywell teamed with retailer Neiman Marcus to offer this pedestal-model $10,000 minicomputer for home use. After a 2-week programming course, the housewife "by simply pushing a few buttons [can] obtain a complete menu organized around the entree." The "kitchen" version is pictured in Dag Spicer, "If You Can't Stand the Coding, Stay Out of the Kitchen," *Dr. Dobb's Journal* (12 August 2000); available at **www.ddj.com/184404040**. (Photo courtesy of Charles Babbage Institute.)

"intersection rhetoric," where arguments from one sphere or one group of users could be applied to another sphere or user group. (See Figure 8.3.)

## Nonhegemonic Men and Women

The dominant or hegemonic discourse presented men as computer skilled and women as indifferent. However, there were also two other groups in this period—a group of female users and a group of male nonusers. How do these fit into the hegemonic discourse?

In several reports, women were actually portrayed as the "superusers" or the main user group for office computers, both in the private and the public sector (Fig. 8.4). "Secretaries have in many places become the companies' racers in computing." It was noted that "many female secretaries do the computing for their male leaders," and many of them "are more competent than their superiors with regard to computers and technology" [33]. Thus, it appeared that the secretary was not "automated" out of a job. Instead, the secretary's job was reevaluated, and the "punching lady" was transformed into a new, though still female, "office manager" with a more responsible job, higher wages, and higher status [34]. Together with observations about women being well represented or dominant in "low level" computer work, such as routine work and word processing [35], these reports acknowledge women as an important user

Figure 8.4. Women as "superusers" of office computers. NCR's model 299 accounting computer, designed for multipurpose data processing, offered "automatic features and simplicity of programming" for small businesses. (Courtesy of Charles Babbage Institute.)

group for office computers (see Chapter 9 in this volume). Nonetheless, despite the clear acknowledgment of their computer skills, these women office workers did not alter the hegemonic discourse about computer use, which remained focused on women nonusers. This important group of female computer users could in effect be ignored owing to the perceived difference in the 1980s between a secretary's computer, deemed a mere "word processing machine," and a "general" computer [36], together with how women's use was limited to operating the technology. Using male-oriented computer expertise as the norm for "computer competence" would wipe this (female) group off the map. These women computer users were made visible as women, but in the hegemonic discourse their computer use did not count for much.

The hegemonic discourse also effectively ignored the male nonusers, or "the stone age leaders," as they were called. In the computer magazine *Datatid*, this curious group was quite prominent throughout the 1980s and 1990s, but they were entirely invisible in *Aftenposten* until the mid-1990s. In 1995 *Aftenposten* profiled a number of "renowned" nonusers—all of them in high positions, and all of them men. One of them, apparently not so happy with being interviewed, stated that "I think of myself as smart enough to master this, but with so many computer competent people around me I do not want to spend time on it" [37]. This claim is in line with what *Datatid* found in 1985 among leaders in Norwegian computer companies, who appeared busy with other things and so left the computer to be handled by the secretary [6]. These

Figure 8.5. Male nonusers of computers: the busy business leader? Perhaps one, or two, male nonusers of computers pictured here at Argonne National Laboratory (ANL negative no. 145-84-10 #22A).

male leaders presented their nonuse of computers as a *deliberate choice*. This choice was apparently accepted, at least through the end of the 1990s. A journalist writing in *Aftenposten* in 1999 acknowledged that he recently started using email after being rebuked by a business associate: "Do you live in the stone age!" This article made fun of leaders and people in high positions who did not use computers, especially those not using email. Another nonuser would tell people that he had a PC in his office, followed by a whisper: "But I don't use it!" Another report claimed that the Internet revolution was awaiting the leaders to realize that the world was about to change. Many of these male leaders got a PC in their office in the early 1990s, it was claimed, because "it looked pretty," but many of them still wrote by hand [38]. Apparently some of the male leaders acquired the *status* of the computer quite early without actually using it. The consequence of their nonuse was described as no more severe than the risk of receiving business communications on paper through "snail-mail," as before, a far cry from the dire consequences described for women nonusers.

These prominent men were obviously not the only male nonusers in the 1980s and 1990s, but they were the only group made visible. Despite the leaders' visibility as men, they were not discussed "as gender," and their gender was not used as an argument or explanation for their behavior. They did not affect the general image of men as computer competent, but were instead excused based on a different discourse—the discourse of the busy business leader (Fig. 8.5).

## CHALLENGING THE HEGEMONIC DISCOURSE: RECONSTRUCTIONS AND NEW VOICES

So far we have seen how the hegemonic discourse was created through a systematic pattern of making female nonusers and male users visible, while simultaneously male nonusers and female users remained discursively invisible. The "intersection rhetoric" increased the visibility of women's lack of knowledge by permitting the use of observations or arguments from one arena, group, or level of use to be valid explanations for another arena, group, or level of use. By this overemphasis of gender, a conception of gender as the primary difference was sustained, and differences within the genders as well as other differences, such as age or income, were made seemingly unimportant [39]. Even when the male nonusers entered the scene, they did not face the threat of being excluded from important activities. And when the hegemonic discourse was occasionally challenged, it was met with doubt, disregard, or even contradiction. These discursive logics all worked to homogenize the discourse through including meanings that supported the hegemonic discourse, while excluding meanings that threatened it. However, it is important to note that discourses do change, despite their seemingly stable and fixed qualities. In this section we will see attempts to rewrite the discourse before 2000 as well as the entry of new voices and new meanings after 2000.

## How to Change Things if Gender Is a Primary Difference

One of the recurring questions following the worries about women's low interest in computers, in particular, computer education, has been the question of *how* to include women. The trend in computer education in Norway has to a large degree followed the rest of the Western world: a low proportion of women students grew slowly across the early 1980s, but decreased markedly toward the mid-1990s [40]. Numerous initiatives to recruit and retain women had temporary and local effects in the late 1990s [25,41], but the numbers of women are once again decreasing and are today lower than in the late 1980s in the most technical computer education in faculties of technology and natural sciences [42].

I have analyzed elsewhere the discursive constructions in computer education and initiatives to recruit more women into this field, illustrating a "gender-blind," a "masculine," and "feminized" discourse of computing [25], and there are examples of each of these in *Aftenposten*. We find the gender-blind discourse blaming women for making the wrong choices, and the masculine discourse encouraging women to "think in new ways" or to "close the milk shop and pedicure and start in the computer business" [43]. We even find a more feminized version trying to rewrite the meaning of computing as less technical and more social—in accord with women's supposed "social abilities." While the first two discourses tried to change women, the last one is the most interesting in this context, as it definitely tried to change the discourse of computing to make room for women. This is the one we will focus on here.

Reports discussing women's low participation in computing education and low interest in computers frequently tried to explain this fact, as well as how to change it, by conceptualizing men and women as essentially different. Men and women have different attitudes toward computer technology, it was claimed. It was assumed that men have a playful and exploring attitude while women are driven solely by need, not by enthusiasm or inquisitiveness [44]. Men get addicted, and they love the technology for itself, whereas women ask what they can use it for. Boys are interested in "finesses and technique" while girls are interested in "communication, email and information retrieval," arguments well known also from earlier research [45–48]. Men and women were also described as having essentially different qualities, and several entries claimed that women in certain ways were *better* than men with regard to computing: "women are better in comprehending the users' situation. Men have a tendency to lose themselves in exciting details" [49].

A contemporary campaign echoed these very arguments to recruit women to computing. Here women were lauded for their excellent communication abilities, while men were acknowledged as "the technical geniuses." This description of men and women coincided with an attempt at redefining computing. One business representative claimed that many computer jobs were "not technical at all," and another expert claimed that "the characteristics associated with girls … creativity and to be good at teamwork" would lead to success in the computer business [25,41]. The arguments were perhaps well intended in the way they made room for women and described computing as something women could manage as well as or, in some instances, better than men. However, the underlying argument was that computing was not *really* about technology, but about something else. Women were still not considered "technical geniuses." Thus, women might study computing or work in the computer industry, but not for the same reasons as men.

Emphasis on the social aspects also surfaced in a rare description of a group of female computer engineers. They were described as experts, but as a negation of male computer experts: they did not talk incessantly about technology and they were certainly not nerds. "Instead they talk about weddings, children, men … about a lot of things that often occupy women in their late 20s and early 30s" [50]. The female computer engineers emphasized that they "worked with people"—just as they assumed other young women wanted to. Besides, computer companies did not always want the male computer geeks, it was claimed, but rather preferred women who could "listen to users and their needs." Thus, the message was that the computer industry needed women because they were *not* like male experts. Still, it seems, they were not valued for their technical expertise.

As far as we can see, women confront a number of "double standards" in computing. They face difficulties in establishing an identity as "computer expert" in part because they lack ready-made images to identify with or role models [3,51]. The suggestion that computing is incompatible with femininity [52] creates an imbalance that may lead women to maintain a distance from male computer experts in attempts to restore the balance. Rewriting computing to be more in line with the assumed "female qualities" and preferences offers an alternate co-construction of gender and computers. However, not everyone is entirely happy with this attempt to write technology out of computing, nor with the negative image it creates of men [41]. And the alternative construction does not really include women in the technological aspects of computing.

## New Voices After 2000

The hegemonic discourse seems rather stable through the late 1990s, while attempts to recast the discourse in this period occur primarily with concerns about the low proportion of women in computer education. After 2000, we find new discursive constructions alongside the dominant discourse. Different meanings can exist side by side, resulting in something like a polyphonic musical choir of different and seemingly contradictory voices [53]. After 2000 we can find this polyphonic choir with echoes of previous voices as well as new voices. The newspaper articles on gender and computing since 2000 can roughly be divided in four main topics: (1) criminal men, (2) computers for everything and everybody, (3) differences between computer users, and (4) women in IT education/business. The articles within these four topics also relate to gender in distinctive ways.

The articles about criminal men are all very brief, as though they were barely worth mentioning. Continuing from the earlier period, it is still men who are associated with criminal use of computers. Yet in this period the young male hacker, formerly the computer wizard of the 1990s, lost some of his status. His criminal deeds are now described as "boyish pranks," and he is no longer celebrated for his arcane knowledge. Instead, his computer knowledge is "normalized," since anyone can find recipes for hacking on the Internet [54]. Thus, the call to "forget the hacker" [55] is partly achieved—by redefining him away from being someone with exceptional computer skills to an "anybody" using commonly available information. The young male hackers or nerds have lost their hegemonic position as the celebrated computer wizards.

One of the most notable differences since 2000 is the embrace of computers as being everywhere, used by everyone, and for everything. The earlier period also saw similar claims, in particular, during the early 1980s, although mostly referring to the future. The more recent news articles seem to reflect practices already present and realized, and they construct the categories of "everywhere" and "everything" more actively, not as a vision but through stories of people's actual use of computers. The category of "everybody" is actively constructed as a discursive group that includes many *new* users of computers. Thus, we meet young people, old people, men, women, grandmothers, people looking for a date, office workers, prisoners, and prostitutes as the new user groups; and they use computers for a broad spectrum of activities including work, hobbies, communicating in new ways with family and friends as well as with strangers on Internet services. The new "everybody" still confronts the image of the "original" computer experts, that is, the nerdy men. In challenging the "nerdy men," the most "unlikely" users are called upon, such as, for instance, "your aunt," "your mummy," "women over 60"—images that clearly challenge the image of the "real" computer user as solely male [56]. These new images clearly counteract the invisibility of women computer users.

Some of the new computer users are presented as marginalized females, such as prostitutes and female prisoners. In their stories, computer technology has gained a vital position in making them able to participate in and become successfully integrated in society. Even though men per se still do not figure as either nonusers or new users, new male users are presented in this period, such as male craftsmen. Craftsmen did not consider computers important, but now they realize that running a business without computers is about to become impossible, or at least embarrassing.

The new spectrum of users challenges two of the most important discursive constructions from the earlier period: the dominant position held by primarily young males as the "real" computer users; and the image of women as nonusers along with the invisibility of female users. Thus, these new stories challenge the gendered inclusion/exclusion pattern of the earlier hegemonic discourse, creating discursive space for both male and female computer users.

This expansion of computer users clearly involves a number of different users with a number of different social features. The newspaper articles referred to above do not explicitly discuss in which ways they are different. This is, however, the topic in a series of other articles and in these, gender again is described as the main differentiating feature. The old, pre-2000 voices emphasize that girls have less technical skill than boys do, and that girls want to maintain distance from the nerd label, emphasizing the gender gap of the hegemonic discourse. In dramatic contrast, the new, post-2000 voices observe that the gender gap is about to close. Women have "invaded the internet," with gender differences in access and use "surprisingly small" [57]. However, women turn out to use the Internet in different ways, since "contact with friends and acquaintances are more important than tangible results." Men, on the other hand, "want action and results," banking services, and "window-shopping," and boys are "most eager to use the net for creating contacts." Inconsistencies in descriptions of the various preferred activities seem to indicate that the descriptions of men's and women's online preferences involve gender expectations more than actual activities.

One "Internet expert" confidently claims that "everyone" who wants to use the Internet today can do so, and gender is no longer the most important difference. Several articles follow this pattern: a journalist trying to sketch a picture of gender as the main difference (i.e., following the previous hegemonic discourse) is contradicted by an "expert" pointing out that the situation has changed. One expert agrees that there are some differences between girls' and boys' interests, but "when entering working life, the computer knowledge of both genders is about equally good" [58]. Another expert claims that it is primarily "myths" about gender that create expectations of girls' and women's lack of skills: "In reality, boys and girls have a very equal level of knowledge" [59].

Another example of old gender gaps being closed, while new ones are opened, comes from a researcher commenting upon her own study showing that girls' and boys' uses of the computer are converging. "More boys are chatting … and more girls are playing PC games" [60]. But still, the differences are large "both in what they do and how much time they use," and she continues: "I believe that it will always be like that, because it is based on fundamental differences in interests between the genders." Despite the closing of old gaps, new ones appear, indicating the importance of gender in sorting the world, and also how easily this sorting mechanism can appear as a documentation of "nature," an unchangeable and rigid structure.

These articles illustrate how the hegemonic discourse is no longer in harmony with the observable practices of people. It is continually being challenged and renegotiated in ways that seek to revalue girls' and women's relationship to computers in more positive terms, that is, as less different from the (male) norm. These articles also remind us that gender is not a purely biological feature, but it involves categories that include meaning, values, and expectations. While old gender gaps might be closing, new ones appear and reinstall gender as a main differentiating feature.

The fourth and final main topic since 2000 is the ongoing focus on girls' and women's low level of participation in computer education and the computing workforce. Here the "nerdy men" is still a repeated image (although not with such a celebratory tone), and we find echoes of the feminized discourse emphasizing computing as mostly about people and communication, which is assumed to interest women more than technical aspects. Women are also wanted in the IT business because "they think a little bit different and supply new perspectives" [61]. But the most interesting development in this discourse is new images of *men* fighting the image of the nerd/hacker/geek, which has been seen as one of the main problems for women in education and industry [41,52,62]. These new men are not isolated or asocial, nor do they have a "single-minded devotion to computers" [52]. Quite the contrary, they are active in various social activities and organizations, and "not engaged with the computer all the time." The new men "talk about other things than their computer" and even "have a tan in the summer" [63]. The invitation to women is still not based on women being technically competent, but rather reflects a truism about women in professional contexts representing "something special" purely based on gender. Most notably, what is being reconstructed here is not so much women or computer education—but rather men. All the same, the hackers or "computer idiots" still exist and "we need them" [64].

A number of articles focus specifically on female leaders who make up around 4% to 5% of the IT industry in Norway. Female leaders are wanted for their "female competence" and to secure the "needs of half the users" [65], even if both of these observations remained rather vague and unspecified. Women, however, "don't know the code" of the IT business, and in recognizing this, a mentoring project initiated by a network for women in IT identified male "agents" as mentors for female "talents." One of the mentors could report that his (female) "talent" had become "more rational and less emotional" [66]. Thus, there is a desire to increase the number of women in leading positions, to create role models, and to help them learn the codes. This assistance is expressed by very rigid gender constructions, however, where women are marked as different from the male norm. Women can never win the competition with men's culturally acquired professional competence based on their "nature" as women [67]. And paradoxically, women are invited for some special values they have as women, but to achieve the top positions they have to become less like women and more like men, for instance, in learning the codes of the (male) business.

The presentation above has focused on the new discursive constructions, although, it should be emphasized, the press also in this period continues to write about girls and women who have less interest, less experience, and less computer skill than boys and men. The most pronounced continuities are concerning the different computer users and the persisting low proportion of women in computing education and work. These are also the fields where gender seems to be most stubbornly reproduced, often in essentializing ways, making it appear as if it "will always be like that" owing to men's and women's "natures" [68]. We have also seen new discursive constructions, in which discursive continuities operate side by side with new voices. The new voices introduce new and more varied groups of computer users. They try to restore some kind of gender balance by claiming things have changed and by introducing the new social men (with a tan) who are assumed to make the IT world more attractive to women. The expansion and diversification in these accounts make women less evident as *the* nonusers of computers, even as the young teenage boys have lost some of their former status as computer wizards, softening the gendered pattern of visibility/invisibility of skills.

## HOW CAN WE UNDERSTAND THE CHANGE?

In this chapter we have seen how perceptions of the relationship between gender and computer technology developed in popular discourse. Overall, the findings are perhaps not surprising, since the computer's masculine associations as well as the low proportion of women in computing are well known [69–71]. This chapter's focus on discourse reveals how and when this strong connection between masculinity and computers emerged, as well as suggesting how and why it has changed most recently.

Across the period from 1980 to today, we can see three main phases in the cultural appropriation of computers. First, in the early 1980s, before the dominant discourse took hold, the perceptions of gender were unclear and ambivalent, and they could even be distinctly hospitable to women. This was even more explicit in the Norwegian computer magazine *Datatid*. The magazine frequently suggested that the computer offered special opportunities to women by creating new jobs in or near the home for women with caregiver responsibilities [6]. This phase, expressed strongly in the professional literature, soon gave way to a flood of popular-culture accounts where computers and computing were clearly gender-typed as masculine. We have seen how men were increasingly perceived as active users while women were perceived as problematic nonusers. The explicit gender-typing and the pattern of visibility/invisibility were major driving forces in establishing the hegemonic discourse of the late 1990s. The third period, since 2000, was more expansive; the discursive changes were closely tied to the spread of computers throughout society, expanding the image of computer users in ways that challenged the previous pattern of visibility/invisibility.

These historical patterns raise at least three questions. First, why in the first phase did the computer appear as ambivalent or even gender neutral? Even though computers were not entirely new in the 1980s, computers in the home and in the office were new to most people. In the early 1980s office workers perceived the computer as novel and exciting, but their excitement disappeared within just a few years [72]. Also, early on, the computer was symbolically flexible enough to be associated with either the female office worker or the male office leader. Later, in the mid-1990s, Norwegian girls expressed a similar symbolic ambivalence about the Internet, making the researchers conclude that the Internet had not (yet) achieved the same strong associations to masculinity as the computer [48].

Although it has been claimed that young girls can "sense" the masculine character of computers, disposing females to reject them [73], this chapter indicates quite the opposite: computers did *not* enter culture with a ready-made masculine symbolism attached. Instead, personal computers began with an unclear, ambivalent, and somewhat confusing gender-typing. It is worth speculating why this might be so. While technology in general had connections to the heavy and noisy mechanical technology so deeply rooted in a working class masculinity, the personal computer was also linked to the secretary's typewriter. Computer keyboards presented a challenge to male executives accustomed to dictating letters rather than typing them (see Chapter 9 in this volume). Judy Clapp, one of the female computer pioneers, related one male executive's first computer experience: "He got his computer and called me to come up and see him using it. I walked in and he was leaning back on his desk with his secretary in front of the computer. He was dictating and she was typing!" [74].

Second, why and how did the computer *become* clearly masculine through the 1980s and 1990s? It would be naive to expect a definitive answer to such a complicated question. In the accounts presented in this chapter, at least, gender was used not merely to mark differences between men and women, but also as an ordering structure that made men's and women's actions visible and invisible in a certain pattern. Because of this ordering structure, what was made discursively visible is not necessarily the "true" story (recall the invisible legions of male nonusers), but rather a partial story filtered through gendered cultural expectations. When men—or rather a distinct minority of computer-savvy men—were taken to represent the norm of active computer use, women appeared as deviants while men not conforming to the norm became invisible. The obsessive focus on gender as the main difference, even when reporting about a closing gender gap, suggests that gender is the fundamental category we use to structure our perception of society and, accordingly, our expectations about computers. The persistent focus on gender differences also makes it difficult to see commonalities and similarities in men's and women's experiences with computers [68].

Third, why do we find such discursive variation since 2000, perhaps even indications of change in the dominant discourse? The gender ambivalence of the early 1980s might be ascribed to the newness of the computer, a difference in kind. Since 2000 there has been an important difference in degree, and "more is different" [75, p. 149]. The use of computers and the Internet grew rapidly between 1994 and 2000, at which point 71% of the Norwegian population (between 9 and 79) had access to a home computer and 52% had access to the Internet. By 2007 computing technology had become as pervasive as radio and television: fully 87% of the population had access to a computer and 83% to the Internet. Now, the main difference in access and use is no longer between men and women, but between young and old (respectively, 83% in age groups 45 and below and 28% in age groups 65 and above). It seems new technology becomes most interesting when it's become trivial and available for everyone to use [75, p. 105]. Despite the massive growth during the 1980s and 1990s, it is primarily in the period after 2000 that computers and the Internet reach this phase of pervasiveness. Thus, the image of the user changes from young male enthusiasts to "everyone" using it for "everything." Not only are more people using computer technology, but also there is a new way of perceiving computer technology. "[T]he generic concept of ICT is less meaningful to young people. They prefer to talk about specific activities that they perform using ICT. ... The issue is no longer whether or not to use ICT, but what activities you need ICT to do" [56]. In the 1990s, "access" was a keyword in discussions about gender and ICT, with an underlying assumption that "access to the technology and information about its brilliance will make the women 'change side'" [76]. The dominant concern about the gender gap is no longer in access and use, but rather women's continuously low participation in computer science [77]. Increased access and use has not resulted in more women so far choosing computer education. However, the developments since 2000—the "difference in degree" and trivialization of the computer—might also be important for this to be realized. In this chapter we have seen not only spurs to change and variation, but also how discourses can suppress variation by persistently steering our vision toward male enthusiasts and female reservation. What we have seen here is something like a Bakhtinian choir, illustrating how discourses, even when they appear to be stable, should be seen as temporary fixed structures that will always be in motion, moved—although slowly—by our choices, statements, interpretations, actions, and research.

# REFERENCES

**1.** Statistisk sentralbyrå [Statistics Norway]; available at **www.ssb.no/utniv/** (accessed 20 March 2009).

**2.** Joan Wallach Scott, *Gender and the Politics of History* (New York: Columbia University Press, 1988).

**3.** Hilde Corneliussen, *Diskursens makt— individets frihet* [The power of discourse—the freedom of individuals] (Ph.D. thesis, Department of Humanistic Informatics, University of Bergen, 2003).

**4.** Merete Lie, "Gender and ICT," in Merete Lie, ed., *He, She and IT Revisited* (Oslo: Gyldendal Akademisk, 2003), pp. 9–33.

**5.** This work is part of a larger research project, and analysis of the computer magazine *Datatid* also contributes to this chapter.

**6.** See Hilde Corneliussen, "Gender in Norwegian Computer History," in Eileen M. Trauth, ed., *Encyclopedia of Gender and Information Technology* (Hershey, PA: Idea Group Reference, 2006), pp. 630–635.

**7.** About 340 news entries from *Aftenposten* between 1981 and 2007 were retrieved. Not all of them appeared to be relevant; about 200 of these news entries are included in the empirical material analyzed in this chapter. Articles from *Aftenposten* since 1984 are available at **www. retriever-info.com/en/**, a subscription archive for Scandinavian media.

**8.** 9 July 1995 ("year we connected to the Internet"). Unless another source is named, all dates given in this format refer to *Aftenposten*. All quotes from Norwegian newspapers are translated by the author; 14 January 1983, 11 November 1983 (1980s as time of change).

**9.** Merete Lie, "Gender in the Image of Technology," in Merete Lie and Knut H. Sørensen, eds., *Making Technology Our Own? Domesticating Technology into Everyday Life* (Oslo: Scandinavian University Press, 1996), pp. 201–223.

**10.** 31 January 1984 (driving force).

**11.** 13 December 1982 ("language of the future", "illiterates of tomorrow"); 7 November 1981 ("typical household tasks").

**12.** 12 January 1996, 5 October 1997, 7 March 1999 (access and use); 22 February 1985, 24 December 1985, 11 July 1986, 17 March 1987 (choice of education); 17 October 1996, 11 March 1999 (the classroom); 30 March 1994 (computer parties); 29 August 1997 (home); 5 August 1982, 11 March 1983, 5 February 1986, 24 September 1999, 3 October 1999 (school); 10 February 1987 (work); 7 January 1996, 29 May 1998 (Internet); 23 October 1985, 5 March 1987, 22 May 1989, 5 February 1997, 5 October 1997 (problem for society).

**13.** 16 December 1987, 16 October 1994, 5 September 1997, 7 March 1999 (low level of participation).

**14.** 29 August 1997, 11 March 1999.

**15.** 5 October 1997 ("Women do not give a toss," Norwegian population).

**16.** 8 June 1997 (technophobia).

**17.** 5 March 1988 (extraordinary skills); 16 October 1994 (love for the computer).

**18.** This focus is also highly present within research on men's relationship to computers: for example, Sherry Turkle, *The Second Self: Computers and the Human Spirit* (New York: Simon and Schuster, 1984); Leslie Haddon, "Researching Gender and Home Computers," in Knut H. Sørensen and Anne-Jorun Berg, eds., *Technologies and Everyday Life: Trajectories and Transformations* (Oslo: Norwegian Research Council for Science and the Humanities, 1991; Report No. 5); Jörgen Nissen, *Pojkarna vid datorn 89* (Stockholm: Symposion Graduale, 1993); Ulf Mellström, *Män och deras maskiner* (Nora, Sweden: Bokförlaget Nya Doxa, 1999); Tine Kleif and Wendy Faulkner, "'I'm No Athlete [but] I Can Make This Thing Dance!'" *Science, Technology, & Human Values*, Vol. 28, No. 2 (Spring 2003): 296–325.

**19.** 26 November 1988 ("wizards"); 15 December 1996 ("dragged out of the boy's room," young geniuses, "hacker generation"); 15 February 1986, 26 November 1988 ("the boy's room").

**20.** 28 July 1994 ("lived for their work"); 2 May 1995 (technical language); 13 December 1982 (language of the future); 2 May 1995 (leaders of society).

**21.** 26 November 1988, 12 November 1996, 27 January 2000 (illegal copying); 30 June 1991, 25 June 1994, 1 November 1994 (violence and sex in computer games); 23 November 1995 (negative effects of games).

**22.** 29 February 1992, 29 September 1993 (computer viruses); 24 May 1985, 11 April 1987, 26 January 2000 (hacking of computer systems); 5 February 1992, 25 June 1994, 16 March 1995, 27 January 2000, 18 May 2000 (violence and sex on the Internet).

**23.** 15 December 1996 (offices resembled a boy's room).

**24.** 4 October 1998 ("boy's room competence course").

**25.** Hilde Corneliussen, "Konstruksjoner av kjønn ved høyere IKT-utdanning i Norge," *Kvinneforskning*, Vol. 27, No. 3 (2003): 31–50.

**26.** Wendy Faulkner, "The Power and Pleasure?" *Science, Technology, & Human Values*, Vol. 25, No. 1 (2000): 87–119.

**27.** Knut H. Sørensen, "Love, Duty and the S-Curve," *Strategies of Inclusion* (SIGIS, 2002).

Available at **www.rcss.ed.ac.uk/sigis/public/ documents/SIGIS_D02_Part1.pdf** (accessed 30 June 2009).

**28.** 12 June 1993.

**29.** 25 September 1993.

**30.** 26 March 1995 (computer phobia).

**31.** 5 October 1997 (women are spectators).

**32.** 5 October 1997 ("losers of the future").

**33.** 17 December 1985, 16 October 1994, 4 August 1996 ("super users"); 16 October 1994 ("racers in computing"); 4 August 1996 (female secretaries computing for male leaders); 14 August 1996 (more competent).

**34.** 2 December 1985 (not "automated" out of a job); 8 September 1989, 14 August 1996 (office manager). This was, however, not supported by research from the late 1980s. See Bente Rasmussen, "Datateknologi—en trussel eller nye muligheter," in Merete Lie et al., eds., *I menns bilde* (Trondheim: Tapir forlag, 1988), pp. 73–87.

**35.** 17 December 1985, 15 May 1986, 17 March 1987 ("low-level" computer work).

**36.** See Merete Lie, Anne-Jorunn Berg, Hjørdis Kaul, Elin Kvande, Bente Rasmussen, and Knut H. Sørensen, "Har teknologi noe med kvinner å gjøre?" *Sosiolog i dag*, Vol. 14, No. 1 (1984): 23–39.

**37.** 26 March 1995 ("renowned" nonusers).

**38.** 22 November 1999 ("stone age", "But I don't use it!"); 11 April 2000 ("it looked pretty").

**39.** See Knut H. Sørensen and Hege Nordli, "Mobil moral og kjønn i endring?" *Kvinneforskning*, Vol. 29, No. 1 (2005): 57–72.

**40.** See Maria Charles and Karen Bradley, "A Matter of Degrees: Female Underrepresentation in Computer Science Programs Cross Nationally," in J. McGrath Cohoon and William Aspray, eds., *Women and Information Technology: Research on Underrepresentation* (Cambridge: MIT Press, 2006), pp. 183–203, for a cross-national comparison of the gender composition of computer science programs in Norway and 20 other industrial countries.

**41.** Vivian Anette Lagesen, "Advertising Computer Science to Women (or Was It the Other Way Around?)" in Merete Lie, ed., *He, She and IT Revisited* (Oslo: Gyldendal Akademisk, 2003), pp. 69–102.

**42.** *Computerworld*, available at **www.idg.no/ computerworld/article103648.ece** (accessed 25 March 2009).

**43.** 10 February 1987 (gender-blind discourse); 24 December 1985 (masculine discourse—"think in new ways"); 11 July 1986 (masculine discourse—"close the milk shop").

**44.** 16 December 1987, 16 October 1994, 4 August 1996 (driven solely by need).

**45.** 9 May 1997 (communication).

**46.** Sherry Turkle, *The Second Self: Computers and the Human Spirit* (New York: Simon and Schuster, 1984).

**47.** Margrethe Aune, "The Computer in Everyday Life," in Merete Lie and Knut H. Sørensen, eds., *Making Technology Our Own? Domesticating Technology into Everyday Life* (Oslo: Scandinavian University Press, 1996), pp. 91–120.

**48.** Tove Håpnes and Bente Rasmussen, "Gendering Technology," in Merete Lie, ed., *He, She and IT Revisited* (Oslo: Gyldendal Akademisk, 2003), pp. 173–197.

**49.** 5 October 1997 ("comprehending users' situation").

**50.** 16 March 1997 ("wedding, children, men").

**51.** Hilde Corneliussen, "'I Don't Understand Computer Programming Because I'm a Woman!' Negotiating Gendered Positions in a Norwegian Discourse of Computing," in Konrad Morgan et al., eds., *Human Perspectives in the Internet Society: Culture, Psychology and Gender* (Boston: WIT Press, 2004), pp. 173–182.

**52.** Sherry Turkle, "Computational Reticence: Why Women Fear the Intimate Machine" in Cheris Kramarae, ed., *Technology and Women's Voices: Keeping in Touch* (New York: Routledge & Kegan Paul, 1988), pp. 41–61.

**53.** Mikhail Mikhailovich Bakhtin, "The Problem of Speech Genres," in Caryl Emerson and Michael Holquist, eds., *Speech Genres and Other Late Essays* (Austin: University of Texas Press, 1986), pp. 60–102.

**54.** 25 January 2001, 16 November 2001. There are no examples of girls being associated with computer criminality, and there is not a linguistic equivalent to "boyish pranks" about girls; 7 October 2001 (computer knowledge "normalized").

**55.** Helen Jøsok Gansmo, Vivian Anette Lagesen, and Knut H. Sørensen, "Forget the Hacker?" in Merete Lie, ed., *He, She and IT Revisited* (Oslo: Gyldendal Akademisk, 2003), pp. 34–68.

**56.** Helen Jøsok Gansmo, Vivian Anette Lagesen, and Knut H. Sørensen, "Out of the Boy's Room?" *NORA: Nordic Journal of Women's Studies*, Vol. 11, No. 3 (2003): 132.

**57.** 28 March 2006 ("invaded the internet").

**58.** 11 April 2001.

**59.** 14 March 2005.

**60.** 4 June 2004.

**61.** 4 June 2004 ("new perspectives").

**62.** Bente Rasmussen and Tove Håpnes, "Excluding Women from the Technologies of the Future?" *Futures*, Vol. 23 (December 1991): 1107–1119.

**63.** 22 March 2004 (not computing all the time); 23 July 2006 (summer tan).

**64.** 23 July 2006 ("computer idiots").

**65.** 12 September 2004 ("female competence").

**66.** 2 November 2003 ("less emotional").

**67.** Ruth Woodfield, *Women, Work and Computing* (Cambridge, UK: Cambridge University Press, 2000).

**68.** Robert W. Connell, *Gender* (Cambridge, UK: Polity, 2002), p. 68.

**69.** Jane Margolis and Allan Fisher, *Unlocking the Clubhouse: Women in Computing* (Cambridge: MIT Press, 2002).

**70.** Merete Lie, ed., *He, She and IT revisited* (Oslo: Gyldendal Akademisk, 2003).

**71.** J. McGrath Cohoon and William Aspray, eds., *Women and Information Technology: Research on Underrepresentation* (Cambridge: MIT Press, 2006).

**72.** Merete Lie, "Computer Dialogues," Skriftserie / Senter for kvinneforskning, No. 2 (Trondheim: Norges teknisk-naturvitenskapelige universitet, NTNU, Senter for kvinneforskning, 1998).

**73.** Jörgen Nissen, "Det är klart att det är grabbar som håller på med datorer!" in Elisabeth Sundin and Boel Berner, eds., *Från symaskin till cyborg* (Stockholm: Nerenius & Santerus Förlag, 1996), pp. 141–161.

**74.** Denise Gürer, "Women in Computing History," *Inroads—SIGCSE Bulletin*, Vol. 34, No.

2 (Special Issue on Women and Computing, 2002): 116–120.

**75.** Clay Shirky, *Here Comes Everybody: The Power of Organizing Without Organizations* (New York: Penguin Press, 2008).

**76.** Helen Jøsok Gansmo, "Towards a Happy Ending for Girls and Computing?" (Trondheim: Department of Interdisciplinary Studies of Culture, Faculty of Arts, Norwegian University of Science and Technology, 2004), p. 87. [Norwegian University of Science and Technology, Ph.D. thesis in Department of Interdisciplinary Cultural Studies].

**77.** J. McGrath Cohoon and William Aspray. "A Critical Review of the Research on Women's Participation in Postsecondary Computing Education," in J. McGrath Cohoon and William Aspray, eds., *Women and Information Technology: Research on Underrepresentation* (Cambridge: MIT Press, 2006), pp. 137–180; Mara H. Wasburn and Susan G. Miller, "Still a Chilly Climate for Women Students in Technology: A Case Study," in Mary Frank Fox, Deborah G. Johnson, and Sue V. Rosser, eds., *Women, Gender, and Technology* (Urbana: University of Illinois Press, 2006), pp. 60–79.

# Constructing Gender and Technology in Advertising Images

## Feminine and Masculine Computer Parts

**9**

ARISTOTLE TYMPAS, HARA KONSTA, THEODORE LEKKAS, AND SERKAN KARAS

It is commonly assumed that the computer is somehow masculine, the product of a highly masculine subculture of computing, and that consequently the computer excludes women. This assumption prevails in existing gender studies of computer advertisements. As a result, inquiries into the gender–computing relationship tend to focus on the aspects of computing work and education from which women are excluded. In this chapter, we adopt a somewhat contrarian viewpoint. We try to show that the computer is not uniformly masculine since it contains certain components that are strongly linked to feminine images and presumed feminine traits. At the same time, we maintain, women are not so much excluded from computing; they are included in computing but through a specific gender-stereotyped manner. As we show through an extensive analysis of 1500 computing advertisements, there is a dramatic overrepresentation of women shown working at the keyboard-input and the printer-output parts of the computer. We believe that these advertising images have been consequential in constructing the public image of the computer and in shaping, or at least reinforcing, gender-specific relationships to the computer.

By focusing on the links between computing education and computing work, we can understand how exactly women are included in computing. For example, during the mainframe era, women in the Greek banking sector as elsewhere ended up in disproportionately large numbers at office positions doing the immense job of routine data entry—even when they had computing educations equivalent to men. Senior and junior managers, conservative and progressive union representatives, and the women themselves found it "natural" that men would design computer configurations and avoid routine office computing. This division of computing labor inevitably reproduced a salary gap between men and women (see Chapter 4 in this volume). Notably, this gap was formed despite remarkably similar male–female educational backgrounds. After all, before the 1980s, there was no university computing education in Greece [1].

The feminine–masculine gender difference in computing work persisted through the emergence of formal university computing education in Greece. Maria Karamesini collected comprehensive statistics on university graduates, including 499 men and 176 women who graduated with an informatics-related science or engineering degree between 1998 and 2000. The employment of those graduates has been equally high for men and women, 88% for both. Similarly full-time employment has been almost the same for men (97%) and women (94%). A somewhat higher percentage of women than men (96% vs. 82%) found permanent as compared to temporary work [2]. From a quantitative perspective, women are clearly included in computing work just as frequently as men.

But there are important differences in the computing work of men and women. In this Greek sample the percentage of men in manufacturing (3.5%), construction (3.3%), transportation, communication, and related industries (9.8%) is about double that of women (1.1%, 1.7%, and 5.1%, respectively). Men are dominant in real estate, business, and entrepreneurial activities (39% vs. 25%). By comparison, women are more prevalent in the lower wage service sector, where the percentages of women who found work in the financial (4.6%) and state institutions office-type environment (13.1%) are double that of men (2.5% and 6.1%, respectively). Very likely, a female Greek computer science graduate could end up keyboarding and printing in an office. Her only practical alternative would be to teach in secondary or primary education, following a typically feminine work path. Indeed, the percentage of women in secondary education (45%) is almost double that of men (26%). In fact, nearly half of all women computer graduates work as teachers. By contrast, the percentage of women who at minimum tried a career in computer-related engineering is around one-third that for men (13.9% vs. 32.2%).

Male informatics graduates in this sample hold executive positions at more than double the rate for women (3.6% vs. 1.7%). Only a tiny percentage of Greek women graduates have been self-employed (1.6% vs. 11.4% for men). Far more women work in the safer, but lower-paying public sector office and teaching jobs than men (63% vs. 41%). These differentials, not surprisingly, result in considerable salary disparities: the majority of men (63.7%) made more than 1100 euros per month, whereas the majority of women (57.2%) made less than this amount. At the lower end of the payscale, 6.2% of men made less than 900 euros, while 9.4% of women did so.

Women comprised around one-quarter (27%) of the Greek computer science and engineering 1998–2000 graduates. Informatics students at Greek universities 5 years later (2003–2004) included 13,513 males and 4491 females (again about 25%). (This percentage drops to about 14% in the population of doctoral students, where there were only 222 women and 1382 men.) These figures actually compare well to computer science departments in the United States and in several European Union countries, even ones ranking higher than Greece in the United Nations Gender-Related Development Index. How can a country ranking lower in a gender-equity index have a comparable, if not higher, percentage of women computer science students than a country that ranks higher in the gender index? We meet extreme versions of this paradoxical phenomenon in several other countries: Malaysia (ranked #58) and Turkey (#79) seem to be doing substantially better than Greece (#24) or the United States (#16) in the measures of women in university computing education [3,4].

There are an unusually large number of women in Malaysian computer science departments—over 50% in some cases— but the results fall far short of a "cyberfeminist utopia" [3]. Malaysian women choose computer science as an entrance into traditional office work, not as an escape from it. It seems that the much-anticipated "coming gender revolution in science" in Malaysia, Turkey, or other countries as a result of university system expansion may be accompanied by "status decline" [5]. As in the Greek case, women can end up at lower paying computing jobs even after starting with the highest possible computing education. Relatively speaking, in these countries the effect of gender becomes more visible *after* a top computing education; in a country such as the United States, *before* it.

Greece is actually a middle case. In Malaysia, women desire university computing education to make it to the office [3]. In the United States, women end up in low-paying office jobs because of educational choices and tracking. For whatever reason, U.S. women are not attracted to computer science university education. Yet they are included in computing education, if we include the vast multitude of nonuniversity computing training paths followed by women [6]. Through different educational routes, women in the United States, Greece, and Malaysia (and many other countries as well) end up disproportionately in lower-status and lower-paid computing work at the keyboard and the printer. In the United States, the route is simply more direct from nonuniversity computer training to low-paying computing work. Regardless of the route followed, women all over the world continue to end up at the keyboard and the printer of the office computer, thereby reproducing in the era of the electronic computer a gender pattern that was introduced during the era of mechanical and electrical typewriters and calculators/tabulators (see Chapter 4 in this volume) [7].

In emphasizing women's lack of attraction to computing, we are emphasizing their active agency. (By contrast, studies focusing on "exclusion" imply their more or less passive response to coercion, which we find problematical.) They are agents, however, who act by being immersed in a certain imaginary order regarding what is natural when it comes to computing [8]. Indeed, study after study of the shrinking proportion of U.S. women studying computer science (see Chapter 2 in this volume) find that women themselves describe the situation as natural: university education in computing "just does not look like a natural choice for women" [9]. The phenomenon has been disheartening for policymakers. Given that women themselves seem to agree to limits, how can they escape their historical placement in computing work at the keyboard and the printer and the low salary that comes with it?

Their poor placement in computing work is even assumed to be "natural" by women who have received the best computing education. Had the Greek female informatics graduates been coerced in any way into office or educational work, they might have been unhappy. But they are not. The most telling finding about the 1998–2000 Greek computer science and engineering graduates is not that women end up at-low paying office and teaching computing jobs in disproportionate numbers. Rather, it is that female graduates believe that this outcome is natural. Despite earning substantially less than men graduates, women graduates overwhelmingly believe that their work matches their educational qualifications (87.0%). In fact, men hold a similar belief about their own work (87.5%). The percentage of women who believe that their job offers positive prospects for moving up the career ladder is only slightly lower than that of men (56% vs. 62%). Identical proportions of women and men are unhappy about their jobs (14.4%). Even more tellingly, more women are happy with their work than men (75% vs. 73%) [2]. A recent comparison of 1957 female and male engineering students who majored in computing at the University of Patras over a period of 21 years found similar results [10].

This chapter seeks to understand this gendered difference in computing work and salaries, to understand why a woman finds it "natural" to end up at the keyboard and the printer after undergoing university education in computing (e.g., Greece, Malaysia, and Turkey) or, alternately, after avoiding university education in computing altogether, such as in the United States and many other OECD countries with substantial male "overrepresentation" in computer science [11]. The 17 countries range widely in a calculated male "overrepresentation" rate; that is, the proportion of male computing students "above" the national university population of men. On the lower side is the United States (at 2.10), ranging upward through Austria, Belgium, Czech Republic, Denmark, Germany, and Slovak Republic (all above 5.0). Other countries with substantial male overrepresentation include Australia, Finland, France, Hungary, Netherlands, New Zealand, Norway, Spain, Switzerland, and the United Kingdom (between 2.1 and 5). In this study, the countries with the "least" male overrepresentation are Turkey (1.79), Sweden (1.95), South Korea (1.92), and Ireland (1.84); Greece and Malaysia were not included in the data.

We posit that there is an imagined difference, not a natural one. Specifically, we have sought to understand the construction of an imagined difference in the public image of computing. We examine how this image has been constructed in and through computing advertisements.

## METHODOLOGY

We believe that our method for examining the public image of computing formed through advertising is a means to better understand the placement of women in regards to information technology. Earlier studies sought to document the masculine image of the computer [12]. In effect, the existing literature on the gender–computing relationship in advertisements assumes that the computer is fully masculine. These studies focus on the way men and women compare in advertisements, either quantitatively (number of appearances) or qualitatively. Some of the qualitative themes have been how tall men are pictured next to women, how the eyes of women are directed to these taller men, how the arms of the taller men are protecting these women, or how old/prudent men are pictured next to young/careless women [13]. Quite logically, these studies look only at the male–female relationship in computing advertisements, not at the male–*computer*–female relationship. For this literature the computer is a closed or even absent black box. The process of the construction of computing images and practices—through the co-construction of computing and gender—receives no attention. In contrast, we are interested in *how* the computer *mediates* the male–female relationship—and in how this mediation interacts with the male–female relationship in order to construct both the computer and gender. As we see it, examining the co-construction of computing technology and the gender relationship requires an integration of perspectives from gender studies, labor studies, and the history of technology. Given that we look at advertisements, we also draw selectively on media studies, popular culture studies, and cultural studies more generally. Our interdisciplinary endeavor has benefited considerably by reading studies on the gender–computer relationship in computing advertisements (cited in Ref. 13).

In our research, we examined 1500 advertisements published in *Computer for All*, the longest-running Greek home computing journal. (We thank Konstantinos Rizopoulos, Dimitrios Kourouvakalis, and their colleagues at the Evgenides Institute Library for their help in accessing the issues of *Computer for All*.) Published monthly since 1983, this journal has been a prime medium for domesticating computing technology in Greece. Its columns reported innumerable comparative tests and responded to numerous issues raised by readers [14]. To survive in Greece, *Computer for All* had to balance between covering the amateur and the professional, the newcomer and the experienced expert, the hobbyist enthusiast and the profit-seeker. It had to be, simultaneously, a journal for scientific readers and casual readers. *Computer for All* translated articles from international magazines and also published articles written locally. Similarly, the advertisements drew on ones available internationally as well as ones produced nationally. In many of them we found products of international computer companies that were advertised through the mediation of their Greek representatives.

Home computing publications were rather new in 1983. To examine an earlier history of computing advertisements, Aspray and Beaver utilized trade journals from the advertising industry [15]. They found that between the 1950s and the 1970s the advertising image of the computer user changed dramatically, reflecting the computer's radical transformation from a room-size mathematical machine, installed in just a few places in the richest countries, to a desk-sized minicomputer used by tens of thousands around the world. This transformation has been aptly called an "unforeseen revolution" [16]. The post-1983 period that we focus on witnessed a different unforeseen revolution, as the computer evolved from an autonomous unit for word processing, game playing, and spreadsheet accounting into a multipurpose networked device [17].

Our study concludes in 2003 when the transition of the computer to a networked device for email and web browsing was well underway. The years after 2003 were also marked by the transition from the paper-based version of home computing journals to a hybrid print-electronic one. These electronic versions of recent years have become a different media genre. Home computing journals now look like a vast web portal that may be accessed at will, based on thematic or other criteria. This ongoing transformation is also affecting the structure, content, and context of computing advertisements. This transformation deserves its own study, which would have to address the a posteriori repositioning of advertisements in the various places of home computing journals' electronic version. Our study is limited to the print era of home computing journals.

Had we chosen to place our emphasis on the change in computing *technology*, we could easily show a pattern of rampant change being the defining characteristic in the history of computing technology—whether a technical history of computing based on changes in computer circuitry and software applications or a social history based on changes in the perceptions and uses of the computer. Looking at computing advertisements and focused on gender, we were led to a different emphasis. Our argument in this chapter points to continuity, not change. More accurately, it points to continuity over change. From a gender perspective, impressive technical change in computing technology has been coupled by equally impressive social and cultural continuity.

## MEN ON THE PHONE

One of the most persistent advertising themes has been the portrayal of men as being on the phone instead of working with the computer: talking rather than keyboarding. There are innumerable examples. In a 1993 advertisement of a DTK computer, the man was seated in front of the computer but talking on the phone [18]. The Greek soccer star Dimitris Saravakos posed in the same manner in a 1988 advertisement of Hantarex Vegas (represented in Greece by Seicon) [19]. Men talking on the phone can be found in advertisements of hardware components, which ranged from screens to modems; the same can be found in advertisements for software, ranging from general support by a software house to special-purpose software for stockmarket brokers [20]. In these advertisements, it is unclear whether men ever did any "work" on the computer itself.

When men were actually in some physical contact with the computer, they did so in order to click a mouse button rather than to work at the keyboard, to control the computer rather than to type. This is implied by the fact that they were using only one hand, while the other hand was holding the phone, reaching out to the desk corner where the phone was, or simply resting [21]. The 1984 advertisement of Apple's Lisa computer showed a man clicking on the computer and touching his head in a manner that implied thoughtfulness. He did not have to worry about doing much more because, as the text of the advertisement explained, "[t]he computer works just like you" [22].

In some advertisements, men did not use their hands at all. In the 1989 advertisement of Profex, which was selling Commodore, Amiga, Amstrad, and other personal computers, a man in his bathing suit used his feet to touch the screen while sitting on a comfortable chair, relaxing his one arm on the chair and holding a drink with the other. The accompanying text read: "Work by

Letting Them Work" [23]. In a similar 1985 advertisement for an IBM PC, through a Greek dealer, a man rested on a comfortable chair with his arms around his neck. A drawing of the computer unit was placed at the opposite corner of the advertisement [24]. In the 2000 Datamedia's wireless network advertisements we find a similar detachment. On the top half of the advertisement a man was relaxing with his arms around his neck. In the bottom half there was a set of wireless network devices, hierarchically placed, with the phone on the top [25].

Men were consistently portrayed to be relaxed and comfortable around computers. They had a cup of coffee, a pair of glasses, or an open book on their desk [26]. They had plenty of space to move freely. This was frequently indicated by the detachment of the computer desk from an enclosed office space—an office with visible walls. The man–computer–desk ensemble was often liberated from the boundaries of a traditional work place [27]. In the 1989 advertisement of Tobasi Company, the man, the computer, and the peripherals were not placed in an office at all but on the top of a mountain [28].

We have so far introduced advertisements that showed only men and computers. Before we turn to advertisements including women, we may inquire why men were so often on the phone. Important clues can be found in a set of advertisements that showed an office space with men on the phone juxtaposed with a separate space where women were waiting. In the lower half of a Philips PC advertisement from 1988, there was a desk with a man who sat comfortably, talked on the phone, and didn't even look at the computer screen. This part of the advertisement was about the Philips home PC, described as the "perfect personal computer." On the upper half another Philips PC was the "perfect professional computer." The man shown in this part of the advertisement was also on the phone and also not looking at the computer. A woman was shown walking up a staircase—from some place below—to arrive at the man's space (Fig. 9.1) [29].

A Microsoft Office version for Greek users from 1998 showed the same juxtaposition of men and women. Men on the phone were near a computer while women at some separate place waited for their call. In this advertisement, we see only the shadows of the women, separated from the men by a glass window [30]. In a 1985 advertisement for a Televideo Systems minicomputer, a drawing depicted several persons in an abstract open-space office. The leading person, a man, talked on the phone and held a pen. He did not look straight at the screen. Incredibly, there was no keyboard whatsoever on his desk. By contrast, the woman placed in a row behind him had output and input equipment on her desk [31].

Phones rarely appear in advertisements showing computers, men, and women together in a closed-space environment, near each other physically. Perhaps no phone was needed because men were directly dictating their instructions to women. Here and in other cases, images of gender and computers were shaped by what was excluded and not only by what was included. The phone was also absent from settings with only women or only men. The suggestion was that the phone was not needed for communication solely between men or between women. In computing advertisements, at least, the phone was a sort of Dictaphone through which men gave orders to women.

Figure 9.1. Woman ascending to the man's space. (Source: *Computer for All*, Vol. 61 (1988): 12.)

## THE KEYBOARD VERSUS THE MOUSE

If placing both hands on the top of a rectangular keyboard seemed a forbidden act for men, gripping a round mouse was positively recommended. Unlike typing on the keyboard, which signified routine laboring, clicking on the mouse could signify something that might be equivalent to piloting a sailboat, governing in the open space rather than working in a closed room. We see this clearly in a 2001 advertisement for the Logitech cordless mouse, which showed a male sailor holding the boat's steering wheel with his left hand and the mouse with his right (Fig. 9.2) [32]. The analogy between the two was in a way foreshadowed by a 1991 Acer advertisement that juxtaposed a picture of a man sailing and a second picture of a computer [33]. A 1992 advertisement showed a man with a Linotype desktop publishing computer. He was sitting in an open-space desk that was equipped with the typical signs of comfort (e.g., a cup of coffee).

Figure 9.2. Mobile man with computer mouse. (Source: *Computer for All*, Vol. 203 (2001): 157.)

He was not touching the keyboard but his right hand was grasping the mouse while his left simply rested on the desk [34].

In sharp contrast to men, women were always shown facing the computer screen directly and most often typing with both hands. They were crammed into tight, bounded spaces in enclosed offices. In the 1985 advertisement of the Greek hotel management system Infoplan, a woman concentrated at her work, looking directly at the computer screen while keyboarding data. A Charlie Chaplin figure was pointing to a similar computer placed on a desk

Figure 9.3. Chaplin makes routine assembly-line work into "fun." (Source: *Computer for All*, Vol. 31 (1985): back cover.)

a few meters away from her (Fig. 9.3) [35]. Infamous in Greece for his protest against routine assembly line work in *Modern Times* (1936), Charlie Chaplin was added to several Greek computing advertisements to promote the idea of the computer being something "fun" to work with. But fun was to take place at very different desk settings for men and women. A poster of Charlie Chaplin decorated the wall in the 1991 advertisement of Axis, the Greek representative of Copam computer peripherals. The man was again not touching the keyboard. He was rather relaxing by resting his legs on the desk. He was not looking straight at the computer. The way he held his pen and the placement of a globe and compass next to the computer added to a feeling of relaxation, which the Charlie Chaplin wall poster reinforced [36].

The men–mouse versus women–keyboard associations remained a standard advertising trope into the Internet age. In the four-picture set used in the

2001 advertisement for the Internet service provider Groovy Net, a woman in the second picture was leaning toward the keyboard and typing, while a man in the fourth picture was only holding a phone. No other artifacts were shown in either picture. In the other two pictures only teenagers were shown, in both cases boys. The exclusion of girls is obviously suggestive. But we find it even more suggestive that the boys were not actually typing on the keyboard, even though there were keyboards in front of them [37]. It was as if the screen itself was enough!

The 1985 Hotel Plan advertisement typified an advertising image of women who were keyboarding, concentrating on the screen, sitting in closed-office settings, and having limited space available to them. There were many variations. The 1986 IMC-Prince IBM clone advertisement, addressed to those interested in office mechanization, featured a stereotypically small Asian woman. The woman–computer combination was introduced as "The Little Bigshot." As was customary in advertising images of female computer desks, flowers were shown [38]. Flowers were something like the feminine equivalent of the man's cup of coffee. In some advertisements an instruction book was added on the woman's desk, presumably so the woman could review instructions or copy data from it. When men were shown to read something, usually an engineering or financial graph, they had their legs crossed and they looked obviously relaxed. The 1985 Alpha Micro PC advertisement for an upgrade board offers a classic example [39].

In men–computer–women configurations, the women were usually seated while the men were standing above them. The 1983 advertisement of the Greek representative of the DRS-20 ICL computer systems was rather typical [40]. We find other early examples in the 1984 advertisement of an authorized dealer of Apple's Lisa, in the 1985 advertisement of Corona's representative Delmar Ltd., and in a 1989 Macintosh advertisement [41]. The 1985 Casio advertisement featured a slight variation: a standing woman stood as a relay between a standing man and a keyboarding woman [42]. The 1985 advertisement for the Lotus SmartSuite software representative in Greece (Byte Computer) showed another variation: a group of men, one mediating woman, and one woman in front of the computer [43].

Uses of the computer beyond the office environment were featured in the 1988 advertisement of an assist arm computer accessory by the Greek representative of Liarco and the 1997 advertisement of SONY Trinitron screens [44]. In both advertisements the man and the woman were sitting, either next to each other (1997) or against each other (1988), in which case the keyboard was placed in front of the woman. The man leaning against her could obviously not type on the keyboard. In the 1997 advertisement the woman had both hands on the keyboard while the man had one hand in between them. Yet, he too could not type because he looked at her, not the screen.

Placing women in closed offices, giving them little space to move, locating them in lower positions, sitting rather than standing, looking straight at the screen while having their hands on the keyboard—all these implied that women were doing the routine work of a secretary or data-entry clerk. This interpretation can be confirmed by considering an important exception to this rule. When the user of the computer was clearly a high-status creator (e.g., a scientist or engineer), the person sitting in front of the computer was nearly always a man [45]. Some advertisements made explicit reference to automatic design, like the OrCAD advertisement by the Greek representative (micro-tec) [46]. Here, the man was seated in front of the computer and the computer screen was full of technical and economic diagrams and drawings. In striking contrast, when women faced the computer, the screen contained lines of typed text or data.

The computer screen might be seen as a mirror of the user. When it was placed in secretarial environments a man would have to avoid this (secretarial) mirror. He could recognize himself in it only if he was a creator-designer. Given the keyboard–female versus phone–male contrast, the gendered advertisements of the computer considered so far clearly overlap with the manual-versus-mental division of computing labor. This is an obvious point. The manual–female computing connection contained an extreme variant in which only a human finger was shown. We find this pattern from early on—when an input key was touched by such finger—through more recently with touch-screens [47]. Signs like jewelry and the red-painted fingernails left no doubt this was a feminine job.

We have so far considered advertisements depicting various forms of productive computing work. To conclude this section, we may also consider images of computing reproduction, that is, computing education. Advertisements of Greek computer training schools, aiming at those lacking university educa-tion, consistently showed female students with keyboards. The male teacher was usually standing. Adult men were rarely shown to be taught by women. Only boys were regularly shown sitting while their female teachers were stand-ing, at a school or at home (in which case the teaching was done, stereotypi-cally, by the mother). The advertisements for Constantinou Computer Studies in 1985 and for Control Data Greece in 1986 typify this pattern [48].

Several of the themes identified in office environments were also present in educational advertisements. In a 1989 advertisement for Control Data Greece, a man sat next to a woman and, while she keyboarded, he read [49]. The "mediating woman" theme also appeared in the 1985 advertisement for the Data Rank Corporation [50]. When both the man and the woman were students, as in the 1991 advertisement of the Corelco training schools, the woman clearly did the keyboarding work [51]. In the 1985 advertisement of General Systems, which showed a boy and a girl learning at home with their mother, the girl looked at the computer screen while the boy held the computer manual [52].

Adult male students were rarely shown, but when they were the adver-tisement was about training higher-level computing technicians or program-mers. In 1984 a training school called Advanced Computer Education featured only male students—and only training in programming [53]. In a subsequent advertisement for the same school, secretarial training was also advertised and then women were shown [54]. A comparison of these two advertisements further shows a difference between the hardware used to train men as compared with the hardware used to train women. When the students were men, the computers shown were larger and varied, and the space was less structured, resembling an artisan workshop. By contrast, women were trained in a more uniform educational and orderly environment, through the use of generic PCs.

# THE PRINTER VERSUS THE HARD DRIVE

At the printer-output end of computing, we also find a dramatic overrepresentation of women. A 1997 Hewlett-Packard (HP) advertisement showed a robot-servant that carried the printer output to a man who was sitting comfortably in an open-space office, holding a pen, and with a nearby telephone. The new HP printer was advertised as "the most disciplined servant" this man ever had [55]. But who did this serving in the absence of such robots? A 1997 advertisement for OKI printers, with three men standing around one woman sitting in front of the computer, left no doubt as to who was to execute the order: "OK! PRINT IT" [56]. An alternative featured a woman standing in front of the printer while the men sat around. We find an example in the 1986 advertisement of Televideo Systems, represented in Greece by Delta Computer Systems (Fig. 9.4) [57]. There was maximum distance between men and printers. Men were in contact only with the printer output; they clearly did not work with the printer. In a 1999 advertisement of the Greek representative of Lexmark, a comfortably sitting man was looking at a printout. The printer itself was placed in the lower part of the page, outside the picture that showed the man [58].

For a suggestive image of the gendered division of computing labor that was promoted by the placement of women and printers, we can look at the advertisement on the cover of the August 1984 issue of *Computer for All*. The cover image was actually an advertisement of the journal's own contents. To promote the introduction of computers in Greek hotels—the special theme of this issue—a picture of a hotel reception was chosen for the cover. The hotel reception desk divided the enclosed space of the female receptionist and the more open space of the male guest. The woman was holding the printer output, preparing to give it to the man [59]. In many advertisements only the printer and a woman were shown. A typical early advertisement was that of Technoland in 1987 [60]. In a series of 1998 Canon advertisements, we see an extreme instance. The new Canon printers were introduced as "explosive" by young women who actually held explosives in their hands, or in their mouth, while posing seductively [61].

Such explicitly sexual themes were quite common in printer advertisements. In a 1997 advertisement of Epson's representative in Greece, a young woman placed amidst a sea of printers provocatively showed her tongue. The printer's resolution was tattooed on her arm. Showing her tongue appeared to be equivalent to paper issuing from a printer [62]. In a 2000 advertisement by Intersys, a Canon representative in Greece, a man and a woman were lying in their bed. He was reading a newspaper that covered his face. The setting implied a man who had lost sexual interest in his wife. The new Canon color printer, placed at the lower right of the advertisement, was to change their situation. In the real bed the woman was shown only in black and white. By contrast, her image coming out of the printer was in bright color. It showed her upper body in a seminude position and alluring pose. The text explained that the husband now could have "everything … at home too" [63].

The color–woman–printer association featured several stereotypic variants. In a 1993 Hewlett-Packard advertisement, an attractive woman with green eyes watched her own face coming out of a color printer. The face of the woman

# με ἕναν από τους
# 25 COMPUTERS της

## TeleVideo

ΓΕΝΙΚΟΙ ΑΝΤΙΠΡΟΣΩΠΟΙ
### *Delta Computer Systems*

Figure 9.4. Women get the order to "print it." (Source: *Computer for All*, Vol. 33 (1986): 147.)

and the printed page were mirror images, with the beauty of the one transferring to the other. The text promoted the new printer as a means to make the profile of a business more attractive [64]. A 1990 drawing of a woman who cried because she didn't know that "a MITA laser printer could have saved him!!!" offered one emotional situation, while a 1992 advertisement for STAR's representative Infoquest depicted a calm woman dreaming next to the printer [65]. All these images linked the female–printer ensemble to emotional or sexual situations, and utilized rather crude gender stereotypes to do so.

When men were connected to printers in a manner similar to that of women, they were uniformly portrayed as silly looking, boyish, and nonserious, as if they were not real men. Bright-colored or loose baggy clothes indicated their ambiguous place. We find typical variants of this theme in the 1986–1987 Star printer advertisements by info-quest, in the 1992 advertisement of Microtek TrueLaser, and in the 1996 advertisement of Tally printers. A 1993 Canon advertisement showed a man dressed in bright colors and chained on a chair [66]. A 1999 advertisement for Kyocera printers showed a seminaked man— only his genitals and head were covered—who was cursing his printer problems. The advertisement indicated that he lost his clothes because he paid too much for the printer ink and paper. His body was not in the least athletic, but typical of a middle-age businessman. (The owner-possessor of the printer was always shown to be a man [67].)

In contrast to printers, advertisements for hard drives featured only serious looking men. "There is only one way to construct a hard drive: my way," we read in a 1990 advertisement for Kalok hard drives. It showed a mature hard-drive designer-creator sitting in a director's chair (Fig. 9.5). Endurance was singled out as a key technical feature of this hard drive [68]. In the 1997 advertisement of Western Digital hard drives, also showing only a man and a hard drive, the accompanying text stressed professionalism in general [69]. A Bull advertisement of the same year linked the strength of the server to a team of U.S. football male players [70]. Quite unlike the colorful male clowns sometimes associated with printers, only ruthlessly professional males were associated with hard drives.

## WOMEN ON THE SCREEN

In addition to connecting female hands to the keyboard, advertisements connected female faces to the computer screen. In a 2001 Hitachi computer monitor advertisement, the woman and the screen were explicitly presented as mirror images. A picture of a woman who was sending a kiss, placed in a framework in the shape of a heart, was put next to the computer screen. The computer screen was a desirable substitute for the here-today-gone-tomorrow woman: "At least the screen will still be here after five years," reads the text [71]. A 1987 advertisement for Amstrad computers showed a woman on the monochrome screen. The main line read: "Challenge to compare" [72]. Faces of Asian women featured in advertisements of the Datamicro monochrome screen computers in 1990 (Figure 9.6) and of ActionTec colored camera cards in 1999 [73]. Closer to the present, we find computer screens frequently advertised independently from computer systems. These advertisements often showed a satisfied female face on the screen, such as the 2003 CTX computer screen [74].

When the advertisement showed a computer screen that was embraced by a woman (instead of the woman being shown on the screen), there were often symbols of feminine friendliness on the screen. In the 1985 advertisement series by Busisoft, women who were dressed in red embraced the computer screen while the screen showed a feminine red heart [75]. In an advertisement (also in 1985) of a Greek computer supply store, a woman embracing a computer screen included the drawing of a smile [76]. By contrast, when men

Υπάρχει μόνο ένας τρόπος, για να κατασκευάσεις ένα σκληρό δίσκο: ο δικός μου!

Πριν χρόνια οι βιομηχανίες σκληρών δίσκων πήραν τα σχέδια που υπήρχαν για τους δίσκους των 14'' και προσπάθησαν να τα εφαρμόσουν στα μοντέλα των 3.5''. Το αποτέλεσμα ήταν ένας ανεπαρκής και αναξιόπιστος σκληρός δίσκος.

**Έτσι άρχισα από μηδενική βάση να κατασκευάζω τον τέλειο δίσκο**

Οι σκληροί δίσκοι KALOK 3.5'', είναι ανθεκτικοί γιατί έχουν, κατά 56%, λιγότερα εξαρτήματα. Αυτό τους κάνει τους πιο αξιόπιστους δίσκους στην αγορά, με φθορά μικρότερη του 0.5%.

**Εκτός του ότι είναι πιο αξιόπιστοι, κοστίζουν και λιγότερο.**

Ήταν ευκολότερο να κατασκευαστούν δίσκοι σύμφωνα με τα δικά μου σχέδια. Κι αφού για μας το κόστος κατασκευής ήταν χαμηλό, χαμηλό είναι και το κόστος αγοράς.

**Τώρα μπορείτε να διαλέξετε!**

Οι σκληροί δίσκοι KALOK των 3.5'' και των 20, 30, 40 και 80 MB φορτώνονται και εξάγονται σε μεγάλες ποσότητες.

**Σας εγγυώμαι, πως όταν δοκιμάσετε ένα KALOK, που έχει κατασκευαστεί με τον δικό μου τρόπο, ποτέ δεν θα γυρίσετε πίσω.**

Figure 9.5. Male computer designer in the director's chair. (Source: *Computer for All*, Vol. 84 (1990): 183.)

appeared in monitor advertisements, the image on the screen inevitably showed technical or business drawings. In a 1995 advertisement of Philips monitors, a technical design of a car was shown on the screen while the shadow of a thinking man was placed behind [77]. In 1999 Philips advertisements for flat-screen monitors, a man was sitting on a desk that had screens with business-related tables and charts [78]. In the 1992 advertisement of Taxan high-definition monitors, a martial arts Asian fighter was standing above a computer screen filled with business charts [79]. In the rare advertisement that showed a male face actually on the computer screen, it was that of a teacher. For example, the man

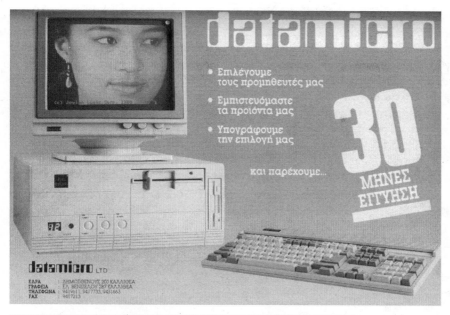

Figure 9.6. Connecting female faces to the computer screen. (Source: *Computer for All*, Vol. 85 (1990): 17.)

pictured in the 1995 series of advertisements of Eriqson Soft Education was identified as one of the best computer trainers in Greece. The trainee, who was holding the educational material outside the monitor, was a woman [80].

We mentioned earlier the frequent replacement of the keyboarding woman by her fingers. There was a similar replacement on the computer screen, with the female eye substituting for the full female face. This type of replacement became more frequent in recent years with the availability of computer screens sold independently, of computer cameras and scanners, and of imaging software. The Pinnacle Systems 2002 advertisement is representative of imaging processing techniques [81]. A Panasonic monitor advertisement of 1996 is a typical scanner advertisement [82]. In the case of scanner advertisements the eye was clearly the focus. Here, often, glasses were added on the female eye in advertisements, suggesting perhaps the glass screen in the device itself as well as the (female) labor in using the scanner. A 1998 Agfa advertisement showed a woman alongside pictures of scanners and related apparatus. She was positioned in a manner that put her eyes, with glasses lowered, in the center of the advertisement [83].

## CONCLUSION

In these advertised images of the computer, the screen often shows an image of a female eye or a whole female face. This is a mirror image of the female eye that looks straight at the screen while using the keyboard. In computing advertisements, it is quite striking that men do not look at this feminine part of the computer (screen). The construction of gender in the advertised image of the computer comes full circle with the image of men talking on the phone when sitting near the computer. Men are not working with the computer; they are in control of computing work. It is the females who do the computing work. Men are on the phone, whereas women are on the screen.

This strongly gender-specific pattern was not followed when an engineer or a manager was shown: only then the image on the computer screen was changed from a female eye or face (or the lines of typed-in figures or text) to a financial or engineering chart. Similarly, the pattern of showing the women sitting and keyboarding and the men standing and dictating—or using a phone to dictate—was broken only when the sitting male was a student of a standing female teacher. In this case women were depicted as providing education to boys and only rarely to adult men.

For men, holding the computer mouse was seemingly the only alternative to holding the phone. The mouse is a masculine input-equivalent of the feminine keyboard. The image of the computer–gender relationships in advertisements runs full circle. The hard drive and the invisible masculine mind are juxtaposed with the printer and the disclosed feminine body. Encased as it is, the computer part that mediates between input and output, that is, the part that contains the hard drive, makes an invisible connection to the keyboard-printing work of women. In computing advertisements and, in reality, it is men who design this part.

Noticeably, unlike the digitally restricted motions of the keyboard and printer, the phone and the mouse can be moved freely without constraint. This advertising arrangement places women closer to the standardized, routinized, and digital side of computing, the side that is already analyzed and awaits passive computation. Men are placed at what has always been the expensive side, that of the analog computing required to actively produce the computing analysis (the analogy between the computed and the computable). This follows a historically deep pattern of imaging men as "analysts" and women as "computers" (also called "computors") [84].

In this chapter, we have interpreted images in computer advertisements from a perspective that connects gender construction to the way men and women have been related in advertising images as well as to the way the computer mediated in this relationship. As a closing example, we may take a popular 1996 advertisement for the Computer Trade Center that featured the top model and gymnast Eleni Petroulaki. Wearing a gymnast suit that looked more like a bathing suit, Petroulaki was measuring the size of a computer's central processing unit. "Size is decisive," she cautioned in the text of the advertisement, "Measure your needs properly." On the lower right of this advertisement Petroulaki's face was shown in the screen (Fig. 9.7) [85].

Gender was explicitly imported into this advertisement through the masculine measure that Petroulaki held as well as her stereotypically feminine dressing. In this chapter, we have been interested in an implicit construction of gender, which takes into account what the model held and wore but moves on to relate it to the image of the computer. These images construct the computer as having two different sides. The one part is constructed through the screen image of the face of the female model. This would be the mirror image of the model if she were to look at it from the distance of a keyboarding user. Sitting

Figure 9.7. "Size is decisive" advises the model-gymnast. (Source: *Computer for All*, Vol. 151 (1996): 199.)

at the keyboard and looking at the computer would be natural to the model. We know it because her face shines in the mirror image. Her inclusion in this part of the computer is, indeed, natural. By contrast, the other part of the computer is constructed through her exclusion, which likewise might appear "natural." The encasement excludes her body from this part of the computer, just as the screen includes her image in the other part of the computer. The keyboard–screen part is constructed in analogy to her. The other part is constructed by her measurement, by her digitalization. In turn, this constructs the one computer part as feminine (inclusion of the female model) and the other as masculine (exclusion of the female model). In this way, the computer constructs gender.

# REFERENCES

**1.** Maria Stratigaki, *Gender, Labour, Technology* (Athens: Politis, 1996) [in Greek].

**2.** Maria Karamesini, *The Placement of University Graduates in the Job Market: Greek Graduates of 1998–2000.* (Athens: Dionikos, 2008), pp. 302–303 [in Greek].

**3.** For Malaysia, see Vivian Anette Lagesen, "A Cyberfeminist Utopia?" *Science, Technology and Human Values*, Vol. 33, No. 1 (2008): 5–27.

**4.** For Turkey, see Maria Charles and Karen Bradley, "A Matter of Degrees Female Underrepresentation in Computer Science Programs Cross-Nationally" in J. McGrath Cohoon and William Aspray, eds. *Women and Information Technology: Research on Underrepresentation* (Cambridge: MIT Press, 2006), pp. 183–203.

**5.** Henry Etzkowitz, Stefan Fuchs, Namrata Gupta, Carol Kemelgor, and Marina Ranga, "The Coming Gender Revolution in Science," in Edward J. Hackett, Olga Amsterdamska, Michael Lynch, and Judy Wajcman, eds., *Handbook of Science and Technology Studies*, 3rd edition (Cambridge: MIT Press, 2008), pp. 412–413.

**6.** For examples, see, respectively, Maria Charles and Karen Bradley "A Matter of Degrees: Female Underrepresentation in Computer Science Programs Cross-Nationally," and Karen Chapple, "Foot in the Door, Mouse in Hand: Low-Income Women, Short-Term Job Training Programs, and IT Careers," in J. McGrath Cohoon and William Aspray, eds., *Women and Information Technology: Research on Underrepresentation* (Cambridge: MIT Press, 2006), pp. 183–203 and 439–470.

**7.** For aspects of this earlier history, see also Margery W. Davies, *Woman's Place Is at the Typewriter: Office Work and Office Workers, 1870–1930* (Philadelphia: Temple University Press, 1984); Sharon Strom, *Beyond the Typewriter: Gender, Class, and the Origins of Modern American Office Work, 1900–1930* (Urbana: University of Illinois Press, 1994); Francisca de Haan, *Gender and the Politics of Office Work in the Netherlands, 1860–1940* (Amsterdam: Amsterdam University Press, 1998); and David Alan Grier, *When Computers Were Human* (Princeton, NJ: Princeton University Press, 2005). Time-honored cultural assumptions about the manual dexterity of women as naturally appropriate to routine machine work found expression in women doing the data entry.

For the mechanization of work based on gendered assumptions, see Katherine Stubbs, "Mechanizing the Female," *Differences*, Vol. 7, No. 3 (1995): 141–164.

**8.** On the ideology as the prerequisite of agency within a certain political economy of work, see Warren Montag, *Louis Althusser* (London: Palgrave-Macmillan, 2003).

**9.** For key literature, see Henry Etzkowitz, Carol Kemelgor, and Brian Uzzi, *Athena Unbound: The Advancement of Women in Science and Technology* (Cambridge: Cambridge University Press, 2000); Jane Margolis and Allan Fisher, *Unlocking the Clubhouse: Women in Computing* (Cambridge: MIT Press, 2002); Janet Abbate, "Women and Gender in the History of Computing," *IEEE Annals of the History of Computing*, Vol. 25, No. 4 (2003): 4–8.

**10.** Aristidis Ilias and Maria Kordaki, "Undergraduate Studies in Computer Science and Engineering," *ACM SIGSCE Bulletin*, Vol. 38, No. 2 (2006): 81–85.

**11.** See Maria Charles and Karen Bradley, "A Matter of Degrees: Female Underrepresentation in Computer Science Programs Cross-Nationally," in J. McGrath Cohoon and William Aspray, eds., *Women and Information Technology: Research on Underrepresentation* (Cambridge: MIT Press, 2006), p. 190.

**12.** See, for example, the review in Lecia J. Barker and William Aspray, "The State of Research on Girls and IT," in J. McGrath Cohoon and William Aspray, eds., *Women and Information Technology: Research on Underrepresentation* (Cambridge: MIT Press, 2006), pp. 38–42.

**13.** The studies we have benefited from include the following: Mary Catherine Ware and Mary Frances Stuck, "Sex Role Messages Vis-à-Vis Microcomputer Use: A Look at the Pictures," *Sex Roles*, Vol. 13, Nos. 3–4 (1985): 205–214; William Aspray and Donald B. Beaver, "Marketing the Monster: Advertising Computer Technology," *Annals of the History of Computing*, Vol. 8, No. 2 (1986): 127–143; Donna J. Haraway, *Simians, Cyborgs and Women: The Reinvention of Nature* (New York: Routledge, 1991); Judith A. Wiles, Charles R. Wiles, and Anders Tjernlund, "A Comparison of Gender Role Portrayals in Magazine Advertising: The Netherlands, Sweden and the

USA," *European Journal of Marketing*, Vol. 29, No. 11 (1995): 35–49; Merete Lie, "Gender in the Image of Technology," in Merete Lie and Knut H. Sørensen, eds., *Making Technology Our Own? Domesticating Technology into Everyday Life* (Oslo: Scandinavian University Press, 1996), pp. 201–223; Juris Dilevko and Roma M. Harris, "Information Technology and Social Relations: Portrayals of Gender Roles in High Tech Product Advetisements," *Journal of the American Society of Information Science*, Vol. 48, No. 8 (1997): 718–727; Nancy Nelson Knupfer, K.M. Kramer, and D. Pryor, "Gender Equity On-line: Messages Portrayed with and About the New Technologies," in Robert E. Griffin, J. Mark Hunter, Carole B. Schiffman, and William J. Gibbs, eds., *Vision Quest: Journeys Toward Visual Literacy* (Pittsburgh: Omni Press, 1997), pp. 391–399; Eva Turner and Fiona Hovenden, "How Are We Seen? Images of Women in Computing Advertisements," in Rachel Lander and Alison Adam, eds., *Women in Computing* (Wiltshire: Cromwell Press, 1977), pp. 60–71; Kevin M. Kramer and Nancy Nelson Knupfer, "Gender Equity in Advertising on the World Wide Web: Can It Be Found?" in *Proceedings of Selected Research and Development Presentation at the 1997 National Convention of the Association of Educational Communications and Technology* (14–18 February 1997): 169–180; Nancy Nelson Knupfer, "Gender Divisions Across Technology Advertisements and the WWW: Implications for Educational Equity," *Theory into Practice*, Vol. 37, No. 1 (1998): 54–63; Zoe Sofia, "The Mythic Machine: Gendered Irrationalities in Computer Culture," in Hank Bromley and Michael W. Apple, eds., *Education, Technology, Power: Educational Computing as a Social Practice* (Albany: State University of New York Press, 1998), pp. 29–51; John C. Marshall and Susan Bannon, "Race and Sex Equity in Computer Advertising." *Journal of Research on Computing in Education*, Vol. 21, No. 1 (1988): 15–27; Candace White and Katherine N. Kinnick, "One Click Forward and Two Clicks Back: Portrayal of Women Using Computers in Television Commercials," *Women's Studies in Communication*, Vol. 23, No. 3 (Fall 2000): 392–412; Katherine Kinnick, Candace White, and Kadesha Washington, "Racial Representation of Computer Users in Prime-Time Advertising," *Race, Gender and Class*, Vol. 8, No. 4 (2001): 96–114; N.A. Misu, "The Cultural Construction of the Computer as a Masculine Technology: An Analysis of Computer Advertisements in Korea," *Asian Journal of Women's Studies*, Vol. 7, No. 3 (2001): 93–114; Lori D. Wolin, "Gender Issues in Advertising: An Oversight Synthesis of Research, 1970–2002," *Journal of Advertising Research*, Vol. 43, No. 1 (March 2003): 111–129; Eva Gustavsson and Barbara Czarniawska, "Web Woman: The Online Construction of Corporate and Gender Images," *Organization*, Vol. 11, No. 5 (2004): 651–670; Nicola Döring and Sandra Pöschl, "Images of Men and Women in Mobile Phone Advertisements: A Content Analysis of Advertisements for Mobile Communication Systems in Selected Popular Magazines," *Sex Roles*, Vol. 55 (2006): 173–185; Nicola F. Johnson, Leonie Rowan, and Julianne Lynch, "Construction of Gender in Computer Magazine Advertisements: Confronting the Literature," *Studies in Media and Information Literacy Education*, Vol. 6, No. 1 (2006): unpaged (electronic journal), available at **www.utpjournals.com/simile/simile.html**; and Doris U. Bolliger, "Perceived Gender Based Stereotypes in Educational Technology Advertisements," *Tech Trends*, Vol. 52, No. 3 (2008): 46–52. For woman–machine representations, see Julie Wosk, *Women and the Machine: Representations from the Spinning Wheel to the Electronic Age* (Baltimore: Johns Hopkins University Press, 2001).

**14.** For how home technology journals ushered in the localization-domestication of technology, we recommend the essays by Joseph C. Corn, Carroll Purcell, and Susan Douglas in John L. Wright, ed., *Possible Dreams: Enthusiasm for Technology in America* (Dearborn, MI: Henry Ford Museum and Greenfield Village, 1992).

**15.** William Aspray and Donald B. Beaver, "Marketing the Monster: Advertising Computer Technology," *Annals of the History of Computing*, Vol. 8, No. 2 (1986): 127–143.

**16.** Paul E. Ceruzzi, "An Unforeseen Revolution," in Joe Corn, ed., *Imagining Tomorrow: History, Technology, and the American Future* (Cambridge: MIT Press, 1986), pp. 188–201.

**17.** For histories of this open-ended transformation, see Leslie Haddon, "Researching Gender and Home Computers," in Knut Sørensen and Anne-Jorun Berg, eds., *Technology and Everyday Life: Trajectories and Transformations* (Oslo: Norwegian Research Council for Science and the Humanities, 1991; Report No. 5); James Sumner, "What Makes a PC? Thoughts on Computing Platforms, Standards, and Compatibility," *IEEE Annals of the History of*

*Computing*, Vol. 29, No. 2 (2007): 88; Thomas Haigh, "Remembering the Office of the Future," *IEEE Annals of the History of Computing*, Vol. 28, No. 4 (2006): 6–31. For the historiography of computing, see Thomas J. Misa, "Understanding How Computing Has Changed the World," *IEEE Annals of the History of Computing*, Vol. 29, No. 4 (2007): 52–63.

**18.** *Computer for All* 1993.109.151 (This and the following are citations to the <year> . <issue> . <page number> of *Computer for All*.) Contact the authors for these additional images not printed here.

**19.** *Computer for All* 1988.55.96–97.

**20.** For screen advertisements, see *Computer for All* 1999.175.43. For a modem, see *Computer for All* 2000.191.233. For general and special-purpose software, see *Computer for All* 1996.150.213 and 1995.132.8–9.

**21.** For examples, see *Computer for All* 1991.94.127, 1996.150.213, 1992.107.165, and 1996.150.93.

**22.** *Computer for All* 1984.11.71.

**23.** *Computer for All* 1989.70.99.

**24.** *Computer for All* 1985.30.71.

**25.** *Computer for All* 2000.189.121.

**26.** For examples, see *Computer for All* 1992.107.165, 1998.164.109, and 1991.94.25.

**27.** For examples, see *Computer for All* 1996.150.93, 1992.107.165, and 1996.150.93.

**28.** *Computer for All* 1989.66.107.

**29.** *Computer for All* 1988.61.12.

**30.** *Computer for All* 1998.164.109.

**31.** *Computer for All* 1985.26.45.

**32.** *Computer for All* 2001.203.157.

**33.** *Computer for All* 1991.96.22.

**34.** *Computer for All* 1991.88.133.

**35.** *Computer for All* 1985.31.back cover.

**36.** *Computer for All* 1991.90.23.

**37.** *Computer for All* 2001.200.237.

**38.** *Computer for All* 1986.37.75.

**39.** *Computer for All* 1985.27.7.

**40.** *Computer for All* 1983.3.27.

**41.** See, *Computer for All* 1984.10.75, 1985.29.3, and 1989.68.89, respectively.

**42.** *Computer for All* 1985.22.17.

**43.** *Computer for All* 1995.140.155.

**44.** *Computer for All* 1988.63.219 and 1997.155.39.

**45.** For a sample, see *Computer for All* 1984.11.62, 1984.12.36, 1984.12.113, 1984.18. back cover, 1985.26.145, and 1987.45.94–95.

**46.** *Computer for All* 1990.83.91.

**47.** For an early example, see *Computer for All* 1983.1.2. For a more recent set, see *Computer for All* 1995.141.6 and 1996.149.33.

**48.** See *Computer for All* 1985.27.100 and 1986.37.69.

**49.** *Computer for All* 1989.71.20.

**50.** *Computer for All* 1985.28.20.

**51.** *Computer for All* 1991.93.81.

**52.** *Computer for All* 1985.25.33.

**53.** *Computer for All* 1984.11.54.

**54.** *Computer for All* 1984.16.50.

**55.** *Computer for All* 1997.158.13.

**56.** *Computer for All* 1997.161.29.

**57.** *Computer for All* 1986.33.147.

**58.** *Computer for All* 1999.175.27.

**59.** *Computer for All* 1984.16. front cover.

**60.** *Computer for All* 1987.51.163.

**61.** *Computer for All* 1998.168.2 and 1998.173.226.

**62.** *Computer for All* 1997.155.25.

**63.** *Computer for All* 2000.191.71.

**64.** *Computer for All* 1993.111.11.

**65.** *Computer for All* 1990.83.11 and 1992.99.31.

**66.** *Computer for All* 1986.37.8, 1987.43.138, 1992.100.31, 1993.112.67, and 1996.151.39.

**67.** *Computer for All* 1999.177.191.

**68.** *Computer for All* 1990.84.183.

**69.** *Computer for All* 1997.163.39.

**70.** *Computer for All* 1997.159.212.

**71.** *Computer for All* 2001.197.117.

**72.** *Computer for All* 1987.50.16.

**73.** See *Computer for All* 1990.85.17 and 1999.179.219.

**74.** *Computer for All* 2001.203.21.

**75.** *Computer for All* 1985.24.17 and 1985.25.3.

**76.** *Computer for All* 1985.23.173.

**77.** *Computer for All* 1995.139.133.

**78.** *Computer for All* 1999.175.43.

**79.** *Computer for All* 1992.108.33.

**80.** *Computer for All* 1995.136.37 and 1995.137.53.

**81.** *Computer for All* 2002.213.165.

**82.** *Computer for All* 1996.150.13.

**83.** *Computer for All* 1998.169.3.

**84.** Aristotle Tympas, "The *Computor* and the Analyst" (Ph.D. thesis, Georgia Institute of Technology, 2001).

**85.** *Computer for All* 1996.151.199.

# Women in Computing

# The Pleasure Paradox
## Bridging the Gap Between Popular Images of Computing and Women's Historical Experiences

# 10

I still think, of all the fields open to women, computer science is the most wonderful one. First of all, as a programmer, no one knows what sex you are, what color you are, what your gender preferences are; they just know: Does it work or not? Did you get it done? Is it fast enough? And therefore, it is *the* field where you are judged by the output—that's it. ... So I love it for women.

—Paula Hawthorn, United States, started computing work in 1960s

Almost every day it's fun to go to work—and I don't hear very many other people say that about their jobs. I loved what I was doing when I was programming. ... Once I had kids, being a manager was so easy and so fun, and you get to do so many different things, and you get to leverage all these smart programmers who can produce things. ... And it's interesting, because it's always new. ... So how can you have a better job?

—Ann Hardy, United States, started computing work in 1950s

*Gender Codes: Why Women Are Leaving Computing*, Edited by Thomas J. Misa
Copyright © 2010 the IEEE Computer Society

Women's pleasure in computing is an aspect of history that has gone largely unexplored. Most studies of the underrepresentation of women in computing focus on negatives, such as discrimination, hostile climates in classrooms and workplaces, and ways in which girls are discouraged from getting the necessary preparation in math and science [1]. The quotations above are striking in describing computing not merely as a field where women can survive, but one that is *especially* good for women: one where stereotypes lose their sting, where work is both challenging and social, where parenthood can be an asset rather than an obstacle. Were such experiences historically exceptional, or surprisingly common? Can women's accounts of what appealed to them about computer work in the past suggest strategies for attracting more women in the future? This chapter will draw on interviews with American and British women who began computing careers between the 1940s and the 1980s to identify aspects of the field they found especially welcoming or pleasurable (Fig. 10.1). In focusing on pleasure, I do not mean to imply that my interviewee's experiences in computing were all positive; virtually all of them recalled hardship and discrimination during the course of their careers. My point is simply that the negative aspects have been much better documented than the rewards.

Surveys have shown that the current image of computing deters many women from considering a career in the field [2]. The popular stereotype of computer work tends to emphasize aspects that are unappealing to many women, portraying computer professionals as working in isolation or in hostile, hypercompetitive environments and performing tasks that are disconnected from real-world issues. But this impression is quite distorted, emphasizing traits that are not necessary for, and may even be detrimental to, a productive workplace [3]. The image of computer work as unsatisfying for women is also con-

Figure 10.1. Women working as computer programmers and managers. Mary Lozier Traudt (left) and programmer Alma Smiddy discuss writing of inventory control program at Lozier Corporation in 1971. (Courtesy of Charles Babbage Institute.)

tradicted by women's historical and present-day experiences. Corneliussen [4] describes women's unexpected pleasure in learning to program—unexpected because the women had internalized the cultural message that, as females, they would not enjoy working with the computer. Her sample of Norwegian college students also shows that the masculine stereotype extends beyond the United States and United Kingdom. I suggest that the underrepresentation of women in computing is in part attributable to this mismatch between image and reality.

Historical analysis can help us challenge this male-biased image. First, we can uncover the reality of women's past enjoyment of computing. Second, historical accounts reveal that the image of computing as hostile or unrewarding to women is not intrinsic to the field and, in fact, is a relatively recent phenomenon. The women I interviewed did not see computing as intimidating in the 1950s and 1960s; indeed, the profession was new enough that they had little awareness of *any* popular image, positive or negative. More importantly, the rising demand for computer professionals meant that women were actively courted by employers. Given the rampant exclusion of women from many other scientific and professional fields during this period, computing seemed inviting by comparison. It was not until the 1980s that the male "computer geek" or "hacker" became a widespread stereotype, paralleling—and perhaps contributing to—the decline in women's participation.

Third, we can begin to understand how gender is socially constructed and reconstructed in changing historical contexts. The association of particular attributes of a profession with masculinity or femininity is not static, but fluid; gender codes can change over time—though the privileging of masculinity has been a consistent pattern that reinforces existing power disparities between men and women. Gender stereotypes about computing are embedded in media representations, job descriptions and recruiting, educational practices, and workplace culture (Fig. 10.2); yet women do not simply passively conform to such stereotypes. Instead, popular perceptions about computing, the skills it requires, and the pleasures it offers provide cultural frameworks or discourses that women draw on to make sense of their own experiences [5]. Moreover, as women construct an identity as "female computer expert" they include not only gender traits but also various other aspects of their personality, such as an interest in mathematics, that may mitigate the effects of sex-typing [6].

Any study of women in computing must qualify what is meant by the terms "women" and "computing." Here I draw on oral history interviews I conducted with 52 programmers and computer scientists. This sample was selected to provide a diverse range of experiences, including computer science as well as programming; British and American contexts; government, industry, and academic employment; various class and educational backgrounds; and well-known figures as well as ordinary ones [7]. The United Kingdom and United States were chosen because they were the countries most active in computing in the early decades covered by this study. While women from both countries provided remarkably similar descriptions of why computing appealed to them, there were some cultural differences that affected their access to computing careers. For example, until the 1960s most British schools were single-sex, and the girls' schools tended to offer fewer math and science courses than the boys'. Some interviewees also felt that cultural barriers to women in management were

*It just happens...*
*Control Data Corporation*
*has a future for you.*
*We've got the door...open it!*

Figure 10.2. Gender stereotypes in job recruitment. Computer companies such as Control Data appealed directly to young women seeking careers. Despite the traditional motifs (such as pink or purple tones), women did gain job opportunities that could transcend the gender stereotyping. (Courtesy of Charles Babbage Institute.)

stronger in the United Kingdom than in the United States (see Chapter 5 in this volume).

To highlight possible gender barriers, the sample focuses on areas of computing that are now considered highly masculinized—programming, computer science, and to some extent management—rather than areas such as data entry, documentation, or customer support, in which more women have been found. My sample also does not include any nonwhite women, who did participate in computing in the early decades but not in large numbers; and it obviously does not represent the views of women who were discouraged or excluded from ever entering the field [8]. There is no claim here to represent a universal female or computing experience; the aim is rather to look for common themes that emerge from the diversity and that suggest underlying gender codes. Even experiences that appear to be atypical are useful in showing what was *possible* for women and what meanings individual women ascribed to such experiences.

Oral history interviews provide a view of the past filtered through the respondent's present consciousness and shaped by narrative conventions [9]. The subjective nature of this evidence is ideally suited to explore issues of perception, emotion, identity, and agency. Women's stories reveal what educational and career choices they saw as available to them, what motivated them to choose computing, and their feelings about important career events. As retrospective evidence, oral histories risk distorting past circumstances (and therefore work best when complemented by contemporary documents), but benefit from the narrator's own historical insights. In telling the story of their computing careers, my interviewees (speaking in the early 2000s) articulated an awareness of current stereotypes and seem compelled to explicitly contradict them, asserting that computing is fun, social, compatible with family life, and well suited to women's tastes and talents. The interviews thus hint at changes over time in the gendering of computing, as respondents show a heightened awareness of how the pleasure they experienced as normal in the past may be viewed as unusual today.

## THE APPEAL AND PLEASURES OF COMPUTING: WOMEN'S STORIES

My interviewees described a diverse range of rewards from computing work: excitement at participating in novel and important projects; pride in meeting the day-to-day challenges of programming or research; feeling appreciated and respected by co-workers; comfort in financial security; pleasure in workplace camaraderie; and satisfaction in service to others. While one might expect many of these feelings to be shared by men, the women's accounts are notable for what they leave out: there is little emphasis on achievements generally associated with male ambition, such as amassing wealth, attaining high rank or status, outshining their peers in technical prowess, or achieving public recognition. Perhaps the women felt that such "masculine" ambitions were inappropriate to a female professional identity; perhaps they simply considered them unattainable in a male-dominated workplace. Regardless, it appears that the enticements that computing offers to women might not be the same as those that are used to recruit men. (See Figure 10.3.)

While each woman's story of why she was initially drawn to computing is different, some general trends emerge. First, many women perceived computing as cutting-edge and glamorous—"new," "exciting," "different"—and were fascinated with the technology itself. The allure of computing contrasted sharply with the limited options for women in the 1940s to 1960s, which were typically teaching, secretarial, or routine calculating work. Second, a number of women who got a taste of programming before they had actually taken a computing job (typically in a college class) found that they enjoyed the *process* of programming: it was "easy" and "fun"; the role of programmer seemed natural or even

Figure 10.3. Women attracted to computer technology and computer science. Burroughs recruitment in 1978 profiled Libby Ryan, a B.S. mathematics major working at the Burroughs engineering center in Tredyffrin, Pennsylvania, who directed software development for large general-purpose computers. (Courtesy of Charles Babbage Institute.)

"fated." A third reason many women chose computing was because they identified as mathematicians and perceived computing to be a similar field. This reflects the fact that scientific programming was a major application area until the 1960s, when business computing became dominant; some interviewees commented that the association of computing with math has now become outdated and may even be an obstacle to women. Finally, almost all of those interviewed mentioned a desire for financial independence and saw computing as one of the best-paying options available to women. In short, as these women surveyed the options open to them at a particular historical moment, they saw in computing an opportunity both to experience pleasure in their work and to construct an identity as an independent, valued professional. Excerpts from interviews illustrate both women's unexpected "love" for programming or computer science and their perception of its superiority to other available careers.

### Excerpts from Interviews: What First Inspired Women to Study or Work in Computing?

I went to work for an insurance company in Boston, Massachusetts—and it turned out to be terrible! ... It was not well-paying; it was not interesting. ... I applied to

Los Alamos [for a computing job, and] they called me for an interview. I was to fly from Boston to New Mexico at their expense—which was incredible! That really shook up the entire insurance company. They even offered me a raise!

—Mary Kircher, United States, started 1950s

[While doing a math degree at Cambridge in the early 1960s, some friends introduced me to programming.] And I thought, really, "I love this! Gosh, you do it with your hands, and you work it out logically, and you get something; and then you correct it, and you have another go, and you stick it in a computer. This is just my thing! I love this!" … I thought really the computing had more zizz, pizzazz: more excitement about it. … I then felt at home. This was where I wanted to be. This is what I want to work in. I loved it.

—Gillian Lovegrove, United Kingdom, 1960s

I took an interest inventory test after about two years in college, and unlike most people—this is not a common experience—computer technology was head and shoulders above anything else. So it was like I was handed it on a silver platter, and I took my first class. … and I loved it! I'm very passionate about what I do, and that's such a great way to start, because I *chose* what I do. It's because I love it. … It really was a passion from the time I started.

—Telle Whitney, United States, started 1970s

I liked computers a lot. I think that often people come to computer science from two different ends of things: either the math end of things, where you have appreciation for the aesthetics—and theoretical computer science is a really great venue for that—and then people also come from the engineering side of things. … I came more from the math side of things, so for me it was the aesthetics of it that really appealed to me.

—Fran Berman, United States, started 1970s

Once in the field, women found numerous rewards; some confirmed their initial impressions of computing, while others were more unexpected. In terms of material rewards, virtually all of the women I interviewed were very satisfied with the pay they received, which was typically far more than they had ever expected to earn (though often less than that of their male co-workers). Regarding the day-to-day work itself, my interviewees enjoyed the intellectual challenge of programming or theoretical computer science, and they described the "puzzle-solving" aspect as especially fun and absorbing. Many women extolled the constant novelty of being in a fast-changing field and reported that they never felt bored with their work.

## Excerpts from Interviews: Fun, Challenge, and Novelty

I like problem-solving, and it was clear that my math interest was probably no different than why I do crossword puzzles. Those are word games, and these are number games. So I thought [programming] was interesting.

—Adele Goldberg, United States, started 1960s

[Stanford] was a very exciting environment. The new ideas: there was no limit to new ideas, and that was very exciting! Remember, it was also a time when the whole area of computer science was still in diapers, so to speak, and artificial intelligence was just being born. We were all very naive; we oversimplified the problems; but we were terribly excited! … You'd try anything, and everything was new.

—Ruzena Bajcsy, United States, started 1960s

I discovered this whole new area that is so much fun: like playing puzzles, but at a somewhat different scale. For example, when you analyze the operations of data structures, you are playing a very well defined game, too. If you are playing with very huge data structures or networks like these Internet graphs, you have a lot of zeroes and ones. If you are going to purely deal with zeroes and ones, a huge amount of digits is not going to mean anything; it would be hard to find a diamond in the rough, or anything of that nature. So you have to take advantage of its relations, to help with your game.

—Fan Chung Graham, United States, started 1970s

Women also derived pleasure from a sense of accomplishment, which they defined in a variety of ways. Like men, they took pride in pioneering new research areas or a new industry. Where women seem to differ from their male colleagues is in the high value they placed on having their work contribute to solving real-world problems—which might range from turning abstract theories into usable software, to providing tools for firefighters and air traffic controllers, to building atomic bombs for national defense, to helping business users satisfy their customers. While women relished the immediate "fun" of working with machines or abstract theories, most of my interviewees also wanted to see a connection between their technical work and the needs of real users.

## Excerpts from Interviews: Excitement of Pioneering, Satisfaction of Meeting Users' Needs

[My three-person team] all went to the [ALGOL 68] conference. … To say we made an impact wouldn't be overstating it—because all these people were academics and in universities, and they had been defining this language, but nobody had been actually writing a compiler for it. So we found that when we turned up at this conference, we had the world's first ALGOL 68 compiler—which absolutely thrilled the people who had written the language.

—Susan Bond, United Kingdom, started 1960s

[At University College London I helped program the first UK node of the Internet.] It was really exciting! … When we actually got it working, and started sending emails—it was one of the first things we started to do—I was probably one of the first people in this country ever to send an email, back in 1974. And that was really thrilling. You could see the potential. It was amazing.

—Sylvia Wilbur, United Kingdom, started 1970s

[I worked] on the first air traffic control system prototype, was heavily involved in the specification and oversight of the implementation and the testing of the second prototype of today's air traffic control systems. … [W]hen the prototype was completed, and we were ready to test the system, the FAA sent thirteen working air traffic controllers to participate in our test and evaluation of this system. … So we had a marvelous opportunity to really understand what the application was, and how real air traffic controllers could or could not use what we had built for them. … I don't look at the computer as sort of a fancy toy. To me, it's a tool. And I think a lot of women look at computers that way.

—Marlene Hazle, United States, started 1950s

There is no better sense of satisfaction than walking into a workplace and finding someone using this tool that you made—and using it effectively! Our little database machine, the Britton-Lee machine, was this fast machine that you used with a VAX as a front end. There was a guy in Texas who was way behind on a project and had promised it for a certain amount of money to a customer. So he bought one

Figure 10.4. Woman computer scientist working with colleagues. In 1980 Burroughs profiled Diane Chikoski, another mathematics major, who was director of programming for small computer systems. "Tasks are assigned according to talents, interests, and career goals," she noted positively. (Courtesy of Charles Babbage Institute.)

of our machines and attached it to this VAX that was underperforming, and now he's able to do this project really fast. It saved his job. So he named his daughter Brittany Lee! I'm not kidding. There's nothing better, absolutely nothing better. Imagine having such an effect!

—Paula Hawthorn, United States, started 1960s

Contrary to the current stereotype of computing as the domain of anti-social "nerds," the social aspects of their jobs provided many rewards to women. They spoke of the pleasure of working with people who were compatible and "fun"; they also valued working with colleagues whom they admired for their intellect or leadership skills (Fig. 10.4). Conversely, women appreciated receiving respect for their own skills and approval for their interest in technical matters, rather than discouragement for violating gender norms. In a culture that often portrayed "technical" and "feminine" as opposites, computing could be a welcoming home for women who wanted to embrace an identity as a technical enthusiast—provided male colleagues were accepting. Women's accounts of social life on the job highlight how a shared interest in and commitment to the practice of computing could forge bonds of friendship and respect among co-workers.

## Excerpts from Interviews: Social Pleasures of Computing

I think the camaraderie was one of the outstanding things about those days. We worked together, we played together—days, nights, weekends—we were all together, and we had no precedent for anything we did. We had to invent every solution, and that's something I think that made an equality among the people. ... So it was a total life of doing something very exciting and recognizing no distinctions among people—so yes, the secretaries were as much a part of the team, and the computer operators, and all the other people—because we were all working on solving a problem, and getting something done for the first time.

—Judy Clapp, United States, started 1950s

I was always a very one-sided math and science person ... which made it sort of hard, in those days. Nobody was supposed to be good in math, and *particularly* not girls. ... I got into [computing] knowing I was unusual, to put it mildly, because I was interested in and very good at math. So I just did my thing, and fortunately, early on it was not a problem. I was one of the group, and treated like one of the group, not like somebody special or strange.

—Lois Haibt, United States, started 1950s

Consideration of social life on the job raises the question of workplace gender discrimination. While every woman I interviewed could recall episodes of egregious or subtle sexism, several of them commented on what they saw as the relative fairness and gender neutrality of the field, given the mores of the time. They believed that programmers and computer scientists were largely judged on the quality of their work, and that this minimized gender bias. At the technical level, therefore, they generally felt that merit was rewarded and women were recognized for their contributions. But gender equality evaporated at the management level: while some women were able to rise to positions of real power, many more encountered glass ceilings and closed doors when they tried to move beyond purely technical positions. As my interviewees perceived it, then, the problem was not necessarily with computing *per se*, but with a male-biased management culture that permeated nearly every industry.

Like their male peers, women who did advance to management roles appreciated the recognition and financial rewards that followed, as well as the power to implement their ideas. It is striking, however, how much emphasis the women placed on the joy of building a team and helping each employee do his or her best work. They tended to view an executive position less as an opportunity for an individual to exercise power and more as a mandate to maximize the potential and satisfaction of one's employees. They often characterized success as something shared among co-workers, rather than being solely individual, and several women described mentoring employees or students as one of their major accomplishments.

When interpreting these self-reports, one must keep in mind that the articulation of "nurturing" values conforms to culturally acceptable models of femininity and may therefore be exaggerated. On the other hand, these are not merely abstract sentiments but are grounded in specific experiences in the women's professional lives when they were given the opportunity to act on those values. Computer work offered some women a chance to define leadership as a mutually supportive exercise—a vision that is notably absent from the popular image of computing.

Overall, these accounts of pleasure and success in computing challenge both masculine and feminine stereotypes. They defy feminine stereotypes because the women enjoyed immersing themselves in technology, being on the cutting edge, and working all-out to achieve a goal, which are typically seen as masculine preferences. They also reject male-oriented stereotypes about success, because the women see success as more than "winning" against other people or gaining personal acclaim, power, or fortune; their definitions of success include making a difference to society, mentoring others, and working with people they like. Women who were successful in computing seem to have shared an ability to ignore negative stereotypes about science and gender (e.g., "girls don't do math") and construct an identity as "female computer professional" that drew on more positive cultural beliefs ("computing is challenging and cutting-edge"; "women work well with others"). Just as important, there was no single recipe for finding pleasure in computing; women with diverse interests and personalities could feel at home there. Some women particularly enjoyed working "close to the machine" and immersing themselves in technical details (perhaps with little social interaction), while others were thrilled to study the theoretical aspects of computer science, and still others preferred a role in project management with more personal interaction.

### Excerpts from Interviews: Social Rewards of Leadership

[I managed a project at IBM on parallel compilers that] became a very, very, very well-known system and group of people—just stacks of papers; we just poured ideas out all over the place! ... I was able to provide a good environment for them. ... I felt we had to build a system where we could validate our ideas, as a group; and I made sure that every person had their own space in it. ... They could do the experimentation and get themselves established professionally—because that was a bunch of young people there—with their own name on pieces of this. ... It was absolutely fantastic; it was a great team. It was described as one of the most successful groups in [IBM] Research at the time.

—Fran Allen, United States, started 1950s

[The company I founded] got some people started in careers, and that was very satisfying, too. ... There are people who have had much more creative and meaningful things to do than they would have otherwise, and that's a nice feeling.

—Elsie Shutt, United States, started 1950s

[As Superintendent of Computing and Software Research at the Radar Research Establishment] I was very proud of my Division. That's probably a female attribute; I don't suppose men feel the same. But they were really good—at the end I had five or six Individual Merit Scientists in the Software Division. And what I learned from [my predecessor] was that the art was to protect your people and let them get on with producing something in their research, while staving off the attentions of the bean counters!

—Susan Bond, United Kingdom, started 1960s

[My software startup] was a woman's company—of women, for women—and we learned to support each other. That's partly my management style, that you would have a team, and sometimes *you* would be the leader and *I* would be the auditor, and other times *I* would be the leader and *you* would be auditor and somebody else would be the technician; and we really learned to use each other's skills to work together. ... Most of the women have moved on and up.

—Steve Shirley, United Kingdom, started 1960s

## IMAGE VERSUS EXPERIENCE: POLICY LESSONS

If computing offers so many rewards for women, why are they so underrepresented? An extensive literature documents the various barriers women face, from outright hostility, to glass ceilings, to a lack of accommodation for family life [1]. To some extent, the women I interviewed encountered all of these obstacles. But I will argue that another significant deterrent to women is the one-sided image of computing they encounter long before they enter the job market. The women I interviewed were clearly aware of the current "male geek" image of computing, and many were vociferous in denouncing it.

## Excerpts from Interviews: Don't Believe the Image!

I think that it's important not to pay too much attention to the stereotype that you somehow have to be one of these geeky guys, which is completely ridiculous. Not everybody's like that; most people aren't like that. ... The stereotype is just a stereotype, it's not reality; and you shouldn't let that hinder you. ... And there are great things to be done. It's hard, sometimes, to see it: the way computing and technology are often taught, we lose the connection with the impact of what we're creating. It's a really good idea to think about all the incredible things that could be done with all of this, if you care about that.

—Anita Borg, started 1960s

All the [school guidance] counselors seem to think that everybody who goes into computer science is just nerdy, and so women shouldn't want to do that, because these women aren't nerdy. They let nerdy women do it, but not just ordinary women! And it's just not that way; once you get into it, it's not like that. ... I just wish that somebody would get out and explain to the counselors in the schools that this is a *good* thing for women to be doing; they're not going to spend their life behind a computer. ... It's *so* much more social.

—Ann Hardy, started 1950s

My usual advice is for [women] not to get intimidated. In a way, in science—it's not entirely black or white, but it has clear definitions, and if you get it, you are on equal ground. When I first went to college, I ran into these guys—I'm pretty sure that in every class there are a few—who seemed to already know everything! Later on, I found out that it was not the case. In fact, the worst thing that can happen is that you pretend you know something and you don't.

—Fan Chung Graham, started 1970s

The dissonance between the stereotypes and the historical reality of women's experiences in computing suggests several policy approaches.

**1.** *Reframe the Popular Image of Computing.* Women will not be drawn into computing unless they can imagine an identity as a female computer professional that is consistent with personality traits they value—which for many women includes being creative, well-rounded, and sociable. Computer professionals, employers, teachers, and school guidance counselors should emphasize how computing work relates to the real-world needs of society, as well as the fun, intellectual excitement, and camaraderie it can provide. While hostile workplaces do exist, they should not be accepted as an inevitable or justifiable part of computing culture to which women must adapt.

One theme that emerges from the historical record is that women evaluate computer work in the context of their other career options. In the 1950s, when overt gender discrimination severely constrained women's choices, programming (and later, computer science) stood out as an appealing and rewarding field. Today they must compete with a far wider range of occupations. But the same comparative advantages that drew women in the past—good salaries, intellectual interest, respect for their technical skill—could still attract women today, if we can override the message that these rewards are reserved for men.

2. *Discard Narrow Gender Stereotypes and Accommodate Diversity.* Women's accounts illustrate that the profession needs and can accommodate a diversity of personality types: those who want to be immersed in technology can find like-minded souls who will not patronize them, while those who want a more social experience can enjoy exercising their communication and management skills along with their technical expertise. There is room for women who love math and for those with verbal skills; the work can be very abstract or closely linked to concrete problems; programmers and computer scientists can choose to be married to their work or have a balanced family life. Employers, teachers, and school guidance counselors should recognize and publicize that diverse types of people can enjoy computing—and that those personality types cross gender lines. Many women derive satisfaction from "masculine" feats of technical mastery and spending long hours alone with the computer; conversely, many men enjoy a cooperative and sociable work environment.

3. *Reconsider Reward Systems.* The computing profession as it currently exists provides many rewards that women have identified as valuable: the intrinsic satisfaction of fascinating work; team solidarity; and appreciation for their technical skill and performance. But the accomplishments women see as most important are not necessarily those that receive the most recognition. Teamwork and social skills are rarely rewarded in proportion to their productive value: after all, a cleverly engineered product may be useless if it does not get to market because of bad management, or if it fails to meet the customer's needs due to poor communication. Women's firsthand accounts show that the particular ways they defined "success" and experienced satisfaction did not always follow the dominant career model based (implicitly) on male priorities and experiences. Activities that many women have found significant, such as mentoring students and employees, communicating with colleagues and customers, or engaging in professional service, may not be acknowledged or encouraged. Employers who want to retain talented workers should recognize and reward the communications and social skills that women (and men) bring to the job. Managers should resist the tendency to tie perceptions of good performance to masculine stereotypes—for example, equating obsessiveness with technical mastery, or aggressiveness with leadership.

4. *Restore the Fun to Computing.* Interviewees' descriptions of what initially attracted them to computing suggest that we should offer

Figure 10.5. "Computer science is the most wonderful" field. Heather Gilbert, a Stanford mathematics major who also gained a Master's in computer science, started at Burroughs as a system analyst in 1969. After several assignments at company headquarters in Detroit, she transferred to Pasadena, Calif., where in 1978 she oversaw management systems. (Courtesy of Charles Babbage Institute.)

today's young women the chance to try programming in a way that they will find fun and exciting (Fig. 10.5). Recent research indicates that women today find computer technology less interesting and cutting-edge than they did in the past, especially those who have not experienced using the computer creatively. Bair and Marcus [10] found that college women interviewed in 2002 saw computers as routine and boring: "Computers don't have the same novelty or create the same interest as they once did." They relate this to the fact that the women's experience with computers tended to be with mundane tasks such as word processing, while their male peers had more experience with entertainment applications and tended to see computers as more exciting. The same research shows that this negative perception often changes when the women learn programming in a supportive environment and discover for themselves the pleasure of mastering a technical challenge. To maximize the appeal for women, programming exercises should be connected to real-world problems, and students should have a chance to interact with end-users, both to appreciate the challenge of understanding users' needs and to have the satisfaction of pleasing a client. Positive firsthand experience with skilled computer work is the surest way to refute masculine stereotypes and perhaps convince more young women that "of all the fields open to women, computer science is the most wonderful one."

# REFERENCES

**1.** See, for example, Tracy Camp, "The Incredible Shrinking Pipeline," *Communications of the ACM*, Vol. 40, No. 10 (1997): 103–110; J. McGrath Cohoon and William Aspray, eds. *Women and Information Technology: Research on Underrep-* resentation (Cambridge: MIT Press, 2006); Jennifer DiSabatino, "Glass Ceiling for Women in IT Persists," *Computerworld* (15 May 2000): 12; Chuck Huff, "Gender, Software Design, and Occupational Equity," *Inroads: SIGCSE Bulletin*,

Vol. 34, No. 2 (2002): 112–115; Lori Kendall, "'The Nerd Within': Mass Media and the Negotiation of Identity Among Computer-Using Males," *Journal of Men's Studies*, Vol. 7, No. 3 (1999): 353–369; Jane Margolis and Allan Fisher, *Unlocking the Clubhouse: Women in Computing* (Cambridge: MIT Press, 2002); Karen Stabiner, "Where the Girls Aren't," *New York Times Education Life* (12 January 2003): 35. These issues are also discussed in other chapters of this volume. For more general works on the exclusion of women from science and engineering, see Margaret Rossiter, *Women Scientists in America: Before Affirmative Action, 1940–1972* (Baltimore: Johns Hopkins, 1995); Ruth Oldenziel, *Making Technology Masculine: Men, Women, and Modern Machines in America, 1870–1945* (Amsterdam: Amsterdam University Press, 1999); Margaret A. M. Murray, *Women Becoming Mathematicians* (Cambridge: MIT Press, 2000).

**2.** See Tracy Camp, "Survey Says!" (1998); available at **www.mines.edu/fs_home/tcamp/ results/paper.html**; Ellen Spertus, "Why Are There So Few Female Computer Scientists?" MIT Artificial Intelligence Laboratory (August 1991); available at **people.mills.edu/spertus/Gender/ why.html**.

**3.** On the gap between female students' perceptions of the traits needed by IT workers and the experiences of actual IT professionals, see Bettina Bair and Miranda Marcus, "Women's Interest in Information Technology," in Carol J. Burger, Elizabeth G. Creamer, and Peggy S. Meszaros, eds., *Reconfiguring the Firewall: Recruiting Women to Information Technology Across Cultures and Continents* (Wellesley, MA: A. K. Peters, 2007), pp. 161–175.

**4.** Hilde Corneliussen, "'I Fell in Love with the Machine': Women's Pleasure in Computing," *Journal of Information, Communication and Ethics in Society*, Vol. 3, No. 4 (2005): 233–241.

**5.** For an elaboration of this point using Anthony Giddens's structuration theory, see Sue H. Nielsen, Liisa A. von Hellens, Jenine Beekhuyzen, and Eileen M. Trauth, "Women Talking About IT Work: Duality or Dualism?" in *Proceedings of ACM SIGMIS Conference '03* (Philadelphia, 10–12 April 2003), pp. 68–74.

**6.** I explored how women who identified as mathematicians were able to find solidarity with male programmers in Janet Abbate, "Proto-feminism and Programming: Gender Politics in Computing Before the Civil Rights Era," paper presented at Society for the History of Technology Annual Meeting, Washington, DC, October 2007.

**7.** On sampling for range, see Roberts S. Weiss, *Learning From Strangers* (New York: Macmillan, 1994); and Paul Thompson, *The Voice of the Past: Oral History*, 3rd ed. (Oxford, UK: Oxford University Press, 2000).

**8.** See Jane Margolis, *Struck in the Shallow End: Education, Race, and Computing* (Cambridge: MIT Press, 2008).

**9.** On narrative analysis of oral histories, see Mary Chamberlain, "Narrative Theory," in Thomas L. Charlton, Lois E. Myers, and Rebecca Sharpless, eds., *Handbook of Oral History* (Lanham, MD: AltaMira Press, 2006), pp. 384–407; Mary Jo Maynes, Jennifer L. Pierce, and Barbara Laslett, *Telling Stories: The Use of Personal Narratives in the Social Sciences and History* (Ithaca, NY: Cornell University Press, 2008); Paul Thompson, *The Voice of the Past: Oral History*, 3rd ed. (Oxford, UK: Oxford University Press, 2000).

**10.** Bettina Bair and Miranda Marcus, "Women's Interest in Information Technology: The Fun Factor," in Carol J. Burger, Elizabeth G. Creamer, and Peggy S. Meszaros, eds., *Reconfiguring the Firewall: Recruiting Women to Information Technology Across Cultures and Continents* (Wellesley, MA: A. K. Peters, 2007), p. 171.

# Programming Enterprise
## Women Entrepreneurs in Software and Computer Services

# 11

JEFFREY R. YOST

$F$ew chief executives have been higher profile than Hewlett-Packard's (HP) leader from 1999 to 2005, Carleton "Carly" Fiorina. In 1996, as AT&T Executive Vice President for Corporate Operations, she oversaw the largest initial public offering in the United States to that time—Lucent [1]. Her achievements at AT&T and Lucent helped propel her to the top leadership post at HP. With this appointment, she became the first woman to run a Dow 30 company and the first woman CEO and Board Chair of an IT giant [2]. A board battle with Walter Hewlett (son of co-founder William Hewlett) over Fiorina's decision to acquire Compaq, and other differences of opinion on strategy, contributed to her controversial ouster.

A year before Fiorina took over at HP, Margaret "Meg" Whitman became CEO of a small web-based auction firm, eBay. Whitman led this company for a decade, turning it into an e-commerce powerhouse. It brought together buyers and sellers of nearly every imaginable product in a virtual marketplace, taking a commission on each sale and operating with extremely low overhead. As the dot.com collapse of 2000 to 2002 decimated many e-commerce firms and scarred countless others, eBay emerged relatively unscathed. In fiscal 2006 eBay had nearly $6 billion in revenue and more than $1.2 billion in net income [3]. In January 2008 Whitman stepped down from eBay.

*Gender Codes: Why Women Are Leaving Computing*, Edited by Thomas J. Misa
Copyright © 2010 the IEEE Computer Society

While no other women have reached the level of recognition and stature in the IT world as Fiorina and Whitman, fully one-tenth of Fortune's 2008 "50 Most Powerful Women" were high ranking executives at IT giants—from Safra Catz, the co-president of Oracle, who oversees day-to-day operations for this leading enterprise software firm, to Ginni Rometty, IBM's Senior Vice President for Global Business Services, who runs the $18 billion division critical to IBM's future growth [4]. One of the primary reasons these leading women IT executives have been in the spotlight, however, is because many glass ceilings remain firmly in place and there are relatively few women in these top posts. Another important reason is that these achievements, while rare and generally the result of overcoming numerous obstacles, are a complete break from the past. From the origin of the computer industry in the early 1950s—and the software and services industry roughly a half-decade later—through the 1980s there were meaningful though varying barriers to the entry for women into large computer and software companies, and almost insurmountable ones to moving high up the corporate ladder at these firms.

This chapter is focused on an alternative path of women to leadership positions in the IT world. It concentrates on women entrepreneurs from the 1960s through the 1980s in the software and computer services industries—the companies they founded and ran and their leadership within trade associations for these industries. There are many challenges to unearthing this important history. Virtually no archival resources exist to provide records on these firms, and little archival material is available on IT trade associations. An exception to the latter is the ADAPSO Records at the Charles Babbage Institute. This collection and a series of oral histories with women IT entrepreneurs are the foundational resources for this chapter.

The history of women IT entrepreneurs is not only uncharted terrain; it is also a subset of the larger history of women entrepreneurs that has been grossly understudied. (There is a growing literature on women entrepreneurship in the past decade—and a surge of scholarship on women and microenterprise in the developing world. This literature generally analyzes contemporary situations or recent events, advocates particular policies or practices, and ignores longer-term historical developments [5].) Among the factors contributing to the dearth of historical literature on women entrepreneurs are the particular trajectories of the fields of business history and women's history. Long following the lead of Alfred Chandler, business historians have focused on large firms [6]. Even as the field has recently broadened, the literature that examines the origin of small businesses is almost exclusively limited to studies of the few firms that grew to become corporate giants [7]. Meanwhile, the fields of women's history and gender history have grown rapidly in the past three decades, along with histories concentrated on race and class, as part of the "new social history." In this environment, women's labor history has thrived as a field [8]. But few historians have focused on women elites in the business world [9]. Hence, the history of women who founded and led small to mid-sized software and computer services businesses, and provided leadership to trade associations in these industries, has remained outside the dominant currents of women's history and business history.

This chapter will first examine the broader environment for IT employment for women. It will then turn to three case studies of women (Luanne

Johnson, Grace Gentry, and Phyliss Murphy), who ran successful small software and computer services businesses for years (Argonaut Information Systems, Gentry, Inc., and Phyliss Murphy & Associates), and also were leaders in two trade organizations: the Association for Data Processing Services Organizations (ADAPSO) and the National Association of Computer Consultant Businesses (NACCB). (In discussing the NACCB, it will also profile the long-time executive director, Peggy Smith—who previously was one of three founders of an IT consultant brokerage.) These case studies not only demonstrate the insight, creativity, resourcefulness, and skill of these enterprising women to found and lead their businesses, but also the unique capabilities they brought to trade associations to enable them to add value to their member companies.

## WOMEN'S EMPLOYMENT IN LARGE IT ENTERPRISES

By the 1960s the universe of computer occupations not only included those at computer firms (like IBM, Control Data, etc.), but also the computer or data processing operations of numerous companies in a growing number of industries (including insurance, banking, and aerospace). At both computer companies and firms with computer departments, computer occupations ranged from keypunchers and operators to programmers, systems analysts, and computer engineers.

Keypunchers were a new form of clerical workers; they were low paid and predominantly women from the start. The computer operator category changed over time—generally declining in responsibility, skill, prestige, and earnings—from those who did complex plug board programming in the late 1940s ("ENIAC girls") to those who did routine mechanical and clerical tasks in the 1960s. (Deskilling and division of labor accelerated during the 1960s and operators of computers typically came to be similar in responsibilities and status to other types of machine operators (programming was left to the programmers and there was not a career path to advancement; see Chapter 5 in this volume) [10, pp. 63–83].) Further up the hierarchy were programmers and systems analysts. By the 1950s and 1960s programmers were clearly higher than operators, but it was a new occupation of somewhat uncertain stature and midlevel compensation [11]. In these years, it was usually lower paid and lower status than computer engineers, and it required less education. Programmers came from a range of fields and did not always need a college degree to get hired—often scoring well on an aptitude test was enough. Systems analysts sometimes graduated from the ranks of skilled programmers and, over time, increasingly had college or graduate training in mathematics, business, engineering, or computer science. (More gradations have developed, including "software engineers" and, more recently, "software developers." For the period covered in this chapter, most software workers fell in the programmer, systems analysts, sales, or executive ranks.) They analyzed problems, procured equipment, designed and oversaw data processing systems, and supervised a number of programmers. They also served as intermediaries between the decision-making users of data (business analysts/managers/executives) and the programmers [10, pp. 63–83].

In the mid-1950s the first software services firms arose to serve mainframe computer customer organizations. By the 1960s the services industry was thriving and included service bureaus (i.e., IBM's spin-off Service Bureau Corporation, General Electric's GEISCO, Tymshare, Inc.), facilities management firms (i.e., Electronic Data Systems), and diversified providers (i.e., Computer Science Corporation, University Computing Corporation). In the early to mid-1960s a number of services companies began producing software products (i.e., Applied Data Research's Autoflow) [12]. Within a few years some firms were founded as software products businesses (i.e., Cullinane Corporation) [13]. Beginning in the mid-1970s an increasing number of IT services businesses supplied independent contractors to client organizations, representing a new area of the services industry (and a focal point of this chapter). All of these segments employed (or contracted with) numerous programmers and systems analysts.

Given this chapter's focus on the software and computer services industries, it will concentrate on the occupations of programmers, systems analysts, and software/services top executives. Some of the small group of women who programmed the ENIAC or other mainframes for the government in the late 1940s continued to work at major computer firms in the 1950s, but women's entry into the ranks of programmers generally was difficult during that decade. Joan Greenbaum, a programmer who later wrote on management theory in data processing, quoted a female physics graduate from the late 1950s: "The aerospace industry was growing fast and I really wanted to be a programmer, but women weren't 'good enough' to be programmers. We were hired at 20 percent less than men and only allowed to set up the test cases" [10, p. 87]. By the 1960s opportunities opened up substantially for women as there was almost a perpetual "software crisis" resulting in, and partially defined by, a shortage of programmers. (Joan Greenbaum found it difficult obtaining professional work after graduating from college in 1963 in other fields, but after scoring well on a programming aptitude test, quickly received a programming job and, as she perceived it, instantly became a "professional." The professional status of programmers, however, was contested terrain (see Chapter 6).) At this time, scoring well on aptitude tests could often lead to entry into the programming field for women, but hiring biases in favoring male applicants did not disappear, nor did biases in compensation or opportunities for advancement.

A survey published in *Computerworld* indicated that, in 1974, 13% of systems analysts and 20% of programmers were women [14]. A half-dozen years later, data from the 1980 census showed significant growth in these numbers: 22% of systems analysts and 31% of programmers were women [15]. In absolute terms, this represented major growth—as the number of programming jobs and systems analyst jobs increased by 94% and 80%, respectively, during the 1970s [15]. Increasingly in that decade, some employers ran advertisements that were specifically targeted at hiring women programmers (compare Fig. 1.1, 6.1, and 10.2) [16]. In general, there were geographical and industry differences and women tended to have higher relative representation in the lower paid, end-user industries as opposed to positions at computer and software companies [17].

A study of the earnings gap in the leading state for computer employment, California, indicated that female computer specialists (programmers and systems analysts) earned only 72% of male computer specialists. The researchers (Donato and Roos) conducting this study adjusted this raw figure for a variety of individual (age, education, etc.) and structural factors (industries, industry sectors, etc.) and concluded that women still only made 89% the compensation of men [15]. That women found it more difficult to gain employment at computer and software firms, and that throughout at least much of the industry women programmers and systems analysts made less than men, leads us to the cases of three women who initially worked for sizable corporations/organizations but then took a different path—starting their own software and computer services enterprises.

## ARGONAUT INFORMATION SYSTEMS

Luanne Johnson was born in 1938 and raised in Orville, Ohio. Her father was a teacher; and she grew up with a deep interest in writing. She was an education major at Bowling Green State University when she took a sponsored trip to California as vice president of a Christian fellowship student organization. She loved California from the moment she arrived, especially the San Francisco Bay area, and decided to stay. Soon after, she got married. Having strong typing skills, Johnson was hired as a department secretary at University of California–Berkeley. She soon left Berkeley for several secretarial jobs in the private sector, before becoming a legal secretary with a downtown Oakland firm. Divorced by that time, and raising a daughter, she wanted the higher salary of legal secretaries. (This section, unless noted otherwise, is from the Luanne Johnson Oral History [18].)

In the early 1960s, a librarian friend encouraged her to take a programming aptitude test. She scored well and followed this with night school programming courses to earn a certificate from Heald College. Before long she was hired by Alameda County as a programmer trainee, along with two male trainees. While the two men complained about the compensation, she was making more than she had made as a legal secretary and was grateful for the opportunity to take programming courses at IBM—including Autocoder, FORTRAN, COBOL, PL1, and RPG. Alameda County transferred programmers around as needed on projects; and before long she was programming court calendars—the only group that had to take nightshifts from time to time. When Johnson, the only woman on this project, could not find a sitter, she would have to take her daughter to work at night and bundle her up to sleep on the couch in the women's room, propping the door open with a box of IBM punch cards. The insensitivity to scheduling a single mother this way soon led her to seek other opportunities.

Through a friend, she learned of a programming job at a freight company. Soon she had several years of full-time programming experience and began to jump around, changing jobs four times in the next 5 years, each time for higher compensation. The rapid growth of computer and computer services firms helped define the "go-go years" of the late 1960s—a period of seemingly endless opportunity [19]. Johnson knew that her skills were in demand and did not worry about job security, working for several start-up services firms because the work was exciting and paid more, and believing there would always be other programmer jobs just around the corner.

In 1969 she joined Comm-Sci, a small computer services company consisting of the founder Bill Adair, programmer Tom Mosely, and a few contractors. They had developed a payroll system on a contract and were looking to market the program to other customers. Johnson was brought in to work with a customer to develop an accounts payable system. She had taken a number of extension accounting courses at University of California–Berkeley and, thus, was in a good position to understand not only the programming but also the customer needs with such a system.

According to Johnson, Adair was a charismatic leader but lacked follow-through on business details. Sometimes customers were provided services and not invoiced. More commonly, interested potential customers never received follow-up attention. Frequently, resources were purchased without any type of budgeting process. Mosely was a highly gifted programmer who wrote concise, elegant COBOL code for tax and accounting programs. The simplicity of the code made it easy for customers to add to and modify elements. Johnson learned much about programming from Mosely.

In 1971, Adair called Mosely and Johnson, still the only two employees, into his office and told them that he had some personal problems to deal with, that he was shutting the business down, leaving town, and that they would have to find new jobs. That night Johnson thought about the business and saw real value to the new concept of software products. She went back to Adair and offered to buy the rights (for a small royalty on future sales for 2 years) to the two systems—payroll and accounts payable. He agreed to her offer, as he had no plans for the software; and Johnson became an entrepreneur in the software products industry. Johnson named the firm Argonaut Information Systems, after Argonaut Pawn Shop, which she passed by on her way to work each day—choosing the name, in part, to appear near the front of a section of the telephone directory (Fig. 11.1).

Figure 11.1. Argonaut Information Systems' Chair Luanne Johnson. (Courtesy of Luanne Johnson, 1986.)

Looking back, Johnson said it all happened too quickly for her to be scared. She rapidly put the finishing touches on the accounts payable system and began selling that and the payroll system. She was aware that software products were growing rapidly from Larry Welke, who traveled the country to learn of software products to add to his International Computer Products (ICP) *Software Directory*—an influential publication that helped the software products industry take off by listing many of the software products available nationally and internationally. In its first half-decade, many Fortune 1000 companies subscribed to Welke's *ICP Software Directory* (launched in 1967) to learn of new products to purchase for their data processing departments, while software companies subscribed to better understand the competitive landscape [20]. (The quarterly directory started with free listings to gain broad participation and sold annual subscriptions for $25. It took off in 1968 after *Kiplinger Washington Letter* ran a short piece encouraging firms to buy software "rather than re-inventing the wheel." For many years it was the standard source to learn about available software products.)

In the applications services trade, Johnson believed the industry was shifting. Applications services businesses were trying as never before to reuse as much code as possible. However, most customers continued to require substantial help with installation, customization, and training. This was gradually beginning to diminish as "code … [became] … more flexible and robust and had more options." Johnson's goal was to quickly get her products' code in such good shape that they could sell as close to "off the shelf" as possible. She also felt major progress could be made by writing better documentation, to obviate the need for training. These were her early priorities with the firm, along with selling aggressively and creating a stronger organization. She made some sales just by following up with potential customers initially contacted by Adair. Other than the ICP Directory, little marketing was necessary to build the business.

One benefit Johnson believed she would have in owning a company was greater flexibility and the opportunity to work less than full time. She was remarried at this point, running a household, and raising her daughter. While there may have been a bit more flexibility, she ended up working long hours. Johnson ran this one-person business out of a room in her house for the first year, using three or four independent contractors off and on to assist with installations. The business was extremely low overhead; and there was no need for start-up capital. Thanks to the ICP Directory, sales were national from the start—her first customer was in St. Louis. In its first year Argonaut Information Systems had roughly $60,000 in gross revenue. The business began to grow and, by the second year, Johnson hired an administrative assistant. With this, she moved the operation out of her home and opened a small office. Within several years she hired programmers and had a staff of four or five. On several occasions when customers were late with payments, she would have to borrow money to make payroll. No bank would lend her money, so she borrowed funds from her father.

As the software products industry took off in the mid- to late 1970s, large firms such as Management Science America (MSA) began launching major marketing campaigns for their products. (Management Science America and Informatics, Inc., were the largest U.S. software products firms in the late 1970s.

By then, both had software products revenues exceeding $30 million annually. The industry overall was composed of a handful of large firms and many small ones. In 1979 there were an estimated 1095 software products companies, with average annual revenue of just over $1 million [21].) Such large software firms, however, were targeting their marketing and sales to Fortune 500 customers. While these firms sometimes offered the same product features as Argonaut Information Systems, Johnson successfully focused on mid-sized and smaller firms and organizations. Much of her business came from companies that had installed IBM equipment. Soon they realized they had uneven demand and that valuable computing resources were often idle. They decided to capitalize on this by purchasing software from Argonaut to run some of their back office accounting functions in-house.

In the Bay Area there was an unusually well-developed base of independent contractors (ICs), which sometimes provided substantial competition. At times ICs, with even less overhead, would come in and do customized software for less than Argonaut charged for its products. Argonaut, however, was selling well nationally so that losing some local business was not a big problem. In general, Argonaut did particularly well in towns that did not have a major airport—places where none of the large software products and services companies would regularly fly in to make sales calls.

In its first decade Argonaut's marketing was primarily limited to the *ICP Software Directory* (listings were free) and smaller ICP publications that emerged (that charged a modest fee). Argonaut did a bit of advertising in large trade publications like *Computerworld*, but generally Johnson believed that ICP was sufficient. Looking back, she believed it was the only marketing that paid off. Argonaut did not participate in trade shows. Johnson estimates that at least 90% of her customers originally learned about Argonaut from the ICP publications. This provided plenty of business to keep her small staff and contractors busy.

On Larry Welke's (ICP) advice, Johnson attended her first ADAPSO conference in 1973 in San Diego and joined the association. ADAPSO had been launched in 1961 as a service bureau trade association. It soon became the leading trade association for computer services firms broadly and, by 1972, had also become the leading trade organization for the newly emerged software products trade. ADAPSO members were extremely open and shared information on successes and failures. Johnson later reflected, "I got my MBA from ADAPSO. It was an amazing environment to go in there. People from competitive companies would sit on panels and say, 'Well, here's the mistake I made. … here's what to look out for.'" In the long run, ADAPSO proved of greater interest to her than Argonaut.

Johnson might have had an opportunity to greatly expand her firm, but this is not what she wanted. In the early 1980s the firm had grown to roughly 15 employees. By this time it was generating millions of dollars of revenue each year. Johnson hired a marketing guru with a master's degree from Harvard to help with the business. Increasingly, she felt pressure from her employees to grow the firm. They wanted a larger organization with more layers of management, a firm where there would be opportunities for advancement and promotion. Johnson's interest had always been in developing robust products, with excellent documentation, that could sell virtually off the shelf. She had succeeded in this. Given that her employees wanted something different from the business, she decided it was time to exit and sold her firm, although she served as a consultant off and on with the enterprise for a half dozen years. She also remained active in ADAPSO and would go on to become the president of this organization (discussed in trade association section).

# GENTRY, INC.

Like Luanne Johnson, Grace Marie Hill was born in 1938. She grew up in Dallas and in Gilmer, Texas. A strong student at Hockaday Preparatory School in Dallas, she earned a scholarship to Harvard (Radcliffe) University. She majored in social relations with the goal of completing her undergraduate degree, going on for a doctorate, and becoming a professor. Following her first year at Harvard, she married Richard Gentry, who had just graduated from Texas A&M. Within a year they had their first child. Determined to pursue a career (and with strong support from Richard), she continued to take classes at the University of Arizona and University of California–Berkeley as the family moved first for Richard Gentry's Air Force pilot training and, later, for him to start graduate school in physics at Berkeley in 1960. (This section, unless otherwise noted, is from the Grace Gentry Oral History [22].)

Richard Gentry, who soon decided he wanted to enter the workforce rather than continue in graduate school, joined IBM's San Francisco branch as a systems engineer. He trained IBM customers in programming at the IBM Education Center for 4 years before transferring to the Government, Education and Medical Division (GEM). At GEM, he worked on data processing systems for Alameda County and soon distinguished himself by developing on his own time what came to be known as the Gentry Monitor, a highly efficient transaction processing system [23]. This system was the basis for IBM's successful Filing and Source Data Entry Techniques for Easier Retrieval, or FASTER [23].

Meanwhile, Grace Gentry had become disillusioned with sociology at Berkeley and decided to pursue an academic career in statistics. Richard, knowing the future of statistics would be computer-based, suggested Grace gain computer experience and brought home a copy of IBM's Programming Aptitude Test, on which she excelled. He also got her into a 2-week customer training programming course at the IBM Education Center.

Knowing the government was one of the best places, especially for women, to get advanced programming training, Grace Gentry took federal and local government exams. Scoring and interviewing well, she was offered positions with a dozen federal departments in 1967. She took an overload of classes to complete her degree in a semester and took a Management Intern position with the Social Security Administration (SSA). After advancing in the SSA but not wanting to move to Baltimore, Maryland, Grace Gentry was contacted by the University of California (UC) Statewide Electronic Data Processing Center and hired as a business analyst. Business analysts interviewed users to determine their needs and translate them to systems analysts, who in turn oversaw the programmers. With certain projects and deadlines, Grace Gentry worked as a systems analyst or did programming, teaching herself to use various programming languages. This led her to later jokingly reflect that she went backwards—from business analyst to systems analyst to programmer—but this broad experience would prove invaluable in later running an IT services contracting firm.

One day at UC Statewide, after Grace had developed a successful report writer for the university's admissions departments, her boss's boss congratulated her. She asked him how he heard about it, to which he replied, from a discussion in the men's room. Grace Gentry responded, "Well see, that's one of the problems. You guys go in there and piss together, and you chat and yak. How are we women ever supposed to be successful when we can't go in there with you?" This got around and another male employee soon said, "Hey, Grace, would you step into the men's room? I have something to tell you." While it was a joke enjoyed by all, the fact that communications and decisions often occur in male-gendered spaces (whether the men's room, boardroom, golf course, private club, or sporting events) at corporations and organizations was (and still is) quite real and can impact women's opportunities to succeed and advance.

At the start of the 1970s, Richard Gentry left IBM to work for William Millard's Systems Dynamics (SYSDYN). Millard, who had been head of Data Processing for Alameda County when Richard Gentry had done work for the county through IBM, later became famous for founding personal computer pioneering firm IMS Associates (IMSAI—in 1975) and fathering the field of personal computer retailing by co-founding ComputerLand (1976) [24]. His first venture, SYSDYN, however, failed in 1972. Soon after, a contact at Alameda County offered Richard Gentry consulting work, but for the county to hire him, he had to incorporate. This led to the formation of Richard E. Gentry, Inc., initially a one-person operation.

Projects grew with Alameda County; and Richard Gentry was asked to provide additional contractors. Grace Gentry had by that time moved from UC Statewide to Bank of America—as it began to actively recruit women for management positions. A manager at Bank of America told her that the bank felt it had missed out on hiring the best minorities and did not want to make the same mistake with women.

Although Grace Gentry saw opportunities at Bank of America, she left to help Richard with the Alameda County contract. Her experience at UC Statewide had left her with numerous women friends who had strong technical skills and experience. Within a year Grace and Richard Gentry had hired five women as independent contractors. While the company name was Richard E. Gentry, Inc., some called them "Wonder Women, Inc." Later, the name was officially changed to Gentry, Inc.

Within a couple years, as the number of contractors working at the firm expanded, Grace Gentry stopped working on contracts and devoted full-time hours to running the business. Richard Gentry worked for the firm as a lead consultant. While he would have preferred it just be the two of them working as contractors, he went along with Grace's decision to expand and run the enterprise. In the mid-1970s she had no models to offer guidance. If there were other brokerages hiring ICs for programming and system analysis, she did not know of any.

The initial hires were all women, which not only highlights the importance of personal networking, but also the risks involved in independent contracting—particularly in the early years when it was an uncharted business model. The firm only hired programmers and analysts with years of experience.

Figure 11.2. Grace Gentry at her home office (kitchen table) at Gentry, Inc. (1974–1977). (Courtesy of Grace Gentry.)

Grace Gentry reasoned that men would not want the uncertainty of this type of arrangement—even if it paid more in the short run. What would happen when the contract they were working on ran out? Would there be others? Wouldn't any potential advantage from a higher hourly rate be eaten away with health insurance and other costs? What was the path to career advancement? For married women the proposition was often seen quite differently: the family health insurance was commonly covered by their husbands' jobs. To earn a higher wage and have flexibility to enter and exit the workforce was a real advantage. There could also be tax advantages to operating as a self-employed business.

The firm had virtually no overhead. Grace Gentry ran it out of her kitchen for more than a half decade prior to leasing and later buying an office building in Oakland (see Fig. 11.2). The Gentrys' son, who was in high school, did the payroll. His younger sister took on this duty after he left for college. For analyst/programmers, the firm originally charged $12 per hour to clients. They paid $10 per hour to the contractors and did payroll only after collecting from clients. (This translated to $20,000 a year gross. A substantial salary for an experienced programmer at the time was around $10,000 to $14,000 a year. The first year the U.S. Bureau of Labor Statistics added the occupation of programmer was 1984. The midlevel salary for a programmer at that time was $27,158—or $12,867 adjusted back to 1974 (programmer salaries likely grew more than inflation) [25].) Thus, there was a delay in getting paid—a factor that mattered far less when it was secondary rather than primary income.

Gentry, Inc.'s rates to clients were a fraction of what clients had to pay IBM, Lambda, or other large services consultant enterprises for similar talent. Occasionally, potential clients wanted to check out the facilities—"kick the tires" as Grace Gentry put it. She would just confidently explain to them it was run from their home and that is why they were able to supply such talent at a rate sometimes only about one-third of what the giants would charge. Grace Gentry intentionally focused on serving smaller and mid-sized companies and organizations that were more price sensitive and often only needed one to several people (business the large firms generally avoided). The IT services giants, having to pay their salaried employees on the sidelines when projects ended and having other large overhead expenses, could not approach Gentry, Inc.'s rates for talented experienced programmers and systems analysts.

Within several years, one of Grace Gentry's contractors mentioned that her husband, an ex-IBM employee working for a smaller company, was not happy with his current situation and might want to work for Gentry, Inc. After he signed on, many other men soon followed—recognizing the advantage of getting paid for *all* the hours they actually worked, earning higher income, and betting on themselves and their skills to find the next job if necessary. Some younger, single male contractors went without buying health insurance, maximizing their net income.

Much like the uncertain professional status for programmers, which had contributed to its being at least marginally more open to women than many professions in the first decade (mid-1950s to mid-1960s) of the computer industry, the financial risks and uncertain status of IC programmers and systems analysts had facilitated women's entry into the field in this industry segment's first decade—the 1970s. By the 1980s, the model was more established; and there were numerous IC computer services brokerages emerging in urban areas throughout the United States. Many of these businesses were quite small, while a minority, including Gentry, Inc., grew to be mid-size enterprises with more than 100 contractors. The mix shifted toward male independent contractors and probably was roughly the same as the broader IT services industry. Grace Gentry's hiring all women in the first years was the result of her network of skilled contacts. It was about hiring highly competent contractors she could trust to excel for their clients. While the pool of candidates may have favored women in the early years (with men questioning the stability and status of IC jobs), this soon changed. Throughout, Grace Gentry hired the best candidates she knew or could recruit for the job regardless of gender.

Grace Gentry also took major steps to make independent contracting a career and not just a short-term job. Her contractors often worked with the firm for many years. Growing up, she had done various door-to-door selling jobs and was skillful at obtaining contracts from new clients. Early on, all the contracts they had were with Alameda County. She quickly saw the risk that this posed to her firm and her contractors. She aggressively sold her company's services in the public and private sectors, and diversified her base of industry clients. This enabled the firm to weather multiple recessions and maintain work for her contractors.

Grace Gentry also took the initiative to help her contractors extend their skills and make career advances similar to those they might make as employees at a larger firm. She would let programmers working on a project advance to systems analysts (charging the lower programmer rates) as they learned new responsibilities on the job. This helped the client save money, and helped the contractor retool upward, and in the long run also helped Gentry, Inc. With the next job she would be able to hire them out as systems analysts, charge the higher rates, and offer them the higher compensation. She learned that contractors were far more loyal if they had opportunities to advance their status and compensation.

In the late 1970s Grace Gentry sought to further diversify her company by adding new businesses, including a software products division and a third-party products division. With the latter, Gentry, Inc. supplied Hewlett-Packard equipment and sold software and services to create complete turnkey systems to meet clients' needs. Like many traditional services companies (that had employees rather than ICs), Gentry, Inc. sought to exploit the economies of reusing code by moving into software products. With these divisions, Gentry, Inc. hired technicians (programmers, analysts, project managers) as employees for the first time. (Gentry, Inc. already had some salaried sales and office staff.)

In 1979 Gentry, Inc. created a report writer called REX and followed this with a similar, more advanced, product the following year called PAL—both for the HP 3000 minicomputer. Gentry, Inc. was diligent at conducting customer surveys and updating the product. Grace reflected that it was rewarding to be a technical leader, but also somewhat frustrating, as competitors would see the new upgrades to Gentry's products at an annual trade show and add all the same features to their products.

As personal computer sales increased during the 1980s, it hurt HP's mini-computing business and the sales of Gentry, Inc.'s software products and turnkey solutions. When Grace Gentry suggested that her developers create report writers for PCs, they discouraged her from pursuing this, telling her, "We're going to do you a great favor … [and] … look for other jobs because you shouldn't do this. You cannot win against Microsoft." By that time the original contracting services division was clearly supporting the software products division, and the latter was sold off without profit. The turnkey business, also dependent on the success of HP minicomputers, quickly succumbed to a similar fate. While the products and turnkey businesses had helped support the contracting business at times, by the mid-1980s contracting was supporting the other two. (Although the independent contractor model allowed brokerages such as Gentry, Inc. to quickly downsize if contract work diminished, Grace Gentry always worked harder than ever to sell to businesses and organizations during such times and keep all the skilled contractors employed. She believed keeping the talent was of fundamental importance to the long-term success of the business.)

In 1986 Senator Patrick Moynihan introduced legislation—Section 1706 of the 1986 U.S. Federal Tax bill—that forever changed the landscape of the IT contracting industry. This section required that "technical service firms" that supply ICs to clients would no longer be granted employment tax-safe havens that apply to all other types of businesses using ICs. It, in effect, outlawed the IT independent contractor brokerage business model of Gentry, Inc. and similar firms. The bill was politically motivated and long fought for by trade organizations representing large IT services businesses that only used salaried employees [26]. To mobilize to try to fight this legislation, a number of IT services independent contractor brokerages, including Gentry, Inc., launched the trade association, the National Association of Computer Consultant Businesses [26]. (A fuller discussion of the NACCB is in the section on trade organizations in the latter portion of this chapter.)

Several years after Section 1706 hit the books, Gentry, Inc. switched to an employee-based model to avoid escalating historic tax liabilities in case the firm was ever found in violation of the code. The Gentrys' equity stake in their Berkeley home provided the payroll cash that allowed them to convert [26]. The legislation led some computer services brokerage businesses to shut down. The NACCB had a legal defense fund to protect firms that continued with a contracting model or had potential back taxes prior to converting to the employee model. By 1995 there were more than 125 member companies in the NACCB. Most were one-branch operations that served a single urban/regional (75-mile radius) market. About a quarter had annual revenue under $3 million, another quarter between $3 and $7 million. Approximately 15% had annual revenue exceeding $20 million [27].

The number of employees at Gentry, Inc. hit an all time high of around 200 in the middle to late 1990s as Y2K fears skyrocketed. In July 1998 Grace and Richard Gentry decided to retire and sold the firm to Personnel Group of America (PGA) for $12.5 million in PGA stock [28]. Many of their contractors/employees were longtime friends who knew that both Grace Gentry and Richard Gentry had taken no salary during rough economic times in the past (the recessions of the early 1980s and early 1990s) to keep them employed. These friends were thankful that the Gentrys sold, as they believed this pioneering firm would have gone under trying to keep everyone employed when the greatest challenge to date soon hit the IT industry, the so-called dot.com collapse.

## PHYLISS MURPHY AND ASSOCIATES

Phyllis Murphy was born in 1939 and grew up in Quincy, Illinois. She graduated with a degree in accounting from Western Illinois University. Upon completion of her degree she applied to numerous accounting firms in Chicago, and eventually was hired by a small company on Chicago's west side. A year and a half later she took a position in accounting with real estate management firm Draper and Kramer. In 1966 she was asked if she wanted to learn to program. When she inquired what this was, she was told computers "will do exactly what you tell them to do." She remembered thinking, "this could be love." She took a four and a half day programming course at Univac and then began wiring panels on a Univac 1004. She soon became Draper and Kramer's Director of IT. She recalled that at the professional meetings she attended for IT managers, she was often the only woman. (This section, unless otherwise noted, is from the Phyliss Murphy Oral History [29].)

Murphy left the firm in 1972 to gain expertise in data bases and networked computer systems—working for a service bureau firm for two and a half years. In 1974 she joined Consumer Systems, an IT services consultancy with major offices in Chicago and Minneapolis. She started as a consultant but soon began to manage IT projects for large clients, including a project to move insurance giant Banker Life and Casualty from a pure manual system to an online COBOL system. By 1978 Murphy was leading a group of 145 consultants for Consumer Systems. That year her husband had an opportunity to advance his career in Southern California; and they moved to Los Angeles. Phyliss Murphy agreed to head the much smaller Los Angeles office. She was the only woman to head an office for Consumer Systems.

Murphy found the Los Angeles operation and IT services environment to be far different from the Midwest. The sales personnel were largely ineffective and had no corporate training—unlike sales staff for Consumer Systems in Chicago and Minneapolis who were all trained at the Chicago headquarters. There were more IC consultants, and long-term relationships between IT service firms and client organizations were less typical in Southern California. Meanwhile, Consumer Systems was diversifying into a range of unrelated businesses and not adequately funding the Los Angeles office.

Given this situation, Murphy left Consumer Systems in 1981. She was very selective in seeking out a new employer. She briefly joined a permanent placement firm to help them hire staff to train IT specialists and to better learn the IT services terrain of Los Angeles. Having investigated many firms, and seeing problems (poor sales infrastructure, bad financial management, disrespectfulness, or poor back office) at each, she decided to start her own IT services business.

In 1981 Murphy launched her company. In a business where reputation and trust are critical, she wanted to ensure that clients could easily identify her with the firm and named it Phyliss Murphy and Associates. She used roughly 60% salaried employees and 40% ICs—feeling a mix worked well in Southern California (Consumer Systems had only salaried employees). She had gained experience working with large clients in the past, and she sought and received business from both large and small companies/organizations.

While understanding and responding to regional differences in establishing her business (such as using 40% ICs), she believed she managed her business in a Midwestern manner—focusing on honesty, integrity, and fiscal conservatism—that set her firm apart from many in the area. For more than a year she ran the business from her home, conducting interviews at a local Denny's restaurant.

By the third year Murphy had more than 20 employees/contractors and had tried out four salesmen—two who worked out—and had moved to lease office space. She always felt that quality sales staff was the greatest challenge in the computer services business. While she did not enjoy making sales calls, she did it regularly to close contracts. (With anticipated gridlock on the freeways during the 1984 Summer Olympics, Murphy shifted temporarily to have her sales staff primarily work the phones rather than make in-person sales calls. This experiment proved highly successful and ever since she has had her sales staff focus on calls, setting up face-to-face meetings when clients request it.) With her accounting background, she managed all the finances and accounting herself. Early on, she secured major contracts with large enterprises such as US Borax, which set up opportunities with many others. In contrast with Johnson's firm and Gentry's firm, Phyliss Murphy tried to target larger businesses, believing they were more professional and reliable than smaller enterprises in the greater Los Angeles area and that larger firms (generally far more than $500 million in revenue annually) understood supplemental technical staffing and were more focused on successfully completed IT projects than monitoring every minute of consultants' time.

Starting her business in the 1980s, the independent contractor model was already well established. Often both male and female services consultants preferred this model; it could lead to more compensation, it allowed them to manage their own money, and it resulted in the pride and independence of self-employment. Her employees and ICs generally had 6 years industry experience for the more junior positions and 8 to 10 years or more for senior employees/contractors. From the beginning, her business was roughly composed of 20% women and 80% men and had substantial ethnic/racial diversity. In the early years, Murphy believed that her being a woman helped, because she stood out; but in time it was neither a disadvantage nor an advantage—she believed the success of the business rested on delivering strongly for clients.

Oftentimes larger computer services businesses that were concentrated in other regions would seek to enter or expand in the Los Angeles market through acquiring local small to mid-sized computer services providers. Murphy related that these big firms often did not understand the Los Angeles environment in services (investing in expensive marketing campaigns, etc.) and frequently their newly created Los Angeles business/branch office would shut down within a few years. This occurred with acquisitions by Boca Raton-based Compustaff, and some other large services providers, and kept the environment favorable for small to mid-sized businesses such as Phyliss Murphy & Associates.

In 1987 Murphy became very actively involved with the NACCB. She started a chain letter outlining the history behind and the injustice of Section 1706. As a result, she became among the most high-profile critics of the legislation and was quoted in the *Wall Street Journal* and other publications. Taking on this role, she knew she had to switch to an all-employee only model right away—fearing IRS audits, of which four came in rapid succession.

Of all she gave to aid the efforts of the NACCB, she felt she received even more. As a result of the NACCB, she wrote conversion fees into every contract, purchased group insurance, and learned much that contributed to her firm's bottom line. Murphy successfully navigated her business through the extremely tough period from 2000 to 2002 and continues to own and run this successful enterprise. In reflecting upon her 28 years leading the business, she emphasized that the industry has been "great … for women," and she has no plans to retire.

## ADAPSO AND NACCB

Given the opportunity to demonstrate their many skills to colleagues and competitors, these women entrepreneurs (Luanne Johnson, Grace Gentry, and Phyliss Murphy) all became leaders in trade organizations. Here, they perhaps had greater understanding and ability than male leaders to help facilitate environments of trust, ethical practices, and sharing of information—the cooperation critical for such associations to add value by taking advantage of the collective wisdom of members and coordinating a united front to battle outside threats from competing industry segments and unsupportive legislators.

Luanne Johnson had been an active member of ADAPSO since 1973 and after she sold Argonaut Information Systems in 1980 (and stopped consulting for the enterprise in 1986), she accepted the invitation from this trade association to run the newly formed ADAPSO Foundation. ADAPSO had reached its 25th anniversary and formed the foundation as a way for the industry and organization to give back to the community. Under Johnson's leadership the foundation focused on various initiatives to help disadvantaged and disabled children.

Over the years Johnson had gained the respect of John Imlay, President of Dun & Bradstreet Software Services, Larry Welke (ICP), and other powerful individuals within ADAPSO. Following her short and successful stint heading the foundation, Johnson was asked to be executive director of ADAPSO in the late 1980s. ADAPSO by that time had grown into a massive trade association with hundreds of member firms—including nearly all the large players in software and services. It was a multidivisional association—with divisions for Information Systems Integration, Information Technology Services, Networked-Based Services, Software, and Vertical Applications & Remarketers—each with its own board [30]. Johnson had a degree of trepidation, but with strong encouragement from Welke and Imlay, and feeling she would always wonder "what if" had she declined, she signed on and moved from the San Francisco Bay area, her home for decades, to Washington, DC [18].

In the late 1980s and the start of the 1990s Johnson worked with the board to develop and implement a long-term plan focused on enhancing attention to membership services through a new Membership Services Department, as well as to boosting the image of the organization and increasing membership levels, communication, and education. ADAPSO, a major lobbying organization by this time, sought to promote "greater fairness in competition and regulation"—but this was a challenging task given the diversity of the association and industry segments with competing interests [30].

The software products industry had grown tremendously. There was also pressure to change the association's name—in large part because it reflected just the data processing services industry. In 1991 ADAPSO became the Information Technology Association of America (ITAA). That same year a woman became Chair of the Board for the first time, Judith Hamilton, and Johnson's title was changed from Executive Director to President.

Johnson and Hamilton's elevation to the top leadership of ADAPSO/ITAA represented a significant break with the past. Since the 1970s ADAPSO had some women members, many of whom were quite influential at the committee level. However, they tended to come from small companies and had difficulty moving up through the organization. Beginning in the 1970s, ADAPSO increasingly became an organization of mid-sized to very large companies, and its leadership generally was in the hands of certain leaders from these large firms—nearly all male. Judith Hamilton, in contrast, came from one of the accounting and services giants, Ernst & Young, and along with Johnson represented a new era of women's participation in the top leadership of the association. Both worked to maintain and extend ADAPSO/ITAA's role in sharing ideas through roundtables (where chief executives of noncompeting firms discussed policies, practices, and outcomes) and conferences, expanding international programs, and representing the organization's interest in a unified way to the government. In 1995 Johnson retired from her position as president but continued to work on international issues within the World Information Technology and Services Alliance, an organization she helped create to promote international cooperation and exchange in the software and services fields.

NACCB was a much different organization than ADAPSO. It was significantly smaller, had far less funds, was launched a quarter century after ADAPSO, and represented a very specific industry segment: IT consulting services brokerages. It also had been born out of a single issue, fighting Section 1706 of the 1986 tax bill. Within a few years, however, it expanded its scope. Grace Gentry, who had helped to found the organization, was an early president of NACCB and pushed strongly on not only 1706, but also to enhance membership services and benefits. She was a strong proponent of industry roundtables for executives to learn from each other's strategic and organizational successes and challenges. NACCB was ideally suited for roundtables since most member businesses were quite similar but operated in different geographies and thus were willing to share extensive information on their firms.

Phyliss Murphy had been the leader of one of the two predecessors of NACCB—the SC-SCBA (Southern California Software Contracting Businesses Association), a similar regional organization formed in the early 1980s that focused on industry challenges posed by state law. She, too, was a strong voice within the NACCB in the formative years. Both Gentry and Murphy were important forces in pushing for a NACCB standard "Code of Ethics," and Gentry created an industry survey—a highly useful tool for members in defining strategies and practices.

There were a number of computer services consultant businesses, particularly outside the organization, that engaged in activities that injured the reputation of the industry—such as hiring away talent from their own client organizations, submitting contractor's resumes for a job without first determining the contractor's availability or interest in that job, and similar unprofessional practices. By the early 1990s NACCB had a Code of Ethics in place that member companies had to honor. A description of the code was provided to clients and potential clients. Potential clients were encouraged by NACCB member companies to make certain that competitors adhered to the code, even if they were not part of NACCB. This helped elevate the overall ethical practices of the entire computer services consulting industry.

In its first decade, most NACCB members were small to mid-sized companies, and there were a significant number of women involved. In the early 1990s another woman entrepreneur, Peggy Smith, became the first Executive Director of the NACCB. Smith had worked at one of the large computer services consulting businesses, Lambda Technologies, in the early 1980s. General Electric's GEISCO timesharing business expanded into the consultant business at the start of the decade and acquired Lambda. In 1982 Smith transferred from Philadelphia to open GEISCO's consulting office in Greensboro, North Carolina. She was dissatisfied with GEISCO's lack of understanding of the consulting business and inadequate support for her operation and left to form her own company with two other individuals from the business. Having significant success but disagreeing on strategic direction with her partner in the late 1980s (the first partner had already exited), she sold out her share. She was an active NACCB member; and Grace Gentry recruited her to consult on growing NACCB membership in 1989. She went on to work on a number of issues and activities for the organization in the first half of the 1990s [31].

In 1995 she was officially hired as NACCB's Executive Director and soon secured an office in Greensboro for the trade association. She was instrumental in organizing and helping program NACCB annual conferences and industry roundtables and working with the organization's legal department led by Harvey Shulman, in Washington, DC (the home office later moved to Washington, DC). While most of the rotating presidents of the NACCB were men, Gentry, Murphy, and Smith had an enormous early impact on this small but rapidly growing and successful trade association. Smith was responsible for organizational practices that boosted the momentum of the NACCB's growth. Currently, of the three, only Murphy is still active in the organization. The NACCB has continued to grow rapidly and now consists of not only smaller and mid-sized firms but many of the giants in the computer services field.

## CONCLUSION

Women are distinctly absent from the existing historical literature on entrepreneurial leadership in the software and computer services industries [32]. Even trade journal literature and existing archival resources provide no real sense that women were any part of the dynamic risk-taking culture critical to the formation of new businesses and the thriving new trades in computer services and software. The dominant tendency in business history and entrepreneurial studies to focus only on large businesses, or on the small businesses that grew to become giants, contributes to the notion that IT firm creation was exclusively a male domain. Yet when small to mid-sized companies and lesser-known industry segments, such as the brokerage side of the computer services consulting business, are examined, it becomes clear that women entrepreneurs contributed substantially.

Women such as Grace Gentry, Phyllis Murphy, Luanne Johnson, and Peggy Smith all had worked within IT departments or divisions of mid-sized to large corporations and organizations and, to varying degrees, saw limitations in advancement to leadership roles or met with inadequate funding and lack of respect. Each of these women demonstrated vision, courage, and a mixture of self-reliance and cooperative leadership styles to launch and grow new computer services and software products businesses between the 1960s and 1980s.

While at times these women faced higher hurdles—for instance, Luanne Johnson could not get any kind of credit line early on, and Peggy Smith after getting remarried was asked to have her husband co-sign for her existing line despite his having no role in the business (something that definitely would not have occurred in reverse)—they all persevered and had considerable success. In interviewing these women, they all stressed that the IT world, with the exception of large firms, focused on achievement and results rather than gender in hiring contractors or buying software products. Because there were fewer women than men in the IT business, especially in the early years, their skills and demonstrated results stood out and helped them secure and retain clients and customers. In the words of Phyliss Murphy, her ability to deliver results *and* her gender "stood out."

Like small enterprise, trade associations, and especially leadership within these organizations, has been vastly understudied [33]. (Few historians have followed business historian Louis Galambos's strong lead in doing rigorous analysis of trade association—as he did for the cotton textile trade.) All four of these women provided substantial leadership to trade associations, adding value to member companies. Johnson and Smith held ongoing top executive posts within ADAPSO/ITAA and the NACCB, respectively. Gentry and Murphy helped found the NACCB and SC-SCBA, and both contributed mightily to the NACCB for many years—Gentry serving as an early president, and Murphy actively involved to this day.

Much as women computer scientists are important as role models to women students in colleges and universities, the histories of women IT entrepreneurs can serve as models for future women founders and leaders of IT businesses. This chapter, which first outlined some of the barriers to women's climb up the ladder in large computer and software businesses and organizations, highlights the important early role of entrepreneurial women in fundamental segments of the IT industry (computer services consulting and software products) and its leading trade associations between the 1960s and the mid-1990s. While these women's achievements were not made without overcoming obstacles, their technical and leadership skills came to the fore, were highly valued, and tended to bring opportunities and reward rather than discrimination and rejection. Most of all, this study is intended as a small first step to recovering the early role of women IT entrepreneurs, and a reminder of the importance of preserving records of these developments before they are forever lost.

# REFERENCES

**1.** "Lucent's Initial Offering Nets $3.025 Billion," *New York Times* (4 April 1996): D8.

**2.** Hewlett-Packard Corporation, *Annual Report* (2000). HP had a net income of nearly $3 billion in 1998.

**3.** eBay, *Annual Report* (2007).

**4.** "50 Most Powerful Women in Business," CNN/*Fortune*; available at **money.cnn.com/magazines/fortune/mostpowerfulwomen/2008/index.html** (accessed 12 December 2008).

**5.** See Nancy M. Carter, Colette Henry, Barra Ó Cinnéide, and Kate Johnston, eds., *Female Entrepreneurship* (London: Routledge, 2007); Jeanne Halladay Coughlin and Andrew R. Thomas, *The Rise of Women Entrepreneurs* (Westport, CT: Quorum Books, 2002); Robyn Eversole, "Change Makers? Women's Microenterprises in a Bolivian City," *Gender, Work & Organization*, Vol. 11, No. 2 (March 2004): 123–142.

**6.** Chandler's primary books defining his focus on the "managerial revolution" and the emergence and growth of large vertically integrated firms are *The Visible Hand* (Cambridge: Belknap Press, 1977); and *Scale and Scope* (Cambridge: Belknap Press, 1990).

**7.** For shifts to go beyond Chandler's focus on large vertically integrated firms, see Naomi R. Lamoreaux, Daniel G. Raff, and Peter Temin, "Beyond Markets and Hierarchies: Toward a Synthesis of American Business History," *American Historical Review*, Vol. 108, No. 2 (April 2003): 404–433.

**8.** Of the many quality works, two early standouts are: Alice Kessler-Harris, *Out to Work* (Oxford: Oxford University Press, 1981); and Thomas Dublin, *Women at Work* (New York: Columbia University Press, 1979).

**9.** There have been many quality historical studies of women's leadership in philanthropic and benevolent societies, politics, science, and medicine. For example, Louise W. Knight, *Citizen* (Chicago: University of Chicago Press, 2006); Elisabeth Griffith, *In Her Own Right* (New York: Oxford University Press, 1984); and Evelyn Fox Keller, *A Feeling for the Organism* (San Francisco: W. H. Freeman, 1983). Histories of women and business entrepreneurship are rare and tend to be on the 19th century or first half of the 20th century (prior to the advent of the computer industry). See

Wendy Gambler, "A Gendered Enterprise: Placing Nineteenth-Century Businesswomen in History," *Business History Review*, Vol. 72 (Summer 1998): 188–218; Susan M. Yohn, "Crippled Capitalists: The Inscription of Economic Dependence and the Challenge of Female Entrepreneurship in Nineteenth-Century America," *Feminist Economics*, Vol. 12, No. 1–2 (January/April 2006): 85–109; Kathy Peiss, "'Vital Industry' and Women's Ventures: Conceptualizing Gender in Twentieth Century," *Business History Review*, Vol. 72 (Summer 1998): 219–241.

**10.** Joan M. Greenbaum, *In the Name of Efficiency* (Philadelphia: Temple University Press, 1979).

**11.** Occupation status varied between firms. For the battles for authority and status in corporations' early computer centers see Thomas Haigh, "The Chromium-Plated Tabulator: Institutionalizing an Electronic Revolution, 1954–1958," *IEEE Annals of the History of Computing*, Vol. 23, No. 4 (October–December 2001): 75–104.

**12.** Martin Goetz Oral History, conducted by Jeffrey R. Yost (3 May 2002), Charles Babbage Institute, University of Minnesota; available at **www.cbi.umn.edu/oh/**.

**13.** John Cullinane Oral History, conducted by Jeffrey R. Yost (29 July 2003), Charles Babbage Institute, University of Minnesota; available at **www.cbi.umn.edu/oh/**.

**14.** Jack Stone, "The Human Connection" *Computerworld* (4 July 1977): 17.

**15.** Katharine M. Donato and Patricia A. Roos, "*Gender and Earnings Inequality Among Computer Specialists,*" in Barbara Drygulski Wright ed., *Women, Work, and Technology: Transformations* (Ann Arbor: University of Michigan Press, 1987), pp. 291–317.

**16.** Katharine M. Donato, "Programming for Change? The Growing Demand for Women System Analysts," in Barbara F. Reskin and Patricia A. Roos, *Job Queues, Gender Queues* (Philadelphia: Temple University Press, 1990), pp. 167–182.

**17.** Myra H. Strober and Carolyn L. Arnold, "Integrated Circuits/Segregated Labor: Women in Computer Related Occupations in High-Tech Industries," in Heidi I. Hartmann, Robert E. Kraut, and Louise A. Tilly, eds., *Computer Chips and Paper Clips* (Washington, DC: National Academy Press, 1987), pp. 136–182.

**18.** Luanne Johnson Oral History, conducted by Jeffrey R. Yost (12 August 2008), Charles Babbage Institute, University of Minnesota; available at **www.cbi.umn.edu/oh/**.

**19.** The meteoric rise and subsequent fall of the stock of H. Ross Perot's Electronic Data Systems was a central tale of James Brooks' *The Go-Go Years* (Hoboken, NJ: Wiley, 1974).

**20.** Lawrence Welke, "Founding the ICP Directories," *IEEE Annals of the History of Computing*, Vol. 24, No. 1 (January–March 2002): 85–89.

**21.** Martin Campbell-Kelly, *From Airline Reservations to Sonic the Hedgehog: A History of the Software Industry* (Cambridge: MIT Press, 2003), pp. 18–19, 127.

**22.** Grace Gentry Oral History, conducted by Jeffrey R. Yost (11 August 2008), Charles Babbage Institute, University of Minnesota; available at **www.cbi.umn.edu/oh/**.

**23.** Richard Gentry Oral History, conducted by Burton Grad (24 May 2006), Computer History Museum; available at **www.computerhistory.org/collections/oralhistories/**.

**24.** Millard's leadership of IMSAI and Computer-Land is chronicled in Paul Freiberger and Michael Swaine, *Fire in the Valley*, 2nd ed. (New York: McGraw-Hill, 2000).

**25.** Carl Prieser, "Research Summaries: Occupational Salary Levels for White-Collar Workers, 1984," *Monthly Labor Review* (1984): 43–45.

**26.** Harvey Shulman Oral History, conducted by Jeffrey R. Yost (30 March 2007), Computer History Museum; available at **www.computerhistory.org/collections/oralhistories/**.

**27.** 1995 NACCB Operating and Compensation Survey (copy provided to author by Grace Gentry).

**28.** Grace Gentry Oral History, conducted by Luanne Johnson (24 May 2006), Computer History Museum; available at **www.computerhistory.org/collections/oralhistories/**.

**29.** Phyliss Murphy Oral History, conducted by Jeffrey R. Yost (18 December 2009), Charles Babbage Institute, University of Minnesota; available at **www.cbi.umn.edu/oh/**.

**30.** ADAPSO Annual Guide (1990), ADAPSO Records, Charles Babbage Institute, University of Minnesota.

**31.** Peggy Noell Oval History, conducted by Jeffrey R. Yost (29 January 2009), Charles Babbage Institute, available at **www.cbi.umn.edu/oh/**.

**32.** Martin Campbell-Kelly, *From Airline Reservations to Sonic the Hedgehog: A History of the Software Industry* (Cambridge: MIT Press, 2003). This is an excellent history of the software products business and the first decade of the services industry. Its cases are made up by the first business in the overall software and services industries and the players that grew to become large firms—these were all headed by men.

**33.** Louis Galambos, *Competition and Cooperation* (Baltimore: Johns Hopkins University Press, 1966).

# Gender Codes
## Lessons from History

# 12

THOMAS J. MISA

The fascination with personal computing in the 1980s widened the audience for popular books on computer programmers and their personalities. Yet, oddly enough, these popular accounts tended to narrow the image of computing. And this image has a man's face. *Programmers at Work* (1986) presents 19 interviews with "brilliant programmers," *Out of Their Minds* (1995) celebrates the lives and discoveries of 15 great computer scientists, while more recently *Beautiful Code* (2007) takes the aesthetic pulse of 38 "leading programmers." These books profile a total of 72 computer scientists; and among them just one woman, Laura Wingerd, a software product manager [1]. Somehow the editors and publishers unaccountably passed over such leading women figures as Jean Bartik, Francis (Betty) Holberton, Jean Sammet, Fran Allen, and Barbara Liskov. (Each of these women have won such notable accolades as the IEEE Computer Pioneer Award, the Association for Computing Machinery's Turing Award, widely acclaimed to be computing's Nobel Prize, or being named a Fellow of the Computer History Museum.) Given women's clear presence in the practices, communities, and institutions of computing that are amply documented in this book, why did the public image of computing become so male? Three examples illustrate the workings of media bias and institutional blindness.

Let's first consider the singular Robert X. Cringely, a journalist and media personality whose magazine columns, best-selling book, and television programs have done much to perpetuate specific stereotypes about gender and computing. Cringely is the pen name of Mark Stephens, who wrote the monthly computer-gossip column at *Infoworld* from 1987 to 1995. His best-selling *Accidental Empires* (1992) spawned the popular PBS series "Triumph of the

Nerds" and did much to elaborate and entrench the male nerd stereotype. *Accidental Empires* relates "how the boys of Silicon Valley make their millions, battle foreign competition, and still can't get a date" and includes at most a half-dozen women among its numerous dramatis personae: among them, "a blonde suit in her twenties named Jennifer Seman" who goofs up a software license. His follow-on "Nerd TV" series in 2005 also pushed women to the sidelines. After unaccountably selecting a 23-year-old woman fashion model as the central figure for the 9th episode of the series, Cringely eventually featured for the 13th episode a truly accomplished woman, Judith "Judy" Estrin—an entrepreneur active in the microprocessor, networking, and software industries and for a time Chief Technology Officer for networking giant Cisco Systems [2].

Secondly, institutional blindness in at least one notable case accounts for *why* women's accomplishments in computing were seemingly rubbed out. Two of ENIAC's women programmers were removed from the scene—literally cropped out of the picture—when the U.S. Army placed the ENIAC machine with one male operator at the center of its 1946 recruiting campaign (Fig. 12.1). Young men were told: "The ENIAC is symbolic of many amazing Army devices with a brilliant future for you!" The cropped image in an October 1946 advertisement in *Popular Science Monthly* pointedly overlooked the hundreds of women who had assisted the war effort. These women were no longer wanted since the "Army needs men … for scientific work" and "enlistments are open

Figure 12.1. Women with pioneering ENIAC machine. Women working on ENIAC at the Moore School (full view) were cropped out for a 1946 U.S. Army recruiting advertisement (inset), in which only Corporal Irwin Goldstine remained (airbrushing took out the second man at back). (Source: U.S. Army photo; available at ftp.arl.army.mil/ftp/historic-computers/.)

Figure 12.2. Frances (Betty) Holberton with Univac LARC-2 supercomputer (c.1961). A key software pioneer, Frances Holberton (1917–2001) programmed the ENIAC (1942–1946) and created software for the UNIVAC at Eckert–Mauchly Computer Company and Remington Rand (1947–1953). At the Applied Math Laboratory (1953–1966) of the U.S. Navy's David Taylor Model Basin, a large-scale test facility for ship design, she supervised advanced programming and helped create the computer language COBOL. (Courtesy of Charles Babbage Institute.)

... to ambitious young men" [3]. In the Army, and elsewhere in American society, women who had taken up nontraditional roles in the war effort were now directed back to traditional women's roles as stay-at-home mothers. It took decades to properly recognize the ENIAC women for their programming what was arguably the first electronic computer. Finally, in 1997 all six—Kathleen McNulty Mauchly Antonelli, Jean Jennings Bartik, Frances Snyder Holberton (Fig. 12.2), Marlyn Wescoff Meltzer, Frances Bilas Spence, and Ruth Lichterman Teitelbaum—were inducted into the Women in Technology International's Hall of Fame, and several have subsequently received additional recognition.

Consider, as a third example, the depiction of women in *Wired* magazine, where beginning in the 1990s Nicholas Negroponte, Stewart Brand, George Gilder, John Perry Barlow, and others defined an emerging digital culture. "*Wired* is about the most powerful people on the planet today—the Digital Generation," its cofounder proclaimed. While promoting digital culture as a universal force shaping the contemporary world, the magazine presented a highly skewed masculine perspective. Its covers frequently featured well-known (white male) computer entrepreneurs or objectified images of women. In 15 years of monthly issues there were just two cover-story profiles of accomplished women in its pages and no less than five cover stories about Bill Gates. *Wired* is labeled outright as a "men's magazine" by Nikki Douglas, long-serving senior editor of Grrlgamer.com [4]. Whether through media bias or institutional blindness, the absence of women from the public images of computing certainly reinforced the perception of computing as a masculine domain [5].

This chapter assembles the lessons to be learned from the other chapters in this book. To put our findings in a nutshell, we believe that computing's present-day dilemma with gender—the place of men and women in its practices and institutions and images—has a great deal to do with computing's history. A stiff dose of accurate history, dispelling the male-centered mythology broadcast by Cringely and *Wired* and other popular media accounts, is one positive result of this volume. We can review this accomplishment in greater detail.

## WOMEN IN COMPUTING

This book aims to illustrate the varied participation of women in all aspects of computing throughout its history. Even while many observers over the years have portrayed "the computer" in masculine terms, the historical reality is much more complex. Women were involved with computing literally from the moment of creation, and their stories need to be known more widely. Computer history is slowly catching up. For example, Grace Murray Hopper is justly celebrated as a founder of automatic programming—owing to her work at Harvard's pioneering Computation Laboratory, the ENIAC-successor Eckert–Mauchly Computer Corporation, and at Univac, the first commercially successful computer company. She also played a key role in creating COBOL and standardizing FORTRAN (Fig. 12.3). Hopper was even named as the Data Processing Management Association's first "man of the year" in 1971 (as noted in Chapters 3 and 6 in this volume), the first of her many significant honors and awards. Recently, with the annual Grace Hopper Celebration of Women in Computing, she has become an icon with literally thousands of webpage entries. Yet, amazingly enough, the first serious scholarly biography about Hopper was just published in 2009 [6].

The achievements and celebrations of many additional women in computing are still awaiting full treatment. Chapters 10 and 11 in this volume are notable efforts to recount the experiences of women computer-science pioneers as well as women information-technology entrepreneurs. We hope that telling their stories is a step toward a more accurate and complete image of computing. Yet for each of these justly celebrated women, there were thousands of women who worked as ill-paid keypunch operators or computer operators. An important historical lesson is that the "information revolution" that we most frequently associate with electronic digital computers, emerging in the 1950s, has an older and deeper history. Information was transformed from continuously varying qualities or measurements into standard quantified units, that is, digitized, and literally punched onto cards much earlier than the invention of electronic computers that came along to speed up the calculations and sorting of this information. Already by the 1920s, a generation after Herman Hollerith tabulated the 1890 U.S. Census, a sizable punch-card industry had sprung up in the United

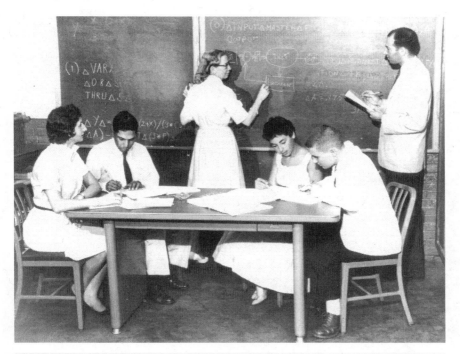

Figure 12.3. Grace Hopper as prophet of high-level programming languages. Grace Hopper (1906–1992) programmed Harvard's Mark I computer (1944–1949) and helped developed the UNIVAC (1949–1966), for which she wrote the world's first compiler in 1952. Her ideas on higher-level programming inspired COBOL. She directed the Navy Programming Languages Group (1967–1977), eventually retiring as Rear Admiral. (Courtesy of Charles Babbage Institute.)

States and also across the industrial countries of western Europe [7]. In most places the industry had a largely female workforce, and in the 1950s when electronic business computers were introduced by Remington Rand, IBM, and other companies, these computers were literally grafted onto or merged into a company's existing punch-card operations. In this way, electronic business computing did not create "new" gendered work conditions. Instead, business computing was strongly shaped by existing gender expectations, policies, and practices in the workforce (see Chapters 3, 4, and 5 in this volume).

And these gendered patterns from one generation have a long shadow. The specific gender norms of the mechanical punchcard era persisted well into the electronic computing era. Succeeding generations of women in computing confronted the established fact that women working in offices had defined gender roles as typists, clerks, stenographers—and, for years, workers who punched data onto cards. Conversely, men processed these punch cards and managed the punch-card workforce. As Hicks shows in Chapter 5, women were energetically recruited into the British government workforce undergoing computerization—until the moment when computing jobs were assigned significant managerial responsibility and women were in effect barred from them. The status seeking that often accompanies professionalism lent a different path to

Figure 12.4. Women programmers and systems analysts. In recruiting publicity, Burroughs featured Roz Westra, a 1978 computer science graduate, who worked as a senior systems analyst in Irvine, California, on hotel reservation software. (Courtesy of Charles Babbage Institute.)

the same general result in the United States, as professional organizations in data processing, programming, and librarianship adopted practices and professional practices that "coded" the upper rungs of the profession as masculine, even as many women continued to labor in rank-and-file positions (See Chapters 3, 4, 6, and 7).

Women were prominent in the first generation of computer programmers, owing something to the field being new and undefined. Their ranks in the computing profession grew steadily across the late 1960s and 1970s. It bears repeating that during these decades computing was unusually open to women—compared with medicine, law, and engineering. Women worked as highly skilled programmers and systems analysts as well as lower-paid operators and maintenance workers (Fig. 12.4). By the mid-1980s, when women's proportion in computing education peaked at 37% in the United States, computing was the most gender-balanced of any of the engineering professions. All the same, there have been several distinct barriers to women's full acceptance in the ranks of computing. It seems useful to acknowledge these barriers—sexism, narrow images, and even overly restricted conceptions of gender—and to suggest they should be confronted in reform efforts of today. (Media-driven stereotypes, an important part of the gender gap, are discussed in the following section.)

## IMAGES OF GENDER AND COMPUTING

Sexist humor and macho work culture, while by no means unique to computing, is identified as one key factor at play when women leave computing [8]. Recent interviews with 2500 men and women in the science, engineering, and technology professions present evidence of "a macho culture where women are very much outsiders, and where those who do enter are likely to eventually leave," with nearly two-thirds of women reporting harassment on the job [9]. In the computer-game industry "work conditions remain overtly hostile to female employees," according to Henry Jenkins and Justine Cassell (and as noted in Chapter 1 sexism lives on in computer gaming and industry trade shows) [10]. At MIT students were reportedly "shocked, confused, and amused" when, without warning, the "home page for a pornographic web site was displayed on the projection screen at the front of the auditorium" for the introductory course on Structure and Interpretations of Computer Programs. Controversy ensued concerning the appropriateness of frontal (female) nudity and the promise of "full screen, top resolution" pictures in a computer science course. Eventually, MIT issued an apology clearly stating that "it is not acceptable … to use instructional material that needlessly offends" [11].

The pervasive *image* of the solitary male programmer, so wrapped up with computing as to be "dreaming in code," is not universally attractive or inviting. There have been, at times, extreme elements within the computing cultures that have taken pride in creating a masculine world of their own (Fig. 12.5). This image of the separate (masculine) world had its origin with the early notion of the programmer-priesthood. As John Backus, the inventor of FORTRAN once put it: "many programmers of the freewheeling 1950s began to regard themselves as members of a priesthood guarding skills and mysteries far too complex for ordinary mortals" [12]. The priesthood image proved irresistible for publicity efforts, and many media accounts over the years have perpetuated some version of it. Indeed, the strongest of all the gendered images in computing

Figure 12.5. Computerization and mass media. Computer system by Geodatic, Inc., of Princeton, New Jersey, prepares "personalized replies to prospective customers" responding to *Playboy* magazine advertisements (1970). (Courtesy of Charles Babbage Institute.)

that shape our perceptions of the present and our expectations of the future is the latter-day priesthood of "nerds."

Modern computer nerds were most likely born with MIT's notable hacker culture of the early 1960s, as such diverse writers as Joseph Weizenbaum, Sherry Turkle, Steven Levy, and others have outlined. The seminal loci were a group of programmers that formed around the early TX-0 and PDP-1 computers, the Tech Model Railroad Club, and soon enough the MIT Artificial Intelligence Lab. In the mid-1970s the *National Lampoon* issued its "Are You a Nerd?" poster (and immediately at MIT at least one such self-identified nerd "glanced at the poster, then put on my [heavy black framed] glasses ... hiked up my polyester slacks an extra half-inch, and assumed The Pose"). Nerds have never enjoyed a stable identity, however [13]. Several different terms—grind, gnurd, hacker, tool, dweeb—have over the years described someone with an overwhelming attraction to the inanimate technical world. The *New Hacker's Dictionary* (1993) provides two broad definitions. Positively: "someone who knows what's really important and interesting and doesn't care to be distracted by trivial chatter and silly status games." Less positively, defining the closely related "computer geek": "one who fulfills all the dreariest negative stereotypes about hackers: an asocial, malodorous, pasty-faced monomaniac with all the personality of a cheese grater." The terms "nerd" and "geek" today form potent if sometimes ambiguous images [14]. One can find them rattling through popular culture, computer advertising, and mass media in many forms (see Chapters 8 and 9 in this volume).

The media obsession with the conflict that male computer nerds supposedly experience with traditional gender roles may itself contribute to the gender gap in computing. The nerd image identifies something odd with young men who "flaunt ... their thin, underdeveloped bodies" and who appear to be uninterested in young women, but this simply cannot be the whole story. A wider concept of *gender* itself would be helpful in investigating, for instance, how gay men and lesbian women experience the "macho" culture of computing and negotiate its assumptions about proper gender behaviors. In reality, computer nerds or hackers do not all conform to the narrow image of a solitary heterosexual or asexual male. "Hackerdom easily tolerates a much wider range of sexual and lifestyle variation than the mainstream culture. It includes a relatively large gay and bisexual contingent," according to the *New Hacker's Dictionary* (1993). "Hackers are somewhat more likely to live in polygynous or polyandrous relationships, practice open marriage, or live in communes or group houses. In this, as in general appearance, hackerdom semi-consciously maintains 'counterculture' values." Lynn Conway further suggests the need for a nontraditional concept of gender. The co-author with Carver Meade of a pioneering textbook on VLSI design fabrication, Conway underwent a gender transition from male to female and later was publicly "outed" in 1999. In 18 different languages besides English, Conway's web site on transgender issues has received nearly 3 million hits [15].

Images expressing anxieties about gender roles in computing have a long history. In the early years of mainstream personal-computing use, many worried that women were somehow falling behind while men, having mastered the personal computer, would dominate the jobs that required its use. Journalists,

Figure 12.6. Anxieties about gender roles in computing. Herb Grosch as "computer wizard" using a General Electric computer to compute lunar orbits, with female assistant identified only as "Ann." (Courtesy of Charles Babbage Institute.)

then, focused on the *minority* of young men who were true computer experts, overlooking the vast majority of men who, just like most women, were not expert users. Women got their own journalistic treatment, with a focus on their lack of expertise and considerable hand-wringing about their future. It's as if a preconceived idea was already in the heads of the journalists (Fig. 12.6). As noted earlier, the image of male computer experts forming a distinct separate society with its own culture and ethos circulated in Weizenbaum's *Computer Power and Human Reason* (1976), with its striking portrait of the "compulsive programmer"; Stephen Levy's celebratory *Hackers: Heroes of the Computer Revolution* (1984); and Robert Cringely's popular books and TV programs.

Reinforcing the circulation of images, cultural norms were embedded also in the "programmer aptitude tests" and personality profiles that IBM and other leading computer companies used in identifying, hiring, and training computer programmers. As Nathan Ensmenger makes clear in Chapter 6, such norms emerged even in the entire absence of reliable knowledge about who was a good prospect for training as a programmer. The personality profiles offer an egregious instance of illogical circular reasoning: somehow programmers were believed to have certain specific personality characteristics, and so individuals fitting these characteristics were hired, and so the next generation of programmers indeed had these characteristics, however flimsy the original rationale for them. This illogical process led to real-world consequences and entrenched certain cultural norms in programming.

In the case of programmer aptitude tests and personality profiles, we can trace the path that led from ungrounded assumptions to certain consequences. It is not so easy to trace the complex paths that images take through the popular media. Early ideas about what computing "ought" to look like, however these came about, seem to dispose editors to commission stories in a certain way. Such media treatments can become self-fulfilling prophesies, with pioneering stories setting up the categories or personalities that define or frame subsequent stories. It is abundantly clear that certain types of stories about the (masculine) computer world became permanent fixtures in popular culture. Male geniuses figure large in the world created by Cringely and *Wired* magazine.

For popular culture, an origin moment of the lone male computer genius was a 1971 piece in *Esquire* magazine, in which author Ron Rosenbaum profiled the colorful and quixotic John Draper. In "Secrets of the Little Blue Box," Rosenbaum played up the personality of Draper, but rather left to the shadows the community of blind teenagers who had initially discovered that the plastic whistle from Captain Crunch breakfast cereal emitted the precise tone that unlocked the phone system [16]. These blind teenagers taught the amazing feat to John Draper, and he quickly designed and built "blue boxes" for manipulating the phone system. And the phone system, as Draper well knew, "is nothing but a computer." Draper, soon enough famous as Captain Crunch, taught these secrets to two prank-loving California teenagers who launched their careers making and selling blue boxes in the Berkeley dorms. They were Steve Wozniak and Steve Jobs, and the rest is history. (Rosenbaum even maintains that his *Esquire* piece introduced Jobs and Wosniak to the existence of "blue boxes.") Subsequently, many popular books, movies, and internet sites about computing featured the colorful and quotable Captain Crunch. A high point of sorts was Captain Crunch's appearance (played by Wayne Péré) in the fictional docudrama *Pirates of Silicon Valley* (1999). One way or another, a mythic Captain Crunch echoes through to today. Some years later, Rosenbaum appraised his own "part [in] the creation of a true American hero … [a] genuinely significant-mythic American icon" [17]. Another well-known *Esquire* piece, "The Tinkerings of Robert Noyce," by Tom Wolfe (1983), profiling the co-founder of electronics giant Intel, helped define Silicon Valley in popular culture. Is it a coincidence that the men's magazine *Esquire* spawned these male-centered mythic images?

## SHADOWS OF STEREOTYPES

Gender-based computing stereotypes persist in news and advertising media, and computing reform efforts need to recognize the process through which mass media sources of many types create, reinforce, and occasionally modify such stereotypes to the general public [18]. In Chapter 8, Corneliussen documents the process through which Norwegian newspapers established stereotypes in the Norwegian public consciousness between 1980 and 2007. Possibly to create controversy or just to spark readers' interest, newspapers focused on gender *differences* in computing, portraying men as embracing computer skills and women as computer-phobic. Once established, the stereotypes became self-fulfilling prophecies by rendering invisible the people who did not fit the stereotype, such as female computer users and the large number of computer-phobic males. This media perception of a "good story" might explain why the large number of women in the history of computing have for so long gone largely unnoticed and unrecognized: the ENIAC women described by Ensmenger in Chapter 6, the satisfied women computer programmers described by Abate in Chapter 10, and the successful women computer entrepreneurs described by Yost in Chapter 11. Commonly accepted stereotypes—and the select facts that fit them—are by their nature easy to remember because they oversimplify complex realities and frequently reinforce one another and are therefore easy to remember (Fig. 12.7). But the real people did not fit the stereotype and therefore were soon forgotten in public discourse.

While stereotypes can be remarkably persistent, they can and do change over time. Corneliussen documents how the media's discourse on computing changed over time from "computers for all" in the early 1980s, to "men are computer geniuses" while "women are computer-phobes" in the 1990s to "women have invaded the internet" and "male computer nerds can have a tan too" in the 21st century. Reform efforts to change these stereotypes can draw on historical studies of computing practices, involving women and men, as well as give appropriate publicity to the evolving practices of computing. It is little reported in the mass media, for instance, that young women are active users of

Figure 12.7. Media images strengthened gender stereotypes. Stylized publicity images, such as this one for NCR's Century 100 computer (1967), often portrayed male managers—this one wearing an unrealistically expensive suit—directing female support staff. (Courtesy of Charles Babbage Institute.)

the Internet (creating content and not just surfing the web) as well as increasingly prominent as computer gamers.

While some computing stereotypes may be common across many cultures, there may also be country-specific variations. This volume makes a preliminary reconnaissance of this terrain. Differences in gender norms existed between the punch-card departments of German and American businesses, as discussed in Chapter 4. Gender discrimination persisted in Britain so strongly as late as the 1980s to attract the legal sanction of the European Community. Chapter 9 documents stereotypes appearing in Greek computer advertisements between 1983 and 2003. Men are consistently depicted as relaxed in the context of computers, and in control, without actually doing any of the associated "busy work," while women are depicted as carrying out the instructions of men through interacting with keyboards and printers. The Greek images of men as relaxed and in control around computers, but not actually using them, are at odds with the Norwegian stereotype of men as computer users and technical experts analyzed in Chapter 8. Similarly, the Greek images of women as the primary users of (office) computers seem to diverge from the Norwegian stereotype of women as nonusers of computers. Whether these images and stereotypes are "converging" with the spread of the Internet—or persisting despite it—is something that we simply don't know. Since these media images have complex effects in society, concerted efforts are needed to counteract the existing stereotypes that have placed women, as well as men, in narrow gender-specific roles [19].

## REFERENCES

**1.** Susan M. Lammers, *Programmers at Work: Interviews with 19 of Today's Most Brilliant Programmers* (Redmond, WA: Microsoft Press, 1986); Dennis Shasha and Cathy Lazere, *Out of their Minds: The Lives and Discoveries of 15 Great Computer Scientists* (New York: Copernicus/Springer, 1995); Andy Oram and Greg Wilson, eds., *Beautiful Code: Leading Programmers Explain How They Think* (Cambridge: O'Reilly, 2007).

**2.** Robert X. Cringely, *Accidental Empires: How the Boys of Silicon Valley Make Their Millions, Battle Foreign Competition, and Still Can't Get a Date* (New York: Addison-Wesley, 1992), quote p. 264. On "Cringely," see www.wired.com/wired/archive/6.12/cringely_pr.html, www.pbs.org/cringely/nerdtv/transcripts/013.html, and www.infoworld.com/t/platforms/sco-strikes-gold-verizon-just-strikes-728. *Infoworld*, after firing Stephens, who was the third Cringely to write the column (the second reportedly was a woman), secured rights to the name, and so a later version of Robert X. Cringely® carries on the legend.

**3.** Contrast the "classic" picture of ENIAC at ftp. arl.army.mil/ftp/historic-computers/jpeg/eniac2.jpg, clearly showing two women and Corporal Irwin Goldstine, with the Army's 1946 advertisement printed as figure 2 in Jennifer S. Light, "When Computers Were Women," *Technology and Culture*, Vol. 40, No. 3 (1999): 455–483 on p. 476. muse.jhu.edu/journals/technology_and_culture/v040/40.3light_figures.html.

**4.** Melanie Stewart Millar, *Cracking the Gender Code: Who Rules the Wired World?* (Toronto: Second Story Press, 1998), pp. 96–107, quote p. 71. For *Wired* covers, see www.wired.com/wired/archive/covers.html. Nikki Douglas, "The Future of Games Does Not Include Women" (5 April 2006); available at www.grrlgamer.com/article.php?t=futureofgames (accessed 26 June 2009).

**5.** Notable for including numerous women in a history of software is Steve Lohr's *Go To: The Story of the Math Majors, Bridge Players,*

Engineers, Chess Wizards, Maverick Scientists and Iconoclasts—The Programmers Who Created the Software Revolution (New York: Basic Books, 2001). Unfortunately, Publisher's Weekly wrote: "Lohr's learned narrative never quite engages the reader … this account of reputed fringe visionaries lacks flash and loopiness," which, in a strange way, suggests why Cringely is such a success.

**6.** Kurt W. Beyer, Grace Hopper and the Invention of the Information Age (Cambridge: MIT Press, 2009).

**7.** Lars Heide, Punched-Card Systems and the Early Information Explosion, 1880–1945 (Baltimore: Johns Hopkins University Press, 2009).

**8.** J. McGrath Cohoon and Jie Chao, "Sexism—Toxic to Women's Persistence in CSE Doctoral Programs," Computing Research News, Vol. 21, No. 1 (January 2009); available at www.cra.org/CRN/articles/jan09/cohoon_on_sexism.html.

**9.** Lisa Belkin, "Diversity Isn't Rocket Science, Is It?" New York Times (15 May 2008).

**10.** Henry Jenkins and Justine Cassell, "From Quake Grrls to Desperate Housewives," in Yasmin B. Kafai et al. eds., Beyond Barbie and Mortal Kombat: New Perspectives on Gender and Gaming (Cambridge: MIT Press, 2008), pp. 5–20, quote p. 13; and Dmitri Williams, Nicole Martins, Mia Consalvo, and James D. Ivory, "The Virtual Census: Representations of Gender, Race and Age in Video Games," New Media & Society, Vol. 11, No. 5 (2009): 815–834.

**11.** Dan McGuire, "Pornography Display in 6.001 Provokes Debate on Decency," Tech News (27 February 1998); available at tech.mit.edu/V118/N8/aporn.8n.html. For the official apology, see www.mit.edu/activities/safe/cases/mit-demo-pics/penfield.txt.

**12.** John Backus, "Programming in America in the 1950s: Some Personal Impressions" in N. Metropolis, J. Howlett, and Gian-Carlo Rota, eds., A History of Computing in the Twentieth Century (New York: Academic Press, 1980), quote p. 127.

**13.** Benjamin Nugent provides an alternate geneology, tracing "nerd" to the campus culture of Rensselaer Polytechnic Institute in the mid-1960s and to the Saturday Night Live characters played by Bill Murray and Gilda Radner in the late 1970s. See his American Nerd (New York: Scribner, 2008), pp. 55–66. "Nerd" and "geek" are from Eric S. Raymond, compiler, The New Hacker's Dictionary (Cambridge: MIT Press, 1993); available online at www.ccil.org/jargon/jargon.html.

**14.** Ron Eglash, "Race, Sex, and Nerds: From Black Geeks to Asian American Hipsters," Social Text, Vol. 20, No. 2 (2002): 49–64; and several web sites available at www.nerdgirls.org, www.nerdgirls.com, and www.girlgeeks.org.

**15.** Eric S. Raymond, compiler, New Hacker's Dictionary (Cambridge: MIT Press, 1993); Sherry Turkle, The Second Self: Computers and the Human Spirit (Cambridge: MIT Press, 2005), quote p. 183. Lynn Conway's web site is at ai.eecs.umich.edu/people/conway/. For analysis, see Judith Butler, Bodies that Matter (New York: Routledge, 1993); and Catharina Landström, "Queering Feminist Technology Studies," Feminist Theory, Vol. 8 (2007): 7–26.

**16.** Ron Rosenbaum, "Secrets of the Little Blue Box," Esquire (October 1971) is available at Captain Crunch's web site, www.webcrunchers.com/crunch/stories/esq-art.html, and at www.lospadres.info/thorg/lbb.html (May 2009). For Rosenbaum's claim about Jobs and Wosniak, see www.slate.com/id/28402/entry/28403/ (May 2009) and www.youtube.com/watch?v=AgD3a4ulwaE (August 2009).

**17.** Ron Rosenbaum, "Pynchon and Crunch: Heroes of the Underworld Wide Web," New York Observer (4 February 2001); available at www.observer.com/node/43941 (May 2009).

**18.** Kaylene L. Clayton, Liisa A. von Hellens, and Sue H. Nielsen, "Gender Stereotypes Prevail in ICT: A Research Review," SIGMIS-CPR '09 (New York: ACM, 2009), pp. 153–158.

**19.** At Carnegie Mellon, Carol Frieze taught a course "Understanding and Challenging the Images of Computing" in the spring of 2009; available at www.cs.cmu.edu/~cfrieze/courses/index.html (May 2009). For the ACM's initiative "New Image for Computing," see www.acm.org/membership/NIC.pdf (accessed August 2009). In 2007 the IEEE launched a new publication, Women in Engineering Magazine.

# Gender Codes
## Prospects for Change

# 13

CAROLINE CLARKE HAYES

$W$hy have the proportions of women earning undergraduate computing degrees, and working in the computing workforce, been dropping since the mid-1980s—when women's participation in nearly all other technical disciplines is on the rise? This question is of great concern to educators, employers, funding agencies, and the U.S. federal government because a sizable, diverse, and creative information technology workforce is critical for continued participation in the high-tech, global economy. Contributors to this volume aimed to shed light on this question, if not to answer it completely, providing insights into possible causes of the current situation and outlining ways to reverse this trend.

It is important to remember that women are scarce only in some aspects of computing. To think of "computing" as a single profession, as such, hides the richness and complexity of the true situation, and this framing may also obscure solutions. For many decades, women have comprised the majority of many low-status, low-paying segments of the computing workforce such as data entry and word processing. Conversely, women have persistently been underrepresented in high-status, high-paying segments such as hardware design and upper level management. There are many professional layers within computing, each with its own distinct story.

This volume identifies several of these layers, and tells the story of each layer's evolution with respect to gender roles over time. By following the evolution of several segments of computing, in several countries, and identifying the multiple forces that shaped them, we can begin to understand the forces shaping the current situation and how those forces might be realigned.

The primary areas of recent concern are the falling proportions of women in undergraduate computer science programs, and the white-collar professional computing jobs for which those degrees prepare them, such as software developer (programmer) and systems analyst. In undergraduate computer science programs the percentage of women earning bachelor's degrees fell dramatically from its peak in 1984 at 37% women to less than half this level. Furthermore, the 2007 HERC/HERI freshman interest survey indicates that it is likely to fall further by 2010, possibly leveling out at 10% women [1]. These proportions are similar to the gender proportions in the fields of electrical and mechanical engineering, the most strongly male-dominated of the technical disciplines.

In white-collar computing jobs, there has also been a similar drop that roughly parallels the one in undergraduate education. The proportion of women employed as systems analysts and software developers fell from a peak of 38% in 1987, 3 years after undergraduate enrollments peaked, down to 29% in 2005. The recent losses in female bachelor degree graduates since 2002 are not yet reflected in the workforce, but one can expect that they will be.

These demographic changes are substantial, and they are entirely unlike the patterns observed in other fields of science, technology, engineering, and mathematics (the so-called STEM fields). According to National Science Foundation data, the proportion of women bachelor degree graduates in STEM fields has steadily been rising over the past four decades, from 25% women in 1966 to 51% in 2006. Moreover, women are not disappearing from all segments of computing. In the United States, many of the low-status computing tasks such as data entry and word processing continue to be largely female (see Chapters 3 and 4). While this is not necessarily good news, there is good news in some high-status computing areas. The proportion of women is actually increasing among computer science doctorates and full professors [2]. We emphasize this to combat the common but oversimplified view that women are disappearing from all sectors of computing. They are not.

## POSSIBLE EXPLANATIONS

There are numerous hypotheses as to why the proportion of women is shrinking in several important segments of computing. We will explore the strengths and weaknesses of three hypotheses: a lack of female role models; an unappealing, masculine nerd culture; and negative, masculine stereotypes of computing.

### Lack of Female Role Models

One could argue that a lack of female role models in computer science is a major contributing cause. Thus, one might expect that increasing the proportion of women faculty in computer science might increase undergraduate women's interest in signing up for a computer science major. In fact, the proportion of women among computer science faculty has been increasing for the last 20 years, yet the proportion of women undergrads has fallen drastically. Increasing faculty role models has clearly not been sufficient, by itself, to increase the proportion of women undergraduates. There must be additional forces at work.

## Masculine Nerd Culture

The male-dominated "nerd" culture is often blamed for chasing women out of computing. However, a male-centric culture alone does not explain why the proportion of undergraduate computer science women is decreasing; there are many other male-dominated "nerd" cultures in fields such as engineering and physics, and yet the proportion of women in these fields continues to increase, not decrease. So perhaps the more appropriate question would be: Is the culture of computer science (CS) *more* hostile to women than that of other STEM fields? If CS culture is more hostile, then one would expect to see a disproportionate drop-off in the proportion of women in computer science as they advance in education level and career stage. Figure 13.1 shows that the drop-off in computer science is average compared to other STEM fields.

Figure 13.1 shows the difference between the predicted proportion of female faculty and the actual proportion. The "actual" is based on Nelson's faculty data for the top 100 departments in various STEM fields. The "predicted" is based on the historical pipeline of Ph.D. graduates and is calculated from the National Science Foundation data tracking Ph.D. graduates over the previous 35 years (1966–2001). Fields with the smallest proportions of women, such as the engineering disciplines, appear to be the best at recruiting and retaining women with doctoral degrees into the faculty ranks. Furthermore, fields such

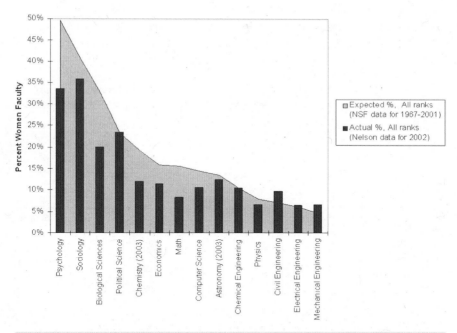

Figure 13.1. Retention of women from doctoral to faculty levels: Expected versus actual percentage of U.S. women faculty, 2002. Data from National Science Foundation, *Science and Engineering Degrees: 1966–2006* (Arlington, VA: National Science Foundation, 2008); and Donna J. Nelson, "A National Analysis of Diversity in Science and Engineering Faculties at Research Universities" (15 January 2004).

as psychology and the biological sciences, which have graduated relatively large proportions of women with doctoral degrees for a long time, do not appear to be particularly successful at recruiting and retaining these women as faculty [3]. This figure raises many additional questions such as: Are engineering disciplines making a greater effort to recruit and retain women faculty? Clearly, additional investigation is needed.

However, the key point for this discussion is that the "shrinkage" of women with increasing rank is no worse in computer science than in the majority of STEM fields. Women are just as likely to advance to faculty ranks in CS as in other STEM fields.

## Negative Stereotypes

The "computer science geek" is typically portrayed as an antisocial white male, highly skilled and intelligent, with little attention to personal hygiene. This image is not terribly appealing to either men or women, but it is likely more unappealing to women. The geek image does not necessarily match reality; while such people exist, the average person actually in computer science is not like the "geek." Thus, it may be external *perceptions* of computer science culture that deter many women, more so than the actual culture.

The computer geek image has been around for many years. Why should women be more deterred by it now? Indeed, for 20 years, smaller and smaller proportions of undergraduate women have been choosing computer science as a major, as shown in Figure 13.2. Only 1% of all undergraduate women graduated in computer science in 2006. By contrast, at 5.5%, the proportion of undergraduate men graduating in computer science was approximately the same in 2006 as it was in 1986.

What has changed? Early in computing's history the general public was not particularly aware of what computer programming was, nor what people in

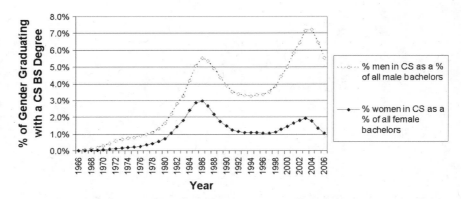

Figure 13.2. Proportion of all undergraduates earning computer science degrees: popularity of computer science as a major. (Data from National Science Foundation, *Science and Engineering Degrees: 1966–2006* (Arlington, VA: National Science Foundation, 2008).)

that profession were supposed to be like. This was certainly true in the mid-1960s: "The best bit was that no one knew what I did as it was so new" (see Chapter 5). However, by the early 1980s, the increasing popularity and success experienced by computer science also increased media attention and public awareness of computer science stereotypes. Public and media attention on computing certainly increased since the 1980s as computers have crept into almost everyone's daily activities.

Thus, what has changed is the public awareness of computing stereotypes. We suggest that negative male-centered media images may have turned increasing numbers of women away from computing careers (and also some men). Chapters 8, 9, and 12 illustrate specifically how newspaper and advertising media have created, perpetuated, and modified computing images and stereotypes. Clearly, more research is needed to determine the timing, prevalence, and nature of computing images in the media.

## REVERSING CURRENT TRENDS

If the popular image of computer science is a significant factor in the gender gap, then changing or modifying the popular images may be a crucial strategy. While it may be difficult to erase the already established computer geek stereotype, it may be possible to modify it or augment it with other more positive images of computing.

Fortunately, people can hold multiple, possibly conflicting images and stereotypes of a single profession, simultaneously. For example, in the mid-1990s during the Internet craze and the dot.com bubble, several computing stereotypes coexisted simultaneously including the "evil hacker," the whiz-kid nerd, and the twenty-something entrepreneur-millionaire who was hip yet so respected that he could get away with wearing a T-shirt and jeans to critical business meetings.

The changing prevalence of each of these images may have a strong impact on career choices. Thus, in the mid-1990s, the positive male computer entrepreneur-millionaire image may have counteracted the negative male computer geek image for men, but likely less so for women, since both images were male. This may explain the upsurge of interest in computer science for both men and women during the late-1990s dot.com bubble, although more so for men. That upsurge ended abruptly when the dot.com bubble burst in 2000.

The lessons are that both positive and negative images can coexist, and that positive male images may positively influence both genders, even if one gender responds more strongly than the other. Is it possible for computer science to introduce new, positive images of computing that can counteract the existing negative ones? And if one is to do so, how can they be introduced effectively?

## INTRODUCING NEW IMAGES: APPROACHES TO CHANGE

History has shown that some approaches to change are more effective than others. We discuss two broad categories.

## Approaches Based on Existing Stereotypes

Corneliussen in Chapter 8 describes three types of discourse about gender and computing: *gender blind*, which in effect blames women for making the wrong choices in not taking up computing more actively; *masculine*, which encourages women to think in new ways about computing and to fit into the established culture; and *feminine*, which attempts to rewrite the meaning of computing as "less technical" and "more social" in a discourse that aims to make computing more appealing to women—if one believes the stereotypes.

Each of these three approaches relies on and perpetuates existing stereotypes that may be problematic. A "gender blind" approach fails to take into account current and very real social and cultural differences between men and women, and as it attempts to motivate through blame, it is unlikely to inspire anyone. Alternatively, both the "masculine" and "feminine" approaches potentially insult women who are already in computing (Chapters 10 and 11), and may alienate both men and women who are potentially interested in computing but do not fit stereotypes (Chapter 8). Finally, the attempt to recast computer science as nontechnical, taken by the "feminine" approach, is a bit like attempting to recast the ocean as "not really so salty." It is not an effort destined for success. Whether men or women, people interested in computer science will be interested in it for its technical nature, among its many other appeals.

## Gender-Independent Approaches

Gender-independent approaches are those that do not make assumptions about the inherent interests and backgrounds of each gender (such as all women like pink and are afraid of technology, or all men like football and love technology), although they may implicitly leverage demographic differences. Carnegie Mellon University (CMU) has employed a successful gender-independent approach that simultaneously increased the number of women and the diversity of ideas and personalities among the men in their programs (see Chapter 2). Modifying the admissions process was the key in CMU's effort to increase the proportion of women in their undergraduate computer science program. CMU's admissions focused less on past programming experience and more on leadership, while keeping grade and test standards high [4]. Differences in background were evened out by making background courses available. This approach is gender independent because it neither aims to recast computer science as less technical, nor does it make assumptions about the interests or backgrounds of either men or women.

While it is not entirely clear why this approach worked or what additional factors shaped the results, the removal of prior programming-experience requirements was certainly important. At that time, men were more likely than women to have had prior programming experience (recently this is changing). The removal of background requirements may have removed barriers for women, while also opening the program up to men from more varied backgrounds. The end result was good for both groups. Whether intentional or not, the program encouraged diversity of ideas as well as better gender balance.

The National Academy of Engineering has identified a gender-independent approach to change the image of engineering [5]. This approach could easily be adapted to computer science. (The ACM's recent initiative, "New Image for Computing," aims at similar results [6].) The NAE project was initiated in response to concerns about the adequacy of the U.S. technical workforce, and its lack of diversity, and draws on market research techniques. In general, the public has a limited understanding of what engineers do: images may come to mind of men driving trains, of tinkering with machines while wearing dirty coveralls, or using calculators while sitting at drafting tables. Most people don't realize that "engineers help shape the future" or "engineering is essential to our health, happiness and safety," to cite two of the messages tested by the project.

Don Giddens of Georgia Tech, chair of the committee that produced the NAE report, states that "we want to emphasize how an engineering career provides an opportunity to change the world rather than over-emphasize the obvious need for strengths in math and science" [7]. While this approach emphasizes the human and social aspects of engineering, which may well be of interest to women at this time in history, it is gender independent in that it does not assume that *only* women care about these aspects of engineering. Such strategies can increase the diversity of interests found in both women and men in the student body. Moreover, since the human and social aspects are inherent to engineering (if underappreciated by the larger public), this is not simply recasting engineering to appear more "friendly" to women. Georgia Tech emphasizes to prospective students that "engineers change the world." While many factors likely influence a student's decisions to come, Georgia Tech graduates a very large proportion of women in engineering [8].

## Examples of Image-Changing Strategies

People outside computer science, including young women considering career choices, get their impressions of what people in the profession are like through many sorts of media images in movies, advertising, newspapers, television, and promotional materials. Images may come in the form of written stories, depictions of characters in movies, or photographic images on web sites, advertisements, or other places. Images of many types *do* have an impact on the implicit biases that people hold. People may or may not be consciously aware of their own biases, yet they impact the way in which people make decisions [9].

However, images can also be used to change these biases. The Implicit Association Test assesses a person's implicit associations between paired concepts, like "race" and "criminal," or "race" and "president." Malcolm Gladwell (a mixed race Jamaican-American) describes how repeated daily exposure to positive images of African Americans improved his IAT scores, indicating that he now held more positive associations with African Americans [10]. More positive and more female images of computing might be used in the same way to change the public view of computer science.

While it may not be possible to directly influence the computing images that commercial advertisers, the press, or Hollywood choose to use, professional computing organizations, government organizations (such as the National Science Foundation), universities, and companies employing computing professionals can choose the computing images they use in their advertising and promotional materials and web pages. Art is another interesting vehicle for presenting images that change people's viewpoints because of its power to reach people at an emotional and concrete level. Nancy Johnson exhibited portraits of women engineers in 2006 at the Phibbs Center for the Arts in Hudson, Wisconsin. These portraits will eventually be housed near the engineering and science dean's office at the University of Minnesota, where students, faculty, and staff can see them on a daily basis. The same can be done for computer scientists. The public, especially young people who have not yet made career choices, needs to be exposed to such images, whether contemporary or historic. It is equally important to change the impressions that men have of computer science if one is to change the overall culture or the impressions held by society as a whole.

However, such images additionally have to be placed in additional forums where young people can see them regularly: on YouTube, in coffee shops that house art exhibits, or as a rotating exhibit hung in the hallways of K-12 schools (not just high schools). Through exposure, attitudes might be changed.

## The Importance of Local Change

Even when one cannot change the whole of society, one can often change one's local institution or department. Social change happens through many avenues, including individual and local changes. It is also important to keep in mind that numerical change is not the only important goal; cultural changes that help women (or other underrepresented groups) to feel comfortable and productive in their environment are also important. Significant cultural changes may be possible in a specific department or group, even when achieving gender balance is not.

## PATHS FROM THE PAST TO THE FUTURE

Much remains to be done. The studies and analysis of computing's history contained in this volume provide a better view of the sometimes forgotten but bold roles that women have played throughout computing's history, for example, as the world's first programmers and as business entrepreneurs who found opportunity in risks that most men were not willing to take. They have also provided insights into how computing's current "shrinking women" crisis came about and may provide important guidance in identifying corrective strategies. However, more historical investigation needs to be done in order to truly understand how we arrived at the present. This knowledge is power in shaping a healthy and competitive future for computing [11].

Some of the research that still needs to be done includes further investigation of the hypothesis that rising public awareness of male "computer nerd" and "evil hacker" images factored into the recent 20-year decline in the proportion of women. This will require studies of computing images in news and advertising media, as well as historical interviews with people from the general public to understand computing awareness, attitudes, and perceptions of the general public (e.g., people outside computing).

It is also important to investigate why both women and men entered (or left) computing at various times in history. For example, looking at Figure 13.2, one can see that the recent 20-year shift in the undergraduate gender balance resulted both from a smaller share of women and a larger share of men choosing CS. It is important to understand what affected the choices of both of these groups. While it is hard to get a comprehensive picture of how many women were in computing before the National Science Foundation started to track degrees in 1966, or the Bureau of Labor Statistics started to track computing jobs in 1971, it is still important to understand the dynamics and attitudes of this time.

Historical studies may help change the existing image of computing. Stories and profiles of women in computing gathered through oral history interviews can be presented to the students, researchers, and interested members of the public through a rich variety of existing and new-media forms, ranging from photographic exhibits of successful women to videos on YouTube. Such stories may have the power to counteract the misbegotten idea that computing has always been about men, and may help to attract a more diverse group into computing's future.

# REFERENCES

**1.** John H. Prior, Sylvia Hurtado, Jessica Sharkness, and William S. Korn, "The American Freshman National Norms for Fall 2007." Higher Education Research Institute, Graduate School of Education & Information Studies (University of California, Los Angeles, 2007).

**2.** National Science Foundation, Division of Science Resources Statistics, *Science and Engineering Degrees: 1966–2006.* (Arlington, VA: National Science Foundation, 2008); National Center for Women and Information Technology, *NCWIT Scorecard 2007* (Boulder: University of Colorado, 2007).

**3.** Both civil engineering and electrical engineering are more successful in hiring women than is biology, according to 1999–2003 data from the National Academy of Science; see Neil Munro, "Science Faces Title IX Test," *National Journal Magazine* (4 July 2009).

**4.** Lenore Blum and Carol Frieze, "The Evolving Culture of Computing: Similarity Is the Difference" *Frontiers: A Journal of Women Studies*, Vol. 26, No. 1 (2005): 110–125.

**5.** National Academy of Engineering, Committee on Public Understanding of Engineering Messages, *Changing the Conversation: Messages for Improving Public Understanding of Engineering* (Washington, DC: National Academies Press, 2008).

**6.** For a preliminary report on the ACM's initiative "New Image for Computing," see **www.acm.** org/membership/NIC.pdf (accessed August 2009). This initiative originally focused on differences between racial/ethnic groups, but its preliminary findings are that gender is the more fundamental determinant of positive views of computing. Specifically, "we found relatively small differences in the responses of Hispanic, African American, and White boys, but the disparity between boys and girls is profound" (p. 7).

**7.** "Changing the Public's View of Engineering"; available at **www.coe.gatech.edu/feature/02_ nae.php** (accessed August 2009).

**8.** Karl W. Ritzler, "Tech Urges Women to Try Engineering," *Atlanta Journal-Constitution* (2 May 2008).

**9.** A. G. Greenwald, D. E. McGhee, and J. L. K. Schwartz, "Measuring Individual Differences in Implicit Cognition: The Implicit Association Test," *Journal of Personality and Social Psychology*, Vol. 74, No. 6 (1998): 1464–1480.

**10.** Malcolm Gladwell, *Blink: The Power of Thinking Without Thinking* (New York: Little Brown and Company, 2005).

**11.** D. A. Lenat and E. A. Feigenbaum, "On the Thresholds of Knowledge," *Proceedings of the International Joint Conference on Artificial Intelligence*, Vol. 2 (1987): 1173–1182.

# Bibliography

Abbate, Janet. "Women and Gender in the History of Computing," *IEEE Annals of the History of Computing*, Vol. 25, No. 4 (2003): 4–8.

Abbate, Janet. "How Did You First Get Into Computing?" *IEEE Annals of the History of Computing*, Vol. 25, No. 4 (2003): 78–82.

Abbate, Janet. "Proto-feminism and Programming: Gender Politics in Computing Before the Civil Rights Era," paper presented at Society for the History of Technology Annual Meeting, Washington, DC, October 2007.

Acker, Joan. "From Sex Roles to Gendered Institutions," *Contemporary Sociology*, Vol. 21, No. 5 (1992): 565–569.

Adam, Alison. "Constructions of Gender in the History of Artificial Intelligence," *IEEE Annals of the History of Computing*, Vol. 18, No. 3 (1996): 47–53.

Anderson, Sonya Lee. "The Data Processing Management Association: A Vital Force in the Development of Data Processing Management and Professionalism" (Ph.D. thesis, Claremont Graduate University, 1987).

Anonymous. "Data Processing Salaries Report—1971," *Business Automation*, Vol. 18, No. 8 (1 June 1971): 18–29.

Anonymous. "Staff Organization and Their Training," *Computing News*, Vol. 5, No. 95 (15 February 1957): 8–11.

Aron, Cindy Sondik. *Ladies and Gentlemen of the Civil Service: Middle-Class Workers in Victorian America* (New York: Oxford University Press, 1987).

Aspray, William, and Donald B. Beaver. "Marketing the Monster: Advertising Computer Technology," *Annals of the History of Computing*, Vol. 8, No. 2 (1986): 127–143.

Association for Computing Machinery. "New Image for Computing"; available at www.acm.org/membership/NIC.pdf (accessed August 2009).

*Gender Codes: Why Women Are Leaving Computing,* Edited by Thomas J. Misa
Copyright © 2010 the IEEE Computer Society

Atkin, Andrea M., Ruth Green, and Laura McLaughlin. "Patching the Leaky Pipeline," *Journal of College Science Teaching*, Vol. 32, No. 2 (2002): 102–108.

Augst, Thomas, and Wayne A. Wiegand, eds., *The Library as an Agency of Culture* (Madison: University of Wisconsin Press, 2003).

Aune, Margrethe. "The Computer in Everyday Life: Patterns of Domestication of a New Technology," in Merete Lie and Knut H. Sørensen, eds., *Making Technology Our Own?* (Oslo: Scandinavian University Press, 1996), pp. 91–120.

Austrian, Geoffrey D. *Hermann Hollerith: Forgotten Giant of Information Processing* (New York: Columbia University Press, 1982).

Backus, John. "Programming in America in the 1950s: Some Personal Impressions," in N. Metropolis, J. Howlett, and Gian-Carlo Rota, eds., *A History of Computing in the Twentieth Century* (New York: Academic Press, 1980), pp. 125–135.

Bair, Bettina, and Miranda Marcus. "Women's Interest in Information Technology: The Fun Factor," in Carol J. Burger, Elizabeth G. Creamer, and Peggy S. Meszaros, eds., *Reconfiguring the Firewall: Recruiting Women to Information Technology Across Cultures and Continents* (Wellesley, MA: A. K. Peters, 2007), pp. 161–175.

Baker, Elizabeth Faulkner. *Technology and Woman's Work* (New York: Columbia University Press, 1964).

Bakhtin, Mikhail Mikhailovich. "The Problem of Speech Genres," in Caryl Emerson and Michael Holquist, eds, *Speech Genres and Other Late Essays* (Austin: University of Texas Press, 1986), pp. 60–102.

Banaji, Mahzarin R., and Anthony G. Greenwald. "Implicit Gender Stereotyping in Judgments of Fame," *Journal of Personality and Social Psychology*, Vol. 68, No. 2 (1995): 181–198.

Baran, Barbara. *Technological Innovation and Deregulation: The Transformation of the Labor Process in the Insurance Industry* (Washington, DC: U.S. Congress, Office of Technology Assessment, 1985).

Barker, Lecia J., and William Aspray. "The State of Research on Girls and IT," in J. McGrath Cohoon and William Aspray, eds., *Women and Information Technology: Research on Underrepresentation* (Cambridge: MIT Press, 2006), pp. 3–54.

Baron, Ava, ed. *Work Engendered: Towards a New History of American Labor* (Ithaca, NY: Cornell University Press, 1991).

Baum, Christina D. *Feminist Thought in American Librarianship* (Jefferson, NC: McFarland & Company, 1992).

Becker, Joseph, and Robert M. Hayes. *Information Storage and Retrieval: Tools, Elements, Theories* (Hoboken, NJ: John Wiley & Sons, 1963).

Beckwith, Laura, Margaret Burnett, Valentina Grigoreanu, and Susan Wiedenbeck. "Gender HCI: What About the Software?" *IEEE Computer* (2006): 97–101.

Belkin, Lisa. "Diversity Isn't Rocket Science, Is It?" *New York Times* (15 May 2008); available at www.nytimes.com/2008/05/15/fashion/15WORK.html.

Beyer, Kurt W. *Grace Hopper and the Invention of the Information Age* (Cambridge: MIT Press, 2009).

Bird, Peter. *Leo: The First Business Computer* (Wokingham, UK: *Hasler Publishing Ltd.*, 1994).

Black, Maurice. *The Art of Code* (Ph.D. thesis, University of Pennsylvania, 2002); available at repository.upenn.edu/dissertations/AAI3072974.

Blum, Lenore, and Carol Frieze. "The Evolving Culture of Computing: Similarity Is the Difference," *Frontiers: A Journal of Women Studies*, Vol. 26, No. 1 (2005): 110–125.

Bolliger, Doris U. "Perceived Gender Based Stereotypes in Educational Technology Advertisements," *TechTrends*, Vol. 52, No. 3 (2008): 46–52.

Brandon, Richard. "The Problem in Perspective," in *Proceedings of the 1968 23rd ACM National Conference* (New York: ACM Press, 1968), pp. 332–334.

Brataas, Anne. "Lack of Women in Computing Has Educators Worried," *Inside Science News Service* (16 June 2008); available at www.insidescience.org/policy/lack_of_women_in_computing_has_educators_worried (accessed August 2009).

Braverman, Harry. *Labor and Monopoly Capital: The Degradation of Work in the Twentieth Century* (New York: Monthly Review Press, 1974).

Brooks, James. *The Go-Go Years: The Drama and Crashing Finale of Wall Street's Bullish 60s* (Hoboken, NJ: John Wiley & Sons, 1974).

Bryan, Alice. *The Public Librarian* (New York: Columbia University Press, 1952).

Burrelli, Joan. *Thirty-Three Years of Women in S&E Faculty Positions*. June 2008, NSF 08-308; available at www.nsf.gov/statistics/infbrief/nsf08308/.

Burris, Beverly H. "Technocracy and Gender in the Workplace," *Social Problems*, Vol. 36, No. 2 (1989): 165–180.

Butler, Judith. *Bodies that Matter* (New York: Routledge, 1993).

Bylinsky, Gene. "Help Wanted: 50,000 Programmers," *Fortune*, Vol. 75, No. 3 (1967): 141.

Camp, Tracy. "Survey Says! Results on the Incredible Shrinking Pipeline" (1998); available at www.mines.edu/fs_home/tcamp/results/paper.html.

Camp, Tracy. "The Incredible Shrinking Pipeline," *Communications of the ACM*, Vol. 40, No. 10 (1997): 103–110.

Campbell, Scott M. "Beatrice Helen Worsley: Canada's Female Computer Pioneer," *IEEE Annals of the History of Computing*, Vol. 25, No. 4 (2003): 51–62.

Campbell-Kelly, Martin. *From Airline Reservations to Sonic the Hedgehog: A History of the Software Industry* (Cambridge: MIT Press, 2003).

Campbell-Kelly, Martin, and William Aspray. *Computer: A History of the Information Machine* (New York: Basic Books, 1996).

Canning, Richard. "Issues in Programming Management," *EDP Analyzer*, Vol. 12, No. 4 (1974): 1–14.

Canning, Richard. "Professionalism: Coming or Not?" *EDP Analyzer*, Vol. 14, No. 3 (1976): 1–12.

Carlson, Scott. "Wanted: Female Computer-Science Students," *Chronicle of Higher Education*, Vol. 52, No. 19 (13 January 2006): A35; available at chronicle.com/free/v52/i19/19a03501.htm.

Carlson, Walter. "ACM and Special Interest Groups," *Data Base*, Vol. 25, No. 2 (1994): 9–12.

Carpenter, Raymond L., and Kenneth D. Shearer. "Sex and Salary Survey," *Library Journal* (15 November 1972): 3682–3685.

Carter, Nancy M., Colette Henry, Barra Ó Cinnéide, and Kate Johnston, eds. *Female Entrepreneurship: Implications for Education, Training and Policy* (London: Routledge, 2007).

Cassell, Justine, and Henry Jenkins, eds. *From Barbie to Mortal Kombat: Gender and Computer Games* (Cambridge: MIT Press, 1998).

Ceruzzi, Paul E. "An Unforeseen Revolution: Computers and Expectations, 1935–1985," in Joe Corn, ed., *Imagining Tomorrow: History, Technology, and the American Future* (Cambridge: MIT Press, 1986), pp. 188–201.

Chamberlain, Mary. "Narrative Theory," in Thomas L. Charlton, Lois E. Myers and Rebecca Sharpless, eds., *Handbook of Oral History* (Lanham, MD: AltaMira Press, 2006), pp. 384–407.

Chandler, Alfred D., Jr. *The Visible Hand: The Managerial Revolution in American Business* (Cambridge: Harvard University Press, 1977).

Chandler, Alfred D., Jr. *Scale and Scope: The Dynamics of Industrial Capitalism* (Cambridge: Harvard University Press, 1990).

Chapple, Karen. "Foot in the Door, Mouse in Hand: Low-Income Women, Short-Term Job Training Programs, and IT Careers," in J. McGrath Cohoon and William Aspray, eds., *Women and Information Technology: Research on Underrepresentation* (Cambridge: MIT Press, 2006), pp. 439–470.

Charles, Maria, and Karen Bradley. "A Matter of Degrees: Female Underrepresentation in Computer Science Programs Cross-Nationally," in J. McGrath Cohoon and William Aspray, eds., *Women and Information Technology: Research on Underrepresentation* (Cambridge: MIT Press, 2006), pp. 183–203.

Civil Service National Whitley Council Committee. *The Marriage Bar in the Civil Service* (London: HMSO, 1946).

Clayton, Kaylene L., Liisa A. von Hellens, and Sue H. Nielsen. "Gender Stereotypes Prevail in ICT: A Research Review," in *Proceedings of the Special Interest Group on Management Information System's 47th Annual Conference on Computer Personnel Research* (Limerick, Ireland, 28–30 May 2009). *SIGMIS-CPR '09* (New York: ACM, 2009), pp. 153–158; available at doi.acm.org/10.1145/1542130.1542160.

Cockburn, Cynthia. "Women and Technology: Opportunity Is Not Enough," in Kate Purcell, Stephen Wood, Alan Waton, and Sheila Allen, eds., *The Changing Experience of Employment: Restructuring and Recession* (London: Macmillan, 1986).

Cohn, Carol. "War, Wimps and Women: Talking Gender and Thinking War," in Miriam Cooke and Angela Woollcott, eds., *Gendering War Talk* (Princeton, NJ: Princeton University Press, 1993), pp. 227–246.

Cohoon, J. McGrath, and William Aspray, eds. *Women and Information Technology: Research on Underrepresentation* (Cambridge: MIT Press, 2006).

Cohoon, J. McGrath, and William Aspray. "A Critical Review of the Research on Women's Participation in Postsecondary Computing Education," in J. McGrath Cohoon and William Aspray, eds., *Women and Information Technology: Research on Underrepresentation* (Cambridge: MIT Press, 2006), pp. 137–180.

Cohoon, J. McGrath, and Jie Chao. "Sexism—Toxic to Women's Persistence in CSE Doctoral Programs," *Computing Research News*, Vol. 21, No. 1 (January 2009); available at www.cra.org/CRN/articles/jan09/cohoon_on_sexism.html.

Connell, Robert W. *Gender* (Cambridge: Polity, 2002).

Corneliussen, Hilde. "'I Don't Understand Computer Programming, Because I'm a Woman!' Negotiating Gendered Positions in a Norwegian Discourse of Computing," in Konrad Morgan, Carlos A. Brebbia, Jose Sanchez, and Alexander Voiskounsky, eds., *Human Perspectives in the Internet Society: Culture, Psychology and Gender* (Boston: WIT Press, 2004), pp. 173–182.

Corneliussen, Hilde. "'I Fell in Love with the Machine': Women's Pleasure in Computing," *Information, Communication and Ethics in Society*, Vol. 3, No. 4 (2005): 233–241.

Corneliussen, Hilde. "Gender in Norwegian Computer History," in Eileen M. Trauth, ed., *Encyclopedia of Gender and Information Technology* (Hershey, PA: Idea Group Reference, 2006), pp. 630–635.

Corneliussen, Hilde. "Konstruksjoner av kjønn ved høyere IKT-utdanning i Norge," *Kvinneforskning*, Vol. 27, No. 3 (2003): 31–50.

Corneliussen, Hilde. *Diskursens makt—individets frihet: Kjønnede posisjoner i diskursen om data* [The Power of Discourse—the Freedom of Individuals: Gendered Positions in the Discourse of Computing.] (Ph.D. thesis, Department of Humanistic Informatics, University of Bergen, 2003).

Cortada, James. *Before the Computer: IBM, Burroughs and Remington Rand and the Industry They Created, 1865–1956* (Princeton, NJ: Princeton University Press, 1993).

Cortada, James. *The Digital Hand, Volume 3: How Computers Changed the Work of American Public Sector Industries* (New York: Oxford University Press, 2008).

Coughlin, Jeanne Halladay, and Andrew R. Thomas. *The Rise of Women Entrepreneurs: People, Processes, and Global Trends* (Westport, CT: Quorum Books, 2002).

Cowan, Ruth Schwartz. *More Work for Mother: The Ironies of Household Technology from the Open Hearth to the Microwave* (New York: Basic Books, 1983).

Coyle, Karen. "How Hard Can it Be?" *Wired_Women: Gender and New Realities in Cyberspace* (Seattle, WA: Seal Press, 1996).

Craig, Harold Farlow. *Administering a Conversion to Electronic Accounting: A Case Study of a Large Office* (Boston: Harvard University Graduate School of Business Administration, 1955).

Cringely, Robert X. *Accidental Empires: How the Boys of Silicon Valley Make Their Millions, Battle Foreign Competition, and Still Can't Get a Date* (New York: Addison-Wesley, 1992).

Cusumano, Michael. "Factory Concepts and Practices in Software Development," *IEEE Annals of the History of Computing*, Vol. 13, No. 1 (1991): 3–32.

D'Auria, Thomas. "ACM Membership Profile Report," *Communications of the ACM*, Vol. 20, No. 10 (1977): 688–692.

Davies, Margery W. *Woman's Place Is at the Typewriter: Office Work and Office Workers, 1870–1930* (Philadelphia: Temple University Press, 1982).

Davis, Clark. *Company Men: White-collar Life and Corporate Cultures in Los Angeles, 1892–1941* (Baltimore: Johns Hopkins University Press, 2000).

Dickson, Katherine Murphy. *Sexism and Reentry: Job Realities for Women Librarians* (Lanham, MD: University Press of America, 1997).

Diebold, John. *Automation: The Advent of the Automatic Factory* (New York: Van Nostrand, 1952).

Dijkstra, Edsger. "The Humble Programmer," *Communications of the ACM*, Vol. 15, No. 10 (1972): 859–866.

Dijkstra, Edsger. "Programming as a Discipline of Mathematical Nature," *American Mathematical Monthly*, Vol. 81, No. 6 (1974): 608–612.

Dilevko, Juris, and Roma M. Harris. "Information Technology and Social Relations: Portrayals of Gender Roles in High Tech Product Advertisements," *Journal of the American Society of Information Science*, Vol. 48, No. 8 (1997): 718–727.

DiSabatino, Jennifer. "Glass Ceiling for Women in IT Persists," *Computerworld* (15 May 2000): 12; available at www.computerworld.com/action/article. do?command=viewArticleBasic&articleId=44826.

Donatao, Katharine M. "Programming for Change? The Growing Demand for Women System Analysts," in Barbara F. Reskin and Patricia A. Roos, eds., *Job Queues, Gender Queues: Explaining Women's Inroads Into Male occupations* (Philadelphia: Temple University Press, 1990), pp. 167–182.

Donato, Katharine M., and Patricia A. Roos. "Gender and Earnings Inequality Among Computer Specialists," in Barbara Drygulski Wright, ed., *Women, Work, and Technology: Transformations* (Ann Arbor: University of Michigan Press, 1987), pp. 291–317.

Döring, Nicola, and Sandra Pöschl. "Images of Men and Women in Mobile Phone Advertisements: A Content Analysis of Advertisements for Mobile Communication Systems in Selected Popular Magazines," *Sex Roles*, Vol. 55 (2006): 173–185.

Douglas, Nikki. "The Future of Games Does Not Include Women" (5 April 2006); available at www.grrlgamer.com/article.php?t=futureofgames (accessed 26 June 2009).

Downey, Greg. "Virtual Webs, Physical Technologies, and Hidden Workers: The Spaces of Labor in Information Internetworks," *Technology and Culture*, Vol. 42, No. 2 (2001): 209–235.

Downey, Greg. "The Place of Labor in the History of Information-Technology Revolutions," *International Review of Social History*, Vol. 48, No. 11 (2003): 225–261.

Downey, Greg. "The Librarian and the Univac: Automation and Labor at the 1962 Seattle World's Fair," in Catherine McKercher and Vincent Mosco, eds., *Knowledge Workers in the Information Society* (Lanham, MD: Lexington Books, 2007).

Dublin, Thomas. *Women at Work* (New York: Columbia University Press, 1979).

Dyer-Witheford, Nick. *Cyber-Marx: Cycles and Circuits of Struggle in High-Technology Capitalism* (Urbana: University of Illinois Press, 1999).

Edwards, Melvin Lloyd. "The Effect of Automation on Accounting Jobs" (Doctor of Education, University of Oklahoma, 1959).

Edwards, Paul N. "The Army and the Microworld: Computers and the Politics of Gender Identity," *Signs*, Vol. 16, No. 1 (1990): 102–127.

Edwards, Paul N., Steven J. Jackson, Geoffrey C. Bowker, and Cory P. Knobel. *Understanding Infrastructure: Dynamics, Tensions, and Design* (Arlington, VA: National Science Foundation, 2007).

Eglash, Ron. "Race, Sex, and Nerds: From Black Geeks to Asian American Hipsters," *Social Text*, Vol. 20, No. 2 (2002): 49–64.

Ensmenger, Nathan L. "From 'Black Art' to Industrial Discipline: The Software Crisis and the Management of Programmers" (Ph.D. thesis, University of Pennsylvania, 2001).

Ensmenger, Nathan L. "The 'Question of Professionalism' in the Computer Fields," *IEEE Annals of the History of Computing*, Vol. 23, No. 4 (2001): 56–73.

Ensmenger, Nathan L. "Letting the 'Computer Boys' Take Over: Technology and the Politics of Organizational Transformation," in Aad Blok and Greg Downey, eds., *Uncovering Labour in Information Revolutions* (Cambridge, UK: Cambridge University Press, 2004), pp. 152–180.

Ensmenger, Nathan L. *The Computer Boys Take Over: Computers, Programmers, and the Politics of Technical Expertise* (Cambridge: MIT Press, 2010).

Ensmenger, Nathan, and William Aspray. "Software as a Labor Process," in Ulf Hashagen, Reinhard Keil-Slawik, and Arthur L. Norberg, eds., *History of Computing: Software Issues* (New York: Springer-Verlag, 2002), pp. 139–166.

Etzkowitz, Henry, Carol Kemelgor, and Brian Uzzi. *Athena Unbound: The Advancement of Women in Science and Technology* (Cambridge, UK: Cambridge University Press, 2000).

Etzkowitz, Henry, Stefan Fuchs, Namrata Gupta, Carol Kemelgor, and Marina Ranga. "The Coming Gender Revolution in Science," In Edward J. Hackett, Olga Amsterdamska, Michael Lynch, and Judy Wajcman, eds., *The Handbook of Science and Technology Studies*, 3rd edition (Cambridge: MIT Press, 2008), pp. 403–428.

Eversole, Robyn. "Change Makers? Women's Microenterprises in a Bolivian City," *Gender, Work & Organization*, Vol. 11, No. 2 (March 2004): 123–142.

Fairchild, Mary Salome Cutler. "Women in American Libraries," *Library Journal* (December 1904): 157–162.

Fantone, Laura. "Final Fantasies: Virtual Women's Bodies," *Feminist Theory*, Vol. 4, No. 1 (2003): 51–72.

Faulkner, Wendy. "The Power and Pleasure? A Research Agenda for 'Making Gender Stick' to Engineers," *Science, Technology, & Human Values*, Vol. 25, No. 1 (2000): 87–119.

Feenberg, Andrew. *Transforming Technology: A Critical Theory Revised* (Oxford, UK: Oxford University Press, 2002).

Field, F. Bernice. "Technical Services and Women," in Russell E. Bidlack, ed., *Women in the Library Profession: Leadership Roles and Contributions* (Ann Arbor: University of Michigan, 1971), pp. 11–15.

Freedman, Janet. "The Liberated Librarian? A Look at the 'Second Sex' in the Library Profession," *Library Journal*, Vol. 95 (May 1970): 1709–1711.

Freiberger, Paul, and Michael Swaine. *Fire in the Valley: The Making of the Personal Computer*, 2nd edition (New York: McGraw-Hill, 2000).

Fritz, W. Barkley. "The Women of ENIAC," *IEEE Annals of the History of Computing*, Vol. 18, No. 3 (1996): 13–23.

Galambos, Louis. *Competition and Cooperation: The Emergence of a Modern Trade Association* (Baltimore: Johns Hopkins University Press, 1966).

Galpin, Vashti. "Women in Computing Around the World," *ACM SIGCSE Bulletin*, Vol. 34, No. 2 (June 2002): 94–100.

Gambler, Wendy. "A Gendered Enterprise: Placing Nineteenth-Century Businesswomen in History," *Business History Review*, Vol. 72, No. 2 (Summer 1998): 188–218.

Gansmo, Helen Jøsok. "Towards a Happy Ending for Girls and Computing?" (Trondheim: Department of Interdisciplinary Studies of Culture, Faculty of Arts, Norwegian University of Science and Technology, 2004). [Norwegian University of Science and Technology, Ph.D. thesis in Department of Interdisciplinary Cultural Studies.]

Gansmo, Helen Jøsok, Vivian Anette Lagesen, and Knut H. Sørensen. "Out of the Boy's Room? A Critical Analysis of the Understanding of Gender and ICT in Norway," *NORA: Nordic Journal of Women's Studies*, Vol. 11, No. 3 (2003): 130–139.

Gansmo, Helen Jøsok, Vivian Anette Lagesen, and Knut H. Sørensen. "Forget the Hacker? A Critical Re-Appraisal of Norwegian Studies of Gender and ICT," in Merete Lie, ed, *He, She and IT Revisited: New Perspectives on Gender in the Information Society* (Oslo: Gyldendal Akademisk, 2003), pp. 34–68.

Gilbert, Jean P., and David B. Mayer. "Experiences in Self-selection of Disadvantaged People into a Computer Operator Training Program," in *SIGCPR '69: Proceedings of the Seventh Annual Conference on SIGCPR* (New York: ACM Press, 1969), pp. 79–90.

Gilchrist, Bruce, and Richard Weber. "Enumerating Full-Time Programmers," *Communications of the ACM*, Vol. 17, No. 10 (1974): 592–593.

Golda, John. "The Effects of Computer Technology on the Traditional Role of Management" (MA thesis, Wharton School of Business, University of Pennsylvania, 1965).

Goldin, Claudia, Lawrence Katz, and Ilyana Kuziemko. "The Homecoming of American College Women: The Reversal of the College Gender Gap," *Journal of Economic Perspectives*, Vol. 20, No. 4 (2006): 133–156.

Goldstine, Herman, and John von Neumann. *Planning and Coding of Problems for an Electronic Computing Instrument* (Princeton, NJ: Institute for Advanced Study, 1947).

Gordon, Robert. "Personnel Selection," in Fred Gruenberger and Stanley Naftaly, eds., *Data Processing … Practically Speaking* (Los Angeles: Data Processing Digest, 1967), pp. 87–88.

Goyal, Amita. "Women in Computing: Historical Roles, the Perpetual Glass Ceiling, and Current Opportunities," *IEEE Annals of the History of Computing*, Vol. 18, No. 3 (1996): 36–42.

Greenbaum, Joan M. *In the Name of Efficiency: Management Theory and Shop-floor Practice in Data-Processing Work* (Philadelphia: Temple University Press, 1979).

Greenbaum, Joan M. "On Twenty-Five Years with Braverman's 'Labor and Monopoly Capital' (Or, How Did Control and Coordination of Labor Get into the Software so Quickly?)" *Monthly Review*, Vol. 50, No. 8 (1999): 28–42.

Greenberg, Herman. "Sex Discrimination against Women in Libraries," in Margaret Myers and Mayra Scarborough, eds., *Women in Librarianship: Melvil's Rib Symposium* (New Brunswick, NJ: Rutgers University Graduate School of Library Service, 1975), pp. 49–82.

Greening, Tony. "Gender Stereotyping in a Computer Science Course," *ACM SIGCSE Bulletin*, Vol. 31, No. 1 (1999): 203–207.

Grier, David Alan. "The ENIAC, the Verb to Program, and the Emergence of Digital Computers," *IEEE Annals of the History of Computing*, Vol. 18, No. 1 (1996): 51–55.

Grier, David Alan. *When Computers Were Human* (Princeton, NJ: Princeton University Press, 2005).

Griffin, Pat. "Introductory Module for the Single Issue Courses," in Maurianne Adams, Lee Anne Bell, and Pat Griffin, eds., *Teaching for Diversity and Social Justice: A Sourcebook* (New York: Routledge, 1997), pp. 61–109.

Griffith, Elisabeth. *In Her Own Right: The Life of Elizabeth Cady Stanton* (New York: Oxford University Press, 1984).

Grundy, Frances. *Women and Computers* (Bristol, UK: Intellect Books, 1996).

Guizzo, Erico. "The EE Gender Gap Is Widening," *IEEE Spectrum*, Vol. 45, No. 12 (December 2008): 23; available at www.spectrum.ieee.org/dec08/6983.

Gürer, Denise. "Women in Computing History," *Inroads—SIGCSE Bulletin*, Vol. 34, No. 2 (2002): 116–120.

Gustavsson, Eva, and Barbara Czarniawska. "Web Woman: The On-line Construction of Corporate and Gender Images," *Organization*, Vol. 11, No. 5 (2004): 651–670.

Haan, Francisca de. *Gender and the Politics of Office Work in the Netherlands, 1860–1940* (Amsterdam: Amsterdam University Press, 1998).

Haddon, Leslie. "Researching Gender and Home Computers," in Knut H. Sørensen and Anne-Jorun Berg, eds., *Technologies and Everyday Life: Trajectories and Transformations* (Oslo: Norwegian Research Council for Science and the Humanities, 1991; Report No. 5).

Hafter, Ruth. "Born-again Cataloging in the Online Networks," *College & Research Libraries*, Vol. 47 (July 1986): 360–364.

Hafter, Ruth. *Academic Librarians and Cataloguing Networks: Visibility, Quality Control, and Professional Status* (New York: Greenwood Press, 1986).

Haigh, Thomas. "Inventing Information Systems: The Systems Men and the Computer, 1950–1968," *Business History Review*, Vol. 75, No. 1 (Spring 2001): 15–61.

Haigh, Thomas. "The Chromium-Plated Tabulator: Institutionalizing an Electronic Revolution, 1954–1958," *IEEE Annals of the History of Computing*, Vol. 23, No. 4 (2001): 75–104.

Haigh, Thomas. "Technology, Information and Power: Managerial Technicians in Corporate America" (Ph.D. thesis, University of Pennsylvania, 2003).

Haigh, Thomas. "Remembering the Office of the Future: The Origins of Word Processing and Office Automation," *IEEE Annals of the History of Computing*, Vol. 28, No. 4 (2006): 6–31.

Halpern, Mark. "Memoirs (Part 1)," *Annals of the History of Computing*, Vol. 13, No. 1 (1991): 101–111.

Hammer, Carl. "Watch Your Statistics," *Journal of Systems Management*, Vol. 21 (1970): 40–41.

Håpnes, Tove, and Bente Rasmussen. "Gendering Technology: Young Girls Negotiating ICT and Gender," in Merete Lie, ed., *He, She and IT Revisited: New Perspectives on Gender in the Information Society* (Oslo: Gyldendal Akademisk, 2003), pp. 173–197.

Haraway, Donna J. *Simians, Cyborgs and Women: The Reinvention of Nature* (New York: Routledge, 1991).

Haraway, Donna J. *Modest_Witness@Second_Millennium: FemaleMan_Meets_ Oncomouse* (New York: Routledge, 1997).

Harris, Brian. *BABS, BEACON and BOADICEA: A History of Computing in British Airways and Its Predecessor Airlines* (London: Speedwing Press, 1993).

Harris, Michael H. *History of Libraries in the Western World*, 4th ed. (Metuchen, NJ: Scarecrow Press, 1995).

Harris, Roma M. "Information Technology and the De-skilling of Librarians; or the Erosion of a Woman's Profession," *Computers in Libraries*, Vol. 12, No. 1 (January 1992): 8–16.

Harris, Roma M. *Librarianship: The Erosion of a Woman's Profession* (Norwood, NJ: Ablex, 1992).

Harris, Roma M. "Understanding Gender Relations in the Librarianship of the 1990s," in Betsy Kruger and Catherine A. Larson, eds., *On Account of Sex: An Annotated Bibliography on the Status of Women in Librarianship, 1993–1997* (Lanham, MD: Scarecrow Press, 2000), pp. xix–xx.

Hearn, Jeffrey. "Notes on Patriarchy, Professionalization and the Semi-Professions," *Sociology*, Vol. 16, No. 2 (1982): 184–202.

Heide, Lars. *Punched-Card Systems and the Early Information Explosion, 1880–1945* (Baltimore: Johns Hopkins University Press, 2009).

Heim, Kathleen, and Katharine Phenix. "The Women's Movement Within Librarianship, 1977–1981," in Kathleen Heim and Katharine Phenix, eds., *On Account of Sex: An Annotated Bibliography on the Status of Women in Librarianship, 1977–1981* (Chicago: American Library Association, 1984), pp. xi–xxxvi.

Hewlett, Sylvia Ann, Carolyn Buck Luce, Lisa J. Servon, Laura Sherbin, Peggy Shiller, Eytan Sosnovich, and Karen Sumberg. *The Athena Factor: Reversing the Brain Drain in Science, Engineering, and Technology* (Harvard Business Review Research Report, May 2008); available at braindrain.hbr.org.

Hildenbrand, Suzanne. "Library Feminism and Library Women's History: Activism and Scholarship, Equity and Culture," *Libraries & Culture*, Vol. 35, No. 1 (2000): 51–67.

Hildenbrand, Suzanne. "The Crisis in Cataloging: A Feminist Hypothesis," in Sheila S. Intner and Janet Swan Hill, eds., *Recruiting, Educating and Training Cataloging Librarians* (New York: Greenwood Press, 1989), pp. 207–225.

Hildenbrand, Suzanne. "Women's Work within Librarianship: Time to Expand the Feminist Agenda," *Library Journal*, Vol. 114, No. 14 (September 1989): 153–155.

Hill, Lester E. "The Machine Accountant and his 'Electronic' Opportunity," *Journal of Machine Accounting*, Vol. 8, No. 1 (January 1957): 12–14, 23–25.

Hoos, Ida R. *Automation in the Office* (Washington, DC: Public Affairs Press, 1961).

Horowitz, Roger, and Arwen Mohun, eds. *His and Hers: Gender, Consumption, and Technology* (Charlottesville: University of Virginia Press, 1998).

Horowitz, Roger, ed. *Boys and Their Toys? Masculinity, Class, and Technology in America* (New York: Routledge, 2001).

Huff, Chuck. "Gender, Software Design, and Occupational Equity," *Inroads— SIGCSE Bulletin*, Vol. 34, No. 2 (2002): 112–115.

Hunt, H. Allan, and Timothy L. Hunt. "Recent Trends in Clerical Employment: The Impact of Technological Change," in Heidi H. Hartmann, Robert E. Kraut, and Louise A. Tilly, eds., *Computer Chips and Paper Clips: Technology and Women's Employment*, Volume 2. (Washington, DC: National Academy Press, 1986), pp. 223–267.

Ilias, Aristidis, and Maria Kordaki. "Undergraduate Studies in Computer Science and Engineering: Gender Issues," *ACM SIGSCE Bulletin*, Vol. 38, No. 2 (2006): 81–85.

Intner, Sheila S., and Janet Swan Hill, eds. *Cataloging: The Professional Development Cycle* (New York: Greenwood Press, 1991).

Irvine, Betty Jo. *Sex Segregation in Librarianship: Demographic and Career Patterns of Academic Library Administrators* (Westport, CT: Greenwood Press, 1985).

Jenkins, Henry, and Justine Cassell. "From *Quake Grrls* to *Desperate Housewives*: A Decade of Gender and Computer Games," in Yasmin B. Kafai, Carrie Heeter, Jill Denner, and Jennifer Y. Sun, eds., *Beyond Barbie and Mortal Kombat: New Perspectives on Gender and Gaming* (Cambridge: MIT Press, 2008), pp. 5–20.

Johnson, F. M. "Control of Machine Accounting Equipment," *Systems and Procedures Quarterly*, Vol. 4, No. 2 (May 1953): 18–22, 26.

Johnson, Nicola F., Leonie Rowan, and Julianne Lynch. "Construction of Gender in Computer Magazine Advertisements: Confronting the Literature," *Studies in Media and Information Literacy Education*, Vol. 6, No. 1 (2006): unpaged (electronic journal); available at www.utpjournals.com/simile/simile.html.

Kafai, Yasmin B., Carrie Heeter, Jill Denner, and Jennifer Y. Sun, eds. *Beyond Barbie and Mortal Kombat: New Perspectives on Gender and Gaming* (Cambridge: MIT Press, 2008).

Karamesini, Maria. *The Placement of University Graduates in the Job Market: Greek Graduates of 1998–2000* (Athens: Dionikos, 2008). [in Greek]

Keller, Evelyn Fox. *A Feeling for the Organism: The Life and Work of Barbara McClintock* (San Francisco: W. H. Freeman, 1983).

Keller, Evelyn Fox. "Gender and Science: Origin, History, and Politics," *Osiris*, Vol. 10 (1995): 27–38.

Kendall, Lori. "'The Nerd Within': Mass Media and the Negotiation of Identity Among Computer-Using Males," *Journal of Men's Studies*, Vol. 7, No. 3 (1999): 353–369.

Kennedy, Helen W. "Lara Croft: Feminist Icon or Cyberbimbo? On the Limits of Textual Analysis," *Game Studies*, Vol. 2, No. 2 (2002); available at www.gamestudies.org/0202/kennedy/.

Kessler-Harris, Alice. *Out to Work: A History of Wage Earning Women in the United States* (New York: Oxford University Press, 1982).

Kessler-Harris, Alice. *A Woman's Wage: Historical Meanings and Social Consequences* (Lexington: University of Kentucky Press, 1990).

King, Geoff, and Tanya Krzywinska. *Tomb Raiders and Space Invaders: Videogame Forms and Contexts* (New York: I.B. Tauris & Co., 2006).

Kinnick, Katherine, Candace White, and Kadesha Washington. "Racial Representation of Computer Users in Prime-Time Advertising," *Race, Gender and Class*, Vol. 8, No. 4 (2001): 96–114.

Klawe, Maria, Telle Whitney, and Caroline Simard. "Women in Computing—Take 2," *Communications of the ACM*, Vol. 52, No. 2 (2009): 68–76.

Kleif, Tine, and Wendy Faulkner. "'I'm No Athlete [but] I Can Make This Thing Dance!'—Men's Pleasures in Technology." *Science, Technology, & Human Values*, Vol. 28, No. 2 (2003): 296–325.

Knight, Louise W. *Citizen: Jane Addams and the Struggle for Democracy* (Chicago: University of Chicago Press, 2006).

Knupfer, Nancy Nelson. "Gender Divisions Across Technology Advertisements and the WWW: Implications for Educational Equity," *Theory into Practice*, Vol. 37, No. 1 (1998): 54–63.

Knupfer, Nancy Nelson, K. M. Kramer, and D. Pryor. "Gender Equity On-line: Messages Portrayed with and About the New Technologies," in Robert E. Griffin, J. Mark Hunter, Carole B. Schiffman, and William J. Gibbs, eds., *Vision Quest: Journeys Toward Visual Literacy* (Pittsburgh: Omni Press, 1997), pp. 391–399.

Koss, Adele Mildred. "Programming at Burroughs and Philco in the 1950s," *IEEE Annals of the History of Computing*, Vol. 25, No. 4 (2003): 40–50.

Koss, Adele Mildred. "Programming on the Univac 1: A Woman's Account," *IEEE Annals of the History of Computing*, Vol. 25, No. 1 (2003): 48–59.

Kramer, Kevin M., and Nancy Nelson Knupfer. "Gender Equity in Advertising on the World Wide Web: Can It Be Found?" in *Proceeding of Selected Research and Development Presentation at the 1997 National Convention of the Association of Educational Communications and Technology* (14–18 February 1997), pp. 169–180.

Laclau, Ernesto, and Chantal Mouffe. *Hegemony and Socialist Strategy: Towards a Radical Democratic Politics* (London: Verso, 1985).

Lagesen, Vivian Anette. "Advertising Computer Science to Women (or Was It the Other Way Around?)" in Merete Lie, ed., *He, She and IT Revisited: New Perspectives on Gender in the Information Society* (Oslo: Gyldendal Akademisk, 2003), pp. 69–102.

Lagesen, Vivian Anette. "A Cyberfeminist Utopia? Perceptions of Gender and Computer Science Among Malaysian Women Computer Science Students and Faculty," *Science, Technology and Human Values*, Vol. 33, No. 1 (2008): 5–27.

Lammers, Susan M. *Programmers at Work: Interviews with 19 of Today's Most Brilliant Programmers* (Redmond, WA: Microsoft Press, 1986).

Lamoreaux, Naomi R., Daniel G. Raff, and Peter Temin. "Beyond Markets and Hierarchies: Toward a Synthesis of American Business History," *American Historical Review*, Vol. 108, No. 2 (2003): 404–433.

Landström, Catharina. "Queering Feminist Technology Studies," *Feminist Theory*, Vol. 8 (2007): 7–26.

Larson, Magali Sarfatti. *The Rise of Professionalism: A Sociological Analysis* (Berkeley: University of California Press, 1977).

Ledbetter, William. "Programming Aptitude: How Significant Is It?" *Personnel Journal*, Vol. 54, No. 3 (1975): 165–166, 175.

Lerman, Nina E., Arwen Palmer Mohun, and Ruth Oldenziel. "The Shoulders We Stand on and the View from Here: Historiography and Directions for Research," *Technology and Culture*, Vol. 38, No. 1 (1997): 9–30.

Lerman, Nina E., Ruth Oldenziel, and Arwen Mohun, eds. *Gender and Technology: A Reader* (Baltimore: Johns Hopkins University Press, 2003).

Lessig, Lawrence. *Code and Other Laws of Cyberspace* (New York: Basic Books, 1999).

Levy, Steven. *Hackers: Heroes of the Computer Revolution* (Garden City, NY: Anchor Press/Doubleday, 1984).

Lie, Merete. "Computer Dialogues: Technology, Gender and Change, " Skriftserie / Senter for kvinneforskning, No. 2 (Trondheim: Norges teknisk-naturvitenskapelige universitet, NTNU, Senter for kvinneforskning, 1998).

Lie, Merete. "Gender in the Image of Technology," in Merete Lie and Knut H. Sørensen, eds., *Making Technology Our Own? Domesticating Technology into Everyday Life* (Oslo: Scandinavian University Press, 1996), pp. 201–223.

Lie, Merete, ed. *He, She and IT revisited: New Perspectives on Gender in the Information Society* (Oslo: Gyldendal Akademisk, 2003).

Lie, Merete. "Gender and ICT—New Connections," in Merete Lie, ed., *He, She and IT Revisited: New Perspectives on Gender in the Information Society* (Oslo: Gyldendal Akademisk, 2003), pp. 9–33.

Lie, Merete, Anne-Jorunn Berg, Hjørdis Kaul, Elin Kvande, Bente Rasmussen, and Knut H. Sørensen. "Har teknologi noe med kvinner å gjøre?" *Sosiolog i dag*, Vol. 14, No. 1 (1984): 23–39.

Light, Jennifer. "When Computers Were Women," *Technology and Culture*, Vol. 40, No. 3 (1999): 455–483.

Lohr, Steve. *Go To: The Story of the Math Majors, Bridge Players, Engineers, Chess Wizards, Maverick Scientists and Iconoclasts—The Programmers Who Created the Software Revolution* (New York: Basic Books, 2001).

Lowenstein, Roger. *Origins of the Crash: The Great Bubble and Its Undoing* (New York: Penguin Books, 2004).

Lowenthal, Helen. "A Healthy Anger," *Library Journal*, Vol. 96 (September 1971): 2597–2599.

Maack, Mary Niles. "Gender Issues in Librarianship," in Wayne A. Wiegand and Donald G. Davis, eds., *Encyclopedia of Library History* (New York: Garland Publishing, 1994).

Maack, Mary Niles. "Women as Visionaries, Mentors, and Agents of Change," in Joanne E. Passet, ed., *Women's Work: Vision and Change in Librarianship* (Urbana: University of Illinois at Urbana–Champaign GLIS, 1994), pp. 105–130.

Maciuszko, Kathleen L. *OCLC: A Decade of Development, 1967–1977* (Littleton: Libraries Unlimited, 1984).

Magrane, Diane, and Paul Jolly. "The Changing Representation of Men and Women in Academic Medicine." Association of American Medical Colleges. *Analysis in Brief*, Vol. 5, No. 2 (2005): 1–2.

Mahoney, Michael S. "The Histories of Computing(s)," *Interdisciplinary Science Reviews*, Vol. 30, No. 2 (2005): 119–135.

Malone, Cheryl Knott. "Imagining Information Retrieval in the Library: *Desk Set* in Historical Context," *IEEE Annals of the History of Computing*, Vol. 24, No. 3 (2002): 14–22.

Mandel, Lois. "The Computer Girls," *Cosmopolitan* (April 1967): 52–56.

Margolis, Jane. *Stuck in the Shallow End: Education, Race, and Computing* (Cambridge: MIT Press, 2008).

Margolis, Jane, and Allan Fisher. *Unlocking the Clubhouse: Women in Computing* (Cambridge: MIT Press, 2002).

Marschke, Robyn, Sandra Laursen, Joyce McCarl Nielsen, and Patricia Rankin. "Demographic Inertia Revisited: An Immodest Proposal to Achieve Equitable Gender Representation Among Faculty in Higher Education," *Journal of Higher Education*, Vol. 78, No. 1 (2007): 1–26.

Marshall, John C., and Susan Bannon. "Race and Sex Equity in Computer Advertising," *Journal of Research on Computing in Education*, Vol. 21, No. 1 (1988): 15–27.

Mason, Mary Ann, and Eve Mason Ekman. *Mothers on the Fast Track: How a New Generation Can Balance Family and Careers* (New York: Oxford University Press, 2007).

Mathews, Jay. "Shaping the Learning Curve Through a Code," *Washington Post* (16 April 2002); available at www.washingtonpost.com/wp-dyn/articles/A58274-2002Apr16.html.

Maynes, Mary Jo, Jennifer L. Pierce, and Barbara Laslett. *Telling Stories: The Use of Personal Narratives in the Social Sciences and History* (Ithaca, NY: Cornell University Press, 2008).

Mazlack, Lawrence J. "Identifying Potential to Acquire Programming Skill," *Communications of the ACM*, Vol. 23, No. 1 (January 1980): 14–17.

McCallum, Sally H. "MARC: Keystone for Library Automation," *IEEE Annals of the History of Computing*, Vol. 24, No. 2 (2002): 34–49.

McCormick, Ernest J., and Robert H. Finn. "Tests for Use in Selecting IBM Operators," *Journal of Machine Accounting*, Vol. 6, No. 2 (February 1955): 12–13, 17.

McGuire, Dan. "Pornography Display in 6.001 Provokes Debate on Decency," *Tech News* (27 February 1998); available at tech.mit.edu/V118/N8/aporn.8n.html.

McNamara, Walter J. "The Selection of Computer Personnel," in *SIGCPR '67: Proceedings of the Fifth SIGCPR Conference on Computer Personnel Research* (New York: ACM Press, 1967), pp. 52–56.

Mellström, Ulf. *Män och deras maskiner* (Nora, Sweden: Bokförlaget Nya Doxa, 1999).

Milecki, Helen M. "Women in EDP Management," *Data Management*, Vol. 9, No. 2 (February 1971): 18–23.

Milkman, Ruth. *Gender at Work: The Dynamics of Job Segregation by Sex during World War II* (Urbana: University of Illinois Press, 1987).

Millar, Melanie Stewart. *Cracking the Gender Code: Who Rules the Wired World?* (Toronto: Second Story Press, 1998).

Misa, Thomas J. "Understanding How Computing Has Changed the World," *IEEE Annals of the History of Computing*, Vol. 29, No. 4 (2007): 52–63.

Misu, N. A. "The Cultural Construction of the Computer as a Masculine Technology: An Analysis of Computer Advertisements in Korea," *Asian Journal of Women's Studies*, Vol. 7, No. 3 (2001): 93–114.

MIT Committee on Women Faculty in the School of Science. "A Study on the Status of Women Faculty in Science at MIT," *MIT Faculty Newsletter*, Vol. 11, No. 4 (March 1999); available at web.mit.edu/fnl/women/women.html.

Mody, Rustom P. "Is Programming an Art?" *Software Engineering Notes*, Vol. 17, No. 4 (1992): 19–21.

Moncarz, Roger. "Training for Techies: Career Preparation in Information Technology," *Occupational Outlook Quarterly* (Fall 2002): 39–45.

Montag, Warren. *Louis Althusser* (London: Palgrave-Macmillan, 2003).

Moore, James P., Jr. "Management Viewpoints on Men, Machines and Methods," in Charles H. Johnson, ed., *Data Processing: 1958 Proceedings* (Atlantic City, NJ: National Machine Accountants Association, 1958), pp. 26–31.

Munro, Neil. "Science Faces Title IX Test," *National Journal Magazine* (4 July 2009); available at www.nationaljournal.com/njmagazine/ad_20090701_1233.php (accessed August 2009).

Murphy, Mary C., Claude M. Steele, and James J. Gross. "Signaling Threat: How Situational Cues Affect Women in Math, Science, and Engineering Settings," *Psychological Science*, Vol. 3, No. 10 (2007): 879–885.

Murray, Margaret A. M. *Women Becoming Mathematicians* (Cambridge: MIT Press, 2000).

National Center for Women and Information Technology. *NCWIT Scorecard 2007: A Report on the Status of Women in Information Technology.* University of Colorado, Boulder, CO; available at ncwit.org/pdf/2007_Scorecard_Web.pdf (accessed March 2007).

National Science Foundation, Division of Science Resources Statistics. *Science and Engineering Degrees: 1966–2006.* Detailed Statistical Tables NSF 08-321. (Arlington, VA: National Science Foundation, 2008); available at www.nsf.gov/statistics/nsf08321/.

Naur, Peter, and Brian Randell. *Software Engineering: Report on a Conference Sponsored by the NATO Science Committee, Garmisch, Germany, 7–11 October 1968* (Brussels: NATO Scientific Affairs Division, 1969).

Nelson, Donna J. "A National Analysis of Diversity in Science and Engineering Faculties at Research Universities," 15 January 2004, available at cheminfo.chem.ou.edu/ djn/diversity/briefings/Diversity%20Report%20 Final.pdf.

Nelson, Donna J. "A National Analysis of Minorities in Science and Engineering Faculties at Research Universities," 31 October 2007; available at cheminfo.ou.edu/~djn/diversity/Faculty_Tables_FY07/FinalReport07. html.

Newmyer, Jody. "The Image Problem of the Librarian: Femininity and Social Control," *Journal of Library History*, Vol. 11, No. 1 (1976): 44–67.

Nielsen, Sue H., Liisa A. von Hellens, Jenine Beekhuyzen, and Eileen M. Trauth. "Women Talking About IT Work: Duality or Dualism?" in *Proceedings of ACM SIGMIS Conference '03* (Philadelphia, 10–12 April 2003), pp. 68–74.

Nissen, Jörgen. *Pojkarna vid datorn: Unga entusiaster i datateknikens värld, Linköping studies in arts and science* 89 (Stockholm: Symposion Graduale, 1993).

Nissen, Jörgen. "Det är klart att det är grabbar som håller på med datorer! Men varför är det så?" in Elisabeth Sundin and Boel Berner, eds., *Från symaskin till cyborg: Genus, teknik och social förändring* (Stockholm: Nerenius & Santerus Förlag, 1996), pp. 141–161.

Noble, David F. *A World Without Women: The Christian Clerical Culture of Western Science* (New York: Knopf, 1992).

Nugent, Benjamin. *American Nerd* (New York: Scribner, 2008).

O'Shields, Joseph. "Selection of EDP Personnel," *Personnel Journal*, Vol. 44, No. 9 (1965): 472–474.

Oldenziel, Ruth. *Making Technology Masculine: Men, Women, and Modern Machines in America, 1870–1945* (Amsterdam: Amsterdam University Press, 1999).

Olson, Hope A., and Amber Ritchie. "Gentility, Technicality, and Salary: Women in the Literature of Librarianship," in Betsy Kruger and Catherine Larson, eds., *On Account of Sex: An Annotated Bibliography on the Status of Women in Librarianship, 1998–2002* (Lanham, MD: Scarecrow Press, 2006), pp. xiii–xxv.

Oram, Andy, and Greg Wilson, eds. *Beautiful Code: Leading Programmers Explain How They Think* (Cambridge, UK: O'Reilly, 2007).

Organisation for Economic Co-operation and Development, Directorate for Science, Technology and Industry, Committee for Information, Computer and Communications Policy. *ICTs and Gender* (March 2007); available at www.oecd.org/dataoecd/16/33/38332121.pdf (November 2008).

Parker, Ralph H. "What Every Librarian Should Know About Automation," *Wilson Library Bulletin*, Vol. 38, No. 9 (May 1964): 752–754.

Paschell, William. *Automation and Employment Opportunities for Office Workers: A Report on the Effect of Electronic Computers on Employment of Clerical Workers* (Washington, DC: Bureau of Labor Statistics, 1958).

Peiss, Kathy. " 'Vital Industry' and Women's Ventures: Conceptualizing Gender in Twentieth Century," *Business History Review*, Vol. 72, No. 2 (1998): 219–241.

Perry, Dallis, and William Cannon. "Vocational Interests of Computer Programmers," *Journal of Applied Psychology*, Vol. 51, No. 1 (1967): 28–34.

Perry, Dallis, and William Cannon. "Vocational Interests of Female Computer Programmers," *Journal of Applied Psychology*, Vol. 52, No. 1 (1968): 31.

Pfaffenberger, Bryan. *Democratizing Information: Online Databases and the Rise of End-User Searching* (Boston: G.K. Hall & Co., 1990).

Phenix, Katharine. "Women Predominate, Men Dominate: Disequilibrium in the Library Profession," *Bowker Annual*, Vol. 29 (1984): 82–89.

Porter-Benson, Susan. *Counter Cultures: Saleswomen, Managers, and Customers in American Department Stores, 1890–1940* (Urbana: University of Illinois Press, 1986).

Prieser, Carl. "Research Summaries: Occupational Salary Levels for White-Collar Workers, 1984," *Monthly Labor Review* (1984): 43–45.

Prior, John H., Sylvia Hurtado, Jessica Sharkness, and William S. Korn. "The American Freshman National Norms for Fall 2007." Higher Education Research Institute; Graduate School of Education and Information Studies, University of California, Los Angeles (December 2007).

"Professionalism Termed Key to Computer Personnel Situation," *Personnel Journal*, Vol. 51, No. 2 (1971): 156–157.

Radford, Marie L., and Gary P. Radford. "Power, Knowledge, and Fear: Feminism, Foucault, and the Stereotype of the Female Librarian," *Library Quarterly*, Vol. 67, No. 3 (1997): 250–266.

Rasmussen, Bente. "Datateknologi—en trussel eller nye muligheter for kvinner på kontor?" in Merete Lie, Anne-Jorunn Berg, Hjørdis Kaul, Elin Kvande, Bente Rasmussen, and Knut H. Sørensen, eds., *I menns bilde: Kvinner–teknologi–arbeid* (Trondheim: Tapir Forlag, 1988), pp. 73–87.

Rasmussen, Bente, and Tove Håpnes. "Excluding Women from the Technologies of the Future? A Case-Study of the Culture of Computer Science," *Futures*, Vol. 23, No. 10 (December 1991): 1107–1119.

Rathgeber, Eva M., and Edith Ofwona Adera, eds. *Gender and the Information Revolution in Africa* (Ottawa: International Development Research Centre, 2000).

Raymond, Eric S., compiler. *The New Hacker's Dictionary* (Cambridge: MIT Press, 1993).

Rees, Alan. "New Bottles for Old Wine: Retrieval and Librarianship," *Wilson Library Bulletin*, Vol. 38, No. 9 (May 1964): 773–779.

Rees, Teresa. *Skill Shortages, Woman and the New Information Technologies* (Luxembourg: Office for Official Publications of the European Communities, 1992).

Reskin, Barbara, and Patricia Roos. *Job Queues, Gender Queues* (Philadelphia: Temple University Press, 1990).

Rhee, Hans Albert. *Office Automation in Social Perspective: The Progress and Social Implications of Electronic Data Processing* (Oxford: Basil Blackwell, 1968).

Rice, John R., and Saul Rosen. "The History of the Computer Sciences Department at Purdue University," in Richard DeMillo and John Rice, eds., *Studies in Computer Science: In Honor of Samuel D. Conte* (New York: Plenum Press, 1994), pp. 45–72.

Rockmael, Valerie. "The Woman Programmer," *Datamation*, Vol. 9, No. 1 (1963): 41.

Rossiter, Margaret. *Women Scientists in America: Struggles and Strategies to 1940* (Baltimore: Johns Hopkins University Press, 1982).

Rossiter, Margaret. *Women Scientists in America: Before Affirmative Action, 1940–1972* (Baltimore: Johns Hopkins University Press, 1995).

Rotella, Elyce J. *From Home to Office: U.S. Women at Work, 1870–1930* (Ann Arbor: UMI Research Press, 1981).

Sable, Arnold P. "The Sexuality of the Library Profession: The Male and Female Librarian," *Wilson Library Bulletin*, Vol. 43, No. 8 (April 1969): 748–751.

Sackman, Hal. "Conference on Personnel Research," *Datamation*, Vol. 14, No. 7 (1968): 74–76, 81.

Sackman, Hal, Warren J. Erickson, and E. E. Grant. "Exploratory Experimental Studies Comparing Online and Offline Programming Performance," *Communications of the ACM*, Vol. 11, No. 1 (1968): 3–11.

Schiller, Anita R., James W. Grimm, and Margo C. Trumpeter. *Characteristics of Professional Personnel in College and University Libraries* (Springfield: Illinois State Library, 1969).

Schiller, Anita. "Women in Librarianship," *Advances in Librarianship*, Vol. 4 (1974): 103–141.

Schuman, Pat. "Status of Women in Libraries: Task Force Meets in Detroit," *Library Journal*, Vol. 95 (August 1970): 2635.

Scott, Joan Wallach. *Gender and the Politics of History* (New York: Columbia University Press, 1988).

Scott-Dixon, Krista. *Doing IT: Women Working in Information Technology* (Toronto: Sumach Press, 2004).

Sellen, Betty-Carol, and Joan K. Marshall, eds. *Women in a Woman's Profession: Strategies. Proceedings of the Preconference on the Status of Women in Librarianship Sponsored by the American Library Association Social Responsibilities Round Table Task Force on the Status of Women (Douglass College, Rutgers University, July 1974)*.

Shasha, Dennis, and Cathy Lazere. *Out of Their Minds: The Lives and Discoveries of 15 Great Computer Scientists* (New York: Copernicus/Springer, 1995).

Shera, Jesse. Introduction to special issue on library automation, *Wilson Library Bulletin*, Vol. 38 (May 1964): 741–742.

Shera, Jesse. "Without Reserve: Of Librarians and Other Aborigines," *Wilson Library Bulletin*, Vol. 38 (May 1964): 781.

Shirky, Clay. *Here Comes Everybody: The Power of Organizing Without Organizations* (New York: Penguin Press, 2008).

Spicer, Dag. "If You Can't Stand the Coding, Stay Out of the Kitchen" *Dr. Dobb's* (12 August 2000); available at www.ddj.com/184404040.

Sofia, Zoe. "The Mythic Machine: Gendered Irrationalities in Computer Culture," in Hank Bromley and Michael W. Apple, eds., *Education, Technology, Power: Educational Computing as a Social Practice* (Albany: State University of New York Press, 1998), pp. 29–51.

Sørensen, Knut H. "Love, Duty and the S-Curve: An Overview of Some Current Literature on Gender and ICT," in *Strategies of Inclusion: Gender and the Information Society* (SIGIS, 2002); available at www.rcss.ed.ac.uk/sigis/public/documents/SIGIS_D02_Part1.pdf (accessed 30 June 2009).

Sørensen, Knut H., and Hege Nordli. "Mobil moral og kjønn i endring? Mobiltelefonen i norske voksnes hverdagsliv," *Kvinneforskning*, Vol. 29, No. 1 (2005): 57–72.

Spertus, Ellen. "Why Are There So Few Female Computer Scientists?" MIT Artificial Intelligence Laboratory. Technical Report 1315 (August 1991); available at people.mills.edu/spertus/Gender/why.html (accessed March 2009).

Stabiner, Karen. "Where the Girls Aren't," *New York Times Education Life* (12 January 2003): 35.

Stepulevage, Linda. "Computer-Based Office Work: Stories of Gender, Design, and Use," *IEEE Annals of the History of Computing*, Vol. 25, No. 4 (2003): 67–72.

Stone, Jack. "The Human Connection," *Computerworld* (4 July 1977): 17.

Stratigaki, Maria. *Gender, Labour, Technology* (Athens: Politis, 1996). [in Greek]

Strober, Myra H., and Carolyn L. Arnold. "Integrated Circuits/Segregated Labor: Women in Computer Related Occupations in High-Tech Industries," in Heidi I. Hartmann, Robert E. Kraut, and Louise A. Tilly, eds., *Computer Chips and Paper Clips: Technology and Women's Employment* (Washington, DC: National Academy Press, 1987), pp. 136–182.

Strom, Sharon Hartman. "'Light Manufacturing': The Feminization of American Office Work, 1900–1930," *Industrial and Labor Relations Review*, Vol. 43, No. 1 (1989): 53–70.

Strom, Sharon Hartman. *Beyond the Typewriter: Gender, Class, and the Origins of Modern American Office Work, 1900–1930* (Urbana: University of Illinois Press, 1992).

Stross, Randall. "What Has Driven Women Out of Computer Science?" *New York Times* (15 November 2008); available at www.nytimes.com/2008/11/16/business/16digi.html.

Stubbs, Katherine. "Mechanizing the Female: Discourse and Control in the Industrial Economy," *differences: A Journal of Feminist Cultural Studies*, Vol. 7, No. 3 (1995): 141–164.

Sumner, James. "What Makes a PC? Thoughts on Computing Platforms, Standards, and Compatibility," *IEEE Annals of the History of Computing*, Vol. 29, No. 2 (2007): 88.

Taylor, Jennifer. "The Decline of Women in Computer Science, 1940–1982" (MA thesis, Harvard University Graduate School of Education, 2005).

Thompson, Paul. *The Voice of the Past: Oral History*, 3rd ed. (Oxford, UK: Oxford University Press, 2000).

Tukey, John. "The Teaching of Concrete Mathematics," *American Mathematical Monthly*, Vol. 65, No. 1 (1958): 1–9.

Turkle, Sherry. "Computational Reticence: Why Women Fear the Intimate Machine," in Cheris Kramarae, ed., *Technology and Women's Voices: Keeping in Touch* (New York: Routledge & Kegan Paul, 1988), pp. 41–61.

Turkle, Sherry. *The Second Self: Computers and the Human Spirit* (New York: Simon and Schuster, 1984; revised edition Cambridge: MIT Press, 2005).

Turner, Eva, and Fiona Hovenden. "How Are We Seen? Images of Women in Computing Advertisements," in Rachel Lander and Alison Adam, eds., *Women in Computing* (Wiltshire, UK: Cromwell Press, 1977), pp. 60–71.

Tuttle, Helen W. "Women in Academic Libraries," *Library Journal*, Vol. 96 (September 1971): 2594–2596.

Tympas, Aristotle. "The *Computor* and the Analyst: Computing and Power, 1870s–1960s" (Ph.D. thesis, Georgia Institute of Technology, 2001).

Valian, Virginia. *Why So Slow? The Advancement of Women* (Cambridge: MIT Press, 1998).

Vegso, Jay. "Freshman Interest in CS and Degree Production Trends." *Computing Research Association Bulletin* (1 October 2007); available at www.cra.org/wp/index.php?cat=33.

Vegso, Jay. "Female CS/CE Students and Faculty," *Computing Research Association Bulletin* (18 June 2008); available at www.cra.org/wp/index.php?p=147.

Waern, Annika, Anna Larsson, and Carina Nerén. "Hypersexual Avatars: Who Wants Them?" in *Proceedings of the 2005 ACM SIGCHI International Conference on Advances in Computer Entertainment Technology* (Valencia, Spain, 15–17 June 2005). *ACE '05* Vol. 265 (New York: ACM, 2005), pp. 238–241.

Wajcman, Judy. *Feminism Confronts Technology* (University Park: Pennsylvania State University Press, 1991).

Wajcman, Judy. "Reflections on Gender and Technology: In What State Is the Art?" *Social Studies of Science*, Vol. 30, No. 3 (2000): 447–464.

Wajcman, Judy. "The Feminization of Work in the Information Age," in Mary Frank Fox, Deborah G. Johnson, and Sue V. Rosser, eds., *Women, Gender, and Technology* (Urbana: University of Illinois, 2006), pp. 80–97.

Ware, Mary Catherine, and Mary Frances Stuck. "Sex Role Messages Vis-à-vis Microcomputer Use: A Look at the Pictures," *Sex Roles*, Vol. 13, Nos. 3–4 (1985): 205–214.

Wasburn, Mara H., and Susan G. Miller. "Still a Chilly Climate for Women Students in Technology: A Case Study," in Mary Frank Fox, Deborah G. Johnson, and Sue V. Rosser, eds., *Women, Gender, and Technology* (Urbana: University of Illinois Press, 2006), pp. 60–79.

Weber, Richard, and Bruce Gilchrist. "Discrimination in the Employment of Women in the Computer Industry," *Communications of the ACM*, Vol. 18 (1975): 416–418.

Weinberg, Gerald. *The Psychology of Computer Programming* (New York: Van Nostrand Rheinhold, 1971).

Weinstein, Matthew. "Computer Advertising and the Construction of Gender," in Hank Bromley and Michael W. Apple, eds., *Education, Technology, Power: Educational Computing as a Social Practice* (Albany: State University of New York Press, 1998), pp. 85–100.

Weiss, Robert S. *Learning From Strangers: The Art and Method of Qualitative Interview Studies* (New York: Macmillan, 1994).

Weizenbaum, Joseph. *Computer Power and Human Reason: From Judgment to Calculation* (San Francisco: W. H. Freeman, 1976).

Welke, Lawrence. "Founding the ICP Directories," *IEEE Annals of the History of Computing*, Vol. 24, No. 1 (2002): 85–89.

West, Martha S., and John W. Curtis. "AAUP Faculty Gender Equity Indicators 2006" (Washington, DC: American Association of University Professors, 2006).

Wexelblat, Richard L., ed. *History of Programming Languages* (New York: Academic Press, 1981).

White, Candace, and Katherine N. Kinnick. "One Click Forward and Two Clicks Back: Portrayal of Women Using Computers in Television Commercials," *Women's Studies in Communication*, Vol. 23, No. 3 (Fall 2000): 392–412.

Whyte, William Hollingsworth. *The Organization Man* (New York: Simon and Schuster, 1956).

Wiegand, Wayne A., and Donald G. Davis, Jr., eds. *The Encyclopedia of Library History* (New York: Garland Press, 1994).

Wilensky, Harold. "The Professionalization of Everyone?" *American Journal of Sociology*, Vol. 70, No. 2 (1964): 137–158.

Wiles, Judith A., Charles R. Wiles, and Anders Tjernlund. "A Comparison of Gender Role Portrayals in Magazine Advertising: The Netherlands, Sweden and the USA," *European Journal of Marketing*, Vol. 29, No. 11 (1995): 35–49.

Williams, Dmitri, Nicole Martins, Mia Consalvo, and James D. Ivory. "The Virtual Census: Representations of Gender, Race and Age in Video Games," *New Media & Society*, Vol. 11, No. 5 (2009): 815–834.

Willoughby, Theodore. "Psychometric Characteristics of the CDP Examination," in *Proceedings of the Thirteenth Annual SIGCPR Conference* (New York: ACM Press, 1975), pp. 152–160.

Wilson, Dolly Smith. "A New Look at the Affluent Worker: The Good Working Mother in Post-War Britain," *Twentieth Century British History*, Vol. 17, No. 2 (2006): 206–229.

Witz, Anne, and Mike Savage. "The Gender of Organizations," in Mike Savage and Anne Witz, eds., *Gender and Bureaucracy* (Cambridge, UK: Blackwell, 1992), pp. 3–62.

Wolin, Lori D. "Gender Issues in Advertising: An Oversight Synthesis of Research, 1970–2002," *Journal of Advertising Research*, Vol. 43, No. 1 (March 2003): 111–129.

Woodfield, Ruth. *Women, Work and Computing* (Cambridge, UK: Cambridge University Press, 2000).

Wosk, Julie. *Women and the Machine: Representations from the Spinning Wheel to the Electronic Age* (Baltimore: Johns Hopkins University Press, 2001).

Wright, John L., ed. *Possible Dreams: Enthusiasm for Technology in America* (Dearborn, MI: Henry Ford Museum and Greenfield Village, 1992).

Yates, JoAnne. *Control Through Communication: The Rise of System in American Management* (Baltimore: Johns Hopkins University Press, 1989).

Yates, JoAnne. *Structuring the Information Age: Life Insurance and Technology in the Twentieth Century* (Baltimore: Johns Hopkins University Press, 2005).

Yohn, Susan M. "Crippled Capitalists: The Inscription of Economic Dependence and the Challenge of Female Entrepreneurship in Nineteenth-Century America," *Feminist Economics*, Vol. 12, Nos. 1–2 (2006): 85–109.

Zunz, Olivier. *Making America Corporate 1870–1920* (Chicago: University of Chicago Press, 1990).

Zussman, Robert. *Mechanics of the Middle Class: Work and Politics Among American Engineers* (Berkeley: University of California Press, 1985).

Zweben, Stuart. "2006–2007 Taulbee Survey: Ph.D. Production Exceeds 1700, Undergraduate Enrollment Trends Still Unclear," *Computing Research News*, Computing Research Association, May 2008.

# Index

Computer training. *See* Education, computer-related; Training, computer-related

Computers
  background, 82
  comparison with punch-card machines, 88
  early history, 3
  gender dynamics of MetLife jobs, 83–85
  impact on women workers, 82–83
  negative impact for women workers, 90–91
  refining of data processing tasks, 85–87
  as ubiquitous, 177–178, 181–182

Computing Research Association, 5–6, 9, 21 (note 2)

Computing work. *See also* Data processing; Programmers and programming
  association with mathematics, 218
  barriers to women's full acceptance, 256–262
  correlation with computer science education, 33–34, 37
  countering stereotypical "male geek" image, 224–226
  culture of computing, 11–12, 121
  currently male-dominated, 119
  growth in U.S. workforce without regard to gender, 36–37
  historical perspective on gendered identity, 120–135
  presence of women early on, 120–125
  proportion of women workers, 4–7, 32–34, 37

Consumer Systems, 242–243

Control Data Corporation, 113, 216

Conway, Lynn, 258

*Cosmopolitan* (magazine), "Computer Girls" article, 115–119, 124, 127, 134, 136

Council on Library Resources, 149

Coyle, Karen, 12

Cringely, Robert X. (pen name), 251–252, 259, 260

Cullinane Corporation, 232

Cultural change, local, 272

Current Population Survey, U.S. Census Bureau, 64–67

Cusumano, Michael, 133

D

Data entry. *See also* Word processing
  accuracy issue, 86–87
  after advent of electronic computers, 85–87
  becomes more taxing chore, 85–87
  follow-on occupation to punch-card workers, 16, 60, 86
  as women's work, 5, 15, 32, 33, 56, 64, 85–88, 91

Data processing
  addition of programming job, 54
  British government requirements, 98
  carryover from office administrative work, 52, 54, 59, 68
  carryover from tabulating machine work, 52
  Census Bureau gender data, 64, 65–66
  chance for men to elevate positions within corporate hierarchy, 56
  comparison with computer science, 51
  data entry task for electronic computers, 85–87
  gender history, 51–66, 76–77, 79, 82, 85–86, 87–89
  jobs in increasing order of pay and prestige, 53–55, 64
  mirroring of punched-card departments, 52, 60, 63–64
  name changes involving "information," 66
  pre-electronic history in Britain, 98–100
  redefined in electronic computer age, 85–87
  salaries and employment patterns, 54–55, 64
  trade literature reinforcement of gender divisions, 60–63
  view of academic computer specialists toward, 60

Data Processing Management Association (DPMA), 51–52, 56, 63, 117, 128, 135, 254

Datamedia, 193

Datamicro computers, 201, 203

Davies, Margery, 124

Davis, Clark, 58

*Desk Set* (movie), 90–91, 146

Detlefsen, Ellen Gay, 146

Dewey, Melvil, 145

Diebold, John, 75

Dijkstra, Edsger, 126

Discourse theory, defined, 166

Discursive logic, 166, 168–174

Doctoral degrees
  proportion of computer science degrees awarded to women, 29, 32, 40–42, 266
  proportion of Greek women doctoral students in computer science, 189
  proportion of women in all fields earning, 41

Domain names, defining, 3

Donkey Kong (game), 13

Dot.com bubble, 35, 36, 46, 242, 269

Douglas, Nikki, 13, 254

Downey, Greg, 132

DPMA (Data Processing Management Association), 51–52, 56, 63, 117, 128, 135, 254

Dragon's Lair (game), 13

Draper, John, 260

DTK computers, 192